Praise for *Chin*

'Frank Dikötter is a remarkable D... trilogy covering the lives of ordina... on extraordinary, painstaking research in local archives and party records ... Now, with *China After Mao*, Dikötter has told the story of the years after Mao's death in 1976 until the arrival of President Xi ... Dikötter, who writes with considerable verve, blasts several holes in the notion that a Marxist-Leninist system can ever bring real reform. The new dictator's reign will not end well, any more than that of his hero' Chris Patten, *New Statesman* Books of the Year

'[A] compelling account ... Appearances can be deceptive, cautions Dikötter, who writes with elegance, verve and occasional anger ... Dikötter, one of the world's pre-eminent China scholars, draws on a wide body of material, including municipal and provincial archives, newspapers and unpublished memoirs, in a pulsating account ... Dikötter himself is a source of countless insights. His account blends a highly readable narrative with a commentary that is as damning about attitudes to China and the glittering prizes that it offers as it is about the way power has been monopolised by elites in Beijing' Peter Frankopan, *Times Literary Supplement*

'*China After Mao* follows the author's prize-winning trilogy on famine, chaos and repression under Chairman Mao Zedong, and it complements his work on the dictatorship ... Breaking with the bland orthodoxy peddled in some of our finest universities, Dikötter says that China today is a Leviathan where a party, fascist in all but name, controls society ... Historians such as Dikötter are there to warn' Michael Sheridan, *Sunday Times*

'A detailed unpicking of the illusion China's rulers perpetuate that the country's economic growth has been driven by reform ... Bracingly direct ... *China After Mao* provides an important corrective to the conventional view of China's rise through reform' Jonathan Fenby, *Financial Times*

'A clear-eyed and detailed account ... Dikötter is one of today's major historians of China: he has been mining Chinese primary sources for decades ... For this volume, he draws on 600 documents from municipal and provincial archives, as well as conventional sources such as Chinese news media ... What we learn is that while power and ideology are constantly contested, the Chinese Communist party, even in its most liberal phases, remained wedded to the Stalinist model that Xi's China increasingly resembles. We also learn, to nobody's surprise, that absolute truths are highly mutable' Isabel Hilton, *Observer*

'Dikötter masterfully blends the micro-level examples from archives with patient explanations of the economic policies and circumstances behind them and bigger picture narratives of the Chinese state. His wry observations and controlled anger contribute to rendering a complex subject very readable' C.C. Corn, *The Critic*

'A useful entry point for readers new to the subject ... To depart from the prevailing narrative of economic success, Dikötter offers a story of financial incompetence and continuous political infighting, along with selected examples of local suffering' Jennifer Altehenger, *Literary Review*

'A merciless assessment of China in the Reform Era, and of those in the west – politicians and "China experts" alike – who have been duped by the regime's deceit and propaganda and beguiled into wishful thinking that its economic reforms would generate a peaceful transition to democracy ... His account is compelling ... In Dikötter's final judgement, the party has reached "a dead end"' Roger Garside, *Prospect*

FRANK DIKÖTTER is Chair Professor of Humanities at the University of Hong Kong and Senior Fellow at the Hoover Institution. His books have changed the way historians view China, from the classic *The Discourse of Race in Modern China* to his award-winning *People's Trilogy* documenting the lives of ordinary people under Mao. He is married and lives in Hong Kong.

CHINA AFTER MAO

The Rise of a Superpower

Frank Dikötter

BLOOMSBURY PUBLISHING
LONDON · OXFORD · NEW YORK · NEW DELHI · SYDNEY

BLOOMSBURY PUBLISHING
Bloomsbury Publishing Plc
50 Bedford Square, London, WC1B 3DP, UK
29 Earlsfort Terrace, Dublin 2, Ireland

BLOOMSBURY, BLOOMSBURY PUBLISHING and the Diana logo are trademarks of
Bloomsbury Publishing Plc

First published in Great Britain 2022
This edition published 2023

ISBN: HB: 978-1-5266-3428-3; TPB: 978-1-5266-3429-0; PB: 978-1-5266-34306
EBOOK: 978-1-5266-3433-7; EPDF: 978-1-5266-5744-2

2 4 6 8 10 9 7 5 3 1

Typeset by Newgen KnowledgeWorks Pvt. Ltd., Chennai, India
Printed and bound in Great Britain by CPI Group (UK) Ltd, Croydon CRO 4YY

To find out more about our authors and books visit www.bloomsbury.com
and sign up for our newsletters

Contents

Preface

In the summer of 1985, when *Back to the Future* became the highest grossing film of the year, I set off to study Mandarin in China as a student from the University of Geneva, Switzerland. The Chinese Ministry of Foreign Affairs assigned me to Nankai University in Tianjin, a large coastal metropolis near Beijing with a population of 5 million (today the city has trebled in size). I flew to Hong Kong where I crossed the border, taking a week to travel up north by train, making friends on the way. One of them could not remember my surname and later sent me a postcard addressed to 'Frank from Holland, Tianjin, China'. The post office had no trouble finding me, since there were only eighty foreigners in town, including seven Dutch nationals and one Frank.

Like all major cities, Tianjin had a network of wide boulevards built in the 1950s with the help of Soviet experts. There was no grid-lock: there were fewer than 20,000 private vehicles in this nation of more than a billion people. But fenced off from buses and trucks and the occasional car, drifts of closely packed commuters quietly pedalled along designated side lanes. Since they got up at the crack of dawn and went back home before dusk, the city fell quiet at nine in the evening. I sometimes had all six lanes to myself, the lampposts shining a dim light on my bicycle at night.

I returned to Nankai University on the occasion of its centennial celebration in October 2019. Tianjin seemed transformed, its skyline ablaze with glittering skyscrapers, its urban sprawl reaching far and wide with a seemingly endless agglomeration of apartment buildings and office parks, some finished, others still under construction.

Wherever one stood, on a clear day the Tianjin Finance Centre could be seen towering almost 600 metres into the sky, its glass glinting in the sunlight like a giant crystal spire. But appearances can be deceptive. My erstwhile teachers and their successors lived in the same shabby, concrete blocks with potted plants crammed onto dusty balconies, the corridors cluttered with battered bicycles used to get around campus. There was one difference, I was told: the children of most professors were now in the United States.

A few years ago the People's Republic of China officially celebrated forty years of 'Reform and Opening Up', the term given to the programme of economic reforms inaugurated by Deng Xiaoping in December 1978. The transformation of an insulated country reeling from the chaos of the Cultural Revolution into the world's second-largest economy is invariably hailed as a miracle. The title of one scholarly tome – *How the Miracle Was Created* – sums up the prevailing view. A cause of concern for some experts, apparently, is not whether there really was a miracle in the first place but whether it might actually have come to an end.

But how would the experts know? After I moved into my dormitory 35 years ago, I noticed that many foreign students spent a great deal of time speculating about what was happening in Beijing. Some of them became China watchers. Their technique was borrowed from Kremlin watchers: lack of reliable information forced them to scrutinise the most abstruse signs for clues about Zhongnanhai, the party headquarters next to the Forbidden City in Beijing, from the position of each leader on the reviewing stand when parades were held in Tiananmen Square and the layout of news articles in the *People's Daily* to the frequency of certain phrases on the radio. I was sceptical and preferred to study the past.

I remain sceptical. Contrary to what one might reasonably expect after forty years of 'Reform and Opening Up', the situation is not so very different today. A few years ago Li Keqiang, China's current premier, referred to the country's figures for domestic output as 'manmade and therefore unreliable'. Experts, of course, know this, and find ways around it. There is, for instance, a 'Li Keqiang index', one the premier used himself to monitor economic performance by scrutinising total electricity consumption. But the fact remains that we know very little. As the China observer James Palmer put it recently, 'Nobody

Knows anything About China: Including the Chinese Government'.[1] Every piece of information is unreliable, partial or distorted. We do not know the true size of the economy, since no local government will report accurate numbers, and we do not know the extent of bad loans, since the banks conceal these. Every good researcher has the Socratic paradox in mind: I know that I don't know. But where China is concerned, we don't even know what we don't know.

Just across the northern gate of Nankai University, on the other side of a congested eight-lane thoroughfare, a large, cavernous building guarded by young soldiers houses the Tianjin Municipal Archives. Access would have been unthinkable when I was still a student. But in 1996 the law regulating access to the archives was amended and increasing quantities of declassified material gradually became available to professional historians armed with a letter of recommendation. Even if the most sensitive information remained safely locked away deep inside the archival vaults, for the first time researchers were allowed to delve into the dark night of the Maoist era.

I spent a decade examining thousands of party records, travelling the length and breadth of the country from subtropical Guangdong to poor and arid Gansu, a province near the deserts of Mongolia. Inside yellowing folders, scribbled in longhand or neatly typed, were secret minutes of top party meetings, investigations into cases of mass murder, confessions of leaders responsible for the starvation of millions of villagers, reports on resistance in the countryside, confidential opinion surveys, letters of complaint written by ordinary people and much more besides. I wrote three books known as the 'People's Trilogy,' on the fate of ordinary people under Mao.

The timing was fortunate. After Xi Jinping's ascent to power in November 2012, the archives began closing down again. Large batches of documents on Mao's Great Famine and the Cultural Revolution have since been reclassified. But, paradoxically, the last couple of years have been a good time to explore the decades of 'Reform and Opening Up'. For years the Chinese people, including every archivist, have been told that nothing short of an economic miracle took place after 1978, one that has left foreign capitalists gasping for breath. A dark cloud hangs over the Mao era, but it dissipates the moment the term 'economic reform' is invoked. Now, for the first time, we can actually use the evidence produced by the Communist Party to examine the history of the Communist Party since 1976.

Every democracy has a host of rules and regulations that determine what official documents can be declassified and when they can be released for public inspection. In theory, most adhere to a thirty-year rule. Around Christmas every year, readers at the National Archives in Kew eagerly await the latest batch of declassified material from the Prime Minister's Office or MI5. In practice, however, government agencies around the world use a variety of exceptions to withhold millions of documents from scrutiny.

The law in the People's Republic of China also follows a thirty-year rule, so readers should in principle be able to consult documents right up to 1992. But China is not a democracy, it is a dictatorship. And the way in which the rules are applied is often dictated locally. As a result, access varies from place to place. In some archives no outsider will ever get past the sentry box by the front gate, as even an anodyne newspaper cutting is treated like a state secret, while in others every document anterior to 1949, when the communists swept to victory, is deemed off limits. On the other hand, across this huge country the size of a continent, some archives are surprisingly open. Every once in a while a local archive will permit some of its readers to peruse a wide selection of primary material all the way up to 2009, well beyond the thirty-year rule.

My account is based on roughly 600 documents from a dozen municipal and provincial archives, but it also draws on more conventional primary sources, from newspaper reports to unpublished memoirs. Foremost among these are the secret diaries of Li Rui who became Mao's personal secretary, spent twenty years in prison for mentioning the famine in 1959 and was then asked to join the Central Committee a few years after the Chairman's death in 1976. For many years he was the vice-director of the Organisation Department (Orgburo in Soviet parlance), a party branch in charge of investigating and appointing party members at every level of government. He became a true democrat, having seen the system from the inside out, but in 2004 was banned from writing for publication. His diaries go up to 2012 and report his conversations with senior party members in great detail. Historians, of course, thrive not only on evidence, but also on a sense of perspective: when both become short, it is wise to step back and let others continue the story. I place that moment in 2012, when Li Rui closes his diary and Xi Jinping steps to the fore.

A wealth of hitherto unavailable evidence allows us to test some common assumptions about the era of 'Reform and Opening Up'. For decades a motley crew of foreign politicians, entrepreneurs and experts have told us that the People's Republic was on the road to becoming a responsible stakeholder, possibly even a thriving democracy. Political reform would succeed economic reform as surely as the cart follows the ox. But at no point has any leader said anything in support of the separation of powers. On the contrary, maintaining a monopoly has repeatedly been defined as the overwhelming goal of economic reform. Here is Zhao Ziyang, praised to this day as the most promising figure inside the party, addressing the Party Congress in October 1987: 'we will never copy the separation of powers and the multi-party system of the West.' A few months earlier, he had explained to Erich Honecker, the leader of East Germany, that once their living standards had been raised, people in China would acknowledge the superiority of socialism. And then, he added, 'we can gradually reduce the scope for liberalisation further and further.' Time and again, subsequent leaders have repeated the same message. In 2018, Xi Jinping warned that 'China must never copy other countries,' least of all the 'judicial independence' and the 'separation of powers' of the West.[2]

Over the past two or three years, numerous observers have somewhat belatedly changed their minds and no longer envisage a Communist Party of China steadfastly advancing towards democracy. But a great many still believe in the past existence of real economic reform with a concerted move from the plan to the market, from public ownership to private enterprise. Yet one has to wonder whether, the official propaganda issuing from Beijing notwithstanding, the term 'economic reform' is accurate. What we have witnessed so far is merely tinkering with a planned economy. How otherwise to explain the fact that the party insists on having Five Year Plans? More to the point, since 1976 the party has continued to retain ownership of all industry and most large enterprises. To this day, the land belongs to the state, a great many raw material resources belong to the state, major industries are controlled directly or indirectly by the state, and the banks belong to the state. In classic Marxist parlance, the 'means of production' remain in the hands of the party. An economy in which the means of production are controlled by the state is usually described as a socialist economy.

Not once after 1989 did the party leaders ever consider opening up their economy to real market competition. The reason was simple: they knew that the moment they did so, their economy would collapse. Time and again, as the record shows, they have done their utmost to constrain the private sector and instead expand state enterprises. They firmly believe in the superiority of the socialist system, as demonstrated in countless statements in public and behind closed doors. After a cluster of villages in Shenzhen, just across the border from Hong Kong, was transformed in 1980 into the country's first Special Economic Zone, Zhao Ziyang clarified: 'what we are setting up are special economic zones, not special political zones, we must uphold socialism and resist capitalism.'[3]

Almost forty years later, 95 of the top 100 private firms belong to current or former party members. Capitalism is about capital: money is an economic good subject to rules on rates of return and profit margins. But in China capital has remained a political good, distributed by state banks to enterprises controlled directly or indirectly by the state in pursuit of political goals. A market, moreover, is based predominantly on the exchange of goods between individuals. How can ownership of these goods be protected without an independent judicial system based on the separation of powers? For years, critics have decried while admirers have applauded the supposed 'transition' towards 'capitalism' in the People's Republic. But if this book proves anything, it is that without political reform market reform cannot exist. The argument over whether trade can or should be 'free' misses the key point, namely that a market without the rule of law, backed up by an independent judicial system and a free and open press, is not much of a market at all. There is no economic freedom without political freedom. Politics determines the nature of economics, not the other way around. Politics is about power and what to do with it: should it be divided among different institutions, with checks and balances, an increasingly complex civil society and an independent media to constrain abuse, or should it be concentrated in the hands of one individual or single party? The former is termed a democracy, the latter a dictatorship.

Dictatorships, like democracies, are not frozen in time. They constantly adapt to a changing world. Mozambique, for instance, decided to seek a rapprochement with the West in 1982, decentralising its economy a year later and allowing family farming to thrive instead of state farms. Multinational companies were invited to set up joint ventures or sign contracts with the government. Samora Machel, a socialist in the tradition of Marxism-Leninism who had led his country to independence in 1975, turned himself into a salesman for Mozambique with the same drive that had made him such a successful guerrilla leader. He courted and embraced corporate executives around the world, offering lucrative deals based on cheap labour deprived of the right to strike. Mozambique was hardly unique. A whole string of dictatorships, from Dahomey to Syria, made a similar wager: in order to avoid economic collapse, they ventured that private agricultural plots, small private urban enterprises and foreign participation would not undermine their political grip. Barry Rubin, who described these regimes in great detail, called them 'modern dictators'. They are a garden variety of 'dictators', generally seen in contrast to another sub-category, namely 'traditional dictators'.[4]

It is sometimes said that state efficiency is more important than state accountability. This is a dubious proposition. Instead of an orderly handover of power, what we see in the People's Republic is bitter back-stabbing and fighting for power among endlessly changing factions. Most of the country's leaders do not understand even basic economics, focusing almost obsessively on one single figure, growth, often at the expense of development. The result is waste on a staggering scale. It is not uncommon, for instance, for state enterprises to subtract value, meaning that the raw materials they use are worth more than the finished goods they produce. Most of all, somewhat paradoxically, a one-party state does not have the instruments to control the economy. Decisions are made by local governments, often in disregard of the greater good, never mind the writ from Beijing.

Has the country opened up during the era of 'Reform and Opening Up'? Compared to the Cultural Revolution, definitely. But barely, relative to the rest of the world. What the regime has built over the past four decades is a fairly insulated system capable of fencing off the country from the rest of the world. Openness means that there is movement of people, ideas, goods and capital. But the state controls all these flows, which are often permitted in just one direction. Millions of people can move out, living and working in the rest of the world, but very few foreigners move in. After forty years of 'Reform and Opening Up' China had fewer than a million resident foreigners, or roughly 0.07 per cent of its total population, the lowest proportion in any country, less than half that of North Korea. (Japan, often decried as a 'xenophobic' country, has 2.8 per cent.) Finished products can move out of China in phenomenal quantities, but relatively few can actually move in. Today, each year one-fifth of humanity can view 36 foreign films sanctioned by the state. Capital can enter but is difficult to take out, as it is stockpiled by a regime which imposes drastic capital controls. As the archives reveal in far greater detail, since 1976 countless rules, regulations, sanctions, bonuses, deductions, subsidies and incentives have been put in place to create what may very well be the most unlevel playing field in modern history.

Undoubtedly, there has been real economic growth. How could it be otherwise when a country emerges from decades of man-made disaster? Yet as recently as June 2020 it came as a revelation to many observers when Li Keqiang, he of the eponymous 'Li Keqiang index', remarked in an aside that in a country where even in the countryside the cost of living is prohibitive, some 600 million people have to manage on less than $140 a month.[5] In truth, everything is not as it seems. Both extraordinary frugality among ordinary people and extravagant wealth controlled by the state co-exist. When party members work for the state, their employer pays for their home, car, children's schooling, trips abroad and much more besides. Ordinary people, by contrast, have had little alternative but to deposit their savings in state banks. The state uses these deposits to advertise the benefits of socialism, building soaring skyscrapers and bullet trains and new airports and endless motorways. It also uses the money to keep state enterprises afloat. Thanks to financial repression, ordinary people's share of the national output is the lowest of any country in modern history. There is a convenient saying for this in Chinese: 'The state is rich, the people are poor.'

The state and its banks can spend or loan with little accountability, squandering on a massive scale and creating a continually growing mountain of debt, albeit one carefully hidden from view. Just how bad is it? We do not and may never know, since even the bean counters employed by the state to write the reports on debt carefully filed in the archives cannot discern everything that happens below the surface.

Many people are masters of appearances. Obfuscation exists at every level of the hierarchy, with fabricated contracts, false customers, fake sales and rampant accounting fraud. How could it be otherwise with no separation of powers, and therefore no independent press or independent auditing, let alone elected officials accountable to their electorate? Regular campaigns are launched against corruption. These began the moment the party came to power in 1949, but since corruption is intrinsic to the system it can only be temporarily abated, not eradicated. Repeatedly, the leadership gathers to proclaim an emergency, demanding a halt to infrastructure building and ordering enterprises to rein in spending.

Approximately one-fifth of all files in the party archives deal with debt, lending to solve the debt, further debt due to the lending and more lending to solve an even larger debt. Boom and bust are supposed to characterise capitalism, but the situation in the People's Republic looks more like boom and an endlessly postponed bust. The party has huge assets at its disposal, not least the savings of ordinary people and a steady stream of foreign investment. It has thrown increasingly large amounts of money at grandiose projects, regardless of return on capital, let alone bad debt. If the economy grows faster than the debt, the debt will be absorbed, but the debt keeps on growing faster than the economy. As Xiang Songzuo, a professor of economics at the People's University in Beijing and erstwhile deputy director of the People's Bank of China, stated in 2019, 'Basically China's economy is all built on speculation, and everything is over-leveraged.'[6]

In every dictatorship decisions made by the leader have prodigious, unintended consequences. The one-child policy was designed to curb population growth: now men greatly outnumber women, while the country has a shrinking labour force. Many directives enforced by the regime likewise have unforeseen outcomes because across the hierarchy so many party members attempt to deflect, delay or simply turn a blind eye to orders from above. After 1978 the central government devolved greater power to local governments, hoping that this would encourage them to introduce more economic incentives, but local governments became more protective of their own fiefdoms, erecting economic barriers to prevent competition. Instead of an integrated national economy with several large steel plants, every village, town and city wanted to have their own steel mill, with hundreds existing side by side in a single province, draining scarce resources from the state.

A local government has a local party secretary: he and not the market is the man (very rarely a woman) who allocates capital, and in a manner designed to increase his political clout. Even when the local economy goes belly up, he knows that he can count on the central bank to bail him out, since the regime fears nothing so much as 'social instability', meaning runs on banks and workers on the streets.

The image that emerges from the archives is not that of a party equipped with a clear vision of how to steer the country towards prosperity. China resembles a tanker that looks impressively shipshape from a distance, with the captain and his lieutenants standing proudly on the bridge, while below deck sailors are desperately pumping water and plugging holes to keep the vessel afloat. There is no 'grand plan', no 'secret strategy', but, rather, a great many unpredictable events, unforeseen consequences and abrupt changes of course as well as interminable struggles for power behind the scenes. All of these, I trust, make for better history.

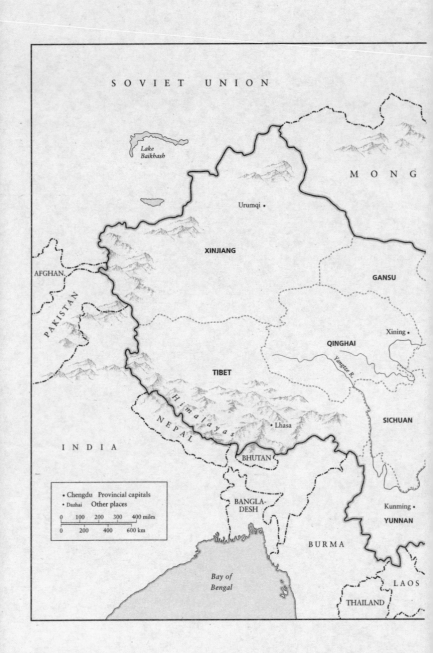

I

From One Dictator to Another (1976–1979)

A vast stone desert called Tiananmen Square lies at the heart of Beijing. In 1976 it was the world's largest paved expanse, easily holding a million people. It was named after the Gate of Heavenly Peace, the southern entrance to the Forbidden City, a sprawling complex of ancient pavilions, courtyards and palaces that had served the emperors of the Ming and Qing dynasties. The T-shaped area in front of the Gate of Heavenly Peace had for several centuries formed part of the imperial approach to the throne, but was originally much smaller. Soon after the Chinese Communist Party conquered the country in 1949, Mao Zedong ordered that the square be enlarged 'to hold a billion people'. Several imperial gates were torn down, medieval structures cleared and sections of the surrounding city wall, their crenellated parapets overgrown with vines and shrubbery, levelled to the ground. The square was quadrupled in size, creating a vast, empty, concrete area the size of sixty football pitches. Chang'an Avenue, running east to west at the top of the square, had welcomed a tram in 1924 but remained a narrow thoroughfare. It was gradually expanded to an eight-lane boulevard, stretching far beyond the city limits. In October 1959, to mark the tenth anniversary of the revolution, a Great Hall of the People appeared on the western side of the square, a Museum of Chinese History on the eastern side. In the middle, a Monument to the People's Heroes, a granite obelisk some 37 metres high, was erected, blocking the traditional north–south approach to the palace. The primary axis of the city was flipped around, now dominated by the intersection of Chang'an Avenue and Tiananmen.[1]

Demonstrations were not allowed under the emperor, but soon after the fall of the Qing in 1911 the area in front of the Gate of Heavenly Peace began to acquire much greater political significance. In 1925, when the country was ruled by the Nationalist Party, a large portrait of its founding father Sun Yat-sen was hung above the gate, replaced in 1945 by an image of his successor Chiang Kai-shek. On 1 October 1949, after Chiang's troops were forced to flee to Taiwan and the People's Republic of China was proclaimed, a portrait of Mao Zedong went up instead.

Protesters also occasionally occupied the square. In 1919, during the May Fourth Movement, some 4,000 students gathered to demonstrate against the terms of the Treaty of Versailles, which handed former German concessions in China over to Japan, an ally of the victors in the First World War. The movement rippled across the country, as protesters called for a boycott of Japanese goods. They also pushed more broadly for science and democracy. In 1912, as China had become Asia's first republic, an electorate of 40 million people had voted for 30,000 electors, who in turn had selected members of the National Assembly and the House of Representatives. But hopes for greater popular representation had been dashed in the following years, and now demonstrators demanded that their country be transported into the modern age under the aegis of 'Mr Science' and 'Mr Democracy' instead of Confucius, the elderly sage who symbolised the old imperial order.[2]

There were further demonstrations on the square, some violently suppressed. On 18 March 1926 the military police were ordered to disperse protesters who clamoured against imperialism, with 47 people dying in the ensuing confrontation. Popular revulsion at the massacre was such that Parliament was forced to pass a resolution of condemnation. A month later the government fell from power. Lu Xun, the country's celebrated writer, called the confrontation the 'darkest day since the founding of the republic'.[3]

Throughout the republican era, the desire for democracy was so widespread that the communists, too, were compelled to embrace the message. The Chinese Communist Party was established in 1921, but membership lingered in the low hundreds for several years. In January 1940, Mao Zedong and his ghostwriter Chen Boda, a bookish but ambitious young man trained in Moscow, penned *On*

New Democracy. The tract pledged a multi-party system, democratic freedoms and protection of private property. It was an entirely fictitious programme, but one that held broad popular appeal, as many thousands of students, teachers, artists, writers and journalists joined the Communist Party in the following years, attracted by the vision of a more democratic future.

One by one, the promises of *On New Democracy* were broken after 1949. All organisations operating outside the purview of the Communist Party – labour unions, student organisations, independent chambers of commerce, civil associations – were eliminated in the first years of the new regime. A literary inquisition ensured that artists and writers conformed to party dictates. As early as 1950, books considered undesirable were burned in giant bonfires or pulped by the tonne. By 1956 all commerce and industry became functions of the state, as the government expropriated small shops, private enterprises and large industries alike. In the summer of 1958 people in the countryside were herded into giant collectives called People's Communes. The land was taken from the farmers, who were transformed into bonded servants at the beck and call of the state.[4]

Popular protests were banned, but Tiananmen thrived as the new political theatre of the country. Carefully choreographed parades were held twice a year on the square, as clockwork soldiers, mounted cavalry, heavy tanks and armoured cars passed in front of the Chairman, watching from the rostrum on top of the Gate of Heavenly Peace. During the Cultural Revolution, in regular mass rallies the Great Helmsman reviewed some 12 million Red Guards, enthusiastically waving the Little Red Book.

***

On one occasion control of the square passed to the people. In 1976 the Qingming Festival, also known as Tomb Sweeping Day, when families traditionally gather to weed graves, touch up headstones and offer flowers to deceased relatives, fell on a Sunday, 4 April. Hundreds of thousands of people streamed into the square, piling wreaths around the base of the Monument to the People's Heroes in honour of Zhou Enlai. The premier had passed away several months earlier on 8 January 1976, thin and shrivelled by three separate cancers. In the eyes of many, Zhou represented a counterbalance to a powerful clique known as the 'Gang of Four', led by Jiang Qing, or Madame Mao. Chairman Mao, the consummate manipulator, had pitted each against the other, ensuring he retained the upper hand.

During the last few years of his life Zhou Enlai had cautiously tried to restore order to the planned economy, open the country and import much-needed foreign technology. In January 1975 he gave one of his final speeches before the National People's Congress, China's rubber-stamp legislature. He called on the country to modernise entire fields that were lagging behind the rest of the world, in particular agriculture, industry, national defence and science and technology.[5] With the blessing of the Chairman, he termed this programme the 'Four Modernisations'. But while Mao approved of modernising the economy, he feared that the moment he died Zhou would undermine his entire political legacy. He used his wife and her allies to isolate the premier, as they lambasted 'blind worship of foreign machinery' and other manifestations of 'revisionism', which in the parlance of the time meant the abandonment of socialism and the restoration of capitalism.

Zhou Enlai was isolated, but an ambitious Madame Mao overreached by trying to extend her grip on the party and the army. In 1974, in order to balance the two factions further, Mao had brought Deng Xiaoping back to power, making him a deputy to Zhou Enlai. Like many leading cadres, Deng had been purged at the height of the Cultural Revolution for following a 'bourgeois reactionary line'. With Zhou Enlai confined to hospital, Deng increasingly took charge. He, too, focused on the economy, but lacked the premier's soft touch as he threatened harsh punishment for railway officials who could not get transportation back on schedule and demanded that industrial leaders meet all the latest production targets. And he, too, attracted the ire of Madame Mao, who used her control of the propaganda machine to churn out a steady flow of denunciatory articles.[6]

One victim of Deng Xiaoping's bruising approach was the Chairman's nephew Mao Yuanxin, a young man who had made a name for himself as deputy party secretary of the provincial revolutionary committee in Liaoning. Deng had pruned the management of the giant Anshan Iron and Steel Corporation, Liaoning's flagship industry, resulting in a streamlined command structure similar to that in exist-ence before the Cultural Revolution. Mao Yuanxin poured poison in his uncle's ear, accusing Deng of representing a whole new bourgeois class stealthily emerging from the shadow of the Cultural Revolution. After Zhou Enlai passed away, the Chairman turned instead to an individual who stood outside the two camps. Burly and amiable, Hua Guofeng was a minor figure but one genuinely loyal to Mao. 'No one else tells the truth like Hua Guofeng,' Mao had once opined.[7] As party secretary of Shaoshan, Mao Zedong's birthplace, he had erected a huge memorial hall dedicated to his master and built a railway to bring in the pilgrims. Deng was allowed to deliver a eulogy to Zhou Enlai and promptly relieved of his duties as vice-premier the moment Hua Guofeng took over.

With Zhou Enlai gone and Deng Xiaoping purged yet again, some feared a return to the heyday of the Cultural Revolution. They were infuriated by the publication on 25 March of an editorial in a newspaper controlled by the Gang of Four in Shanghai, condemning a 'capitalist roader inside the party' who had wanted to help an 'unrepentant capitalist roader' regain power. Everyone who read the piece knew the alleged allies of capitalism were Zhou Enlai and Deng Xiaoping. Protesters took to the streets in Nanjing. In Wuxi, a city near Shanghai, a sea of humanity poured into Red Square, holding portraits of the premier and playing a recording of Deng's eulogy on the public broadcast system. In Beijing, poems attacked 'Jiang Qing the witch'.[8]

On Qingming Festival, a cold, drizzly day, people became openly defiant, occupying Tiananmen Square. Some protesters quietly mourned the premier. One man held a traditional paper umbrella, using it as a reminder that students had demonstrated against their rulers decades earlier, on 4 May 1919. Others were more blunt, clenching a microphone to attack 'the new Empress Dowager' or brandishing a piece of white brocade with a pledge written in blood to defend the premier.[9]

The atmosphere was solemn, as people quietly defied the will of their supreme leader. But the Gang of Four was clamouring for a showdown. During the empire, intrigues and power plays were rife inside the vermilion walls of the Forbidden City, as the emperor surrounded himself with a small army of eunuchs, concubines, soldiers and officials, all scheming to improve their lot. Under Mao, the corridor politics took place inside the Great Hall of the People, overlooking the square to the west. A hulking, intimidating structure inspired by Stalinist architecture, it boasted a vast auditorium drenched in red, capable of seating over 10,000 delegates. Dozens more cavernous conference venues named after the country's provinces provided more generous room for political wheeling and dealing than the former imperial palace across Chang'an Avenue.

The Great Hall of the People was the venue for a National Congress, held every five years to approve the membership of the Central Committee, a body of some 200 top leaders. The Central Committee in turn nominally elected a Politburo, or Central Political Bureau, composed of two dozen members. Day-to-day decisions were made by a much smaller Standing Committee, composed of seven or eight elderly members. The most powerful person was the Chairman. Like much else, the structure reflected the Stalinist principle of democratic centralism, which meant that all political decisions were reached by a voting process which was binding upon all Communist Party members. In practice, the power structure was inversed, as supreme power flowed from the hands of the man at the top of the pyramid. Since there was only one party, expressions of loyalty to its leader were paramount, intimations of dissent dangerous.

The Chairman, aged 82, was too frail to attend the meetings in person and stayed at the Poolside House, one of many residences reserved for senior leaders in Zhongnanhai, an imperial compound with lakes and manicured gardens just west of the Forbidden City. But he was informed of all important events and made all major decisions. A network of underground tunnels ran beneath the square, connecting all the main structures, and messengers ferried up and down between the hall and the compound. Even before Tiananmen was occupied, Mao Yuanxin approached his uncle on 1 April to insinuate that Zhou Enlai's death was being used to foment trouble. He suggested that Deng Xiaoping, already dismissed from his position as vice-premier but still a Politburo member, should be barred from appearing in public on May Day, an occasion always celebrated with much fanfare by every Marxist-Leninist regime. Mao agreed.[10]

Three days later, as crowds occupied the square, the Politburo met at the Great Hall of the People. Hua Guofeng lashed out at 'bad elements' who were stirring up the masses behind the scenes, inciting them to 'attack the Chairman' and 'attack the Centre'. And the denunciations did not come from ordinary people alone, he noted. Hundreds of representatives of state institutions, including officials from the Ministry of Railways and the Ministry of Foreign Affairs, were leaving wreaths in honour of Zhou Enlai. The most active participants came from the Seventh Ministry of Machine Building, a vast, secretive unit which managed the nuclear weapons programme. What was unfolding on the square was deemed nothing short of a 'class struggle', a coded way of stating that counter-revolutionaries were fomenting a coup against the Communist Party.[11]

In the early hours of 5 April, the militia cleaned up the square, quietly loading all the wreaths onto a fleet of trucks and using fire hoses to remove the slogans from the base of the monument. In the morning, enraged demonstrators began streaming back into the square and clashed with the police.

Later that day Mao Yuanxin briefed the Chairman again, reporting that so far some fifty counter-revolutionary incidents had taken place, with attacks on the militia and an assault on the Public Security Office located to the east of the square. The turmoil was 'planned and organised', not only in the capital but in other cities across the country. Deng was the one deliberately spreading 'counter-revolutionary rumours' and 'using the dead to oppress the living'. 'We are being duped,' he blurted out, announcing to his uncle that troops had been put on high alert and were ready to move in. Mao agreed.[12]

Even as protesters fought the militia on the square, Deng Xiaoping was summoned to appear before the Politburo. Zhang Chunqiao, a brooding man who had worked as director of propaganda in Shanghai before becoming a member of the Gang of Four, assailed his opponent, calling him China's Imre Nagy, after the short, stocky, stubborn communist politician who had led the 1956 Hungarian revolt against the Soviet-backed government. Deng remained silent.[13]

By the evening some 30,000 militia were ready, many concealed inside the Forbidden City, others in the Museum of Chinese History to the east of the square. Still Hua Guofeng feared that they had underestimated the gravity of the situation and that the armed forces would be no match for the crowds in the square. But despite repeated concerns from the military, Wang Hongwen, erstwhile head of security in a cotton mill in Shanghai who had risen to glory as one of the Gang of Four, slammed the table and announced that he refused to sign off on the militia carrying anything more than wooden truncheons into the square.[14]

From 6.30 p.m. onwards, warning messages were broadcast continuously through loudspeakers, condemning the protests as a 'reactionary plot' and calling on the crowd to disperse. The message attacked Deng Xiaoping by name. A few hours later, Hua Guofeng picked up the phone and gave the order to the militia to move into the square. The floodlights were switched on, the square sealed off. More than 200 people who remained inside were beaten, dragged away and placed under arrest. From the Great Hall of the People, Jiang Qing observed the events through a pair of binoculars. Later that evening she had a celebratory meal of peanuts and roast pork. Just before midnight, a clean-up crew of one hundred public security officers moved through the square, mopping up the blood.[15]

Mao suffered from undiagnosed Lou Gehrig's disease, which caused a gradual deterioration of the nerve cells controlling his muscles, including his throat, pharynx, tongue, diaphragm and ribs. He communicated through the only person who could understand his slurring speech, namely Zhang Yufeng, a train attendant he had seduced more than twenty years earlier. But his mental faculties remained intact. Until the end he remained a master of intrigue, as transcripts of his meetings amply demonstrate. When his nephew reported back to him at the Poolside House on 7 April, recounting how Zhang Chunqiao had called Deng a Nagy, he nodded his head in approval. The Chairman ordered that the Politburo relieve Deng of all his positions except his party membership. 'Strip him of all his functions,' he said, feebly waving his hand. He further instructed that Su Zhenhua, a general recently rehabilitated after having been purged during the Cultural Revolution, accused of being a 'time-bomb' planted by Deng Xiaoping, be barred from attending the meeting. Mao also excluded Marshal Ye Jianying, an army veteran in charge of the Ministry of Defence. Hua Guofeng, already premier, was to be elevated on the spot to first vice-chairman, making him Mao's designated successor. 'Be fast,' the Chairman ordered, with another wave of the hand. 'Come back when you are done.'[16]

***

A nationwide crackdown followed, as thousands were arrested for counter-revolutionary crimes. Many more were interrogated about their participation in the Tiananmen incident. Across the nation, people were required to denounce Deng Xiaoping, but the campaign fell flat. 'We marched with resentment,' remembered one participant. Everyone was waiting for the end.[17]

It came a few minutes past midnight on 9 September 1976, one day after the Mid-Autumn Festival, when families traditionally gathered under the full moon to count their blessings.

Hua Guofeng held few cards in his hand. He clung onto a scrap of paper on which Mao had scrawled a few lines: 'Go slowly, don't rush. Act according to past directions. With you in charge, I am at ease.' This was the whole of Mao Zedong's testament, although the circumstances in which it was produced remain obscure. The official hagiography claimed that Mao had written these words of wisdom for Hua when they had met Prime Minister Robert Muldoon of New Zealand in late April 1976. But Zhang Yufeng, who was by the Chairman's side during his final years, confided to her diary that Mao had used the message to put Hua Guofeng at ease after he had complained about several provincial leaders.[18]

There was one other problem. Hua Guofeng had been Minister of Public Security during the Tiananmen incident, which did not endear him to the population. But exactly what had happened inside the Great Hall of the People on 5 April remained a closely guarded secret. Few people realised that Hua had deliberately used the incident to discredit Deng and promote his own career. And even fewer knew that it was he who had picked up the phone and ordered the attack on the square. With blood on his hands, Hua had no choice but to ally himself with those opposed to any return to power by Deng Xiaoping.

Hua had one advantage, and he used it to play a weak hand rather well: people underestimated him. A mere two days after Mao's death, Hua Guofeng contacted Marshal Ye Jianying and General Su Zhenhua, the two veteran army leaders who had been banned from attending the Politburo meeting that had sealed Deng Xiaoping's fate. He also reached out to Wang Dongxing, Mao's former bodyguard, who commanded the troops in charge of the leaders' security. On 6 October, on the pretext of discussing the fifth volume of Mao Zedong's *Selected Works*, a Politburo meeting was called. As they arrived one by one at the hall, members of the Gang of Four were arrested. Madame Mao, wily as ever, sensed a trap and stayed away but was later apprehended at her residence.[19]

It was nothing short of a coup. After the coup came a purge, and like any other purge it was a continuation, not a departure, from business as usual. Rallies were held, enemies denounced. In the capital, columns of hundreds of thousands of people waved huge banners denouncing the 'Gang of Four Anti-Party Clique'. They were accused of being traitors, colluding with foreign powers, betraying the country and attempting to restore capitalism. As one participant noted, these were 'exactly the same kind of rallies as during the Cultural Revolution'. Several months later a 115-page verdict based on a close examination of all the available evidence concluded as follows: 'Zhang Chunqiao is a Taiwanese spy, Jiang Qing is a traitor, Yao Wenyuan is an alien class element, Wang Hongwen is a reborn capitalist element.' Jiang Qing and her three fanatical followers became scapegoats. Seemingly overnight, all references to the four were excised from newspapers, books, photographs and films.[20]

A mass rally was held on Tiananmen Square on 24 October, as the leaders made their first public appearance since the coup. Hua Guofeng, now anointed as chairman of the party, quickly took to his new role, moving back and forth along the rostrum, clapping lightly to acknowledge the cheers and smiling beatifically, very much like his predecessor.

His next order of business was to undermine his rival and enhance his own position. Wang Dongxing, the erstwhile bodyguard who knew every palace secret, became his right-hand man. On 8 January 1977, when a few protesters turned up on Tiananmen Square to mark the first anniversary of Zhou Enlai's death, they seized on the incident to launch an inquisition. Li Dongmin, a young man who had put up a poster demanding the return of Deng Xiaoping, was arrested and forced to confess to the existence of a dangerous 'counter-revolutionary clique'. Wang Dongxing took to the phone, ordering the public security services across the nation to investigate every rumour. The authorities in Liaoning province discovered a poster calling on the population to 'resolutely support Deng for premier'. 'Class enemies both at home and abroad are attacking us,' the leadership now thundered, as every party member was enjoined to 'pay attention and stay alert'. In a tense political climate, more witch-hunts followed, with more plots uncovered.[21]

Hua projected himself as the faithful guardian of the Chairman's legacy. Even as the body of his predecessor was being injected with formaldehyde for preservation in a cold chamber deep beneath the capital, Hua Guofeng announced that a memorial hall would be erected on Tiananmen Square, displaying the corpse to the masses in a coffin made of rock crystal. Much as his body was manipulated, Mao's every word was also exploited. In February 1977 several editorials proclaimed: 'Whatever policies Mao decided, we shall resolutely defend; whatever instructions he issued, we shall steadfastly obey.' People disparagingly referred to the policy as the 'Two Whatevers'.

Hua began to model himself on his master. He slicked back his hair and posed for staged photographs, uttering vague aphorisms in the style of the Great Helmsman. His portrait went up in schools, offices and factories. Prominent among these were paintings and posters of a beaming Chairman about to hand over his last will to Hua, who leaned forward in his seat to humbly accept the mission: 'with you in charge I am at ease.' Songs, poems and statues exalted the new leader. But while the propaganda machine churned out slogans exhorting the population to 'Most Closely Follow our Brilliant Leader', the new chairman lacked the institutional authority and political charisma to shore up his power. His clumsy attempt at a personality cult alienated ordinary people and party officials alike.

On several occasions Marshal Ye Jianying suggested that Deng Xiaoping be allowed to assume his former position. Hua demurred. At a party meeting he insisted that the protests on Tiananmen Square the previous year had been counter-revolutionary and that Deng Xiaoping had been castigated as a rightist by Chairman Mao, whose every word must be cherished.[22]

Li Xiannian, a slippery character who had made a career of working with entirely different personalities, now entered the fray. As vice-premier in charge of day-to-day government work, he carried considerable clout. After the fall of the Gang of Four he had acquiesced in denouncing Deng Xiaoping: 'Whoever thinks he is big stuff is bound to fall one way or another. Lin Biao considered himself big stuff, the "Gang of Four" considered themselves big stuff, and Deng Xiaoping also thinks he's big stuff.' But in March Li had a change of heart and joined Marshal Ye at a Politburo meeting in formally requesting a return of Deng Xiaoping.[23]

Hua had to yield. Many party veterans had been humiliated during the Cultural Revolution, and Hua Guofeng's reluctance to examine the record and rehabilitate fallen cadres was out of tune with a widespread desire for change. Most senior officials, besides, were hardened men who had honed their survival skills during decades of dog-eat-dog politics. Even though he had shown greater determination than many had anticipated, Hua was simply no match. Formally, Hua was both premier and chairman, but when he looked around he saw 'another man's men consolidating and increasing their hold on the provinces, on the state machinery, on the army and on the media'.[24] To Hua's great disappointment, in the summer of 1977 Deng returned to power.

***

Hua and Deng alike marched under the banner of Mao Zedong Thought. All veteran leaders harked back to the past. Some wanted to pick up where they had left off before the Cultural Revolution had begun in 1966; others looked back even further, before the cataclysm of the Great Leap Forward in 1958.

Deng went back to 1956. On 25 February that year, Soviet leader and party secretary Nikita Khrushchev had shaken the socialist camp to the core with a secret speech that demolished the reputation of his master Joseph Stalin, who had passed away three years earlier. In Beijing, where the leadership had modelled their regime on that of Stalin, throughout the ranks the speech was received with dismay. Mao, as China's Stalin, viewed de-Stalinisation as a challenge to his own authority. His response came precisely two months later, when he addressed an enlarged meeting of the Politburo on 25 April in a speech entitled 'On the Ten Major Relationships'. China, the Chairman announced, was ready to strike out on its own, finding its own path to socialism. Instead of slavishly following the old Stalinist model, with its lopsided emphasis on heavy industry, China would develop its own version with a more balanced developmental strategy towards agriculture and light industry. It would respond to the needs of ordinary people with appropriate adjustments to their wages. In charting its own course towards socialism, Mao went on, China should borrow science and technology from capitalist countries.

'In the industrially developed countries they run their enterprises with fewer people and greater efficiency and they know how to do business.' This, too, should be an inspiration, as the country could become strong and prosperous only by learning from others.[25]

Mao's speech remained unpublished in his lifetime. Khrushchev had railed against Stalin's cult of personality, and, in Beijing, the Chairman's colleagues used the Russian leader's secret speech to advocate a return to the principles of collective leadership. Mao responded by encouraging freedom of expression among intellectuals, asking the party to 'let a hundred flowers bloom, let a hundred schools contend.' The Chairman believed that the population adulated him and would rally to his side. Instead, the Hundred Flowers resulted in an outpouring of popular anger against the Communist Party, forcing Mao to reverse course and order a clampdown in May 1957. Deng Xiaoping, who like most of his colleagues had bristled at the prospect of allowing ordinary people to speak their minds, demanded sweeping measures, and was placed in charge of a campaign that targeted hundreds of thousands of individuals. Deng acquitted himself admirably, sending countless victims to labour camps in the Great Northern Wilderness, a vast mosquito-infested swamp.[26]

'On the Ten Major Relationships' had struck a resonant chord with Deng and other party members. As the disasters of the Great Leap Forward and the Cultural Revolution unfolded, the speech seemed ever more appealing. It became the inspiration behind the Four Modernisations programme that Premier Zhou Enlai had announced in January 1975. Six months later, Deng Xiaoping approached the Chairman to propose a new edition of the text, which he believed should be included in the fifth volume of Mao Zedong's *Selected Works*. 'This thing really is far too important, it has a great aim and provides great theoretical guidance for the present and for posterity,' Deng scribbled in the margin. Mao allowed the circulation but not the publication of the text.[27]

Hua Guofeng also fervently admired the piece. 'The whole party, the whole army and the whole people should study this brilliant work conscientiously and in a thorough-going way,' he exhorted assembled party members on 25 December 1976. One day later, the *People's Daily* published 'On the Ten Major Relationships' to commemorate Mao Zedong's birthday, giving the official stamp of approval to a broad consensus on the need for sustained economic development following a decade of chaos.[28]

Hua did not need Deng to herald a more pragmatic approach towards the economy. Like most others, he was eager to jolt the country out of its economic torpor. Hua lost no time, calling in November 1976 for a jump in exports to pay for increased imports of foreign technology.[29]

This, too, signalled a return to pre-Cultural Revolution days rather than a step forward. It was a model based on the one developed by Stalin many decades earlier: take grain from the countryside, sell it on the international market and use the foreign currency earned to buy turnkey factories, to be acquired in a ready-to-use condition, to transform an agricultural backwater into an industrial powerhouse. In order to extract more grain, Stalin corralled villagers into state farms and collectivised the countryside. By 1932 an estimated 6 million people had died of hunger following the draining of huge stocks of wheat, corn and rye as well as milk, eggs and meat from the country to finance the Five Year Plan. Even as villagers were reduced to eating grass and tree bark, huge industrial cities were built from scratch. Moscow was transformed, with hundreds of projects designed to rival the skylines of New York. Luxury hotels, new railway stations, a brand-new metro and a string of imposing skyscrapers dazzled the thousands of foreign businessmen busily cutting deals in the capital. Albert Kahn, the head of a firm of American architects, directed the building of hundreds of factories, in effect becoming 'the industrial architect for the First and Second Five Year Plans'.[30]

Just as Stalin had wanted to overtake the United States, in 1958 Chairman Mao was keen to propel his country past its competitors with a Great Leap Forward. Exports were cranked up, as 'larger imports and larger exports' became the catchphrase of the day. To capture more food from the countryside, villagers were herded into giant People's Communes. The leadership went on a shopping spree, purchasing steel mills, cement kilns, glass factories, power stations and oil refineries. Beijing was transformed as tens of thousands of houses, offices and factories were demolished to make way for a vision of towering concrete. While the square received its hall, museum and obelisk, at least 45 million people starved to death.[31]

Most of these imports came from the Soviet Union, on which China had depended for economic and military help since May 1951, when the United Nations had imposed an embargo on strategic imports due to Beijing's role in the Korean War. But in the summer of 1960, China and the Soviet Union fell out. Thousands of Soviet advisers and their dependants were ordered to pack up and leave the country. Scores of large-scale projects were frozen.

Even before the Sino-Soviet rift, China had started dumping products in Asia and Africa. Bicycles, sewing machines, thermos flasks, canned pork, fountain pens: Beijing sold all sorts of goods below cost to demonstrate how far ahead of Moscow it was in the race towards true communism. China also did its best to undercut Japan in soybean oil, cement, structural steel and window glass. Textiles above all became the battlefield for asserting communist supremacy, with products from grey sheeting to cotton prints flooding the international market. As exports towards the Soviet Union decreased, the flow of goods towards the rest of the world swelled even further.[32]

The disaster of the Great Leap Forward left the Chairman fearful of a coup. He worried that even before he died he might be denounced, just as Khrushchev had assailed Stalin. His answer was the Cultural Revolution, which pitted people against each other, forcing them to prove their undying loyalty to the Chairman. Exports were condemned as 'capitalist', with self-reliance hailed instead as the country closed in on itself. Entire provinces sunk into economic autarky as the leadership imposed the principle of self-reliance on the national economy, cutting off many of the trade connections that had linked the country together in a larger whole. By 1970 a task as simple as making a button became a challenge as factories were forced to produce everything locally. Doctrinaire insistence on self-reliance compounded the inability of the planned economy to fulfil even the most basic demands of the population, reaching surreal proportions. In Turfan, the centre of a fertile oasis where Red Guards had converted minarets and mosques into factories, three people had to share one bar of soap every season. Xinjiang was at the remote edge of the empire, but even trading cities along the Pearl River Delta near Hong Kong suffered from shortages of matches, soap, toothpaste, batteries and cotton cloth. Coming so soon after the disaster of the Great Leap Forward, the Cultural Revolution ensured that by 1976 living standards across the nation were lower than on the eve of liberation.[33]

Hua Guofeng focused on foreign trade, but also improved material incentives for workers and a better-organised market, holding conferences on capital construction, industry, railways and transportation, finance and banking, agriculture, and science and technology. One Pekinologist counted more than forty such meetings by the time of Deng Xiaoping's formal return in July 1977.[34]

In August, as the monstrous bulk of the mausoleum for their dead master loomed larger by the day, the party leaders convened in the Great Hall of the People to offer a show of unity at the First Plenum of the Eleventh Party Congress. They were old men who had been thwarted for a decade and were now eager for change. Hua Guofeng seemed crumpled and uneasy, at times shambling in motion. Marshal Ye Jianying appeared senile, standing up and sitting down only with the help of an assistant. Li Xiannian projected boredom, his face occasionally lit by a smile. But Deng looked relaxed and confident, even if his features were heavy with age. All extolled Mao Zedong.[35]

All were also in a hurry. The official goal of the congress, written in the party constitution, was to 'build up the motherland at high speed' and become a 'powerful modern socialist country before the end of this century', an objective that Premier Zhou Enlai had announced with his Four Modernisations of January 1975. The Four Modernisations had in turn been conceived in 1963, when the premier had developed two fifteen-year plans to transform the country by the turn of the millennium into an industrialised power in the world's first rank. The emphasis on a high growth rate to catch up with or surpass certain capitalist countries in a short, predetermined period of time could not have been more Stalinist. This was, in essence, the programme that the leaders would pursue during the following two decades.[36]

So keen were the party elders that they called for a new Leap Forward. The choice of words was perhaps unfortunate, given the disaster of the first Great Leap, but they felt that they must make up for a lost decade. At a Politburo meeting in February 1978, they outdid each other in whipping up the drive for higher targets. Deng Xiaoping wanted more steel, which he viewed as the backbone of heavy industry. Energy was also an issue, and a big power station had to be imported. 'We must go faster,' he opined, urging more imports of advanced technology.[37]

The target for imports of advanced technology up to 1985 had been set at $6.5 billion the previous year, but on Deng Xiaoping's prompting was lifted to $10 billion. It then rose to $18 billion, eventually hitting $80 billion. Well over a hundred large-scale projects were envisaged. In 1978 alone more than 22 turnkey factories were imported from abroad, from huge steel works and modern textile mills to nuclear plants.[38]

For a decade the country had lived in self-imposed isolation. At the height of the Cultural Revolution, the shrill language of class warfare and anti-imperialist struggle had alienated even potentially neutral powers. In 1967 a straw figure with a blackened face was hung in front of the Kenyan embassy, dangling on the gate for many months. The Indonesian and Mongolian embassies endured permanent sieges. The British mission in Beijing was burned to the ground.[39] But the brunt of the attacks during the Cultural Revolution was borne by ordinary people, as a fitful Chairman indulged in a seemingly never-ending cycle of purges and denunciations. For party members at every level of the hierarchy, political survival became an all-consuming task. A mere utterance by Mao could decide the fates of countless people as he declared one or another institution to be 'counter-revolutionary'. His verdict could change overnight, sending his subjects scrambling to prove their loyalty. Everything foreign, moreover, be it listening to classical music or reading a novel, was denounced as 'bourgeois'. As a result, illiteracy rates shot up. As the State Council admitted in 1978, in parts of the country more than half the population could not read, while in some provinces one in three cadres were illiterate.[40] As one astute observer pointed out, 'Hua Guofeng and Deng Xiaoping would have had trouble placing even mid-sized countries on the map'. They had no conception of how foreign countries operated.[41]

Mao, in 1972, had single-handedly shifted the balance of power away from the Soviet Union by seeking a rapprochement with the United States. This came as a shock to many. For decades, China had denounced the United States as an imperialist stronghold bent on enslaving the world. Zhou Enlai himself had set the tone in 1950, becoming an eloquent spokesman for a Hate America Campaign. Cartoons portraying American politicians as bloodthirsty murderers accompanied spiteful slogans spewed from public loudspeakers. Foreign policy took many twists and turns, and in the regime's

endless tirades, calculated vituperation was at times difficult to dis-
entangle from genuine outrage, but for decades the message was clear
enough: people had to hate, curse and despise the capitalists.[42]

Secretary of State Henry Kissinger and other naive admirers
portrayed Mao's gambit as a stroke of strategic genius, but it rested on
one of the great geopolitical misunderstandings of the twentieth century: namely that the United States was a power in terminal decline.
This misapprehension would continue to inform the leadership in
Beijing for decades to come.

Since the acquisition of advanced technology lay at the heart of the
Four Modernisations, fact-finding missions went abroad. As Gu Mu,
one key proponent of trade delegations, later noted, in 1917 Lenin
had sent teams abroad to learn about science and technology. 'We
did the same.'[43] In September 1977 a delegation was dispatched to the
United States. Wang Yaoting, chairman of the China Council for the
Promotion of International Trade, brought along experts in a whole
range of fields, from chemical engineering to metallurgy. The group
had lunch with Vice-President Mondale and visited Mobil, Union
Carbide, Exxon and John Deere & Co., among other companies.
They took a recreational break at Disneyland. Throughout their stay
in the United States they asked no questions about the politics of the
industries they studied. 'They were only interested in technology,'
their American guide explained.[44]

Back home, the delegation reported that the rate of industrial
development in the United States was constantly declining, while
an economic crisis had put an end to the country's postwar expansion. American unemployment was sky-high. Their oil would run out
within a decade. Their trade was creaking under the weight of a record
deficit reaching more than $25 billion.[45]

Other trade missions and study tours went elsewhere in 1978,
touring New Zealand, Japan and Eastern and Western Europe. Their
verdict was the same, summarised by the Ministry of Foreign Affairs
in a nationwide conference on foreign trade in 1979: 'The international
situation is favourable for us as some advanced capitalist countries are
faced with economic decline. They are keen to find an outlet for their
surplus capital, equipment, products and manpower. They are keen
to find new energy sources and raw materials. Their currencies are
inflated, a financial crisis is looming, their unemployment rate keeps

on going up and their economic outlook is gloomy.' As the economist Milton Friedman observed during his visit to China in 1980, even leading experts and bank directors were 'unbelievably ignorant about how a market works'. They droned on about the 'internal contradictions of capitalism'. This was classic Marxism, a philosophy that had for over a century been foretelling the impending demise of capitalism. The conclusion was inescapable. As the Ministry put it, 'we must seize these extremely favourable opportunities.'[46]

***

Hua Guofeng and Deng Xiaoping shared power, balanced by Marshal Ye Jianying in an uneasy triumvirate. From May to November 1978, Hua and Deng confronted each other in a philosophical debate over the meaning of Mao Zedong in an ideological war fought via proxies. Wang Dongxing, who was also in charge of ideology, took up his pen on Hua's behalf. Deng turned to Hu Yaobang, an unorthodox, wiry 62-year-old with a lively if somewhat eccentric mind who would soon shoot to stardom. Mao, always a shrewd observer of human nature, once described Hu as follows: 'Likes to read but only focuses on the surface, likes to talk and makes grandiose statements.'[47]

In 1977 Hu Yaobang had been appointed head of the Central Party School, the top institution in charge of ideological indoctrination. His main mission was to destroy the Two Whatevers, the irreverent name given to Hua Guofeng's policy of closely adhering to Chairman Mao's every dictate. To an outsider, this might have seemed like abstract semantics, but it had very real consequences, as the official verdicts passed during the Cultural Revolution were still in place. When family members and relatives were included, the number of victims approached the 100 million mark.[48] The characterisation of the 1976 Tiananmen protesters as 'counter-revolutionaries' was but one example.

Hu Yaobang came up with the principle of Practice as the Sole Criterion of Truth. It meant that statements must be tested in practice. Pitched battles were fought, much as Protestants and Catholics had torn into each other over the meaning of the Bible. Telephone calls were made, editorials manipulated, repudiations published, information leaked, commentaries introduced to bypass censorship and workshops held, first in Beijing, before long across the nation.

The followers of the Criterion of Truth were accused of cutting down the banner of Mao Zedong. They, in turn, charged the disciples of the Two Whatevers with undermining Mao Zedong Thought, as they dogmatically stuck to every word of the Chairman.

The drama played out in December 1978. In August the previous year, the new leadership had been introduced at the First Plenum of the Eleventh Party Congress. A second plenum generally focused on the consolidation of power, with the third traditionally set aside to introduce a broader vision of the future. The stage for the Third Plenum was the Capital West Hotel, a Soviet-style venue built in 1964 and equipped with special security handled by elite soldiers. It was a favourite haunt of top military officers when holding meetings behind closed doors to hammer out important deals.

Even before the plenum officially opened, handwritten posters began to appear on a long brick wall near an old bus station in Xidan, an intersection along Chang'an Avenue to the west of Tiananmen Square. They attracted a huge crowd of onlookers, warmly bundled up against the cold: ordinary people, who had wearily followed the debates between the two camps in the newspapers, liked Hu Yaobang's slogan in favour of truth from practice. The wall, soon dubbed Democracy Wall, became the focal point for popular discontent with the status quo. Some demonstrators put up detailed accounts of their personal grievances. Others clamoured for the full rehabilitation of senior officials like Peng Dehuai, purged for having stood up to Mao during the Great Leap Forward. Many viewed Deng Xiaoping as the underdog, demanding his restoration to his former functions. Rallies were organised, with some speakers even calling for the study of the separation of powers in the United States. Ren Wanding, a civil engineer who had been persecuted during the Cultural Revolution, established a Human Rights Alliance and published a manifesto demanding basic civil rights for all his fellow citizens. There were calls for universal suffrage, with one electrician from the Beijing Zoo named Wei Jingsheng asking for a Fifth Modernisation, namely democracy, to supplement the party's Four Modernisations. As a Canadian journalist put it: 'They have ended any nonsense about Chinese not understanding what free speech is all about. They know, and they want it.'[49]

Towards the end of November, Deng Xiaoping granted an interview to Robert Novak, a leading American journalist. In a vast room of the Great Hall of the People, a self-confident vice-premier chain-smoked Panda cigarettes and occasionally hawked into a spittoon placed by his chair. When asked about the wall posters at Xidan, he nodded in approval. Novak had the leader's words reported back to the crowd: 'The Democracy Wall is a fine thing.' The protesters went into uproar, as some 10,000 marched to Tiananmen Square for a demonstration lasting well into the night.[50]

The controversy over the Two Whatevers had ignited the fire of popular protest, and the protests in turn encouraged some of the more than 200 delegates to speak out. The assembled party members were supposed to discuss economic policy in a preparatory work conference leading up to the more formal plenum, but some departed from their script and began lobbying for the political rehabilitation of officials purged by Mao. The meeting slipped out of control, with many participants releasing a torrent of anger. Chen Yun, a veteran economist who had played a leading role in economic planning, presented entire lists of people whose names should be cleared. In the middle of the conference, the Beijing municipal party committee reversed the verdict on the Tiananmen events of 5 April 1976, announcing that all those who had been persecuted would have their reputations restored.

Hua Guofeng found himself on the defensive. On 25 November he hastily raised a white flag, embracing the principle of Practice as the Sole Criterion of Truth and reversing himself on a host of other issues. On 13 December he humbly requested that his colleagues no longer address him as 'Chairman'. Marshal Ye Jianying rallied to his defence, praising his sincerity. Hua managed to retain his formal titles as premier and chairman, but Deng took control of the party. He had successfully used the Democracy Wall to fence in his rival and shore up his own position.[51]

***

On 1 October 1970, as National Day was celebrated with processions in every city, Chairman Mao had appeared on the rostrum above the Gate of Heavenly Peace to review the annual parade. For the first time ever an American stood next to him. Edgar Snow, a veteran journalist who had first interviewed Mao Zedong decades ago in Yan'an, was used to signal that major changes were afoot in relations with the imperialist camp. A flicker of hope was instantly kindled among ordinary people, although Americans were slower to pick up the hint. In February 1972, Nixon went to China.

Deng Xiaoping was less subtle when interviewed by Robert Novak, using the journalist to convey a message about normalisation, and repeatedly stressing that Washington and Beijing must collaborate against Moscow. Since every correspondent sent abroad by Beijing was an accredited Communist Party member working for the state, both Mao and Deng believed that their American counterparts were also covert intelligence operatives who would report back to their masters in Washington.

After his return to power in 1974 and again in 1977, Deng had been responsible for foreign affairs. Years earlier, following the Sino-Soviet rift in 1960, Deng had been one of the most vociferous critics of the Soviet Union. Leonid Brezhnev, who assumed power in 1964, was so struck by his vehemence that he called him an 'anti-Soviet dwarf'.[52] Deng, like many of his colleagues, viewed the Soviet Union and Vietnam, not the United States, as his country's main threat. After the United States signed the Vietnam peace agreement and began to withdraw troops from Vietnam in 1973, Deng concluded that Moscow would replace Washington as the dominant global power. The shift required an alliance with Japan and the United States.

Deng went to Japan first. In 1955, the United States had helped the island nation join the General Agreement on Tariffs and Trade, known as GATT, over huge objections from other member states, not least France as well as most Commonwealth members. These countries withheld from Tokyo the Most Favoured Nation status, which would have granted Japan all the concessions, privileges and immunities that member states provided to each other. But low tariffs in the United States meant that exports from Japan surged, as vast quantities of textiles, steel, automobiles, chemicals and electronics were shipped across the Pacific. The trade surplus was used to import and copy foreign technology, build up heavy industry and foster home-grown brands capable of rivalling the best international competitors. A Japanese growth rate of 10 per cent year after year soon prompted talk of an economic miracle. But in 1971, in the midst of a costly war with Vietnam, Nixon abandoned the dollar's peg to gold and imposed a 10 per cent surcharge on imports. The oil crisis two years later marked the end of rapid growth in Japan.

Deng rode a bullet train and visited factories producing the electronics, televisions and automobiles popular across the world. He appeared humble, explaining that his backward country was keen to learn from Japan. He flattered his hosts, brushing aside the memory of the Second World War after they apologised for the suffering their nation had inflicted. He hailed the common heritage between their countries, extending the hand of friendship. A flood of money was released as Japan became China's most generous donor, giving tens of billions of dollars in aid to help build up infrastructure across the country. Having benefited from the Most Favoured Nation status, Japan in turn granted it to China, complete with preferential tariff rates.[53]

But China's most important relationship was with the United States. Even before Deng's tour in January 1979, he had met several delegations from Washington. These visitors were handled as if admission to the inner sanctum of power was a great privilege granted only to a chosen few. As the Hungarian Jesuit László Ladány pointed out in 1974, the communist leaders exploited to the full the aura of mystery enveloping their closed country: 'Many other countries, Japan or India, to mention only two Asian countries, are no less important. Yet no myths attach to modern Japan or modern India. To enter China is an event; to have a talk with a high official is a privilege. This projection of an image of unique grandeur has been highly successful.' Richard Walker, member of a Washington delegation, explained how they were made to wait in their hotel for days on end until the summons finally came, as they were escorted for a personal meeting with Vice-Premier Deng Xiaoping in a state verging on awe. 'Secrecy, unexplained decisions, an aura of cultivated mystery, strict supervision over the foreign guest, the accent of politeness and ceremony, incredible hospitality, attention to details of comfort, and, above all, good food: such are the hallmarks of the Chinese approach to foreign guests, and to foreign relations when carried out in China.'[54]

In Beijing visitors were warned relentlessly about the threat to world peace posed by the Soviet Union. The Soviets were routinely compared to the Nazis, and any kind of relationship with Moscow interpreted as a dangerous policy of appeasement resembling Munich. Russia, called the 'polar bear', was an evil empire bent on world hegemony. 'They are more imperialist than the worst imperialists,'

Hao Deqing, president of the Chinese People's Institute of Foreign Affairs, exclaimed in November 1977.[55] This struck a chord with Cold War warriors in the United States, where the most hawkish voices against the Soviet Union were precisely those who became the most ardent supporters of the People's Republic.

One such was Zbigniew Brzezinski, the Polish-born White House national security adviser known for his rabidly anti-Soviet views. In May 1978 Brzezinski spent three days in China, where his hosts flattered him by calling him the 'polar bear tamer'. At the farewell dinner he opined that 'our shared views outweigh our differences.' As some foreign diplomats observed, he had fallen victim to the local habit of overwhelming guests with hospitality to persuade them to make exaggerated statements. Brzezinski would become a key supporter of military and financial aid to China, abandoning a policy of even balancing between Moscow and Beijing.[56]

Another was Senator Henry Jackson, a staunch anti-communist and leading proponent of human rights. Highly critical of trade agreements with a hostile superpower like the Soviet Union, in 1974 he had sponsored the Jackson–Vanik amendment, limiting economic relations with countries that did not have a market economy and restricted freedom of emigration and other basic rights. Wined and dined in China and suitably awed when finally granted an audience with Deng Xiaoping, Jackson, too, was converted and became a vocal proponent of normalised relations with China. Brzezinski and Jackson shared a vision that rested on the other great geopolitical misunderstanding of the twentieth century, namely that once the People's Republic of China had become developed economically, it would flourish into a democracy.

Deng made many more friends during his visit in the United States. He thrilled the public by donning a cowboy hat at a rodeo in Texas. He circled the arena in a horse-drawn stagecoach, waving to the crowd, and generally charmed business leaders and politicians alike during his stay. Deng Xiaoping had warned that he would answer no questions on human rights, although he happily promised to bring about democracy 'without restriction'. In meeting Jimmy Carter he specifically pointed to the Democracy Wall to prove that Chinese people could freely express a variety of views.[57] Later, back home, he would fume about human rights, sneering at what he considered was the sham democracy of the United States. But in Washington he kept his composure.

The gamble paid off. Deng, unlike Brezhnev, won for his country Most Favoured Nation tariff status, which came into effect a year later on 1 February 1980.[58] This meant that China was granted all the tariff reductions that the United States provided to any other country. Always the consummate showman, Deng Xiaoping embraced Senator Henry Jackson in Seattle.[59] One year later, after the Soviet invasion of Afghanistan, more strategic and military collaboration followed.

**

In Washington, Deng Xiaoping had boasted to Jimmy Carter that his country would teach Vietnam a lesson. Only a few months earlier, on 3 November 1978, the Soviet Union and Vietnam had signed a mutual defence treaty, viewed with suspicion by China. Back in Beijing, Deng wasted no time. On 15 February, the very day that the Sino-Soviet Treaty of Friendship, Alliance and Mutual Assistance signed in 1950 ended, he announced that China would strike back at Vietnam for having attacked the Khmer Rouge of Cambodia. The Khmer Rouge, who had come to power with China's support in 1975, had executed, tortured, starved or otherwise eliminated a quarter of their population, in atrocities that came to an end only after Vietnam invaded their neighbour on 25 December 1978 and toppled Pol Pot's regime.

On 17 February 1979 some 200,000 troops crossed the border into Vietnam. Deng had promised a punitive campaign, not an invasion. The Vietnamese avoided direct combat, allowing the enemy to advance some 20 kilometres towards the city of Lang Son, where bloody house-to-house fighting took place. The People's Liberation Army looted and pillaged as it returned to China. Beijing declared victory, but it was clear to most observers that the entire operation had been a debacle, with a poor command structure and lacklustre communications. One Chinese general privately described the Vietnam offensive as a shambles.[60]

The army's mediocre performance provoked further public unrest. Even before the Sino-Vietnamese War, unprecedented scenes had unfolded around the Democracy Wall, with several hundred villagers demonstrating in the capital on two occasions. On 8 January, the anniversary of Zhou Enlai's death, they had carried banners reading 'Down with Starvation, Down with Oppression, We Want Democracy'. Their faces lined with grief, some dressed in mere rags, a few hobbling along on crutches, they looked nothing like the students who had demonstrated so far. A few days later they brought their misery to the painted gates of Zhongnanhai, demanding the right to work. Contingents of student marchers also paraded around the square, clamouring for human rights. Repercussions were nation-wide. In Changsha and Guangzhou posters in favour of democracy went up. In Shanghai more than 5,000 youths who had been forcibly transferred to the countryside in the wake of the Cultural Revolution staged a demonstration, having illegally returned home and now demanding that they be allowed to stay.[61]

As the debacle in Vietnam unfolded, some protesters began to take Deng Xiaoping to task. Wei Jingsheng, the young man who had proposed a Fifth Modernisation, put up an essay entitled 'Democracy or the New Autocracy?', describing the vice-premier as a new despot.[62]

To criticise Mao was one thing, Deng another. On the evening of 16 March the vice-premier presided over an enraptured audience at the indoor Capital Stadium, where the Boston Symphony Orchestra played John Philip Sousa's 'The Stars and Stripes Forever' as well as more classical pieces to an audience of 18,000 listeners. It was the cultural crown of normalisation with the United States, with yelling, applause, cheers and demands for the conductor, Seiji Ozawa. But hours earlier Deng had hailed the victorious return of the troops from Vietnam in front of several thousand cadres in the Great Hall of the People. He also used the event to condemn the Democracy Wall in harsh terms and label the protesters as 'bad elements'.[63]

Two days later, the propaganda machine loudly condemned 'human rights' as a 'capitalist concept' used to protect 'counter-revolutionaries'. Notices went up in cities where demonstrations had taken place, banning anything critical of socialism, proletarian dictatorship, the leadership of the party, Marxism-Leninism and Mao Zedong Thought. On 29 March, sweeping restrictions were passed in Beijing.[64]

On 30 March, Deng Xiaoping formally promulgated the basic ideological prerequisite for the Four Modernisations, namely the Four Cardinal Principles. 'As long as imperialism and hegemony exist,' he explained, 'it is inconceivable that the dictatorial function of the state should wither away, that the standing army, public security organs, courts, and prisons should wither away. Their existence is not in contradiction with the democratisation of the socialist state, for their correct and effective work ensures, rather than hampers, such democratisation. The fact of the matter is that socialism cannot be defended or built up without the dictatorship of the proletariat.' The four principles were as follows:

1. We must keep to the socialist road.
2. We must uphold the dictatorship of the proletariat.
3. We must uphold the leadership of the Communist Party.
4. We must uphold Marxism-Leninism and Mao Zedong Thought.[65]

A few weeks later, at a central work conference on propaganda and ideology, senior party members rallied around Deng to defend the Four Principles. Hu Yaobang, as Minister of the Propaganda Department, opined that nothing could ever shake Marxism-Leninism and Mao Zedong Thought. Peng Zhen, the erstwhile mayor of Beijing who had been one of the first victims of the Cultural Revolution, explained why Mao Zedong Thought mattered: 'After Khrushchev hammered Stalin to death in the Soviet Union, they still held high the banner of Lenin, whether or not they were sincere in their belief. In China, if we abandon Mao Zedong Thought, then which banner do we hold on to? We must hold high the banner of Mao Zedong Thought. Otherwise it will cause chaos in the ideology of our party, our army and our country's various nationalities as well as in the entire revolutionary camp. It will sadden our friends and gladden our enemies.'[66]

On the sixtieth anniversary of the May Fourth Movement, the leadership turned out in force, united in holding high the banner of Marxism, Leninism and Mao Zedong Thought. The Chairman's mausoleum, closed under the pretext of repairs since the onset of the Democracy Wall, was reopened.[67]

A torrent of propaganda about the Four Cardinal Principles was unleashed in the following months. Dozens of activists were arrested in the capital, some merely because of close association with a foreigner. Wei Jingsheng, who had welcomed foreign reporters, was accused of passing military secrets to foreign powers, even though

the information was publicly available. Although the indictment did
not mention this, what had most galled the authorities was that he
had met with a government official from the United States to propose
linking the Most Favoured Nation status to human rights. In October
he stood shaven-headed before a court, defending himself by pointing
out that the constitution guaranteed freedom of expression. His elo-
quence won him fifteen years in prison. Journalists who had waited
outside in the rain all day gasped when they heard the verdict.[68]

In the early hours of a cold winter day later that year, a small
army of cleaners with twig brooms scrubbed away the last remnants
of free speech from the wall at Xidan. A year later, a secret meeting
on public security warned the leadership against 'an assault by the
ideology of bourgeois liberalisation as well as infiltration by foreign
spies and counter-revolutionary forces'.[69] Peng Zhen moved to elimi-
nate four basic freedoms codified into the constitution, namely the
rights of citizens to 'speak out freely, air their views fully, engage in
great debates and write posters'. The right to strike was dropped from
the constitution in 1982. As one disillusioned observer put it: 'The old
guard reverted to the old way of managing the country.'[70]

Jimmy Carter, who had announced that human rights would be
central to foreign policy in his January 1977 inaugural address, struck
up personal relationships with many Soviet dissidents, from Sakharov
to Sharansky. But he remained silent when it came to the rights of
their Chinese counterparts. In 1987, during a visit to China, a reporter
asked him about Wei Jingsheng. 'I'm personally not familiar with the
case that you described,' he answered.[71]

***

In November 1980 four widely reviled figures appeared in court.
Unlike Wei Jingsheng's star-chamber proceedings, conducted
behind closed doors, Madame Mao and her acolytes faced not only
their judges, but also 880 'representatives of the masses', including
family members of victims of the Cultural Revolution, as well as 300
journalists. It was a show trial that gripped the country, with endless
media analysis of every twist and turn in newspapers, on the radio and
on television.

Even four years after the death of Mao, Beijing was still a drab city,
coated in the dust picked up by winds from the northern plains. The

capital was dotted with bleak and decrepit housing estates, most poorly maintained and rarely painted. Since these were reserved for party members and model workers, ordinary people lived in ramshackle brick houses clustered around a common courtyard with a shared tap and a communal outside lavatory. Sprawling factories ensured that the city was one of the most polluted on earth, with dust and particle levels four times above international standards.[72] One journalist called the city 'diabolically ugly', although he conceded that while much of the imperial grandeur was gone, deliberately torn down by a regime scornful of the past, there were spots of great beauty, whether the Forbidden City or the old Winter Palace, with its lakes, boats and pagoda-style roofs.[73]

When the Ministry of Culture investigated the countryside, it discovered that all the villagers ever did was work, eat and sleep. 'Their lives are extremely dull.'[74] But even in the capital, entertainment was rare. Restrictions on the performance of traditional operas and popular folk songs, banned by Madame Mao at the height of the Cultural Revolution, were gradually lifted after 1976. Reading material became more varied. Shakespeare had been rehabilitated, although readers preferred *Gone with the Wind* and Agatha Christie. Still, most of the volumes found in bookshops were designed for moral edification or instruction, not amusement. Dancing was still a dangerous affair, and for most people recreation meant an occasional trip to the cinema or a walk in the park. Young people listened to pirated music from Hong Kong and Taiwan. The most popular star was Teresa Teng, Taiwan's queen of pop, nicknamed 'Little Deng' by her fans, as she shared the same surname as their leader.[75]

Television had two stations, one national and one local, with little difference between the two in programming, with broadcasts taking up a couple of hours in the morning, a couple in the afternoon and up to four in the evening. Most of the news consisted of silent clips of visiting dignitaries being welcomed at the airport or sitting in big, overstuffed chairs listening respectfully to the country's leaders. Occasionally a foreign film was shown.[76]

Television sets were rare, generally owned by factories and institutions rather than individuals. The reason was simple: the average factory worker would have to invest his entire earnings over five to eight months to pay for a standard Chinese set, while most workers in developed countries could buy two cheap televisions even on a week's pay.[77]

Now, for the first time, a genuine show was being broadcast nation-wide. People from all walks of life were mesmerised. Crowds gathered every night in front of television sets in factories, school buildings and basketball courts, watching the 'bunch of fascist dogs' that the regime encouraged them to hate. Children would every so often shout abuse at the screen, adults throw a few firecrackers to celebrate the Gang of Four's demise. In the morning the newspapers reviewed the performances of both sides, with congratulations for the prosecution and harsh words for the defendants.[78]

It was a carefully rehearsed media circus, with both parties reading from prepared scripts. But an occasional lapse of protocol or flash of anger would create sheer delight, even though a voice-over more often than not interrupted or paraphrased the show. This happened fre-quently when Madame Mao, who showed no contrition, hurled abuse at her accusers. The trial lasted more than a month. On 25 January the verdict was handed down, with three of the defendants sentenced to prison for life, the fourth for twenty years.

Panem et circenses, bread and circuses, was an old principle well understood by modern dictators, but the intense popular dislike for Jiang Qing and her three ultra-radical accomplices seemed real enough. As the travel writer Paul Theroux noted, perhaps the country managed to cope with the guilt of what had happened during the Cultural Revolution by blaming everything on the Gang of Four.[79]

The trial exonerated most of the leadership, since almost every top party official had, at one point or another, taken part in a denuncia-tion meeting. But most of all it allowed the party to absolve Mao Zedong and keep hoisting the banner of Mao Zedong Thought. De-Stalinisation had followed Nikita Khrushchev's secret speech, but there would be no de-Maoification in China.

Still, a formal resolution on Mao's role in history was required. Scores had to be settled, a line drawn under the Cultural Revolution. This was the goal set by the Sixth Plenum, which convened in June 1981, in time to mark the party's sixtieth anniversary of its founding on 23 July 1921. The complex process of producing a comprehensive document on the history of the party had begun over a year earlier, in October 1979. Since a historical resolution would have momentous consequences for all party members, it kept the leaders busy. Ideology, not the economy, was their main preoccupation, not least on the part of Deng Xiaoping, who seized command of the process from the beginning. Teams were assembled, evidence examined and drafts produced, circulated, discussed, revised and fine-tuned on several occasions. There were over a thousand briefing reports, involving close to 6,000 people from state ministers down to municipal party secretaries. At the top of the pyramid, deals were cut and compromises reached, as the resolution had to accommodate a wide range of interests, reflecting an ever-shifting balance of power.

Among the most important contributors was Hu Qiaomu, a leading theoretician who had become Mao Zedong's personal secretary decades earlier in 1941. Hu made a name for himself as a gifted rewriter of history, drafting a resolution on party history in 1945 in which Mao took centre stage. Purged like others during the Cultural Revolution, he was rehabilitated in 1975. Now that the past must once again be edited, Deng Xiaoping, his new boss, called him to the fore. His first draft infuriated Deng, who blamed him for focusing too much on Mao's mistakes during the Cultural Revolution. Hu went back to the drawing board, coming up with an ingenious insight designed to satisfy the requirements of his master: Mao Zedong himself had departed in later years from the scientific system of Mao Zedong Thought.[80]

The final draft barely mentioned Mao's Great Famine and blamed the Cultural Revolution on Lin Biao and the Gang of Four. Time and again, Deng intervened to salvage the Chairman's reputation. 'Some comrades have pointed out that mistakes committed during the Great Leap Forward and the Cultural Revolution by far outweigh those committed by Stalin,' he acknowledged, 'but our evaluation of comrade Mao Zedong and of Mao Zedong Thought is not about the person of Mao Zedong alone, it is inseparable from the entire history of our party.' 'To blacken Mao is to blacken our party,' he concluded.[81] The official verdict was that 'comrade Mao Zedong was a great Marxist and a great proletarian revolutionary, strategist and theorist.' While he made serious mistakes during the Cultural Revolution, his achievements were primary, his mistakes secondary. 'We must continue to uphold Mao Zedong Thought.'[82]

The resolution was designed to terminate, not encourage debate over the party's own past. After its adoption at the Sixth Plenum, academic research on major issues such as the Great Leap Forward and the Cultural Revolution was strongly discouraged, with any interpretation that strayed from the official version viewed with suspicion.

But the document also had other goals. Deng Xiaoping used the resolution to dispose of Hua Guofeng and become paramount leader. In November 1980 he placed Hu Yaobang in charge of chairing a series of bruising meetings with Hua Guofeng, as every aspect of his record was scrutinised. The role he had played in the events of 5 April 1976 came to light, including the fact that it was he who had picked up the telephone to order the militia into the square. Hua was forced to resign, and Hu Yaobang replaced him as Chairman of the Central Committee. Deng became chairman of the powerful Central Military Commission.[83]

In the party resolution, Hua Guofeng was lumped together with the Gang of Four and the Cultural Revolution. As a result, the Third Plenum in December 1978 was consecrated as the 'Great Turning Point in History', when under the guidance of Deng Xiaoping the party finally embarked on the 'correct path for socialist modernisation'.[84] It was a superb piece of propaganda that would be repeated for decades to come.

2

Retrenchment (1979–1982)

Chen Yun, not Deng Xiaoping, was the individual who came best out of the December 1978 Third Plenum. Paradoxically, Deng was weakened at the very moment of his ascendancy. It was Chen who had rallied a majority in pleading for the political rehabilitation of party officials wronged during the Cultural Revolution.

Unlike most of his colleagues, Chen actually came from a proletarian background, having worked as a typesetter at the Commercial Press in Shanghai before joining the Communist Party in 1924. He spent two years in the Soviet Union and specialised in Soviet economics. A dour, colourless man devoted to numbers, he had drawn up the country's first economic plan, with detailed production quotas for every factory. He was also the architect of a state monopoly on grain, imposed on the population in November 1953, that forced the villagers to sell most of their grain at fixed prices to the state. Since the villagers were not permitted to retain more than roughly 13 to 16 kilogrammes of unhusked grain a month for their own consumption, they were effectively put on a starvation diet.[1]

Yet Chen Yun did try to moderate the still more radical policies of the Chairman, which culminated in the Great Leap Forward in 1958. Three years later, in order to extricate the country from widespread starvation, he advocated a 'bird cage' approach to the economy: the bird was the market, the cage was the central plan. But Chen was wary of his master, who described him as 'a man who cannot get rid of his bourgeois character and leans consistently to the right'. By staying out of the limelight, he was spared many of the agonies of the Cultural Revolution.[2]

After spending close to twenty years watching from the sidelines, Chen Yun was now determined to leave his mark. As the main architect of the planned economy, he viewed Hua Guofeng and Deng Xiaoping's rash turn towards foreign imports with deep suspicion. As his daughter later explained, 'You have to understand one thing: My father hates America.'[3]

Chen Yun was hardly alone in harbouring doubts over the speed with which his country was opening up towards the capitalist camp. Other party elders, all of them eager to play a role after years in limbo, joined him. One was Bo Yibo, another powerful economist who had been critical of the Great Leap Forward, freed from house arrest during the Third Plenum. Another was Yang Shangkun, a suave, Sichuan-born army veteran who had also just been released from prison. Even more prominent was Li Xiannian, who had changed his tune and come to Deng's rescue in March 1977. These men and several others, soon known as the Eight Elders, manoeuvred back into position, wielding a great deal of power behind the scenes. They had a disconcerting independence of mind and a readiness to criticise the very man who had engineered their rehabilitation. Deng had to accommodate every one of them.[4]

Deng's stock slipped further in March 1979, as the democracy movement threatened to become uncontrollable. A growing number of cadres across the ranks, alarmed by the protesters, clamoured for a firm hand. Deng, who only months before had praised the campaign, was forced to reverse himself completely. The vice-premier's adventure in Vietnam also raised concerns, as it had revealed glaring weaknesses in the military.

At this moment, Chen Yun decided to intervene. There was a gaping hole in the budget, he pointed out, as the country had gone on a buying spree in 1978, purchasing dozens of turnkey enterprises and a range of advanced technology abroad. State income stood at 112 billion yuan, projected outgoings at 124 billion yuan.[5] In the early months of 1979, state enterprises had undertaken tens of thousands of ambitious infrastructure projects. The accountants led by Chen Yun went on the offensive, sounding the alarm. They pointed out that the funds required to complete all these projects ran to over 100 billion yuan, six to seven times the available budget. Fuel, electrical power and raw materials were lacking. Many of the projects, moreover, were poorly designed, meaning that even when finished they were forced to remain idle or operate below capacity.[6]

To balance the books Chen Yun proposed a period of retrenchment, cutting imports, reining in expenditure and lowering targets for the next three years. Deng Xiaoping, no economic expert, was easily swayed and acquiesced.

'Readjustment' (*tiaozheng*), the official euphemism for the new approach, came like a bucket of cold water. Deng was an old man in a hurry, but so was everyone else. The economy lay in tatters, and people were eager to make up for lost time. Every party secretary had a vision of abundance, whether he was in charge of a factory, a town, a city or a province. They, too, had splashed out since the death of the Chairman, but unlike the top leadership they were not eager to see their own local projects suspended, scaled down or postponed.

A basic skill in any planned economy was the ability to subvert the master plan. The reason for this was quite simple: the plan did not provide enough incentives. Apathy was widespread. Without some accommodation of the profit motive the economy would have destroyed itself. No communist regime anywhere had managed to stay in power without constant infringements of the party line. As the historian Robert Service points out, disobedience in the Soviet Union was not so much the grit that stopped the machinery as the oil that prevented the system from grinding to a complete standstill.[7]

These skills had been all the more important at the height of the Great Leap Forward, when ever higher targets had been imposed on farms and factories across the country. To increase output, grit was added to grain, sand to iron ore. Creative accounting was essential, as numbers on paper could create the illusion of abundance. They could also hide misappropriation of funds. A standard trick was to move investment away from production towards fixed capital, as units treated themselves to new buildings, dance halls and elevators. Endless borrowing from state banks was also a common ploy, even more since no factory was ever allowed to go bankrupt. A network of contacts was essential, as influential officials in the higher reaches of power could help secure extra funds, evade taxation or gain access to scarce resources. Bribes were common. Paradoxically, the planned economy with its dedication to the greater good spawned a system in which the individual and his personal network prevailed. A common practice for state enterprises was to bypass the plan and trade directly between themselves, bartering timber for biscuits or pigs for cement.[8]

It was not just factory managers and party secretaries who displayed endless entrepreneurial guile in devising ways to defraud the state. The Great Leap Forward was so destructive that the very survival of ordinary people came to depend on their ability to lie, charm, hide, steal, cheat, pilfer, forage, smuggle, trick, manipulate or otherwise outwit the state. As one survivor of Mao's Great Famine put it, 'those who stole food survived, those who didn't died.'[9] Obfuscation was the communist way of life, whether for party members or ordinary people.

The new leadership was all too well aware of the problem. In order to stimulate production, Hua Guofeng and Deng Xiaoping passed the right to control state enterprises from the centre to local governments in 1978. Local governments, in turn, allowed their enterprises to retain a share of the profit to invest in growth.

None were keen on retrenchment. They understood one basic flaw of the new system, namely that while a share of the profit could be retained, a deficit could always be turned over to the central bank. They vied to outdo each other, each pursuing their own vision of modernisation. 'Each one builds their own car factory, tractor factory, bicycle factory, sewing machine factory, camera factory and watch factory,' a comprehensive report in Beijing noted.[10] More specific examples were offered: in October 1979 there were roughly 1,500 distilleries at the county level or above; a year later 12,000 new ones had appeared.[11]

Lack of planning on the ground was the main attribute of the planned economy. In Zhejiang, a relatively prosperous coastal province, the provincial planning committee deplored that in 'many towns and cities in our province we lack planning, we distribute our resources irrationally and we tear down and rebuild chaotically'. Few units appeared to respect the policy of retrenchment, as infrastructure projects continued to mushroom. Since all competed for the same limited amounts of coal and oil, one-fifth of all equipment across the province stood idle.[12] Nationwide a third of new projects frequently went without electricity.[13]

Even though Chen Yun and his clique had slashed the state budget for capital construction in April 1979 from 45.7 to 36 billion yuan, investment by local governments doubled to more than 16 billion yuan in 1979 and then trebled to over 25 billion in 1980. In reality, as one accountant pointed out, 'the scope of building by far surpasses this figure.'[14] One leading official explained why, quipping that 'there are infrastructure projects one can see, there are those one cannot see, and then there are those which are blatantly illegal.'[15]

Money was also spent on the workers. Chairman Mao's 'On the Ten Major Relations', published shortly after his death, had dangled the promise of improved material incentives. Hua Guofeng and Deng Xiaoping had made similar pledges, allowing state enterprises to use bonuses to stimulate production. Workers, who had become masters of go-slow techniques during the Cultural Revolution, doing as little as possible, seized the opportunity to clamour for better conditions. In Nanjing, the erstwhile capital of the Nationalist Party, most received a bonus equivalent to 10 per cent of their salary. In Zhejiang it reached more than 12 per cent. And when enterprises ran out of cash, they turned instead to material incentives. In Tianjin, the sprawling industrial behemoth in the north, some factories handed out clothes and textile materials to every one of their workers.[16] The scheme was intended to reward the best workers, but instead all obtained the same bonus, barely increasing their productivity.

All the money lavished on infrastructure and bonuses had an immediate effect on inflation. In a planned economy all prices were fixed by the state and tended to stay the same over time, regardless of availability. People did not pay more, they queued for longer or went without. In Hubei the cost of an egg, a bar of soap or a box of matches had barely budged from 1966 to 1978. But in 1979 and 1980 inflation across the country ran at 5.6 and 6 per cent respectively. These were the official numbers, but the Hong Kong and Shanghai Bank put the figure at a combined total of 37.6 per cent.[17]

Local governments also used their new freedoms to outdo each other in importing advanced technology, prompting great waste. In Nanjing more than 1.7 million yuan was spent on machinery for a cannery which stood idle. Some units went so far as to order foreign appliances before a factory had even appeared, like a 'Buddha awaiting the building of his temple'. Even in the capital a mere one-third of 450 imported precision instruments were ever used. Dozens of high-definition scanners gathered dust. Soviet experts – admittedly biased – estimated that the cost of installing and maintaining advanced equipment was equal to the cost of acquisition. They concluded that 'the expense of acquiring foreign technology on credit outweighs the benefits to the overall economy'.[18]

Above all, state enterprises used the cover of foreign trade to spend scarce currency on luxury goods like sedan cars and television sets.[19] They did so in a great variety of ways, from direct purchases abroad to undercover barter and even smuggling. The State Council reported in May 1980 that more than one million television sets and pocket calculators had been trafficked along the coastline. Fishermen were prime suspects, but even schoolchildren were out to make a profit. In one case an army unit regularly sent a helicopter to collect the goods. In Hainan, a subtropical island off the southern coast, one unit employed 400 people around the clock to deal in foreign goods.[20] In Lilong, conveniently located on the Fujian coast opposite Taiwan, 20,000 people traded in smuggled goods every single day, with hundreds of straw huts erected temporarily to facilitate business.[21] All were a drain on the country's limited foreign currency.

By December 1980 Chen Yun was fuming. Despite all the cuts, the deficit had surged to 17 billion yuan.[22] Chen demanded a return to the measures applied in the wake of Mao's Great Famine: slash the budget, reduce economic growth to zero and centralise all power.[23]

Several of the Eight Elders, not least Li Xiannian, backed Chen Yun's tough position. A new figure also rallied to his cause. Zhao Ziyang, who had joined the Politburo and been appointed premier only months before, homed in on the danger inflation represented. To remedy the deficit, the bank had issued some 13 billion yuan in currency in the last two years, with projections that its printers would churn out a further 9 billion the following year. The total, he explained, was greater than all the currency issued between 1949 and 1978. Consumption outpaced production, and for city dwellers 'real standards of living are actually falling.' He raised the spectre of social unrest, predicting that if the economy was not brought under control 'we will not be able to maintain political stability.' Across Eastern Europe, Zhao pointed out, governments were printing money and borrowing from capitalist countries, leading to declining living standards and popular protests. Workers occupied mines and shipyards across Poland, obtaining the right to establish trade unions that were independent of government control: 'it is a recipe for disaster.'[24]

Zhao Ziyang, the son of a landowner in Henan, had joined the Communist Party in 1938 after the Japanese invasion of the country. He was only nineteen. After liberation he was recruited by Tao Zhu, a ruthless party official sent to Guangdong province in 1952 to replace a local leader Chairman Mao judged to be too lenient towards the local population. Zhao Ziyang helped his boss carry out a ruthless campaign of repression. The slogan was 'Every Village Bleeds, Every Household Fights', with ferocious beatings and random killings taking place across the province. In some places suspects were trussed up, hung from beams, buried up to the neck and torched.[25]

Several years later, when it came to light that, contrary to its anticipated figures, the Great Leap Forward had brought a vast decrease in grain production, Zhao provided the Chairman with a lifeline by alleging in January 1959 that the shortfall was the result of communes secretly dividing their grain output and stashing it away. He launched a pitiless campaign across the province during which villagers were beaten and tortured into revealing any hidden food.[26] But like other party officials, Zhao had a change of heart after the disaster of Mao's Great Famine. He remained a committed communist, but became adept at mitigating some of the party's harsher policies. He could be aloof, although his easy manner endeared him to all levels of the party hierarchy.

In 1975 Zhao was sent to run the country's most populous province, Sichuan, where he looked the other way when villagers sold on the black market foodstuffs over which the state retained a monopoly, including edible oil, grain and meat. In November 1979 he stepped forward as a major exponent of the Four Cardinal Principles, placing the dictatorship of the proletariat firmly at the centre of the party's future work. He repudiated the separation of powers and the democratic system of the 'capitalist camp', describing democracy in the People's Republic of China as the most comprehensive yet achieved in human history.[27] His speech tallied very closely with Deng Xiaoping's own views. A few months later Deng brought him to Beijing.

Zhao's intervention ensured that retrenchment became the order of the day. 'We must retreat the way we did in 1961,' Zhao claimed, referring to the 20 million people who had been sent back to the countryside from the cities to alleviate the burden on the state of having to feed them. Deng Xiaoping had no alternative but to agree to a compromise growth target of 4 per cent. Hua Guofeng became a convenient scapegoat, blamed for having emphasised heavy industry at the expense of light industry.[28]

Prices were frozen, investment curtailed, projects devoted to heavy industry suspended. Factories under construction were left to rot, their equipment dismantled and carted away. Beijing not only put the brakes on local officials, but also cancelled contracts with Japanese, West German and French companies, since these were considered a dangerous over-extension of scarce foreign currency.

One was the Baoshan Iron and Steel Works, located some 25 kilometres outside Shanghai on the southern bank of the Yangtze River. Steel had long been the sacred ingredient in the alchemy of socialism. Hard, shiny, industrial, modern and proletarian, steel was the benchmark of progress. The equation was simple: steel meant industry, industry meant wealth and power, more steel meant greater wealth and power. Deng demanded more of it. The Baoshan complex was designed to be the country's most advanced steel mill, using state-of-the-art technology imported from Japan and shared funding from West Germany and the United States. It was a planning disaster. The riverbank was on soft ground, causing increased construction costs. Since China lacked the high-quality iron ore the sophisticated blast furnaces required, this had to be imported from Australia and Brazil. Then a sandbank at the mouth of the river prevented bulk carriers from reaching the complex, forcing shippers to load every batch of iron ore onto smaller vessels.

Soon enough the cranes stood idle. Thousands of unopened crates packed with precision instruments spilled out of warehouses. Whereas Stage I had been inaugurated with much fanfare in 1978, plans for Stage II were mothballed. Although Japan received financial compensation, the fiasco came as a blow.[29]

For the first time in thirty years, in 1981 China issued bonds to the value of 12 billion yuan, funds needed to cover the deficit and mop up the liquidity caused by printing too much money. The exercise was only partially successful. Despite all injunctions as to the dire consequences of inflation, the money supply continued to grow twice as fast as the supply of goods. Another 5 billion yuan was injected into the economy.[30]

***

The supply of goods had to be increased, but this was no easy task. In a command economy, the plan replaced the market. The state centralised all major economic decisions for the greater good, determining what should be produced, who produced what, how resources should be allocated and what prices should be charged for materials, goods and services. Money, in this system, was passive, merely following the flow of planned products. But China did not have a planned economy. A plan required more than just a vision. It needed massive input from statisticians, since they, rather than the market, determined how many rubber shoes or polyester curtains or bicycle saddles were required. In the wake of the Cultural Revolution, very few statisticians were left standing. The Bureau for Statistics put it in plain language: 'when the statistics are not accurate, it has an effect on how our leaders understand the real situation.' At the height of the Cultural Revolution the bureau itself boasted a mere 200 number crunchers. In 1983 it had 16,000 employees, compared to 220,000 in the Soviet Union.[31]

Since the system encountered obstruction at every level, even with proper numbers the command economy could not function. Factory directors tried to circumvent the plan, leading to the growth of a second economy, also known as the black market, one that grew in size after factories were allowed to keep a portion of their profits in 1978. They sent purchasing agents to buy raw resources, bidding up prices nominally fixed by the state, which in turn led to nationwide supply issues.

One other problem existed. State enterprises did not know how to make, price or sell a quality product. Their performance was based on meeting or exceeding a production target. Whether or not the goods they produced found a buyer was no concern of theirs, but fell into the remit of state retail stores and state trading companies. By 1982, as the State Council put it, there was 'blind production, blind development and blind procurement' at every level, as unsold goods to the official value of 35 billion yuan accumulated in warehouses across the country, representing more than 10 per cent of working capital. This country of widespread poverty paradoxically produced more sewing machines, bicycles and watches than people could buy. In Nanjing 17.5 per cent of locally produced goods were never sold.[32]

The regime was keen to export more in order to pay for increased imports, and state enterprises came under considerable pressure to explore foreign markets. In 1979, having concluded that capitalism was on the decline and the international situation ripe for more exports, the Ministry for Foreign Trade ordered that 'all departments in finance, banking and material supplies must switch on a green light to increase exports.'[33] But making a profit in dollars was easier said than done. Factory directors, used to a captive rather than a competitive market, baulked when they had to sell the same product for less. The trading companies in charge of foreign commerce had to compensate them, while the state in turn had to provide preferential loans and tax rebates to make exports more attractive.

The official exchange rate in 1979 was 1.53 yuan to the dollar, but export goods cost an average of 2.54 yuan to produce for each dollar of sales, meaning that for every dollar earned China lost roughly one yuan. Goods, in other words, were priced higher domestically than in export markets. As the ministry noted, 'the more we export, the more we lose, it is a rate that is extremely unfavourable when it comes to promoting exports and restricting imports.' To address the issue, the currency was devalued to 2.80 yuan to the dollar, a rate reached by adding what the state deemed to be a 'reasonable profit' of 10 per cent, or 0.26 yuan, to the average cost of production.[34] The profit margin, in other words, was not driven by supply and demand, but by a nominal spread determined by the state.

What was termed the new internal settlement rate came into effect in January 1981. At the touch of a button, 80 per cent of exports no longer made a loss. This was, of course, merely an accounting trick, one that meant imports were now more expensive and had to be subsidised.

The internal settlement rate was kept secret. Foreign trade, after all, was regularly described as the forefront of an acute 'class struggle' with the 'capitalist camp'. 'It cannot be made public,' the State Council explained, 'as it would be equivalent to acknowledging that our country has two currencies.'[35] It applied only to outside trade, not to other foreign transactions, including remittances from abroad, tourism, foreign investments and expenditures by diplomatic offices, which continued to use the official rate of 1.50 to the dollar. Whether the internal rate undervalued or overvalued the yuan was difficult to tell, since in the absence of a market nobody could determine the real profit. Enterprises and government institutions alike mercilessly exploited the dual rate system, as clever accountants converted an entry at one rate in the books into a more profitable one using the other.[36]

The internal settlement rate suited the policy of retrenchment, which sought to bridle the ability of local governments to lavish foreign currency on luxury imports. Yet it did not have the desired effect, since, after 1978, local governments could also retain a share of the profit from foreign trade. To transfer their foreign currency share to other state enterprises, for instance to buy more raw materials to make further exports, they had to pass through an official trading system which applied the formal rate of 1.50 yuan to the dollar. As a result, state enterprises with a share of dollars found it more profitable to import, legally or otherwise, goods in short supply on the domestic market. Until the end of 1982 foreign reserves continued to dwindle, while the trade deficit soared.[37]

***

If the economy developed, it did so despite the heavy hand of the state and abrupt policy reversals engineered at the top. Real growth took place in the countryside, far away from the glare of official scrutiny.

People did not stand back and wait for an invitation from above to begin pulling themselves out of poverty. In the countryside in particular, if the Great Leap Forward had destroyed the party's credibility, the turmoil of the Cultural Revolution had undermined its organisation. Even before Mao died, villagers in many parts of the countryside sought to regain control over the land and leach power away from the state. In some cases local officials took the lead, quietly distributing land to the farmers. In others, they merely looked away, exhausted by two decades of revolutionary frenzy. Sometimes a deal was struck, as villagers preserved the fiction of collective ownership by turning over a percentage of the crop to local leaders, who had to deliver grain to the state.[38]

It was a silent revolution that proceeded all across the country, even though it varied from place to place. In Shaanxi province, millions went hungry in 1976, with gangs of beggars roaming the country-side, sometimes eating mud or tree bark in order to survive. Many thousands starved to death. Some cadres merely shrugged, but others preferred to hand over the land and give their villagers a chance to survive on their own wits, rather than watch them die of hunger or steal the grain directly from the fields. In Luonan, a few hours away from the provincial capital Xi'an, the collective assets of entire People's Communes were divided up, as local leaders handed responsibility for cultivating the land back to individual families. Many abandoned two decades of monoculture imposed by a state keen on selling grain on the international market, and instead cultivated crops in high demand on the black market.[39]

While necessity is the proverbial mother of invention, the entre-preneurial spirit also thrived in less deprived regions, nowhere more so than in the subtropical province of Guangdong. In rural markets across the province, villagers conducted a thriving trade in virtually every commodity over which the government maintained a monopoly, from grain, meat, cotton, silk, tea and tobacco to groundnuts.[40]

These practices flourished after Mao's death. For decades the state had paid as little as possible for compulsory deliveries of all essential foodstuffs. A detailed study of 3,000 production teams showed that by 1978 the procurement prices for rice, wheat and corn fell roughly 20 per cent below production costs. Villagers responded by consuming the grain themselves, selling it on the black market or turning instead to more profitable crops. Deliveries dwindled. The State Council estimated its losses at 5 billion yuan in 1976 and at 4.8 billion yuan in 1977. By 1979, in several provinces, including Hunan and Henan, major agricultural producers of rice and wheat as well as millet, sor-ghum and corn, some 70 per cent of all grain reserves were consumed, bartered or sold on the black market.[41]

To cover the shortfall, the country had to purchase up to 12 million tonnes of wheat from Canada and Australia. In 1979, the regime was also forced to increase the price it paid farmers for delivering grain. Since grain could be sold directly on the market for 30 per cent above the official procurement prices, the state had no alternative but to compromise on a 20 per cent increase. The quotas for compulsory procurement also declined drastically, meaning that the state was compelled to pay more for additional deliveries. The same principle applied to well over a dozen more major products, including cotton, sugar, edible oil, pork, beef and fish. In 1980 the prices of sheepskin, jute and timber were also raised.[42]

This meant a huge increase in costs for the state, one that reversed the flow of money. For three decades agriculture had subsidised industry, as the rural population had been forced to sell their produce at artificially low prices but had to buy tools, fuel and fertiliser at a hugely inflated cost. Now the countryside held the cities to ransom.

The procurement prices increased, but selling prices remained roughly the same, since the extra costs could not be passed on to urban consumers. In 1979, the state had to spend some 8 billion to bridge the difference, with the Ministry of Commerce handing over 2 billion yuan just for meat and eggs. 'Think about it for a minute,' the ministry pointed out, 'such a huge amount has to be subsidised, how can we afford it?' Moreover, many people speculated. 'Some of them sell meat and eggs to the state, then they buy back from the state and sell it again to the state.' A whole new realm opened up for lucrative trade, since prices varied across the country. By one estimate, in 1982 the subsidies amounted to 30 billion yuan, one-third of the budget.[43]

These subsidies were designed to consolidate rather than undermine rural collectives. Much as the state hoped to invigorate its urban enterprises by allowing them to retain a share of their profits, in 1978 the government introduced a contract system with the moribund communes, encouraging them to produce more by entitling them to retain and dispose of all their output after mandatory procurement quotas had been fulfilled. The leadership explicitly prohibited the division of the land or the devolution of responsibility for agricultural production to individual households. But farmers had an insatiable appetite for land. The communes transferred the contracts to the villages, which in turn handed over to families responsibility for production. This was privatisation in all but name.

For three years the state waged a losing battle against decollectivisation. The Third Plenum in December 1978 explicitly declared that 'we do not allow family farming, we do not allow the division of land and we do not allow individuals to strike out on their own.'[44] Similar restrictions were repeatedly announced. In March 1980 a concession was introduced, as Yao Yilin, head of the State Planning Commission, suggested that family farming should be allowed in poor, sparsely populated areas where communes were still underdeveloped. 'I agree with Yao Yilin,' Deng Xiaoping declared. 'We can contract some jobs to the brigades, and some to individuals. Let's not be afraid of this, it can hardly influence the nature of our socialist system.'[45]

Later that year, in November 1980, the leadership loudly proclaimed that 'the collective economy is the unshakable foundation of our country's agriculture as it moves forward. Its superior nature cannot be matched by the private sector, and this has been demonstrated by the history of the last twenty years of agricultural development.' A nationwide campaign against decollectivisation unfolded, as leaders thundered against family farming: 'it is the same as dividing up the land and striking out on one's own, we do not allow it.'[46]

The campaign fell flat. As the Ministry of Agriculture acknowledged in January 1981, 78 per cent of households in Guizhou province, 56 per cent in Gansu, 51 per cent in Anhui and 30 per cent in Guangdong were responsible for tilling the land, making all the decisions about what to plant, how to grow it and what to do with the produce. In some places every family operated independently, as 'the collective economy has vanished,' the ministry noted. 'These numbers are on the low side, as they keep on expanding constantly.'[47]

A detailed study of Zhejiang province revealed why private farming was rising inexorably: 'the production of the collectives has not increased for a long time and the benefits accrued to their members are very limited.' One farmer put it more succinctly: 'the collectives are unreliable, so we have no alternative but to parcel out the land and cultivate it ourselves.' Further north, in impoverished Hebei, where malnutrition and starvation were still common, villagers were more blunt: 'there is nothing superior about the collective system.'[48]

In the winter of 1982, the People's Communes were officially dissolved, marking the end of an era. In this great transformation, it was the villagers who took centre stage, as millions upon millions of ordinary people effectively outmanoeuvred the state. For decades, their living standards had stagnated. By 1982 their income had doubled, as they lifted themselves out of poverty. As an astute observer from the East German embassy in Beijing remarked at the time, 'In essence the yearly documents on agriculture adopted by the central government only fix in writing what has already been achieved through a spontaneous process at the village level.' The sociologist Kate Zhou later phrased it slightly differently: 'When the government lifted restrictions, it did so only in recognition of the fact that a sea of unorganised farmers had already made them irrelevant.'[49]

***

The rural population won the freedom to cultivate the land as they saw fit, but they did not own the land. At no point did the state ever envisage relinquishing the fundamentals of Marxism, namely public ownership of the means of production. After the communes vanished, undermined from below, every family was given a lease on the land, to be renewed every fifteen years.

The state withheld another fundamental liberty, namely freedom of movement. In 1955 Zhou Enlai had introduced a household registration system in the countryside, roughly equivalent to the internal passport instituted decades earlier in the Soviet Union. This tied the villagers to the land, ensuring that cheap labour was available for the collectives. It also divided the country into two separate worlds, classifying people as either 'city dwellers' (*shimin*) or 'peasants' (*nongmin*). Children inherited their status through their mother, meaning that even if a village girl married in the city, her children remained 'peasants'. 'Peasants' were treated like an hereditary caste deprived of the privileges that the state granted to its employees, namely city dwellers, from subsidised housing and food rations to access to health, education and disability benefits.[50]

Always fearful of social instability, the regime confined much of the populace to the countryside, including an estimated 100 million, one-third of the entire rural population, who were unemployed or underemployed, paid by the communes to do nothing, or taking turns to work in the fields.[51]

One way to absorb some of this 'surplus labour', the Marxist term the regime employed, was to restrict rural investment. Even after thirty years of propaganda highlighting 'mechanisation in the countryside', with socialist iconography featuring young girls proudly driving tractors through the fields, few machines existed. Rather like England in the 1840s, this was a country fuelled by sweat and powered by muscle. Further rural disinvestment began in December 1978, as the Third Plenum announced that 'peasants should rely on their own strength.' In Gansu, one of the country's poorest provinces where barren hills melted gradually into huge deserts, agricultural investment was cut by half in 1980 and then by half again the following year, dwindling by 1983 to a mere 22 per cent of the 1979 level. Similar cutbacks were imposed elsewhere. As Wan Li, a leading official responsible for agriculture, stated in 1981, 'there is no money for agriculture.'[52]

The regime also deliberately sidestepped providing money for education. Since 1949, the leadership had invested more in infrastructure than in people. Funds were lavished on prestige projects – concert halls, museums, stadiums, entire new cities – while neglecting education in the countryside. Whether working in the capital or a distant county seat in the hinterland, officials were accountable not to those below them, but to their bosses above. Large, striking, tangible signs of power were a sure way of cultivating the illusion of effective governance. This was particularly true of rural areas, where people were treated as mere subjects, a source of cheap labour to be exploited for the benefit of the state. When the leadership met in May 1981 to discuss long-term goals in education, they were fully aware of the extent of illiteracy across the country. In Tongxiang county, Zhejiang, one of the wealthiest places along the coast, 70 per cent of young people could not read even simple characters. As Hu Yaobang pointed out, 'we never had universal primary education,' adding, 'we failed to achieve this over the last thirty years.' But the state could not afford the heavy burden of paying for this, he explained. The economy came first. 'Let the people handle their own affairs,' he counselled, 'let them recruit teachers and build schools.'[53]

The foremost method of soaking up surplus unemployment was to encourage the villagers to work in the collectively owned enterprises, introduced – together with the People's Communes – at the height of the Great Leap Forward. Seeking a communist society of plenty for all, the peasants were expected to transform agriculture and industry simultaneously, in what propaganda termed 'walking on two legs'. Most such enterprises operated on a small scale, employing outdated techniques. Their aim was to enhance economic self-reliance, using local raw materials to meet the demands of local commune members. They milled flour, pressed oil, repaired tools and processed charcoal or limestone. They made tiles, bricks and fertiliser, and also handicrafts, from woven straw pads and twig baskets to ginned cotton.[54]

The Great Leap Forward was a disaster, but the notion of self-reliance flourished during the Cultural Revolution, offering a convenient rationale for leaving people to their own devices. Dazhai became a model to be emulated across the country. Surrounded by dried gullies and steep hills in an isolated corner of impoverished Shanxi, the village had used sheer willpower to pull itself from poverty, refusing all government subsidies. It boasted terraced fields clinging onto hillsides, aqueducts crossing valleys to bring water, walnut and mulberry trees, fruit orchards and piggeries, but also a bean noodle plant, a machine repair shop and other collective enterprises. Dazhai was, of course, a sham, its model villagers the reluctant actors in a play written by the Chairman, its miracle harvests obtained by borrowing grain from other villages. But it was widely advertised, as the spirit of self-reliance was encouraged in every People's Commune through posters, newspaper articles, radio announcements and propaganda films.[55]

Much as farmers quietly used the chaos of the Cultural Revolution to claim back the land, so they used the policy of self-reliance to open local factories and village enterprises. They were supposed to be collectively owned, but many merely used the collective's name to run a business entirely along private lines. All along the coast, underground factories used their earnings to buy grain and meat on the black market, as well as imported goods that the planned economy could not provide, from fish oil to aspirin. They sent purchasing agents to compete with the state sector for scarce resources needed to run their businesses, buying up coal, steel and iron. Even before Chairman Mao passed away, industry dominated parts of the countryside. In Chuansha, a county just outside Shanghai where the local population was mandated by the state to grow cotton, the industrial part of total production increased from 54 per cent in 1970 to 74 per cent five years later.[56]

To help the communes catch up after the lost decade of the Cultural Revolution, after 1978 their enterprises were exempted from tax for three years.[57] Whether or not nominally 'owned by the people', they flourished yet further. In Jiangsu province, the leaders of three counties within cycling distance of Shanghai declined to supervise the economic activities of those under their authority, allowing them to pursue their own livelihoods. Many went from having one job to working several at the same time, fishing and trading while tilling the fields in the evening. By 1983 industry represented 80 per cent of their output.[58]

A similar scenario was common along the coast, nowhere more so than in Guangdong province. One team of observers sent from Shanghai to learn from the rest of the country was taken aback by their findings. In the Pearl River Delta, people walked away from state-mandated grain production. In Dongguan, where the dry soil yielded a pitiful crop, they took up more profitable occupations, many specialising in private transportation, linking up numerous villages across the province. In Shunde, traversed by canals with stilt houses perched over the waterways, the rice paddies were halved in size as people turned to fish farming instead. One village relied on private vehicles, banned by the state, to ferry live fish to market, with ten cars plying produce to the provincial capital. During the early Cultural Revolution years, people in Guangzhou, an oasis in the midst of an extensive river system, had been forced to queue for hours for an occasional batch of dead fish. Now they had access to live produce, with prices declining by 40 per cent from 1979 to 1983. Each day, a small army of peddlers, some on motorbikes, delivered over a thousand tonnes of vegetables to every part of the city.[59]

In Shunde the villagers turned to horticulture, with 10 per cent of the fields covered in flowers. Trade reached all the way to Hong Kong. Demand was such that workers were sometimes hired, a practice the leaders in Beijing decried as 'capitalist'. This was true of one village where 2,000 people banded together in 1982 to set up a sofa factory, selling furniture to the entire nation. As the authors of the report concluded, 'the province follows the market.'[60] The first secretary of Guangdong was Ren Zhongyi, an enlightened leader keen on change. Unlike Zhao Ziyang, he was a true believer in the separation of powers, although wise enough to keep his own counsel.[61]

The entirely unexpected boom in village enterprises had unintended consequences. The cultivators withheld an even greater proportion of their crop from the state, despite increased procurement prices. They found it more profitable to process what they produced in their own local enterprises, small as these may have been, than to sell to the city. The result was fewer raw materials for heavy industry, including factories with new equipment imported at great expense.

In 1975 Shanghai's cotton mills consumed 125,000 tonnes of cotton. Four years later deliveries had dwindled to less than 50,000 tonnes, a drop of 60 per cent. Imports of cotton doubled in 1979 and again in 1980. The decline in tobacco procurement stood at 24 per cent. Deliveries of a whole range of other commodities, from leather to tung oil and pine rosin, fell equally dramatically.[62]

The leadership responded with a policy of retrenchment, curbing demand and cutting imports. But this was increasingly hard to apply in the countryside. Once the People's Communes were dismantled in the winter of 1982, the planned economic system over which Chen Yun and his acolytes presided could no longer control the direction of the rural economy.[63]

**

Birth control was one prominent aspect of the retrenchment effort that would last for decades. Like much else, the impulse to plan everything centrally went back to the Chairman, with babies no exception. Already in 1957 Mao was pondering whether his country had too many people. 'It would be better to have fewer births. Reproduction needs to be planned. In my view, humanity is completely incapable of managing itself. We have plans for production in factories, for producing cloth, tables and chairs, and steel, but no plan for producing humans.' He returned to the same idea several years later, leading to the establishment in 1964 of a Birth Planning Commission. In 1970 this body launched a fully fledged campaign of mandatory birth planning, with propaganda teams spreading far and wide the Chairman's words of wisdom: 'humanity must control itself and reach a planned increase.' In many villages, government workers kept detailed records on women of child-bearing age and harassed those with more than two children. Female sterilisation and mandatory abortion became common, even though the pattern varied enormously from place to place. In Shandong province alone, by 1971 well over a million abortions had been performed. Nationwide, from 1971 to 1976, abortions averaged around 5 million annually.[64]

Numbers soared under Hua Guofeng. In Tianjin in 1978 abortion was common, with 70,000 pregnancies terminated and 108,000 births, an abortion rate of over 40 per cent among women aged 14 to 55. Families who failed to conform had their water cut off, their bicycles

confiscated or their salaries reduced by 10 per cent. In the countryside, the quotas were likewise strictly enforced.[65]

In January 1981, more drastic measures were introduced. Chen
Yun, the architect of retrenchment, was concerned over soaring grain
imports. He warned a September 1980 Politburo meeting that 'one
billion people must feed themselves, but they cannot eat too much,
otherwise everything will be devoured. We need to save some money
for infrastructure.'[66] Back in 1957, a year before the Great Leap
Forward, Chen had put forward similar arguments.[67] This was Marxist
economics at its best, as the state forced ordinary people to cut their
consumption so that their savings could be invested for the greater
good. Deng Xiaoping and others agreed. They found a convenient
justification in the writings of one Song Jian, a former rocket scientist turned demographer who offered a doomsday scenario: China's
population was 'a time bomb waiting to detonate' with hundreds of
millions of peasants who would 'wash away the cities' in a not too
distant future.[68] Zero growth was required as rapidly as possible. His
pseudo-science presented a seemingly objective rationale for the most
draconian birth control policy the world had ever seen.[69]

Party officials were ordered to ensure that couples produced no
more than one child, occasionally two should the firstborn be a
daughter. The policy varied locally, but was strictly applied in such
populous provinces as Jiangsu and Sichuan. Coercion was widespread, abuse common. In the summer of 1981, thousands of women
in east Guangdong were forced to have an abortion, including some
victims who were eight months pregnant. In one commune 316 out
of 325 pregnancies were deemed undesirable by the birth planning
enforcers and terminated.[70]

Even tougher rules were introduced in 1982, targeting not just
adults but also those children born without state permission, who
could no longer be recorded in the household registration system
and in effect become ineligible for all rights of citizenship.[71] People
resisted. In the countryside they tried to hide pregnant women, occasionally blocking access to their village, sometimes assaulting state
representatives. Zhao Ziyang stepped in to defend the policy. 'Some
cadres are beaten and insulted, but they are carrying out a great
task for the people and the country.'[72] Numbers probably peaked in
1983, when 14.4 million abortions were performed, plus 20.7 million

sterilisations and 17.8 million insertions of contraceptive intrauterine devices.[73]

The policy was fine-tuned over the following years, shifting away from blatant coercion to more subtle means of persuasion. Plenty were available, not least in the cities where the state exercised control over jobs, housing, education and health care. For decades to come, every step in life would be determined by compliance with birth control, from promotion in a job to access to a hospital. Birth control in effect meant life control.

3

Reform (1982–1984)

The policy of retrenchment formally ended in September 1982 with the Twelfth Party Congress. One more task remained before 'socialist modernisation' could be accelerated and the country opened up further to the outside world. As Deng Xiaoping explained in his opening address at the congress, it was essential to resist 'decadent ideas from abroad'. 'We shall never permit the bourgeois way of life to spread in our country,' he continued.[1] A few months earlier, speaking at a gathering of military leaders, he had shared his concern over 'corrupt capitalist things from abroad' that were finding their way into the country. 'Serious crimes and major criminals are to be found not only in the economic field but in the political and cultural fields as well.' A crackdown was required, as well as a 'socialist civilisation' capable of inculcating socialist ideals and discipline in the population. Deng sought to clean the house before inviting guests.[2]

What precisely constituted 'socialist civilisation' was somewhat unclear. But when it came to socialist discipline, the regime had a ready answer. In 1963, Mao Zedong had exhorted the nation to learn from Lei Feng, a young soldier who had devoted his life to serving the people, whose posthumous diary was published and studied across the country. Chairman Mao, Lei Feng explained in the pages of his journal, had appeared to him in a vision, saying: 'Do a good job in studying; be forever loyal to the party, loyal to the people!' Lei Feng was a model to be emulated, inspiring slogans, posters, songs, plays and movies. Even storytellers were sent to the countryside to regale illiterate villagers with tales of his selfless exploits and his devotion to the Chairman.[3]

The guiding hand behind building up Lei Feng was Hu Yaobang, leader of the Youth League from 1954 to 1966. A fervent believer in Marx and Mao, Hu had long assigned Nikolai Ostrovsky's classic Bolshevik novel *How the Steel Was Tempered* to Youth League members. In 1963 he discerned Lei Feng's potential, holding him up for emulation in a series of articles published in *China Youth*, the League's official mouthpiece.[4]

In 1980, a few months after Wei Jingsheng and other democracy activists had been dispatched to jail, Hu Yaobang resurrected his hero. The fifth of March was declared Lei Feng Day. Tens of thousands of young people paraded through the Beijing and Shanghai streets to honour the soldier. Postcards immortalising his good deeds were sold in bookshops and post offices across the country. Every day, schoolchildren sang a song praising him. 'Lei Feng is everything for the benefit of others without any thought of himself,' the propaganda machine intoned. Lei Feng would, the regime hoped, counter the growing materialism of young people and inspire them to reject the radios, tape recorders, sunglasses and jeans smuggled from abroad.[5]

A mere two months after Deng Xiaoping's opening address at the Twelfth Party Congress, a new reincarnation of Lei Feng appeared, in the guise of a medical student who died attempting to save an old farmer who had fallen into a manure pit. Zhang Hua was an updated version of Lei Feng, with special newspaper columns devoted to his diaries and school reports. The message was the same: devotion to the greater good, instead of selfish pursuit of personal means, was the hallmark of socialism. Other paragons appeared, from a steel worker who met his quotas ten years ahead of schedule by moving his bedding into the factory workshop, to an opera diva who gave her role to a younger singer. At the National People's Congress in December 1982, Zhao Ziyang extolled two scientists who had worked themselves to death in their selfless pursuit of the Four Modernisations. Hu Qiaomu, the doctrinaire Marxist, called them the 'pride and glory' of the Communist Party.[6]

Instead of inspiring the population, the premature deaths of these martyrs sparked a rare and lively debate in the press. Readers queried whether a college student should aspire to die in a vat of sewage. Others ridiculed selfless acts.[7]

Even as the debate unfolded, Wang Ruoshui, the deputy editor of the *People's Daily*, published an editorial on Marxist humanism, a school of thought that had gained international prominence after the Second World War. Its proponents argued that Marxism was not so much a science as an extension of enlightenment values emphasising the need to allow human beings to realise their full individuality by freeing them from the shackles of political, economic and ideological oppression. Instead of elevating one individual above all others in a dictatorship, Wang argued, socialist humanism held that 'all are equal before the truth and the law,' since 'freedom and dignity are inviolable'. Soon afterwards, as the leadership celebrated the centennial of Karl Marx's death in March 1983, another leading theorist joined the fray. As high priest of the Propaganda Department after 1949, Zhou Yang had in quick succession consigned one writer after another to prison during a great inquisition. He, too, fell victim to his own master and was purged during the Cultural Revolution. A changed man, in November 1979 he openly apologised to his victims. On 16 March 1983, with the blessing of Wang Ruoshui, Zhou Yang published an essay on Karl Marx in the *People's Daily*. Marx had used the concept of alienation to describe how workers became mere tools in a capitalist system. Zhou pointed out that in a socialist system, people could likewise feel socially and politically alienated, while leaders in turn could become alienated from the people they were meant to represent.[8]

This was a direct challenge to the Four Principles the party had enshrined in its constitution months earlier.[9] Hu Qiaomu went on the attack the following day, portraying the debate over humanism as a step towards 'bourgeois liberalisation'. Joining him was Deng Liqun, a party stalwart who headed the Propaganda Department and was known for his fierce opposition to economic reform. On 13 March they compelled Wang Ruoshui to write a self-criticism.[10]

Hu Yaobang, the Number Two in the party hierarchy, remained ambivalent. Nor did Deng Xiaoping speak out immediately, though he watched with increasing concern as Zhou Yang's words emboldened other intellectuals to raise questions regarding the nature of socialism.

Deng Xiaoping had promised a crackdown on crime, and this took precedence over the debate on humanism. First came a clampdown on corruption, as harsh measures including the death penalty were imposed on party members found guilty of smuggling, graft, swindling, tax evasion, embezzlement and theft of state property. By the end of July 1983, some 30,000 party members had been convicted of economic crimes. Several received a bullet in the head, with full television coverage. Others went to prison or were expelled from the ranks. As a spokesman for the National People's Congress trumpeted, opening up to the world had made it all the more necessary to resist 'the corrosive influence of bourgeois ideology' and to eradicate economic crime.[11]

Then came a drive against common criminals. In a series of coordinated raids, thousands of suspects were arrested in the first week of August. In the capital alone, some 3,000 people were rounded up on the night of 6 August and thrown into prison. Two weeks later, a crowd of 60,000 at the Worker's Stadium cheered as thirty convicted robbers, arsonists and murderers, their shaven heads forced down by stern policemen, were sentenced to death. Open trucks took them to the place of execution. Comparable numbers were shot in other major cities. In Tanggu, a port on the Bohai Sea, seventeen people were marched to a hill near the city and executed before a crowd. In a town along the Yangzte River, a young woman called Zhai Manxia was put to death for allegedly having had sex with a dozen partners.[12]

Called Strike Hard, the campaign was a display of state power designed to instil fear. In Beijing suspects of crimes ranging from theft, assault and murder to rape were arrested, although a couple of passersby were also detained so the authorities could reach the requisite number. A few were released, the majority sent to prison or into forced exile in Xinjiang.[13]

The campaign concluded in time to celebrate National Day on 1 October. The moment the festivities ended, the propaganda machine turned its attention to addressing the causes rather than the effects of crime. These were to be found in decadent ideas from abroad. Sunglasses, jeans, long hair, pop songs: these were the outward signs of a pernicious social disease running amok, namely individualism.

The stage was now set for Deng Xiaoping to deliver his set piece. On 12 October 1983, at the Second Plenum of the Twelfth Central Committee, the paramount leader raised the slogan of 'anti-spiritual pollution'. Writers and artists were 'engineers of the human soul', he explained, repeating a term Stalin had used in the 1930s. Their role was to hold high the banner of socialism and teach people to have faith in the party and contribute to the 'magnificent cause of socialist modern-isation'. Some had, instead, corroded people's minds with bourgeois ideas, sowing the seeds of distrust of socialism. 'Do not think that a bit of spiritual pollution is nothing, that it is not worth making a fuss about,' he warned. Without radical measures to eradicate them, dan-gerous ideas from abroad 'will lead more people to walk down a het-erodox road, and the consequences could be dire'.[14]

For several months a campaign against spiritual pollution unfolded. The crackdown was reminiscent of the Cultural Revolution, attacking anything deemed to be 'bourgeois' or 'decadent'. Libraries purged their shelves of controversial books, foreign films were cancelled and teahouses were enjoined to play patriotic songs instead of foreign pop. In Guangzhou, where proximity to Hong Kong had encouraged more openness than elsewhere, pimps and prostitutes were rounded up, with soldiers ordered to take down the pinups from their barracks.[15]

One inadvertent result of the crackdown was to reveal the extent of disillusion with socialism. More than a few party members apparently harboured doubts about Marxism. 'What kind of Communist Party member is a member who has no faith in communism,' one activist wondered. In universities, too, spiritual pollution seemed rife. In one philosophy department alone, eight postgraduate students had taken it upon themselves to refute Karl Marx. Ordinary people likewise seemed uninspired by socialist values. In Gansu province, thousands of kilometres inland, young railway workers professed to be sick and tired of Marxism-Leninism and Maoism. 'I believe in money, not in communism,' one proffered.[16]

The campaign proved elusive, the leadership unsure, even divided. Few people wanted any return to Cultural Revolution witch-hunts. Party activists who took the call to arms too seriously were restrained. Zhou Yang showed due contrition, confessing that he had acted hastily. Wang Ruoshui lost his editorial post at the *People's Daily*. In January 1984, after Hu Qiaomu addressed the issue of humanism and alienation, the debate quietly concluded.[17] It was time to accelerate 'socialist modernisation'.

***

The rural economy had flourished after 1978. Yet the regime, normally far from shy in advertising the merits of its socialist system to the rest of the world, had remained rather coy. It had sought to shore up, not undermine, the People's Communes. The moment they collapsed, the tone changed. In 1983, the propaganda machine advertised one record after another, as ever higher production figures were reached in the countryside, from grain to cotton, sugar and edible oil.[18] For the first time, rich peasants were upheld as models to be emulated. Newspapers, radio and television explained how these pioneers made their money, some in snake farming, others by rearing ducks or cultivating rare medicinal plants. 'To Get Rich Is Glorious' was the new slogan.[19]

The reason for their success, a spate of official comments clarified, was the 'contract responsibility system', with contracts issued to individual rural households. This became the new panacea. In 1978 state enterprises had been allowed to retain a share of profits, an experiment that had yielded mixed results. Party secretaries lavished funds on consumption, not production, passing on the deficit to the state. Inspired by the rural contract system, in May 1984 the leadership introduced a similar structure in six cities. Six months later, at the Third Plenum of the Twelfth Party Congress, the system was officially implemented nationwide.

The new system introduced contracts at two levels. On the one hand, a contract was signed between the state and the manager of a state enterprise, giving the manager, rather than the party secretary, greater power over economic decisions, including production, marketing and investment. The employees, in turn, signed a contract with their supervisor, tying rewards to their performance. People who produced more were paid more. The contract also gave the most enterprising work teams greater leeway to explore the market. Like farmers in the countryside, they could decide to opt out of central planning and produce goods and services exclusively for the market. The system was designed to encourage entrepreneurship without undermining public ownership of state enterprises. It replaced the 'iron rice bowl', namely a guaranteed income and job security, with porcelain.[20]

The contract system appeared one year after the government had tried to introduce a new tax system. In order to decrease the burden on the central coffers, in 1983 state enterprises were required to pay taxes instead of retaining a share of profits. Their funding, moreover, now came from bank loans instead of government loans. The new tax system was approved hastily, since the state had watched its budget decline over the years and desperately needed stable income.[21] It backfired, since even profitable enterprises cooked the books to show a loss instead of a profit on which tax had to be paid. Some, despite all Beijing's stern reprimands, paid bonuses to their workers to increase their debt, while others tried to hide their profits. In Taizhou a radio factory sold its products at a generous discount to local government workers. As the Ministry of Commerce explained after inspecting 2,500 enterprises, hundreds of millions of yuan went unaccounted in a deliberate attempt to defraud the state. A common practice was to set up a 'war chest' with hidden funds.[22]

By late 1983 the managers of deficit enterprises were forced to pledge their commitment to making a profit. In a public ceremony in Heilongjiang, the country's industrial heartland, the managers of the province's 22 largest loss-making factories were assembled and made to sign an oath. They looked dour, with the media describing the campaign as 'military orders to fight to the death'. A few were even sacked. But cheating did not abate.[23] The solution, it seemed, beckoned from the countryside. As Zhao Ziyang opined in the summer of 1984, 'we must transplant vital measures of economic reform in the countryside to enterprises in the cities.'[24]

The goal of the contract system, besides introducing greater flexibility, was to achieve greater growth, not to improve development. In 1977 the leadership, long used to ruling through quotas and targets, had written Zhou Enlai's goal of transforming the country into a leading industrial power by the end of the century into the party constitution. Even though three years of retrenchment had deliberately restrained growth, in 1982 Deng Xiaoping gave new impetus to Zhou Enlai's target, suggesting that the economy should be quadrupled by the year 2000. When asked exactly what percentage level of growth his target implied, Zhao Ziyang and Yao Yilin were uncertain. But Hu Yaobang was better prepared, explaining that an average growth rate of 7.2 per cent would be required. Deng waved his hand, settling on 7 per cent.[25]

This was the target, with corresponding quotas handed out to state enterprises. Since the contract system allowed them to keep their surplus and sell it on the market, entire regions, from counties up to entire provinces, began to vie with each other to reach the target ahead of time.[26] The result was a surge in growth, approximating to something of a miracle. Industrial growth jumped from just over 10 per cent in 1983 to well over 15 per cent in 1984, reaching a staggering 22 per cent in 1985, or so official statistics indicated.[27]

It looked like a repeat of the first inflationary cycle of 1978 to 1982, but this time banks played a very different role. In a planned economy, banks act merely as cashiers, providing money for the economic programmes devised by the state. Besides the central bank, called the People's Bank of China, there were four specialised banks, also owned by the state, but each with its own particular remit: the Agricultural Bank of China, the Industrial and Commercial Bank of China, the Construction Bank of China and the Bank of China. Granted more autonomy by Beijing, all four raised their loan limits. In order to secure a larger base, they set higher lending targets for their branches throughout the country. The money supply surged by some 40 to 50 per cent.[28] Inflation in 1984 alone stood at 23 per cent.[29]

In the province of Henan alone, the four specialised banks lent money 'endlessly', according to one internal report. The Industrial and Commercial Bank of China alone made available a quarter of a billion yuan in six months. A pyramid scheme appeared, as the banks no longer relied on deposits but began lending to each other. 'The specialised banks make short-term loans among themselves with daily interest rates, unstintingly charging a higher interest at every level.' In the provincial capital of Zhengzhou, where two major railway lines crossed the Yellow River, one branch of the Construction Bank extended a loan to a branch of the Industrial and Commercial Bank, which in turn made it available to the Bank of Agriculture, where the loans were repackaged once more and distributed to rural branches. Shell companies and trust corporations appeared to take advantage of easy credit. In Jilin province, a chain of 47 trust companies obtained over 300 million yuan from the state banks, which was lent further down the line to purchase raw materials or consumer goods. Among its customers was the municipal government of Changchun, the provincial capital.[30]

There was an added complication, one that would haunt the banking system for decades to come. No dictatorship ever boasted merely a single dictator: there were many. This was known as the leader principle (*Führerprinzip* in German): one leader stood at the very top, but at every level of the party hierarchy someone was expected to provide leadership. Banks belonged to the state, but local banks had little alternative but to follow the dictates of their local government. Local governments supported local enterprises, and more broadly tried to extract as much as possible from the banking system, knowing that the central government would step in to bail them out. In Huangshi, Hubei province, a state enterprise producing light bulbs ran up half a million yuan of debt while holding unsold stock valued at 3 million yuan. When the bank refused to extend a further loan, the party secretary of the municipal government intervened, excoriating the bank manager for opposing 'economic reform'.[31]

In the old system, state enterprises tried to repay their loans from state banks. But under the contract system, a new breed of managers appeared who refused to honour outstanding debts. One sheet factory in Wuhan had accumulated losses of 1.5 million yuan in 1985. The new owner took over the contract, but not the debt. He was far from alone. When the authorities audited 71 state enterprises in Hubei province, they discovered that most of them had withheld repayments on outstanding loans, amounting to 210 million yuan in arrears. A manager's first priority was himself, followed by the workers and then tax. The bank came bottom of the list. Some new managers were generous, since the money was not theirs. In Yichang, just below the Three Gorges on the Yangtze River, a food-processing factory saw its profits plunge by 12 per cent but increased salaries by 87 per cent.[32]

By the end of 1986, across Hubei province, state enterprises relied on 10 billion yuan in loans. When rural enterprises were included, the amount tripled. But the increase in working capital, 35 per cent overall, by far exceeded the increase in production, which stood at just 9.7 per cent. Every extra 100 yuan invested in fixed assets generated a mere 97.11 yuan. The national average was 100.14 yuan. Admittedly, this represented an improvement on 1984, when working capital in Hubei had surged by 60 per cent, but output by only 15 per cent.[33] Industrial growth, in other words, seemed impressive, but relied on a huge expansion of capital and employment. The easy gains in productivity, which had experienced a sudden improvement in the early 1980s after decades of stagnation, were over.[34] Wang Renzhong, vice-chairman of the National People's Congress, put it succinctly when meeting Erich Honecker, the leader of East Germany: 'we consume more than we produce.'[35]

Since both the leadership and enterprise managers pursued high growth targets, quantity prevailed over quality. Output, in other words, was often shoddy and found few buyers. In Hubei, by 1986 an estimated 1.7 billion yuan worth of goods languished in storage.[36] Nationwide, in electrical appliances alone, goods to the value of 25.5 billion yuan had been written off by the end of 1984. An average factory worker earned 50 yuan a month.[37]

One further reason why quality suffered related to the way production was calculated. The regime used a Soviet method dating back to 1929, assessing value based not on what an enterprise sold, but on its physical output, multiplied by the official price, regardless of sales. Volume, not value, counted. In 1987, for example, the country's iron mills churned out 50 million tonnes of steel, of which only 5 million were fit for purpose. China had to import 20 million tonnes to circumvent the problem. Boosting growth in volume often led not to more wealth but to even greater waste of precious raw materials.[38]

While the output was often questionable, the input was expensive. State enterprises competed for raw materials not just with other state enterprises, but also with the village factories flourishing in the countryside. State agents scoured the country, seeking out additional resources further and further from home and bidding up their prices. A huge structural imbalance between the poor hinterland and the less deprived regions along the coastline was exacerbated. In Gansu, the capital of Lanzhou, department stores offered a better choice of products than before. But a great many of these finished goods, made with raw materials from the region, came from factories along the coast some 2,000 kilometres away. Though poor, in the past the province had enjoyed a steady supply of leather, both real and synthetic. Now local tanneries could not afford to match the prices paid by state procurement agents, whose factories were more heavily subsidised. The same held true for food, as even simple local produce such as soy milk or bean paste became difficult to source.[39]

Some state enterprises along the coast were more competitive, although not necessarily more efficient. One goal of the contract system was to modernise more than 400,000 state enterprises, many of them bloated operations running on massive deficits, with one layer of incompetence piled upon another. All provided free health care, education, housing and entertainment. A few behemoths even operated their own television stations, hospitals and the occasional university. Even though factory managers enjoyed greater leeway than before, they could not dismiss any employees. In the absence of bankruptcy measures, some took advantage of their increased autonomy to expand investment and worker remuneration, regardless of efficiency or productivity. According to Zhao Ziyang himself, including subsidies and bonuses, across the country in 1984 wages increased by 22.3 per cent, a rate well above the increase in production. In the first quarter of 1985 they increased again by 35 per cent.[40] In some cases reform even depressed performance, due to expensive imports, lack of qualified personnel and constraints on raw resources and energy. In Tianjin, by the end of 1985 severe energy shortages meant that for every five factories that continued to operate, two had temporarily to cease production.[41]

Tianjin was the country's third largest city after Shanghai and Beijing, an industrial giant located at the confluence of the ancient Grand Canal and the Hai River, flowing into the Bohai Sea. Yet a report from the municipal party committee noted, 'right now the quality of quite a few factory products is declining and efficiency is falling, while losses are on the increase and waste is severe.' Five per cent of the city's state enterprises produced half of total profits. The situation in Shanghai was hardly better.[42]

Across the country, directives on the contract system received careful study. In Shashi, a busy city on the Yangtze River, both workers and cadres were unimpressed. They pointed out that the state remained in control at every level: 'they talk about delegation of power, but their hand remains firmly in control.' Their verdict was stern: this was old wine in new bottles, or, to use a local expression, 'a different broth concocted from the same medicine'.[43]

***

Much as villagers became adept at evading state control, during the Cultural Revolution individual entrepreneurs thrived in the cities. Well before Mao died, urban subterfuge went in tandem with rural subterfuge. In Shanghai, nominally under the firm grip of the Gang of Four, a seemingly endless stream of private vendors visited the city in 1975, selling farm produce from the countryside. Gangs sold coal, timber and copper, making a threefold profit by exploiting the price differentials between Shanghai and Hangzhou. Market inspectors were powerless: 'they disperse when you charge, but once you are gone they assemble again.' Sometimes state representatives who tried to intervene were taken to task, verbally assaulted or occasionally beaten up.[44]

Popcorn alone attracted some 350 sellers across the city, each making up to ten yuan a day. When coal sales were restricted, people bought from the black market instead. One local official put his wife in charge of sourcing raw materials, while his thirteen-year-old daughter was taught 'how to trade'.[45]

By the end of 1976, more than forty black markets existed, not counting the smaller ones that appeared spontaneously outside department stores, in underground passages or near factory gates. One operated outside the Grand Cinema, an architectural gem with a sweeping marble staircase built by a Hungarian architect in 1928. Another did business in full view of the authorities on People's Square, a vast asphalt esplanade where a racecourse had once stood. A third market was located on the site of the Jing'an Temple, razed and turned into a plastics factory at the height of the Cultural Revolution. Some attracted hundreds of peddlers, offering every conceivable commodity, from edible oil, grain, soap and toys to cookbooks and lewd pictures. The quantities sold, while difficult to estimate, were enormous, including over 2 million boxes of cigarettes.[46]

Not all peddlers were illegal. After 1949 a small number of individuals had been allowed to continue their private trade, repairing bicycles, running a small eatery, selling hot water, making toys at home or operating a street stall. They were termed 'individual households' (getihu), since each person was classified in a household registration system. The state constantly monitored and strictly controlled their activities, clamping down occasionally, denouncing them as 'capitalists' and curtailing their number even further. Before the Cultural Revolution some 34,000 individual traders had been officially tolerated in Shanghai, but by 1976 only 13,000 had managed to survive.[47]

They fulfilled a crucial role, since after several decades of socialism the state still could not provide even basic facilities to its subjects.

When peddlers declined in number during the Cultural Revolution, many people no longer had access to hot water. By 1977 one street with more than 80,000 residents had just three state-owned shops, all of them poorly provisioned. Without the individual hawkers, people had to walk for half an hour to buy supplies. The picture was similar for other services, be it a haircut, laundering a bag of clothes or a small repair. For ordinary people every simple transaction became a major chore.[48]

Most individual traders with an official licence were over sixty years old. In the Hongkou district one 87-year-old had clung stubbornly to his job despite all the campaigns to 'abolish capitalism' and turn him into a state employee. Many suffered from discrimination, meaning that the state institutions on which they depended for their raw materials treated them badly. Black marketeers stepped into the breach.[49]

After the demise of the Gang of Four, they were encouraged to register. Private businesses, defined as household enterprises with more than eight employees, were also tolerated. Numerous restrictions and endless bureaucratic hurdles still kept their official numbers down. When in 1980 the mayor of Shenyang, a large, polluted city in the northern industrial heartland, gradually allowed the illegal traders operating in thirty black markets to sell their goods in public, this was hailed as a minor revolution.[50] Resistance was not over, and many cities nationwide still officially barred peddlers from bringing rural produce to market, insisting on state control over all trade. Until 1983 this was true for Chengdu, a large city in the centre of Sichuan province.[51]

Many private traders therefore continued to dwell in a legal twilight zone. In Shanghai in 1986 there was one registered peddler for every illegal one. They were everywhere, with hawkers erecting some 17,000 stalls on street corners and pavements. One bean counter employed by the municipality estimated that they occupied 8.7 per cent of the total road surface. Some of these structures became permanent.[52]

The situation elsewhere was similar, with cities reverting to their mercantile past, with or without official permission, as if the previous thirty years had never been. No place thrived more than Wenzhou, a port on the East China Sea surrounded by green-blue hills where produce from the hinterland – tobacco, tea, coir, paper umbrellas called kittysols, bamboo and porcelain – had traditionally been ferried down the river on rafts and junks, to be collected and traded further along the coast or overseas. Here as elsewhere, private traders had never disappeared, but after 1976 their numbers soared to 11,000. The city made a few half-hearted attempts to stem a rising tide, but after 1978 decided to go with the flow. Behind imposing mansions built by local merchants before liberation, in a maze of courtyards and temples, entrepreneurs ran small businesses from their homes, sewing clothes, casting iron pots or mending umbrellas, their wares spilling over the pavement and competing for space with stacks of vegetables brought to town by rural traders.[53]

By 1983 the private sector in Wenzhou boasted more than 4,000 enterprises, representing over 40 per cent of all business. 'Every few steps there is a shop,' one report declared. In some cases factory workers were too busy operating a private business from home to turn up at work. State enterprises found it difficult to compete, and failed to meet their targets.[54]

Wenzhou, a city of 300,000 people, caught Beijing's attention. On 1 December 1985 Zhao Ziyang came and spoke. He explained that capitalism would bring long-term contradictions among the people, which might cause social instability, and in turn could prompt political unrest. It was therefore essential to invigorate the state sector and support the collective economy. Hu Qiaomu came a few weeks later, and clarified that the leadership could tolerate the private sector in a small place like Wenzhou. But should the same experiment take place in all of Zhejiang province, this would be a problem: 'China would no longer be a socialist country, it would become a capitalist country.' 'There must be restrictions,' he concluded.[55]

Nationwide, constraints on private entrepreneurs continued, with restrictions on access to capital, resources, energy and transportation, all controlled by the state. The solution, in Wenzhou and beyond, was to become a 'dependent enterprise', pretending to be part of a collective and operating under the flag of state ownership. A private business paid a state enterprise or a military unit a fee to use their name, stationery and bank account. To quote a popular saying, these fake collectives could 'lean back in the cool shade of a big tree', using their relations with a more powerful state entity to avoid becoming the target of an official investigation.[56] Since these businesses also paid taxes through their larger state representatives, some local governments quietly encouraged the practice.

Whether entirely independent or merely dependent, private enterprises flourished after 1984. The contract system allowed an enterprise manager to pass on a contract to one of its more successful work teams, who could explore the market once they had met their state quota. One unintended consequence of this web of contracts and subcontracts was that on the one hand a private enterprise could more easily link up with a state unit, while on the other a state unit could more easily become a private business in all but name.

The result was a flourishing black market, as state units collaborated with dependent enterprises to exploit the price system. At every level two prices existed: a fixed price for raw resources like timber, cotton, tobacco, steel and cement, required by state enterprises to meet their production targets, while the same materials fetched a higher price on the open market. State units passed on their supplies, for a fee, to their dependent enterprises. The state also paid its own enterprises a fixed price for finished goods, while allowing them to sell on the open market any surplus beyond the quota. Here, too, private and public sectors joined hands to make quick profits at state expense. In Hubei province alone, after 1984 more than 8,000 fly-by-night companies appeared, many of them wheeling and dealing on behalf of state units and their dependent private enterprises. As the local authorities noted, in many cases 'the distinction between government and business is not clear.'[57]

The difference between private, collective or state-owned also became opaque. Collective assets could be appropriated overnight and distributed to members of a state unit: they were now nominally 'owned by the people', who sold them on the market.[58] Remnants of the command economy combined with what one economist called 'selected, pasteurised, partial, truncated, restricted and disjointed pieces of market and private property policy'.[59] The outcome was not a mixed system, but a mixed-up one: a 'confused economic system', as Liu Guoguang, a professor of economics and alternate member of the Central Committee, euphemistically termed it.[60]

Whatever the ownership structure, the most profound impact was in retailing, catering, services and transportation. In some cities, private entrepreneurs managed to improve incrementally the lives of ordinary people, by running a barbershop, a bicycle repair, a food stall or a transport business. In others, however, state managers decided that the tertiary sector was not lucrative enough, allowing it to wither even further, with few private households taking up the slack. In Nanjing, to give just one example, the number of repair shops and bathhouses declined substantially between 1983 and 1985, leaving not a single barber to be found in districts with tens of thousands of people.[61]

Even in cities such as Shanghai, where private traders thrived, their efforts were offset by a proportionate decline in state support for public services. The canteens where the vast majority of workers ate were neglected. Many had leaking roofs: 'when it rains outside there is drizzle inside', one inspector noted. Some had no fuel and burned debris and rubbish instead.[62] The infrastructure was crumbling, with the sewage system in the city's older sections dating back to pre-1949.[63] And whether or not they were tolerated, very few private households ever managed to 'get rich.' Most experienced some form of harassment from state representatives, as market inspectors, policemen or local functionaries stepped in to take their cut.

Despite incremental change, by 1987 a mere 22 million people, within a population of more than 1 billion, were officially registered as private employees. Over 15 million of these were in the countryside, where village enterprises alone employed some 90 million people. Even if, by some estimates, half of all private businesses operated under the radar, they remained a modest part of the overall economy.[64]

As the deputy mayor of Wenzhou acknowledged in 1987, in large metropoles like Wuhan, Shenyang and Beijing, the private sector remained small, in some cities almost non-existent. In Wenzhou, the country's 'hotbed of capitalism', two-thirds of municipal income depended on state enterprises: 'we are in the boat of public ownership: if the boat sinks we go down too.'[65]

***

In January 1984 Deng Xiaoping paid a surprise visit to Shum Chun. Watched by millions on national television, he toured the city, inspected an electronics factory and listened to a report from the mayor. He gave his blessing, gravely opining that 'our policy of setting up special economic zones is correct.'[66]

Before his visit, many had viewed the city as an ideologically suspect case operating in a capitalist twilight zone. In December 1980 Zhao Ziyang, Wan Li, Yao Yilin and Gu Mu had chaired a special meeting to warn that 'we cannot allow the country to dissolve into capitalism.' They lambasted hostile foreign forces in the United States and Hong Kong for 'trying to turn Guangdong into Hong Kong'. 'What we are setting up,' they explained, 'are special economic zones, not special political zones.' A few weeks later Chen Yun sternly pronounced that 'foreign capitalists are also capitalists.'[67]

Shum Chun, better known as Shenzhen, shot to fame, as Deng's endorsement spread nationwide by radio, newspaper and television. Much as Dazhai a decade earlier had been a magnet for many thousands of party delegates eager to absorb the revolutionary lessons of self-reliance, Shenzhen became a mecca for party officials keen to learn from its experience in attracting foreign capital and technology. The city of Tianjin alone sent 5,000 people to observe. The massive influx of visitors overwhelmed Shenzhen, although a great many delegates reportedly preferred shopping to listening to lectures.[68]

Shenzhen, back in 1976, was no more than a sleepy backwater with some 30,000 villagers. But it had a railway link with Hong Kong, a mighty financial capital across the border where hundreds of steel and glass skyscrapers competed for a spot in a crowded skyline. Much as Japan and the United States had impressed trade missions and study tours, it was Hong Kong that captured their imagination. Song Ziming and Chai Shufan, sent to New Zealand in August 1977, were taken aback during their transit in the crown colony. A mere rock in the ocean with no natural resources, it apparently produced everything, as raw materials from around the world were unloaded in its busy ports to be fed to 36,000 factories, churning out goods of every conceivable kind, from cheap plastic flowers to advanced computers. Hong Kong was a free port with no duties, its low taxes attracting investment from around the world. Everything in Hong Kong could be used in the pursuit of the Four Modernisations: its port, its banks, its expertise and, most of all, its money. 'Plan for the long term and fully utilise Hong Kong,' Chairman Mao had said years earlier.[69]

This was but one delegation. There were many others, as the crown colony became an informal training ground for the mainland. Shanghai sent teams to study everything from the manufacture of a raincoat to building a skyscraper. In 1978, Guangdong province devoted one study group to each branch of industry and commerce. If there was a model to follow, it was not Japan but Hong Kong.[70]

Hong Kong had long been indispensable to the communist regime as a link to the rest of the world. As the bamboo curtain came down in 1949, the crown colony became China's middleman, importing foreign products and exporting mainland commodities. At the height of the Great Leap Forward, as links with the Soviet Union were curtailed, Hong Kong emerged as the mainland's largest source of foreign currency.[71]

People in Hong Kong, as well as other foreign Chinese migrant communities from Indonesia to California, were termed 'overseas Chinese and compatriots from Hong Kong and Macau'. Although China viewed some as potential spies and capitalist infiltrators, others were cultivated through the United Front, a network of influential people and institutions controlled directly by Beijing. In Hong Kong the regime funded a string of voluntary associations, including a trade union, a chamber of commerce and a news agency, to mobilise support, although much of its network collapsed during the Cultural Revolution.

After 1976, the leadership wished to revive the United Front, but with a new twist. Patriots were not always socialist, Hua Guofeng observed at a September 1979 conference on the United Front, but many capitalists in Hong Kong were patriots. 'If we have a socialist united front they will not come,' Li Xiannian chimed in, 'but we can have a patriotic united front.' By 1981 the message echoed throughout the higher echelons of the party. 'We only have one criterion for overseas Chinese, namely patriotism,' Bo Yibo pronounced.[72]

A charm offensive began, with expressions of contrition over the excesses of the Cultural Revolution, when the property of overseas Chinese had been confiscated. In September 1979, Deng Xiaoping personally ordered restitution of their homes, especially those of wealthy businessmen. It was a quid pro quo, as the beneficiaries were expected in exchange to invest funds and contribute to the Four Modernisations.[73]

The ideal way to attract talent and capital from patriots in Hong Kong was to open a special zone just across the border. Marxist principles need not be violated, the *People's Daily* explained in 1978, since the Soviet Union, where joint ventures with foreign enterprises

had been established in the 1920s, had set a precedent.[74] In the special
zone the state would provide land, buildings and labour, while foreign
companies supplied raw materials, equipment and expertise. This was
the way forward, as foreign science and technology could be imported
without having to pay the full price in invaluable foreign currency.
Shenzhen was in Bao'an county, which had included both the island
of Hong Kong before it was ceded in perpetuity to Britain through
the Treaty of Nanjing in 1842, as well as the New Territories, which
were leased for 99 years in 1898. In September 1978 the State Council
officially declared Bao'an county a free trade zone. Across the Pearl
River, another zone was established in Zhuhai, adjoining Macau. Each
zone received 50 million yuan annually in investment for a three-year
period.[75]

These moves were far from daring. The first export processing
zone, as free trade zones were also termed, had appeared at Shannon
Airport in Ireland in 1959. By 1970 ten countries hosted such zones,
and they continued to boom in the following decade, with 175
established across fifty countries by 1986.

The first joint enterprise established in Zhuhai was a wool-spinning
mill, which did poorly. The brief experiment ended when production
plunged and the factory was closed. In the words of its Hong Kong
owner, 'those people don't like to work very much.' The state paid
the workers, who received desperately low salaries and were largely
illiterate. Foremen and supervisors, who could read and add up,
received exactly the same pay as ordinary employees.[76]

Other ventures fared little better. The most promising factory
in Shenzhen was an automotive assembly plant set up by Harpers
International, the Hong Kong distributor for Ford and Mitsubishi.
A dozen other companies also set up operations to take advantage of
lower wages. In 1979 they were still standing in the middle of empty
fields, linked to a wider grid by a mere dirt track, but hopeful that,
since China had been granted Most Favoured Nation status, the free
trade zones would allow Hong Kong companies to bypass the export
quotas set by the United States by changing their products' country
of origin.[77]

Other teething problems emerged. Many of the poorly paid
workers tried to escape, lured by the bright lights and higher salaries
in Hong Kong. In just ten days in August 1978, some 600 fled across

the border.[78] It was a rising tide. In May 1979 alone, border patrols in Hong Kong intercepted over 14,000. An enormous fence was erected, boosting existing deterrents, including a small army of Gurkhas.[79]

Xi Zhongxun, a veteran party member known for his moderate views, realised that fighting the flood would be difficult. Recently assigned to help south China develop international trade, he proposed that Guangdong and Fujian provinces be granted authority to make their own decisions in foreign commerce – including providing better conditions for workers in the trade zones. 'Let's call them special zones,' Deng declared, recalling the guerrilla zones that the communists had established in border regions before the Second World War. In July 1979 the Bao'an trade zone was renamed Shenzhen Special Zone, a designation later changed to Shenzhen Special Economic Zone. Zhuhai also became a special economic zone, together with Shantou and Xiamen on the coast of Fujian.[80]

Four years later, the only fully operational zone among these four was Shenzhen. Even Shenzhen did not develop quite as the leadership intended. The city was supposed to attract foreign investors and promote overseas exports. Instead, by the time that Deng Xiaoping visited, it imported three times as much as it exported, resulting in a trade deficit of over $500 million. Tourism and real estate, not industry based on advanced technology, constituted the main sources of its wealth. A new floor went up every week, Shanghai noted with admiration, but rapid urbanisation carried a huge cost.[81] The state poured an estimated $1 billion a year into the city to develop its infrastructure, many times the amount the city managed to attract from foreign investors. Shenzhen had, in short, become a flourishing entrepot, with goods imported and exported at preferential rates.[82]

**

Despite the poor performance of the four existing zones, the leadership was eager to open more cities to foreign trade. Zhao Ziyang had read *The Third Wave*, a book published in 1980 by the American futurist Alvin Toffler, who predicted that following the agricultural and industrial revolutions, a third revolution would be based on the computer, from cloning and cable television to the internet. In October 1983 Zhao proposed skipping the second wave altogether, pursuing modern technology along the coast and moving heavy industry to the hinterland. 'Time and tide wait for no one, opportunity knocks but once,' he pronounced. Just as Japan had seized the day with the Meiji Revolution in 1868, now came China's turn to overtake its competitors.[83]

A small study group set up to consider this issue, including Ma Hong, director of the Industrial Economic Institute, and Zhu Rongji, a smart but bruising vice-minister at the State Economic Commission, concluded that *The Third Wave* was a magic bullet the capitalist camp was seeking to use to extricate itself from an intractable economic crisis. The book also departed from the tenets of Marxism. Yet as a strategy founded on the basis of a socialist economy, it represented a huge opportunity to catch up with the external world. Deng Xiaoping and most of all Chen Yun repeatedly stressed the importance of computers to China's future development. *The Third Wave* therefore became mandatory reading for every party official.[84]

On 24 February 1984, a few weeks after his impromptu visit to Shenzhen, Deng Xiaoping called in Hu Yaobang, Zhao Ziyang and several others. 'We should handle economic zones a little faster and a little better,' he opined. A work conference was convened, concluding after several preparatory months of study that more coastal cities must be opened to foreign trade. Lenin had urged his comrades to develop the Soviet Union with capital from foreign capitalists. Deng now opined that foreign capital was not enough, as more joint ventures were required in special zones. On 6 April 1984, fourteen cities, including Dalian, Tianjin, Shanghai, Wenzhou and Guangzhou, were opened, effectively becoming special economic zones, with one proviso. Beijing had poured billions into Shenzhen, but was neither willing nor able to assist the new zones with more funds. 'We give you the freedom to open up,' Zhao Ziyang explained. 'Do not come to Beijing whenever there is a problem.' In effect local governments received greater leeway in foreign trade in exchange for less pressure on the central coffers, a seemingly win-win scenario. 'All we need to do to get results faster is to transfer power to a lower level,' Zhao stated.[85]

To encourage foreign firms to introduce more advanced technologies, the new zones were called Economic and Technological Development Zones.[86] Yet Gu Mu, a key player after 1976 in sending trade delegations abroad, had a warning for the new zones. On 6 April, as the fourteen cities were declared open, he pointed out that suspicion was rife abroad that foreign patent rights were being systematically infringed. He counselled prudence.[87]

Although four years earlier, on 3 March 1980, China had joined the World Intellectual Property Organization, the leadership only paid lip service to the ensuing treaty obligations. Throughout the party hierarchy, theft of intellectual property was actively encouraged. In 1981, for instance, a chemical factory in Shanghai had managed to reproduce fosetyl-aluminum, a compound used as a fungicide and registered in 1977 by the French pharmaceutical company Rhône-Poulenc. After the factory published an article explaining the procedure, the French embassy lodged a protest. Other cases arose, prompting Wan Li, vice-premier of the State Council, to declare solemnly that his country would observe international law when he met a West German pharmaceutical delegation in November 1982. In response, on 25 February 1983 the Ministry of Chemical Industries and the Ministry of Agriculture, Livestock and Fisheries jointly circulated a directive entitled 'On Maintaining Secrecy when Copying Foreign Pharmaceutical Products'. Due to the country's legal obligations, the directive explained, 'we cannot publish in openly available journals, and you must change the name of the product.' Counterfeiting, it further noted, could only be carried out 'under controlled conditions'.[88]

Intellectual property from abroad was collected at the highest level and distributed down the command structure of the planned economy. On 18 March 1983, the Ministry of Chemical Industries sent out a notice encouraging all state enterprises under its remit to send 'leading cadres who are politically reliable', and also conversant with advanced technology, to visit its Bureau of Scientific and Technological Information, which had a reading room with 'special material', defined as 'information on science and technology obtained from abroad through special channels'.[89]

Computers ranked high on the agenda. China's first IBM computer system – an IBM System/370 Model 138 – was installed in 1979 at the Shenyang Blower Works. At that time, computers were heavy machines, with a mainframe the size of a cabinet. There was no patent on the mainframe, leading to what were called clone computers. But the critical software and the technology that gave IBM its competitive advantage were kept secret and protected by patents. The Soviet Union, where clones were built in assembly lines and shipped to allies in the socialist camp, had some of the world's best experts in reverse engineering of computers.[90]

In October 1980 the Shanghai Committee on Computing explored the possibility of copying the entire IBM System 370, an undertaking that would need $2.6 million, a team of five local and foreign experts and a suitable liaison office in the United States. San Francisco was identified as the perfect base, since its mayor, Dianne Feinstein, had established a sister city relationship with Shanghai in January. A delegation would visit 'in the name of friendship'. One month later, the municipal party committee approved the proposal.[91]

Two years later, Shanghai acknowledged that its state enterprises had met limited success in importing and copying complex technologies. 'We need a unified approach towards copying,' one report noted, so that 'the quality of the copied equipment can be guaranteed'.[92]

Counterfeiting became even more important after Alvin Toffler's *The Third Wave* received the seal of approval. In Tianjin, a paper by the Light Industry Bureau put forward the view that counterfeiting was essential if the country was to jump several stages of development. The fourteen new special economic zones, including Tianjin, provided 'ideal conditions for copying consumer goods and advanced technology.' The Yingkou Washing Machine Plant, which had copied Panasonic's products, was just one example.[93]

Time and again, the State Administration on Guarding State Secrets, revived in 1978, enjoined party members to shield their counterfeit culture from indiscreet eyes and ears.[94] Like all central committees, this body had a local branch in every county and city. In 1985, for instance, the Shanghai Committee on Guarding State Secrets provided clear instructions on just what data could be shared with foreign counterparts in joint ventures. This excluded information on 'the importation through unofficial channels of embargoed equipment, instruments, samples, specimens, seeds, intelligence on technology and similar material'.[95]

Foreign delegations nonetheless noted that their counterparts in China had few inhibitions about explaining how they copied patented technologies.[96] No concrete legal sanctions forbade counterfeiting, nor did it incur any moral disapprobation. The notion of private property hardly existed. This was the socialist way of doing things, as the greater good trumped individual rights – especially when they were capitalist.

***

Foreign trade, too, was transformed. Not only were the industrial powerhouses along the coast declared open, but in September 1984 the contract system was introduced in foreign trade across the country. The foreign trade corporations, through which all transactions with foreigners had so far been channelled, lost their monopoly. Thousands of new ones sprang up almost overnight, competing with each other to act as agents for state enterprises. The proportion of foreign exchange vendors could retain from export sale was increased from 8 per cent in 1983 to 25 per cent in 1985.[97]

The result was a boom in imports. They soared by 60 per cent in 1985, driven by demand for colour televisions, tape recorders and microcomputers as well as entire turnkey factories. As Zhao Ziyang said in April 1985, 'you import, and I also import, everyone imports, from assembly lines of colour television sets, refrigerators and washing machines to tape recorders.' 'We cannot continue like this,' he warned. But he could do little to prevent it, since imposing tighter control over foreign currency would have undermined the drive to increase exports.[98] Within a year, the official currency reserves, nursed back to health after a period of economic retrenchment, dwindled from $17 billion to less than $3 billion, barely enough to cover a month of imports.[99]

The situation was a replay of 1978, this time on a larger scale. Imports were duplicated, expensive but inappropriate technologies purchased and vast amounts of money lavished on luxury commodities. Across the country local governments opted for shortcuts, but nowhere more so than in subtropical Hainan, which had a reputation for piracy. Instead of investing in fisheries and plantations, the island's officials decided to exploit their duty exemptions, granted in March 1983 to help end poverty and turn the island into a showcase of economic reform. The local government imported 89,000 cars and trucks, plus millions of television sets and videotape recorders together with cosmetics, food and toys. The harbours were choked. The decree that turned Hainan into a tax-free zone specified that imports were for local use only, but they were resold to the rest of the country, with purchasing agents buying the luxury goods at up to three times the original import price. Local branches of two specialised banks provided the loans funding this scheme. The money was earmarked to develop the island's roads, railways and airports, but was instead traded on the black market for the currency that foreign trade corporations were allowed to retain to import technology. When the central government finally clamped down in the spring of 1985, this was revealed as the biggest foreign currency manipulation in the country's history.[100]

With imports surging, exports did not keep pace. The goal behind the contract system was to encourage more production of export commodities. But the official exchange rate was overvalued. A dual exchange rate had been introduced in January 1980, with an internal settlement rate fixed at 2.80 to the dollar. Over the following years, inflation meant the average cost of earning a dollar abroad gradually rose, reaching 3.20 to the dollar in 1983.[101] Entire factories in Shanghai came to a standstill after they refused to lower their prices further for the export market. The foreign trade corporations, in turn, retaliated by refusing to repay their loans. The state intervened with subsidies, followed by further distortionary policies to offset the adverse effects of the dual exchange rates.[102]

On 1 January 1985 the internal settlement rate was quietly abandoned, with a series of gradual devaluations designed to boost exports. In August 1985 the yuan went down to 2.90 to the dollar. In October four successive devaluations quickly followed, reducing the rate to 3.20. In July 1986 there was a further cut to 3.71, where it stayed until December 1989.[103]

Even this was not enough. Across Tianjin, the industrial giant of the north, the unit cost of $1 of exports was 3.44 yuan in January 1985.[104] The situation was little better in Shanghai, the powerhouse of the south. In virtually every branch of industry, exports entailed losses. Dazhonghua, the city's largest rubber factory, produced tyres for the foreign market at a unit cost of 5.50 yuan for a dollar. Production plummeted, forcing the municipality to introduce new concessions, including reduced taxes and customs duties.[105]

Exacerbating the problem was inflation, which in turn led to a boom in consumption. As lending from specialised banks soared, more money was available to spend on goods. Many enterprises therefore preferred to sell their products at home rather than export them at world prices below production costs. To counterbalance the adverse effects of a distorted official exchange rate and promote export growth, the government introduced a series of compensating measures, from direct export subsidies to indirect expedients, including swap markets, export tax rebates and low-interest export loans.

Buoyed by these measures, the country's export drive regained momentum. Foreign observers, dazzled by the official statistics, wrote of a sleeping giant awakening after years of slumber. The reported value of exports increased from just under $10 billion in 1978 to almost $50 billion in 1988. Exports represented less than 1 per cent of global trade in 1978, but reached 1.7 per cent in 1988. The figure was still below what it had been in 1959, but it transformed the local economy and fundamentally altered China's economic relationship with the rest of the world. This was particularly true of exports of textiles and light manufactured goods, which grew faster than other categories of output.[106]

Japan and the United States were China's two largest markets. Both were eager to contain the Soviet Union, and both had agreed to grant China Most Favoured Nation status, in 1978 and 1980 respectively. Washington, unlike Tokyo, had retained the right to impose countervailing duties should it determine that China's exports were subsidised. Mill owners and other producers in the United States regularly complained that exports from China were unfairly subsidised, prompting the imposition of quota restrictions on the level of Chinese exports, especially textiles.

These new trade barriers were easily circumvented, with exports sent indirectly to the United States via the port of Hong Kong. In 1978, re-exports via Hong Kong represented roughly a quarter of all Chinese goods destined for the United States. By 1984 almost half such exports passed through the crown colony, and by 1988 the value of these indirect exports had soared so high that they surpassed direct Chinese trade with the United States.[107] Key to these trans-shipments was the free trade zone established across the border from Hong Kong in 1978.

***

When the Hainan car import scandal broke in 1985, it tarnished the reputations of all the special economic zones. But Shenzhen was special. From its very inception, the city was designed to pursue a much broader political aim, one absent from all the other trade zones established around the world: the People's Republic of China sought to demonstrate that it could operate two systems in one country. 'What Hong Kong can do, we in Shenzhen can do as well or better,' the *People's Daily* crowed in 1983.[108]

The idea that one country could house at least two systems was first proposed by Marshal Ye Jianying in September 1981, who developed it for Taiwan, the renegade island which the regime vowed to recover. Since Britain's lease on the New Territories would expire in 1997, Marshal Ye's nine-point plan was revised to include the crown colony. Sovereignty would belong to Beijing, while Hong Kong would remain a free port and international financial centre. On 6 April 1982, Deng Xiaoping declared to the British Conservative Party's Edward Heath, who was visiting Beijing, that 'Hong Kong will be managed by its inhabitants.'[109] But the island of Hong Kong had been ceded in perpetuity, and British prime minister Margaret Thatcher was reluctant to relinquish sovereignty. She believed that without some form of administrative control beyond 1997, London would be left with no guarantees, since 'communist governments could not be relied upon to respect agreements.'[110]

Prompted by an outflow of capital from Hong Kong, as well as overtures from Singapore and Taiwan to potential investors, Thatcher set off for Beijing in September 1982. Hu Yaobang was unavailable, entertaining the North Korean dictator Kim Il-sung who also happened to be in Beijing. Zhao Ziyang set the tone by refusing to recognise the treaties signed under the Qing. He gave Thatcher a stark choice, stating point-blank that Beijing would always prefer sovereignty over stability in Hong Kong. For good measure, he also pressed her for a long-term loan at a concessionary rate.[111]

Thatcher's meeting with Deng Xiaoping on 24 September went no better. He was gruff and baulked at the idea of a continued form of institutional presence by Britain after 1997. He queried the idea of administrative control, dismissing it with a flick of the hand. Occasionally he leaned forward to clear his throat and hawk loudly into a white spittoon placed at his feet. He made a threat, saying that he could reconsider the time and manner of recovery if any public disturbances occurred. Nobody quite knew, he continued in a conspiratorial tone, how many banknotes the Hong Kong and Shanghai

Bank of China had actually issued. The hint rattled the Iron Lady: here was one of the most powerful men in the world, manifestly ignorant about how a parliament worked, alleging that she was engineering financial instability to exert pressure on him.[112] On the way out of the meeting, before the television cameras, a visibly shaken Margaret Thatcher tumbled to the ground on the steps of the Great Hall of the People.

On returning to London, she concluded that none of the leaders in Beijing understood international finance or the concept of freedom under a system of law.[113] Her suspicions were soon confirmed. Hours after meeting her, Deng Xiaoping told an intermediary from Hong Kong that, by taking over the colony, Beijing would be able to extract more of its foreign currency.[114] In November he repeated his allegation that London had manipulated the Hong Kong dollar and wondered what other machinations the British would devise.[115]

There were no negotiations, only stern remonstrations and dark warnings, with threats to recover Hong Kong before 1997 repeated time and again.[116] Beijing also imposed a deadline, demanding that an agreement be signed by the end of September 1984. The idea of a special zone was thrust forward relentlessly, although it came with no details and no guarantees. A year before its own deadline, Beijing admitted that it had not prepared a basic law or even studied the legal system of Hong Kong.[117]

On 19 December 1984, the two countries signed a joint declaration, announcing that Hong Kong would become a Special Administrative Region on 1 July 1997. Beijing pledged to leave the colony's separate administrative, financial and legal system unchanged for fifty years. To mark the occasion, the paramount leader gave a speech, entitled 'China Will Always Keep Its Promises'.[118]

Although the declaration did not come quite on schedule for National Day on 1 October, Deng Xiaoping made a triumphant appearance on the rostrum, before a crowd of 100,000 people who had waited in the square since the early hours of the morning. His first words echoed Chairman Mao's most famous slogan, used 35 years earlier: 'The Chinese People Have Stood Up!' 'We have created a socialist society,' Deng continued, 'we have changed the course of human history.' The crowd erupted in applause.[119]

4

Of People and Prices (1984–1988)

In September 1937, Mao Zedong had penned a short essay entitled 'Combat Liberalism'. His target was party members who avoided ideological struggle for the sake of unity. Mao listed eleven forms of liberalism that undermined revolutionary organisations. 'To let things slide for the sake of peace and friendship when a person has clearly gone wrong' was one of them. Others were to 'disobey orders and give pride of place to one's own opinions', 'to hear incorrect views without rebutting them', or 'to work perfunctorily and muddle along'.[1]

On 12 October 1983, Deng Xiaoping had cautioned his comrades against downplaying the danger of spiritual pollution. He invoked Mao Zedong's essay at length, warning that 'no party member can stand above the party and do as he pleases.'[2]

Deng had sided somewhat reluctantly with Hu Yaobang, reining in the campaign against spiritual pollution as it threatened to dampen party members' commitment to the programme of economic modernisation. The literary world regained confidence. Like all state employees in a one-party state, writers were members of an association controlled by the state. And like all associations controlled by the state, there were regular meetings to study and implement the latest policies formulated by the leadership. They also voted, but since they were merely cogs in a machine, they cast only votes for candidates selected by the party. The China Writers' Association held its Fourth Congress from 29 December 1984 to 5 January 1985. Hu Yaobang was invited, Deng Liqun was not, even though he was the head of the Propaganda Department.

Hu Yaobang was a small, delicate man with a bird-like physique, but driven by an intense mind and seemingly boundless energy. He could jump with excitement when speaking to an audience, his arms waving as he gesticulated, his voice sometimes all but out of control. His heavy Hunan accent left some of his listeners bemused. He was fond of using slang. Admirers found his unconventional style refreshing, but his bearing clearly made others uncomfortable.[3]

Speaking at the congress, Hu adopted a liberal attitude. He made a distinction between units directly subordinate to the leadership of the party and other associations, which should be free to vote without interference. He suggested discarding the list of vetted candidates normally provided by the party.

Members voted. Candidates who had been active in the campaign against spiritual pollution were not elected. Ba Jin, a respected novelist whom Deng Liqun had taken to task, was duly voted in. Even more galling was the election as vice-chairman of Liu Binyan, an investigative journalist who wrote critically of the Four Principles. Liu used the opportunity to turn on his foes, who had attacked him for his 'bourgeois' ideas.[4]

The election sent shock waves through the party ranks. Hu Qiaomu and Deng Liqun were incensed. Li Xiannian denounced it as a rebellion against the party. Deng Xiaoping summoned Hu Yaobang. A few days later, on 8 February, a contrite Hu gave a speech at the Central Committee to underline the overwhelming importance of the fight against spiritual pollution. Only socialism could lead to true democracy, while journalists were mouthpieces of the party, the only legitimate representative of the interests of the people. It was a stern message, published in the party organ *Red Flag* a few months later.[5]

In May 1985 Hu once again miscalculated. He gave an interview to Lu Keng, a veteran journalist with the rare distinction of having been imprisoned by both the Nationalist Kuomintang and the Chinese Communist Party that succeeded it. His nickname was 'Big Noise', and he created a minor sensation by publishing the interview in Hong Kong, describing the general secretary as an honest, enlightened soul willing to tolerate dissent. During the meeting the journalist directly touched upon the only formal position retained by Deng Xiaoping, namely his chairmanship of the Central Military Commission. 'Why don't you take over the Central Military Commission while the old man Deng is still alive? If you don't, how will you handle the situation if, in the future, the military commanders oppose you?' Hu responded by saying that with no imminent war on the horizon, he let Deng have the position. When Lu Keng went on to make derogatory comments about Chen Yun, Hu Qiaomu and Deng Liqun, Hu Yaobang remained silent.[6]

Although the interview was heavily edited, the original transcript came to Deng Xiaoping's attention. 'This is completely unacceptable,' he fumed. This was probably the turning point for Deng, who now sought an opportunity to remove Hu.[7]

For several years, as general secretary of the party, Hu Yaobang had tried to rejuvenate the ranks by promoting younger party members. A great many of the more influential ones came from the Youth League, his erstwhile power base. This raised eyebrows.[8] But he also expanded his influence in the armed forces. As Chairman Mao had phrased it succinctly, 'power comes from the barrel of a gun.' Men who had served under Hu in the Shanxi-Chahar-Hebei Field Army before 1949 were appointed to key positions throughout the military. This was, of course, business as usual. Politics, in a one-party state, revolved around endless jockeying for power among ever-changing factions and temporary alliances. No individual could survive on his own. Since loyalty was paramount, all tried to build up a power base by promoting their underlings. When a leading official at the summit was toppled, the entire pyramid below crumbled to the ground. In order to prevent factionalism devouring the party, in as early as 1921 Lenin had outlawed it. Time and again, stern injunctions were issued against 'banding together in gangs', 'forming cliques for private ends' or 'forming factions', yet despite longstanding prohibitions these remained integral to corridor politics at every level of the party machine. But discretion was advisable.

A test came in May 1986. Twenty years earlier, after Khrushchev had denounced Stalin, Mao Zedong had tested the loyalty of his colleagues by suggesting that he might want to step back for health reasons. Instead of begging him to remain, Deng Xiaoping and Liu Shaoqi created a new position of honorary chairman for him, infuriating Mao. Deng now resorted to a similar strategy, overtly wondering whether he should withdraw to make place for a younger generation. Zhao Ziyang grabbed him by his sleeve, imploring him to stay on: 'we rely on you.' Hu, instead, happily agreed with Deng.[9] It was yet another faux pas in a series of blunders.

***

Political protest can be a perilous venture in a one-party state. One tried and tested strategy was to demonstrate on an officially approved day of the revolutionary calendar, for instance May the Fourth. Another ploy was to demonstrate against Japan, since few leaders had the political courage to interfere with nationalist sentiment, whether feigned or real. In this case September the Eighteenth was a good option, as it marked the Mukden Incident, when in 1931 the Japanese Kwantung Army, stationed in north-east China, had staged the episode to justify the full-scale invasion of Manchuria.

On 18 September 1985, in the biggest protest since 5 April 1976, a thousand students converged on Tiananmen Square from several universities, waving banners and shouting slogans against Japan. Their ire had been aroused by Prime Minister Yasuhiro Nakasone, who had paid an official visit to a Shinto shrine honouring the war dead in Japan. 'Down with the second occupation,' they shouted, alluding to Japan's increasing commercial presence. Policemen closed off the square but took no further action.[10]

The protest went unpunished, unusually by communist standards, suggesting support from higher up. A few weeks later demonstrations erupted across the country on twenty other campuses, with major unrest in several cities, including Xi'an, Wuhan and Chengdu. It now became clear that the outbursts were a covert attack on the government's economic policies. This time reprisal was swift.[11]

The instigators of the protests, it appeared, were a 'small minority' of people accused of manipulating the students behind the stage, described as opponents of the open-door policy, degenerate elements in favour of bourgeois liberalisation, dregs of the Gang of Four, underground organisations as well as spies from Taiwan and Hong Kong. The majority of the demonstrators were patriotic but naive. 'We must maintain proletarian discipline and oppose liberalism,' the leadership thundered behind closed doors.[12]

Several hundred students in Beijing were back on the square on 20 November, organising a vigil in front of the Monument to the People's

Heroes. Policemen in jeeps moved into the square and shooed the students away.

When Hu Yaobang urged young people to 'strengthen their belief in communism' and 'strengthen their resistance to bad influences', he failed to quell the unrest. In a new wave of protests, students complained about intimidation by university authorities, inflation, poor living conditions and corruption among party members. 'Down with special privileges,' some shouted, expressing anger towards high officials who profited from the open door to the outside world. On 19 December thousands of Uyghur students took to the streets in Urumqi, the provincial capital of Xinjiang, demonstrating against nuclear tests as well as the number of labour camps for common criminals set up in their province.[13]

The protests petered out, but the leadership was shaken. On 18 September, even as students took to the streets in Beijing, Zhao Ziyang addressed a large party gathering to talk about the next Five Year Plan. In order to keep to the socialist path and uphold the people's democratic dictatorship, he explained, it was essential to fight economic crime while strengthening indoctrination. The country must 'foster ideological education in patriotism, collectivism, socialism and communism', and simultaneously 'oppose and resist bourgeois liberalisation, oppose and resist capitalism, feudalism and other ideologically corrosive influences'.[14]

The Strike Hard campaign was revived. 'Kill a few, produce a shock. We still need ten years to revert to the party's work style of the 1950s. Be ruthless for two years,' Deng Xiaoping recommended.[15]

Again the cities were covered with posters detailing the latest crimes, and again prison vans were seen on the streets, taking criminals to the execution ground. But this time, in an apparent concession to widespread anger over nepotism within the ranks of the party, several family members of ranking officials were accused of rape and duly shot. The leadership was trying to improve its image. 'Those who ought to be killed must be executed according to the law,' the *Beijing Evening News* clamoured.[16]

This was a token gesture. The vast majority of suspects swept up by the system were ordinary people. By June 1986 the prison system was creaking at the seams, with over a million new arrivals swept in following the Strike Hard campaign, confined in crowded and unsanitary conditions. Torture, the vice-minister of justice reported, was 'not uncommon'. Whether they were whipped with leather belts, forced to kneel on broken stones or exposed to heat or cold, 'there are many ways in which prisoners are abused and tortured'.[17]

The campaign against decadent capitalist ideas was also revived. Again the party promised to wipe out 'spiritual pollution', with controversial plays banned and several popular singers forbidden to perform in public.[18]

None of these measures solved a basic contradiction, namely that inflation was gradually undermining the living standards of ordinary people in the cities, even as they watched party members use their political clout to exploit the socialist system for financial gain. The punishment of a few officials and an ideological campaign to instil correct behaviour would bring little genuine reform to a political structure that concentrated power in the hands of party members without genuine accountability.

Students took to the streets again towards the end of 1986, but now they came in much larger numbers. They also openly embraced democracy. Ever since the demise of the Democracy Wall, instead of confronting the regime head-on, political activists had tried to make use of every democratic right guaranteed in the constitution. Like all socialist countries, the regime was based on the principles of democratic centralism, which vested the people's authority in people's congresses, supposedly open to election, that formally represented the supreme authority at both national and local levels. This was a sham, since in the absence of a division of power the National People's Congress could do no more than rubber-stamp the leadership's decisions.

In October 1980 a student in Changsha had stood as a prospective candidate for election to the National People's Congress, describing himself as a 'non-Marxist but in accordance with the scientific socialism of Deng Xiaoping and Zhao Ziyang'. The outcome was predictable. Following his selection, his name was removed from the list of candidates. Demonstrators marched to the provincial party headquarters and held a sit-in, chanting 'down with bureaucracy'. A further eighty went on hunger strike. Elsewhere, too, people had tried to be elected and found themselves quietly excluded from the ballot.[19]

In November 1986, students at the University of Science and Technology in Hefei, the capital of Anhui province, also prepared to participate in local elections for the people's congress. The students were backed by an affable, soft-spoken astrophysicist with large, owlish spectacles named Fang Lizhi, who had toured the country urging students to demand democratic rights rather than wait for the party to bestow them. The provincial party committee, however, had already selected the winners of the election in advance. The students submitted a written petition, which was ignored. Posters went up along a hundred-metre-long wall, including demands for a 'government of the people, by the people and for the people', a phrase made famous by Abraham Lincoln in his 1863 Gettysburg Address. On 5 December, after the authorities tore down the posters, thousands marched on provincial government buildings demanding democratic reform. A few days later, the local authorities backtracked, postponing the election and allowing several students as well as Fang Lizhi to stand.[20]

The students' success caused a ripple effect. Tens of thousands of students took to the streets in a dozen cities, including Wuhan, Beijing, Nanjing and Tianjin. In Shanghai the demonstrations took on their own momentum after Jiang Zemin, the city's party secretary, addressed the students at Jiaotong University. Instead of expressing sympathy, he reprimanded them for being selfish, occasionally pounding the lectern to punctuate his message, enraging the students who unceremoniously hooted him out of the lecture hall. The following day local residents joined the students, parading slogans hastily scrawled on improvised banners made out of bed sheets. On 21 December 100,000 people poured into People's Square, bringing traffic to a halt. It was a festive atmosphere, with demonstrators 'giddy with the sudden sense of freedom and absence of fear', one foreign observer noted. They demanded 'Democracy, Freedom, Human Rights, Opposition to Brutality, and Opposition to Deception', among other things. They dispersed in the afternoon.[21]

On 23 December the *People's Daily* published a conciliatory editorial, appealing for unity and calling students 'our hope and future'.[22] The following day the Central Committee met, denouncing the 'reactionary slogans' of the protesters, who were being manipulated by degenerate elements opposed to socialism and the party. All provinces received a directive to avoid using words that might inflame the situation. They were also instructed to collect incriminating evidence in the form of photographs and recordings of the unrest and to clamp down ruthlessly on any attempt by the students to link up with factory workers.[23] The strategy, heralded a week earlier by Li Ruihuan, the mayor of Tianjin, was to downplay the significance of the demonstrations: 'There is nothing extraordinary about such incidents,' he had said, 'there is no reason for us to lose our composure.' On 25 December a new editorial in the *People's Daily* assured the students that, under the guidance of the Communist Party, political reform would follow economic reform.[24]

Overnight new regulations were passed requiring demonstrators to apply several days in advance of a public event for permission to demonstrate and to provide the names, addresses and occupations of all the organisers.[25] On 26 December, in a closed meeting, Fang Lizhi, Liu Binyan and Wang Ruowang, an author who had denounced the party as mere tyranny, were named as the principal instigators of the unrest, along with 'dregs of the Gang of Four'.[26] The demonstrations fizzled out.

On 28 December, once it became apparent that the unrest had subsided, in a talk at the party Secretariat, Zhao Ziyang condemned 'bourgeois liberalisation' in harsh terms. The situation looked ominous for Hu Yaobang.[27]

Two days later, Deng met Hu, Zhao and several others for a talk. He lashed out at Fang Lizhi, who had openly opposed the Four Principles: 'I have read Fang Lizhi's speech. It is outrageous for a party member to speak like that. Why should this person be allowed to stay in the party?' He was scathing towards democracy: 'We cannot copy bourgeois democracy. We cannot adopt stuff like the separation of powers. Everything will be out of control if we do.' He counselled a firm hand, very much in the way the Democracy Wall had been crushed in 1979. 'Didn't we arrest Wei Jingsheng? Did that hurt China's image?' He praised the way Poland had handled the crisis with the trade unions in 1981, when martial law had been proclaimed to bring the situation under control. 'We should not only talk about using dictatorial means, we should be ready actually to use them.' Most of all, he blamed the disturbances on the 'failure to take a clear-cut stand and maintain a resolute attitude to oppose bourgeois liberalisation'.[28]

On 4 January 1987, Hu Yaobang tendered his resignation, but still had to present himself at a series of gruelling sessions in which the party elders and other senior leaders took turns to probe him, denouncing him for six successive days. Deng Liqun relished the occasion, lambasting his political opponent for over five hours. Yu Qiuli, a veteran military leader, accused him of being a schemer who promoted his own people and had tried to push Deng Xiaoping off the stage. Yang Shangkun, whom Hu Yaobang had rehabilitated, showed no mercy. Neither did Zhao Ziyang, who had most to gain. As early as 1984, he explained, he had felt that his counterpart did not respect party discipline. He worried that in future, without Deng Xiaoping and Chen Yun, he would not be able to carry out his duties. Zhao now cast the final stone: 'I don't think that I can continue to work with you.' On 16 January Hu Yaobang's resignation was accepted by a show of hands.[29]

The most damning accusation made against him was that he had divulged state secrets to the journalist Lu Keng.[30] Still, the party was generous, allowing him to retain his membership. Hu vanished from public view, immersing himself in the collected writings of Marx and Lenin.[31]

During the winter recess, some students smashed small glass bottles. In spoken Chinese these were pronounced 'xiaoping'.[32]

***

It was a coup of sorts. To muster enough support to oust Hu Yaobang, Deng Xiaoping had turned towards the party elders and several military veterans, who continued to sit in on extended Politburo meetings or special work conferences. They carried considerable weight, sometimes even casting a vote or raising a hand, in blatant disregard of the procedures prescribed by the party constitution.[33]

Their power was formalised at the first plenum of the Thirteenth Party Congress, held from 25 October to 1 November 1987. The meeting resolved a conundrum at the heart of the country's power structure: if Deng Xiaoping retired, all the party elders would be obliged to withdraw as well. A resolution was passed, stipulating that on all major issues the Politburo would seek the guidance of Deng and the party elders. It gave the final say over all major decisions to Deng, who formally retired from all his positions. Aged 83, he was now a dictator without a title, except as chairman of the Central Military Commission. Yang Shangkun and Bo Yibo, both aged 79, were granted the right to attend all meetings of the Standing Committee, although they were not allowed to vote.[34] Chen Yun, who was no longer on the Central Committee, served as chair of the Central Advisory Commission. He was 82 years old.

The result was an extremely unstable political system, judged even by the standards of one-party states. A group of old men continued to wield power behind the scenes, squabbling over every decision made by those nominally elected by the Central Committee. A position no longer corresponded to a title, or the title to a job. The leader of the country was leader of neither the party nor the government. For the first time in communist history, someone could hold an important post without belonging to the Central Committee, which in any event had lost much of its clout. As one observer noted, 'communist parties in the Soviet Union and other communist countries must look at China with astonishment.'[35]

After Hu Yaobang's removal, Liu Binyan, Fang Lizhi and Wang Ruowang were expelled from the party. Television programmes intermittently showed mugshots of the three men. Their names appeared in newspaper headlines and in the propaganda blaring from public loudspeakers, together with the slogan 'Resolutely Oppose Bourgeois Liberalisation'.[36]

Zhao Ziyang was unanimously elected as general secretary, taking over from Hu Yaobang. One of his first acts was to bring back Lei Feng, with banners and posters enjoining young people to 'Learn from Lei Feng'. Yu Qiuli, the powerful army veteran, chaired a meeting devoted to the model soldier, flanked by propaganda tsar Hu Qiaomu and other senior leaders. They invoked words of wisdom from paramount leader Deng Xiaoping: 'Anyone who wants to become a genuine communist must learn from Lei Feng's virtue and spirit.'[37]

Several newspapers were shut down, including the *Shenzhen Youth Daily*. In October 1986 it had published a piece entitled 'Crisis! The Literature of the New Era Faces a Crisis'. Its author, a young man named Liu Xiaobo, had launched a devastating attack on establishment figures of the country's literary scene.[38]

Like all its predecessors, the campaign petered out. Zhao Ziyang, it turned out, was no more determined than Hu Yaobang to stamp out foreign ideas. The reason was always the same: few people had any appetite for a mass campaign reminiscent of the Cultural Revolution.

But more importantly, to avoid scaring away foreign investors China had to offer an image of stability. The economy required large amounts of foreign currency, more so than ever before. A first inflationary cycle in 1979 and 1980 had led to several years of economic retrenchment. A second cycle had developed in 1984 and 1985, with a huge expansion in loans by the specialised banks. Import controls were once more imposed on luxury goods in 1986. Purchases of television sets, motor vehicles and household appliances abroad dropped to negligible levels. Capital construction was also reined in, leading to a fall in imports of such materials as cement, copper, aluminium and steel.[39]

It was a half-hearted retrenchment. But a slump in the international market price for oil, one of the country's main exports, forced the leadership to export more commodities at unfavourable prices to compensate for the decline in value. Sales of raw cotton to Japan, for instance, rose by 8 per cent in value but by 45 per cent in volume. As Zhao Ziyang put it to Erich Honecker in June 1987, 'we were forced to export other products, but these products made us very little money.'[40] A sharp drop in foreign investment compounded the problem. Foreigners baulked at tight foreign exchange controls, endless bureaucracy and an impenetrable domestic market.[41]

The efforts to cool the economy, combined with a slump in the price of oil and a fall in foreign investment, produced an unexpectedly sharp decline in the rate of industrial growth. In the second half of 1986, Zhao Ziyang reversed course, pumping more money into the economy to revitalise the growth rate. In October he announced new incentives for joint ventures, including lower taxes. The second inflationary cycle, which had never really ended, gradually morphed into a third one.[42]

Despite more favourable conditions, the number of contracts for foreign investment continued to decline. After Hu Yaobang was dismissed, foreigners worried that the campaign against 'bourgeois liberalisation' would result in more restrictive commercial legislation.

The campaign was quietly abandoned, with additional credit steered towards the state enterprises. Zhao Ziyang was grappling with a contradiction. While tight monetary control was required to rein in consumption, state enterprises nonetheless had to be stimulated, as they relied on bank loans for more than 80 per cent of their working capital. A similar paradox was at work in foreign trade. In order to reduce the deficit, a massive export drive had to be whipped up, requiring all sorts of subsidies, rebates and loans. The money supply went up.[43] As the British embassy stated in a report entitled 'Deja Vu: Overheating in the Chinese Economy', 'there is enough steam coming out of a demented economy to drive a power station.'[44]

Prices rose as the budget fell, a problem that had bedevilled the leadership since 1979. At its heart was the price problem. Under a planned economy, the state fixed all prices. The alternative was to allow buyers and sellers to negotiate what they should pay for a particular commodity. For good reason, this was not an appealing option: the prices of goods that workers in state enterprises consumed would have shot up, while those of the shoddy products they churned out would have tanked. Villagers would have held the cities to ransom, much as they had already forced the regime in 1979 to increase procurement prices for food deliveries. Even more galling, the private enterprises that the authorities barely tolerated would have easily outpriced their state counterparts.

The spectre of mass unemployment and social instability instead led the regime to adopt a gradual approach, awaiting a perfect moment that never arrived. Between June 1981 and August 1982, local authorities and their enterprises were allowed to float the prices of most industrial products within a given range, meaning that a similar product could have many prices.[45] Then, in 1984, state enterprises were given licence to sell at market prices any surplus produced above their quota, introducing a dual price system, with one set of prices for the plan, another for the market. A huge grey zone appeared in which corruption blossomed, as people exploited the price differentials. The system demanded subsidies to maintain the artificial prices fixed by the state, placing even greater burdens on the central coffers. The problem was solved by creating more money, which led to an increase first in market prices, and then, through the magic of the black market, in fixed prices.

In order to reduce state subsidies, in May 1985 prices of a broad range of non-staple foods and consumer goods were allowed to float. Since the country was in the middle of its second inflationary cycle, having created a surge in the money supply followed by double-digit inflation, an overall limit was set on increases in the retail price index. The State Bureau for Prices, the institution in charge of managing prices through a network of local branches, determined that the index should not increase by more than 10 per cent. Deng Xiaoping, at a stroke, lowered it to 9 per cent. Zhao Ziyang made the rounds, spreading the message: 'you must adopt appropriate measures to ensure that the retail price index does not move by more than 9 per cent this year.'[46]

In Tianjin in 1984, subsidies for vegetables had cost the city 40 million yuan, roughly equivalent to the annual salaries of 70,000 workers. Now they shot up by 35 per cent. Controls on prices for furniture were also lifted, except for wardrobes, desks, chairs and beds. The price of a pair of good-quality leather shoes remained fixed at 6 yuan for men, 5 yuan for women.[47]

A greater range of free and fixed prices boosted the black market. In Shanghai alone the municipal Bureau for Prices reported 1,400 price infractions, with the offenders including so-called briefcase companies, makeshift operations that did nothing but exploit the system. As the vice-mayor pointed out, checking and controlling the price of every commodity was an impossible task, not least because the rules changed constantly and varied from one place to another. Some districts even closed their price bureaus, allowing all prices to float. This, in turn, invigorated a black market between districts where prices were enforced and those where they were not.[48]

By 1987 the State Bureau for Prices had relaxed controls on a whole range of prices. Foreigners wrote enthusiastically about a growing share of the free market. But while the state was no longer responsible for allocating a commodity, it did not mean that it operated under market conditions. Provinces, counties, cities, even districts now had the authority to fix prices instead. Local governments, in short, stepped in to take over from the central government.[49]

Since local governments derived income from local enterprises, they protected these through local price controls. In Dazhai, the erstwhile model of self-reliance, the output of two coal mines was sold to the villagers at 8 yuan a tonne, but to outsiders at 21 yuan a tonne.[50] Raw materials were particularly vulnerable, since there was a scramble every time the economy overheated. Trade barriers went up, beside price controls, to prevent speculators from poaching local resources. Trade wars broke out. There was, for instance, a 'cocoon war', as local authorities sent armed police forces and militiamen to guard the borders and prevent their silk cocoons, earmarked for purchase by the state, from being snapped up by outsiders and transported to more profitable regions. Similar conflicts erupted over coal, wool, tobacco, even dried sweet potatoes. 'Regions are at war with one another, and with the central government,' one government adviser opined.[51]

Instead of an integrated economy, a patchwork of independent fiefdoms emerged. When a lorry loaded with five tonnes of grapes left Qufu, the birthplace of Confucius in Shandong province, and headed for Guangze in Fujian province, it had to pass through more than a hundred checkpoints, paying several taxes, administrative fees, quarantine costs and even a contribution to one local fund for agricultural development. By the time the drivers reached their destination eight days later, they had lost not only the entire cargo, but also their own wallets, and even the tarpaulin used to protect the produce from the elements.[52]

Paradoxically, one commodity appeared to have no price, namely money. Total credit tripled from 266 billion yuan in 1982 to 788 billion yuan by the end of 1986, although very little of it was repaid. Lacking market discipline, and with central planners no longer enforcing sanctions, there was merely a mixed economy in which a state enterprise could borrow knowing that it would be bailed out once it was in deficit.[53] Interest rates, which in an open economy indicated the price of money, were a largely ineffective financial tool. Local governments resisted rate increases, since these meant that an enterprise would pay proportionally less in local taxes. And since enterprises depended on loans for their operating capital, any interruption to the flow of money would be disastrous.[54]

In short, by increasingly delegating administrative authority to local governments after 1979, the leadership now depended on local officials to carry out its monetary and fiscal policies. But local officials were more concerned with building up their own economies and improving their own standards of living than in implementing central directives that restricted the flow of money.

By 1987 there was neither a plan nor a market to steer the economy. Instead the country was in the grip of a vicious circle, one explained very well by the local Wuhan branch of the Bank of China: growth in the money supply encouraged greater consumption, but consumption produced inflation, which in turn prompted state enterprises to compete for additional local loans to snap up scarce goods and raw materials in anticipation of future inflation, leading to an expansion of the money supply.[55] The principal architect of this state of affairs was Zhao Ziyang.

The cumulative effect of these local decisions was that inflation undermined the living standards of the majority. Already by the first half of 1987, 40 per cent of urban households had experienced a decline in real incomes.[56] Later that year, the byzantine price system began to show signs of stress. Villagers refused to sell feed for pigs at fixed prices they considered unfair. The supply of pork, which accounted for 85 per cent of all meat consumed, dropped precipitously, forcing the leadership to reimpose rationing in Beijing, Tianjin, Shanghai and Shenyang. Sugar rationing began soon afterwards, with an allowance of one kilogramme per month for each household.[57]

In 1979, the rural population had demanded higher prices for producers, while the urban population had expected lower prices for consumers. Both had been satisfied at the cost of massive subsidies. With the dual price system introduced after 1984, the government succeeded only in alienating both interests, at the cost of even higher subsidies. By 1988 state subvention of housing, health, education and food had increased sixfold compared to 1979.[58]

Industry continued to expand drastically in the first quarter of 1988, with corresponding hikes in prices. Year-on-year inflation, however difficult to calculate with so many different prices for the same goods, reached 19 per cent in June, 24 per cent in July and 30 per cent in August. These were the official figures, but at a Politburo meeting later that year, Vice-Premier Yao Yilin produced a more credible estimate of 48 per cent inflation for the first half of the year. The monetary supply increased by some 40 per cent during the year, as bank inspectors and fiscal controllers were unable to curb inflation and control the flow of state funds that found their way into non-economic investments, from high-rise office buildings to luxury hotels.[59] As deputy minister of finance Xiang Huaicheng noted in April 1988, everywhere state organisations were building extravagant new offices, hotels, restaurants and sanatoriums.[60] Government offices and state enterprises alike embarked on a buying spree, snapping up such coveted goods as television sets and video recorders. Ordinary people could only watch while their own living standards declined.

In impoverished regions of China some cadres were even ferried around in sedan cars to attend conferences on poverty alleviation. Zhao Ziyang himself could see the danger: 'The masses are very dissatisfied, if we don't check this trend ruthlessly there will be no end of trouble.'[61]

The masses increasingly took their dissatisfaction onto the streets, in dozens of incidents around the country, from protest marches by students to petitions presented by workers. In June 1988 the police had to seal off Tiananmen Square amid public discontent over double-digit inflation.[62]

This was the moment Deng Xiaoping chose to propose shock therapy, namely the removal of price controls across a whole range of goods. Zhao Ziyang had repeatedly postponed price reform, assuring the leadership that prices would rise only temporarily. Now he came under pressure from Deng, who realised the extent of corruption caused by the dual price system and was impatient to push through further reform. 'We don't fear big waves,' Deng opined, 'but must march forward against them in order to force our way through.' In July 1988, in a meeting with foreign guests, he again announced his determination to 'smash the obstacle to price reform'.[63]

A few weeks later the leadership held its usual summit away from the sweltering summer heat at Beidaihe, a seaside resort established by foreign missionaries and traders in the late nineteenth century. Zhao Ziyang, charged with presenting the programme for price reform, faced opposition from party leaders who demanded that inflation be slashed by clamping down on capital construction, reining in the money supply and cutting consumption. The main proponent of retrenchment was Li Peng, a Soviet-trained engineer who had served as minister of the power industry after 1979 before his promotion to the Standing Committee of the Politburo in October 1987. Unlike his adoptive father, Zhou Enlai, Li Peng was a dour, rigid technocrat and hardline stalwart.

In March 1988, after extensive backstage horse trading, the party elders had appointed Li Peng as premier, in effect general secretary Zhao Ziyang's counterpart. In what would prove a major miscalculation, Zhao, thinking Li would be easy to handle, had agreed.[64] Li had backing from the hardliners, especially the economist Chen Yun, architect of the earlier retrenchment in 1979. As a heated debate about the merits of price reform unfolded, a stubborn Deng nonetheless refused to give ground. In the end he snapped, slamming the table and telling Li Peng point-blank: 'If you waver you can quit.'[65]

On 19 August, two days after the meeting, the *People's Daily* published an editorial describing the removal of price controls as the key to future economic reform.[66] A wave of panic buying ensued, as people feared that their savings would depreciate even further. There were runs on banks, with depositors forming long queues to withdraw their money and convert it into tangible goods like carpets, television sets, washing machines and refrigerators. In Shanghai, the equivalent of $27 million was withdrawn within two weeks. Officials of the People's Bank of China had to call a news conference to rebut rumours that a ceiling had been imposed on individual withdrawals.[67]

In some cities unrest broke out. In Pingyang, along the coast of Zhejiang, local residents queued up for several days outside all 68 branches of the Agricultural Bank of China. Once the bank ran out of cash, people began assembling in their hundreds to protest against the local authorities. In Wenzhou, Yueqing, Taishun and other cities in Zhejiang, irate crowds trying to withdraw their savings assaulted post office branches.[68]

Customers bought at record rates, turning to previously overstocked goods, from sewing machines and electric fans to pressure cookers. Even the ubiquitous spittoon was vulnerable to hoarding. In Yongjia, on the Zhejiang coast, sales of certain daily necessities rocketed by fifty times the monthly average. In neighbouring Rui'an, sales in August were three times higher than those for the entire year of 1987, as shops were stripped bare of goods such as bed sheets and blankets. There was a rush on edible salt, forcing local authorities to introduce rationing. Throughout the country, from early morning until late at night, department stores were crammed with shoppers spurred by rumours of imminent price rises. In one town every pair of shoes vanished overnight.[69] 'People have lost faith in price reform, they say the party has no future,' Li Rui confided to his diary.[70]

Strikes and showdowns followed. In a single Zhejiang village, more than 800 women in a shoe factory stopped work, demanding higher wages. Dozens of similar incidents occurred across Rui'an county, with workers from flour mills, textile factories, shipyards and wharves up in arms.[71] Everywhere industrial unrest prevailed, even though the right to strike had been abolished in 1982. Several strikes of up to 1,500 workers rocked Shanghai, raising the spectre of social instability.[72]

The experiment with price reform was officially scrapped on 30 August. Even though the run on the banks had only lasted a week, faced with popular unrest, Deng Xiaoping had flinched. Panic buying had, ironically, reduced the stocks of unwanted goods gathering dust in warehouses. It also brought in a substantial amount of money. Deng was apparently just as ready abruptly to decide on a course of action as he was to abandon it, with huge consequences for the country. It was a bungled opportunity, with price reform postponed to another day.

For a decade, Deng had been tugged back and forth between different factions, swinging widely from one economic policy to another, making reform piecemeal, with a redistribution of power from the centre to the regions instead of a concerted move from the plan to the market. His U-turn on price reform further weakened his standing with the party. His protégé Zhao Ziyang took the blame, straining relations between the two.

At the Third Plenum in September, conservative planners under Chen Yun regained control over the direction of the economy. The key term was again 'readjustment' (tiaozheng), a euphemism for retrenchment.[73]

A flurry of directives demanded that capital construction be reined in, consumption cut. 'The national economy faces its most severe and difficult time,' the State Council gravely intoned, 'if we cannot pull through the people will lose faith in the reforms, in the party and in the government.'[74]

Yet even as it announced its new policy of retrenchment, the leadership was sleepwalking into another financial crisis, this time in the countryside, where average incomes had levelled off or even declined after 1985. One reason, besides dwindling investment, was a slump in grain production. In 1979, villagers had forced the state to increase procurement prices for both compulsory deliveries and sales above the imposed quotas. The grain harvest had increased rapidly in 1984, from some 316 million tonnes to more than 400 million tonnes. The state had baulked at the expense of having to pay more not just to the villagers, but also to the cities where food was subsidised. Subsidies ballooned from 7 billion yuan in 1978, equivalent to 6 per cent of the budget, to 23 billion yuan in 1984, or 15 per cent of the budget. In 1985 the leadership abandoned compulsory delivery quotas and replaced them with a contract system, limiting its commitments. The key to the new system was that grain in excess of contractual deliveries no longer qualified for a higher price. Since the state maintained a monopoly on grain and cotton, it was the main buyer on the open market of output surplus to contract, allowing it to begin making savings. In 1985 these amounted to 8 billion yuan. 'We want to create a miracle,' Zhao Ziyang confidently announced as he introduced the new contract system.[75]

Simultaneously, the leadership increased by an average of 25 per cent the price of those raw materials required for agricultural production, including fertiliser, pesticides, plastic sheeting, diesel oil and electricity.[76] Since the cost of production rose even as income dwindled, villagers reacted by cutting back on planting grain. Output instantly dropped to 380 million tonnes in 1985. Three years later it was still below the level reached in 1984. Other crops, too, including hemp, cotton, oil-seeds and sugar, slumped or remained stagnant.[77]

The key word, in the countryside and the cities alike, was 'contract'. It implied a negotiated transaction reminiscent of a market instead of a power relationship intrinsic to a command economy. Yet no negotiations took place, since the state fixed the price of the grain to be delivered at a level it deemed 'equitable'. Nor was there a choice. Farmers were compelled to accept a contract whether or not they wished to. Even when they turned to the market for their surplus production, they still had to sell to the state. Worst of all, in the absence of enforceable legal rights, there was very little guarantee that local officials would respect the contracts which their subjects had to sign. In some rural areas in 1985, the farmers were no longer paid in cash but with IOUs, pieces of paper with handwritten promises of payment.[78]

Over the following years, purchases of grain that farmers produced above the amounts stipulated in their contracts became straightforward requisitions. The state controlled the market, which could be shut down pending delivery of all grain, bought up at the lowest price possible. At every level – village, county, province – local officials began to seal off rural markets and set up checkpoints to prevent farmers from obtaining better prices for their produce elsewhere.[79]

In 1979 villagers had forced the state to increase payments for all deliveries of food, compulsory or not. In 1985 the state was in a position to retaliate and pay less. But the game had no winners. In 1988 the crisis deepened. In some villages children kept watch, banging gongs when they saw government officials approaching. They would find a deserted village with bolted doors. Occasionally a ladder that a grain inspector climbed to examine a granary was pushed over. Violence flared as cars of corrupt officials were set on fire and warehouses with chemical fertiliser looted.[80]

The State Grain Bureau, the official organisation responsible for buying and storing grain, and selling it according to the priorities of the central government, supervised a sprawling network of grain procurement stations employing millions of people. Like all other state institutions, the procurement stations paid no heed to financial losses, which could be passed on to the central government, with deficits increasing every year. The situation came to a head in 1988, when the stations no longer had enough cash to pay farmers for the produce they had contractually undertaken to deliver. Cotton procurement, the responsibility of the State Cotton and Hemp Bureau with its parallel network of purchasing stations, ran into similar difficulties.

Procurement stations could no longer turn to the Bank of Agriculture, making the problem yet more acute. Under constant pressure from local authorities, branches of the bank had extended loans so liberally that they had reached rock bottom. The state bank responsible for agriculture was effectively bankrupt. As one bank inspector said, 'right now capital is like a funnel, it is poured in from above and seeps through the bottom.' He explained how easy it was for a local official to obtain a loan: 'Some cadres walk into a bank to get cash because it is more convenient for them to do so than to go back home and fetch their wallet. They take as much as they want.' In Jingzhou, Hubei province, some 40,000 cadres owed an average of 1,000 yuan each, the equivalent of two years' pay for an average worker. 'And what do they do with the money? They do business, they build a house, they buy luxury goods, they pay for a wedding, some even use it to gamble,' the bank representative clarified. To bypass the lack of funds, farmers were issued IOUs. In Yueqing county, roughly half of all deposits in the 131 branches of the Bank of Agriculture were promissory notes.[81]

The problem was nationwide. In November 1988 an emergency conference was convened in Beijing. 'I would rather print more money than issue IOUs,' Zhao Ziyang pronounced. Fearing further popular agitation in the countryside, he demanded that the banks provide the cash needed to pay the farmers.[82]

The money supply therefore continued to grow, with more than 28 billion yuan being churned out in the last quarter of the year. Despite stern injunctions on retrenchment from the leadership, inflation soon followed.

In August the leadership had announced that prices would be freed. Fearful of both urban and rural unrest, in December it imposed comprehensive price controls. In Gansu province, to take one example, the prices of nineteen types of essential goods were frozen, including rice, flour, oil, sugar, pork, beef, mutton, coal, soy sauce, vegetables, baby milk powder, matches, soap, washing powder, textbooks for schoolchildren, toilet paper and medical fees. Prices for some industrial products, including televisions, refrigerators and bicycles, previously allowed to float, were also reined in.[83] In Shanghai, price increases for daily necessities and non-staple foods as well as 'twenty-six types of industrial consumer goods' were banned. Beijing also expanded control over steel, copper, aluminium and other raw materials. To restrict speculation on agricultural inputs, a monopoly on the distribution of fertiliser, pesticides and plastic sheeting was re-established.[84] To appease a restive population, rather than being directed towards building projects raw materials were commandeered to make up for shortages in consumer products, with steel diverted to make more refrigerators and timber used for matches.[85]

In the first months of 1989, retrenchment began to bite, as economic growth tumbled, the money supply was reduced and one-third of industrial capacity lay idle.[86] State subsidies increased, boosting the budget deficit, while unemployment grew. According to Li Peng, since capital construction had been scaled back, with more than 18,000 projects cancelled or postponed, some 5 million workers had to return to the countryside. The premier hoped that they would find employment in village enterprises. But these had been the first to suffer from drastic cuts in credit and they, too, had to cut their workforce. By March 1989 some 50 million people from the countryside were on the road, looking for work.[87]

There was one consolation for Zhao Ziyang: since Premier Li Peng had been assigned responsibility for the austerity programme, he also became the focus for widespread popular resentment, especially among provincial leaders, since the need for centralisation lay at the very heart of retrenchment.[88]

***

Retrenchment went in tandem with a renewed effort to suppress anything that smacked of 'bourgeois liberalisation'. The main target of the regime was Su Xiaokang, a 39-year-old lecturer at the Beijing Broadcast Institute. Shorter than most northerners, but built like a pit bull with a barrel chest, Su was a fearless journalist who brushed aside all concerns for his own safety to investigate politically sensitive topics, from endemic poverty to corruption within the corridors of power. In February 1988 China Central Television commissioned him to produce a film examining the country's tumultuous history. The six-part documentary was broadcast over the summer, even as panic buying gripped the country. In a reference to a classical poem lamenting the downfall of an ancient kingdom through the folly of its king, *River Elegy* portrayed traditional culture as insular and stagnant. The river in the title was the Yellow River, customarily revered as the birthplace of Chinese civilisation. But Su Xiaokang and his colleagues treated it as a symbol of a stultifying past, its flow impeded by silt and sediment. In the words of an ancient proverb, 'a dipperful of water from the Yellow River is seven-tenths mud.' By contrast, the blue waters of the ocean, into which the muddied waters of the river emptied, represented the future. The message, clear to all viewers, was that the country must modernise by adopting ideas from the West. For good measure, the documentary also lambasted other cherished symbols of the past, including the Great Wall and the imperial dragon.[89]

'*River Elegy* distorts Chinese history, entirely negates the fine traditions of Chinese culture, and vilifies the Chinese people,' the *People's Daily* declared in a front-page editorial one day after the first episode was aired. It denied the accomplishments of socialism, the mouthpiece further alleged, and advocated 'total Westernisation'.[90]

The popular response, by contrast, was overwhelmingly positive. When a revised version was shown later in the summer, the streets of the capital and other major cities were empty. Tens if not hundreds of millions of viewers watched the six instalments every night for a week. Abridged versions of the script appeared in newspapers and magazines, followed by a flood of commentaries, both favourable and critical. One print after another sold out, with sales reaching more than a million copies. In bookshops and pavement bookstalls across the country, videotapes of the original broadcast were snapped up as fast as they could be stocked.[91]

On 27 September Vice-President Wang Zhen, an eighty-year-old retired military official with rigid views who had made a career attacking intellectuals, closed down the debate. Wang, described approvingly by his mentor Deng Xiaoping as a 'bazooka', took aim at the documentary, attacking it for 'vilifying our great Chinese people' and 'cursing the Yellow River and the Great Wall'. 'Intellectuals are dangerous,' he railed, sending ripples of alarm through academic and cultural circles. Every newspaper reproduced his speech.[92]

One week later *River Elegy* was banned, with distribution of the video outlawed and printed copies of the text removed from the shelves and burned in public denunciation campaigns. In the internal circular informing party members of the ban, general secretary Zhao Ziyang curtly noted: 'It is necessary to respect the views of the veteran cadres.'[93] At the Third Plenum of the Thirteenth Party Congress later that month, he repeated that China 'will never copy the separation of powers and multi-party system of the West'.[94]

More trouble came towards the end of November. Ren Wanding, a leading Democracy Wall activist who had clamoured in 1978 for human rights, chose the tenth anniversary of the movement to break his silence. After four years in a labour camp, he remained undeterred, openly demanding free elections and the separation of powers. He made the rounds in Beijing, meeting with students and speaking at a Democracy Salon founded by Wang Dan, a slender, soft-spoken history undergraduate at Peking University. Ren found the younger generation so inspiring that he released a petition addressed to the United Nations Commission on Human Rights, Amnesty International and the Hong Kong Commission for Human Rights, demanding the release of Wei Jingsheng and other democracy activists imprisoned since 1979, in a direct challenge to Deng Xiaoping, who had personally ordered a crackdown on the wall and its followers.[95]

Ren Wanding was not an isolated figure. In December the Propaganda Department sponsored a large conference to celebrate the tenth anniversary of the Third Plenum of the Eleventh Party Congress. Instead of praising the plenum as a 'Great Turning Point in History', Su Shaozhi, former head of the Leninism-Marxism-Mao Zedong Thought Institute, boldly ripped into the campaign against bourgeois liberalisation, calling for the rehabilitation of all its victims, including Wang Ruoshui. Despite efforts to censor Su Shaozhi's speech, on 26 December the *World Economic Herald* in Shanghai published his remarks. To add insult to injury, Su also spoke freely to foreign journalists about the corruption which had flourished since 1984 with the dual price system. 'The party needs to democratise itself but has done little of it,' he said. 'To beat corruption, we need a free press, freedom of opinion and investigative bodies that are independent.'[96]

While *River Elegy* galvanised support for freedom and democracy among millions across the country, some critical reactions to the documentary reflected mounting social tensions and a more general unease over opening the country to the outside world. Communist regimes promised their workers protection from insecurity and uncertainty, with jobs for life and prices that barely budged for decades. But as inflation increasingly undermined living standards, and the iron rice bowl came under attack, people began to feel threatened, their lives seemingly tossed around by forces outside their control. Some lashed out at foreigners, with xenophobia lurking just beneath the surface. The Communist Party itself, drawing much of its legitimacy from the claim that it had ended centuries of foreign exploitation, regularly whipped up hatred of outsiders. The notion that China had been humiliated at the hands of foreigners was branded into the mind of every child and every adult. While official propaganda could be stultifying, nothing was quite as liberating as a flying kick in the face of an arrogant white man by a seething Bruce Lee in *Fists of Fury*. When the endless queuing and jostling for space of the daily grind became too much, when dissatisfaction became unbearable, anger readily cohered around foreign things and people. *People of China, Why Don't You Become Angry?* was one title on sale in bookshops.[97]

Rising social volatility brought increased incidents of open antipathy if not outright hostility towards foreigners. In 1985 demonstrations had erupted against Japan. Now students turned against Africans. In an earlier incident on 24 May 1986, an angry crowd of Tianjin University students armed with clubs besieged a canteen where African students had organised a party to mark the anniversary of the African Union. Those trapped inside were forced to break into an adjoining kitchen as bricks, stones and bottles were hurled through the windows until four o'clock in the morning. 'Beat the foreigners to death,' the crowd chanted at regular intervals.[98]

Similar episodes rocked several other campuses in December 1988. On Christmas Eve a riot broke out in Nanjing after a group of African students reportedly refused to register their female guests, as school regulations required. After a brawl left two Africans and eleven university employees injured, more than 5,000 students marched through the centre of the city shouting 'Beat the Black Devils'. The authorities were forced to call in security troops to maintain order. One week later, hundreds of kilometres to the north, an angry crowd of protesters at the Beijing Language Institute put up posters demanding punishment of an African student who had allegedly insulted a local woman. Two thousand students later boycotted classes.[99]

When the leadership met behind closed doors to review law and order in January 1989, they agreed that the overall situation was grim. Severe inflation had heightened social instability, while the policy of retrenchment had brought huge challenges to the employment structure. Failure to honour rural contracts meant that far less food than required to feed the cities had been procured. Students were restive, some even clamouring for 'freedom' and 'democracy'. In the ethnic belt that ran along the north-western border, from Tibet to Xinjiang, unrest was rife. Despite a tough campaign against crime, law and order were on the decline.[100]

In local folklore, a serpent sits behind the throne of the emperor to ensure that no one approaching from behind can cause him harm. As the Year of the Snake was about to slither in, heightened vigilance was required.

5

The Massacre (1989)

The Beijing of 1989 was still a drab city of tenement blocks and offices, enlivened here and there by remnants of its imperial past. Even so, it had changed since Chairman Mao's death. Blue and khaki were no longer so ubiquitous, as brightly coloured clothes had appeared, with modern suits increasingly worn by party members. Imported cars appeared in larger numbers on the streets, while new buildings and neon signs enlivened the skyline. Originally the Beijing Hotel, located next to Tiananmen Square, had been the main venue for visiting dignitaries, but several new establishments had opened their doors, including the Jianguo Hotel and the Great Wall Sheraton Hotel, a sleek silver structure towering over the capital.

Hawkers, peddlers and itinerant traders were everywhere, offering their wares on pavement corners, sometimes gathering in free markets. Among the more prosperous of these was a narrow lane called Silk Alley, situated between the Jianguo Hotel and the Friendship Store. Unlike the Friendship Store, a hulking complex spread over three floors with shop assistants legendary for their inability to shake off a lifetime of indoctrination in bad manners, Silk Alley was lively. Its 160 small wooden booths, painted in blue with a number in white, offered silk or cotton dresses, pyjamas, blouses, underwear, trousers, shoes, bags, knick-knacks and much else from factories in places as far away as Wenzhou.[1]

The general population, its standard of living lagging behind, tended to view private traders with contempt. Even university students, considered a privileged minority, lived six to a tiny room, with showers once a week. As part of a national effort to save energy, in the middle of the winter the heat and electricity were shut off every couple of days. In crowded canteens students were served concoctions of tofu and cabbage, with generous helpings of rice gruel, slopped out from huge iron vats.[2] Their professors barely received a living wage, forcing some of them to take two jobs in order to make ends meet. A year earlier, in April 1988, a small group of eighteen students from the capital's most prestigious universities had staged a fruitless protest before the Great Hall of the People to demand better treatment for intellectuals.[3]

Migrants from the countryside were also a relatively new phenomenon. Their numbers had surged, with tens of millions nationwide. Lured to the city, where better employment opportunities existed, even if the household registration system prevented them from acquiring permanent residency, they were interlopers, surviving on the margins of urban society. Entire villages came to rely on their remittances, especially as investment in the countryside dwindled and living standards declined. The registration system of the planned economy had tied them to the land, turning them into bonded servants at the beck and call of local cadres in the People's Communes. Now the same system guaranteed a steady supply of cheap labour for infrastructure projects and the exporting factories located along the coast. Migrants enjoyed no rights, no benefits and few protections, and were exploited by local authorities, who could send them back to the countryside at a moment's notice, or instead deploy them on another project where sweat was required. Foreign specialists occasionally lectured on 'social mobility', a fancy term which sounded rather learned, but the migrants bore great resemblance to a hereditary caste permanently locked into poverty.

As retrenchment began to bite, the influx of villagers became harder to control. In Beijing alone, the authorities detained thousands every month, yet the numbers still swelled, encompassing young men looking for work, but also disabled people, petitioners with grievances, street performers, vagrants sleeping rough, even beggars near the Jianguo Hotel.[4]

As the Lunar New Year approached, the regime mounted a huge effort to ensure that shops were provisioned with consumer goods and food. Residents in the capital were allowed to buy an extra pound of meat in state shops, while the supply of cabbage was increased by a quarter. The occasion was subdued, with a few coloured rockets and crackers flickering in the capital's smoggy sky, a dim echo of past fireworks. In Shanghai a complete ban on firecrackers was imposed. Austerity was the order of the day.[5]

The leadership made the rounds, offering New Year greetings and delivering talks to boost popular morale in the face of economic woes. Li Peng addressed an audience of 4,000 party leaders, telling them that economic and political stability was essential, as the country would celebrate the fortieth birthday of the communist takeover in October.[6]

But trouble was not long behind. In April 1988 former president Richard Nixon had published a book entitled *1999: Victory Without War*. Communism, he explained, should be undermined by supporting opponents within those regimes. Deng Xiaoping was not one of them, but Zhao Ziyang showed promise. 'The unanswered question is who is the one among many who has the strength and vision to replace Deng when he finally leaves the scene,' Nixon wrote. 'In a communist country only one can be the leader. Whether that leader is Zhao will depend upon how successfully his skills as a political tactician match those he has already exhibited as an economic one.'[7]

Later that year, on 19 September, after several weeks of panic buying across the country, Zhao Ziyang met the economist Milton Friedman for a candid conversation on reform, an encounter that attracted the attention of several journalists in Hong Kong who had close ties to a Beijing think-tank associated with Zhao Ziyang. 'The Patriarch Should Retire', one editorial boldly proclaimed. Another pronounced that 'those who hope China will walk the capitalist road bet on Zhao Ziyang.' To Beijing conservatives, this seemed suspiciously like 'collusion with external forces', a spectre commonly conjured up in dictatorships, with a clandestine network within the state alleged to be engineering a coup with the assistance of hostile foreign powers.[8]

A few months later, the plot thickened. In early January, Fang Lizhi, who had been cast out of the party in 1987, decided to take Ren Wanding's petition one step further, issuing an open letter to Deng Xiaoping demanding the release of all political prisoners. He personally recommended May the Fourth as a suitable occasion for a general amnesty. On 2 February 1989 Fang published a piece in the *New York Review of Books*, dismissing socialism in a single sentence: 'Forty years of socialism have left people despondent.' Ten days later, more than thirty of China's most prominent authors signed the petition and made it public at Columbia University in New York. The document, according to a secret circular from the Central Committee, demonstrated 'foreign support' for 'reactionary political forces' at home and abroad.[9]

Meanwhile, the US embassy in Beijing had been asked to draw up a list of guests for a large banquet to be hosted by President George H. W. Bush, who wished to attend Emperor Hirohito's funeral in Japan, and decided to visit South Korea and China, too. A decade earlier, from December 1974 to December 1975, Bush had headed the Liaison Office in Beijing, as the de facto American embassy was termed before diplomatic recognition. Bush considered himself something of an old China hand. Deng, the White House explained, was 'an old friend'. Winston Lord, the ambassador, included Fang Lizhi on the guest list, although a cautionary note about the astrophysicist's dissident status was included in his cable to Washington. Although no one in the White House paid any heed, this instantly raised hackles in Zhongnanhai. The protocol official initially dispatched to warn the Americans was ignored. By the time Bush boarded Air Force One in Tokyo, the Ministry of Foreign Affairs had delivered a strongly worded ultimatum. The leadership in Beijing must have concluded that Washington was in cahoots with the domestic forces of bourgeois liberalisation. 'Who IS Fang Lizhi?', an exasperated Bush reportedly shouted to his advisers.[10]

On 26 February the police prevented Fang Lizhi from reaching the Great Wall Sheraton Hotel, where the banquet took place. The incident forced Zhao Ziyang to lecture George Bush on the dangers of meddling in Chinese internal affairs. Zhao also used the occasion to launch an attack on dissidents and their support for the separation of powers.[11]

Although a strong statement, it failed to boost his image. Zhao was already an isolated figure, who surrounded himself with loyal advisers, but had neglected to cultivate potential allies within the party ranks. Even after their relationship became strained after the August 1988 debacle on price reform, Zhao continued to rely heavily on Deng Xiaoping.[12] And even as Zhao narrowed his power base, Li Peng had busily extended his political clout, building alliances with Chen Yun and other party elders, who now took the offensive. In Suzhou, a city of gardens along the Grand Canal a hundred kilometres west of

Shanghai, the veteran planner Li Xiannian publicly lambasted Zhao Ziyang. Others followed suit, further undermining the general secretary in a series of closed-door meetings.[13]

On 20 March Li Peng gave the keynote address at the National People's Congress. He apologised at great length for the 'shortcomings and mistakes' in the party's economic policy, deploring 'the tendency to be too impatient for quick results in economic and social development'. 'We lacked a full understanding,' he continued, 'of the complexity of reform.' All the delegates understood that the premier's apparent mea culpa was aimed at Zhao Ziyang, the architect of reform, slumped in a chair behind the podium.[14]

***

Hu Yaobang's death on 15 April came like a lightning bolt in a clear sky. Weeks earlier he had appeared in good health, playing bridge in his winter retreat in Nanning. On 8 April, while attending a Politburo meeting, he suffered a severe heart attack and was rushed to hospital, where he died a week later.[15]

In death Hu was transformed into a legend, a symbol of integrity for people yearning for change. The very day he passed away, students put up posters at Peking University, the campus that had taken a lead in the December 1986 demonstrations. 'Hu Yaobang is dead, the democratic spirit is dead, Peking University is dead,' one wrote in despair. 'How could you leave us like this?' another exclaimed. A poem lamented: 'The honest man is dead; the hypocrites live on.' A harsher tone also surfaced, with one poster denouncing efforts by the authorities to prevent students from celebrating the seventieth anniversary of May the Fourth. An outpouring of grief likewise erupted at Tsinghua University, where students pasted up wall posters read and copied by hundreds of people. Some of them circulated rumours. One tenacious story held that Hu Yaobang had died of sheer anger over the intolerance of his colleagues at the Politburo meeting. Another alleged that the widely detested Li Peng had so severely remonstrated with him that he had died of heart failure. The same day students began to converge on Tiananmen Square, leaving wreaths around the base of the Monument to the People's Heroes.[16]

On Monday 17 April hundreds of students made their way to Tiananmen Square to pay homage to the leader who had inspired them. Senior party members and leading intellectuals visited the deceased's family members to offer their condolences. In the evening the movement assumed a decidedly political character, as thousands marched in Beijing and Shanghai to demand a reassessment of the events leading to Hu Yaobang's resignation in January 1987.[17]

On 18 April intelligence chief Qiao Shi, one of the five members of the Standing Committee, put the public security apparatus on high alert, explaining that the students were contacting their peers around the country by telephone to 'stir up mass disturbances and turn memorial activities into a spearhead directed against the party and the government'.[18]

The spirits of the dead, according to tradition, torment the living. Even as Qiao Shi's directive made the rounds, Zhao Ziyang had to decide what to do next, a perilous decision, since it was Deng Xiaoping who had forced the former general secretary to step down. The demonstrations threatened to turn against him. Zhao decided to take no further action. That same day, students from Peking University organised a sit-in on the square after they were prevented from hanging a banner on the monument. After sunset, several thousand demonstrators converged on Zhongnanhai, where they denounced the regime and shouted 'Long Live Democracy' and 'Down with the Communist Party'. Several protesters pushed and shoved the guards protecting the main gate leading to the premises of the Central Committee and the State Council. The following day, streamers bearing the words 'Burn Zhongnanhai!' appeared. The protesters returned in the evening, when they mounted a renewed assault on the gate. This time the authorities were prepared, with police storming the crowd and arresting anyone they could apprehend and stuffing them into police buses. Those arrested were driven back to their campuses and released, getting off lightly.[19]

Rain poured down on the city on 20 April. In the evening an official warning was read out on television, denouncing a 'small number of people' who were using Hu Yaobang's death as a pretext to 'attack the party and the government' and 'chant reactionary slogans'. The following day, tens of thousands marched again towards the square, 'clasping hands, singing, waving big red banners'. The plan was to occupy Tiananmen with sufficient provisions of food, water and winter coats to stay the night, since the authorities had announced that the square would be closed during the following day's memorial service. By nightfall an estimated 100,000 people had gathered, and still more groups arrived, carrying wreaths and tributes to the monument. The mood was defiant. 'I am ready to go to jail,' one participant said. The activist Ren Wanding, who had protested on the same square thirteen years earlier, addressed the crowd, praying for 'the awakening of a legal system'. 'The Democracy Wall lives again!' he shouted.[20]

Demonstrations were also held in more than twenty other cities, with students carrying wreaths and portraits of the deceased. In Lanzhou, capital of Gansu province, hundreds of protesters assailed provincial government offices, shouting 'We Want Democracy, We Want Freedom', 'Down with Dictatorship', 'Down with Bureaucracy' and 'Down with the Communist Party'.[21]

The official memorial service was held in the Great Hall of the People at ten o'clock on the morning of Saturday 22 April. Earlier that day more than 50,000 people who had stayed overnight defied a police order to disperse, demanding admission to the hall. The authorities, who could hardly order a crackdown, compromised by allowing them to stay on the square and listen to the memorial address broadcast from the loudspeakers. Rows of soldiers linked arms to block the hall entrance. A lorry driver in the crowd was dismissive of the leaders inside. 'These men aren't communists,' he said, 'they are just feudal old guys who are afraid of the people and despise us.'[22]

Some 4,000 party leaders gathered around the glass-topped coffin containing the remains of Hu Yaobang, dressed in suit and tie. Deng Xiaoping, according to one foreign reporter, looked 'grey, bloated and stunned'.[23] One day earlier, the leadership had refused to honour their erstwhile comrade as a 'Great Marxist', the highest title in the communist pantheon, despite a request from the family as well as admirers of the deceased. Zhao Ziyang, who read the eulogy, instead used the agreed term of 'great proletarian revolutionary and politician', assigning Hu to the same rank as Hua Guofeng. 'He was brave enough to insist upon what he thought was right,' Zhao Ziyang concluded.[24]

Even this was too much praise for some party veterans, who viewed the eulogy as an implicit reversal of the party's verdict. The funeral was too elaborate, one general complained. There was nothing great about the man, another insisted. 'Only Xiaoping is higher than us, seeing farther and more clearly,' one veteran grumbled.[25]

As Zhao Ziyang left the Great Hall of the People, he bumped into Li Peng. Since Zhao was leaving for a scheduled state visit to North Korea the following day, Li Peng suggested another meeting of the Standing Committee. There was no need, Zhao answered, since the demonstrators would soon disperse now that the memorial service was over. A dialogue would appease most of the students. Li retorted that a firm stance was required, since some protesters clamoured for freedom and democracy and were causing turmoil. Zhao was evasive.[26]

In the afternoon, a funeral procession carried the body of Hu Yaobang west along Chang'an Avenue to the Babaoshan Revolutionary Cemetery, as an estimated million people lined the route of the motorcade to pay their last respects.[27]

Over the weekend people protested in several other cities. In Xi'an, the ancient capital in Shaanxi province where an army of terracotta sculptures had been discovered in 1974, some 6,000 people went on the rampage, assaulting government offices, burning an oil tank, setting two buses on fire and hurling rocks at the police. 'Some were standing peacefully, others went crazy, ripping limbs off trees and throwing anything they could at the police,' an eyewitness recounted. After the provincial party secretary wired Beijing for help, 4,000 soldiers were dispatched to impose order. In Changsha, the capital of Hunan, thousands of demonstrators ransacked shops, a hotel and the railway station, demanding that Deng Xiaoping step down. Lampposts were uprooted and windows smashed. In Chengdu in Sichuan province, 10,000 students took to the streets.[28] That same day, Li Ximing, the party boss of Beijing, phoned Zhao Ziyang to ask him to postpone his trip to North Korea. Zhao, instead, put Li Peng in charge. The two briefly met at the railway station in the afternoon. Zhao repeated that the students could be assuaged through dialogue.[29]

On Monday 24 April students across the capital went on strike. Over the weekend they had abolished the official student unions, replacing these with their own autonomous organisations. They took command of the loudspeaker systems on a number of campuses, broadcasting their demands for freedom and democracy. Hundreds of volunteers, crammed into tiny dormitory rooms, churned out thousands of leaflets enumerating their grievances. Teams of students fanned out across the city, distributing the leaflets, collecting funds and rallying the population. In a step too far for the leadership, groups of workers could be seen gathering around posters that the students displayed in public places. In the evening the Standing Committee met again, concluding that there was 'organised opposition' to the party. Li Peng, who chaired the meeting, demanded an uncompromising approach and 'unstinting repression'.[30]

The following morning the leadership gathered again at Deng Xiaoping's residence. 'This is not an ordinary student movement, but turmoil,' the paramount leader observed. 'We must adopt a clear-cut stand and implement effective measures to quickly oppose and stop this unrest. We cannot let them have their way.' The people behind the students, Deng continued, were influenced by liberal elements in Yugoslavia, Poland, Hungary and the Soviet Union. 'Their motive is to overthrow the leadership of the Chinese Communist Party and the socialist system.' The leaders agreed to publish an official statement firmly condemning the student activities. From Pyongyang, Zhao Ziyang telegraphed his approval.[31]

A harsh editorial, broadcast on the evening of 25 April and published in the *People's Daily* the following day, accused 'an extremely small number of people with ulterior motives' of taking advantage of the students to 'poison and confuse people's minds'. 'This is a planned conspiracy,' the editorial continued, aimed at 'negating the leadership of the party and the socialist system.' The tremendous achievements of the last decade to 'revitalise China' would be ruined should the disturbances go unchecked. A ban should be imposed on 'unlawful parades and demonstrations' as well as attempts to link up with people in 'factories, schools and villages'. All illegal organisations established by the students should be disbanded.[32]

***

The editorial was not well received. In an unprecedented act of defiance, the following day a crowd of 150,000 people marched through the main arteries of the city shouting slogans against corruption. For the first time, groups of workers joined their ranks. The population came out en masse to show support, cheering from crowded pavements and overpasses, welcoming the demonstrators like a liberating army. Some carried their own banners, shouting slogans that addressed concerns closer to home, from inflation to graft. They offered loaves of bread wrapped in plastic, bottles of water, packets of ice lollies. Soldiers were stationed all along Chang'an Avenue, some carrying automatic assault rifles, but they intimidated no one, melting away in front of the crowd. The square itself looked like a war zone, with soldiers massed around all the main structures. But the demonstrators walked straight past Tiananmen, bypassing the square entirely, in what seemed more like a well-organised victory parade than a spontaneous protest march, with students showing discipline and restraint. Even the tone was different, as they chanted slogans in favour of the party and the constitution.[33]

Li Peng blundered, circulating some of the confidential comments Deng Xiaoping had made at the meeting in his residence two days earlier, for consideration by party members assembled in study sessions even as the students marched through the capital. Once these leaked, the protesters began to focus on the paramount leader, wondering why the Standing Committee had to report to him. The phrase 'to administer state affairs behind a curtain' began to spread. Deng was displeased with his premier.[34]

After the students' show of force, the regime was forced to change tack and open a dialogue. On 29 April a meeting took place between students and government representatives and was broadcast live on television, which was a rare occurrence. Yuan Mu, a spokesman for the State Council, opened with a stern lecture, repeating the main points of the 26 April editorial. Questions from students followed. When one of them complained about bias in the official press, Yuan Mu retorted that 'as far as I know, press censorship does not exist in our country.' He smirked frequently, which did not endear him to his audience. But his smile disappeared after a slim young man suddenly stood up, decried the dialogue for having excluded the student autonomous organisations and walked out in protest. Yuan Mu tersely replied that the student organisations were illegal. After another participant quoted Article 35 of the constitution, which stipulated freedom of speech and association, the spokesman pointed out that each citizen had a legal duty not to violate state interests.[35]

The dialogue divided the students. Infighting, which had raged all along, began to tear some of their organisations apart. Some delegates viewed the unions established independently from the government as an obstacle to further dialogue and proposed to disband them. Others began to drift away. On 1 May, celebrated as Labour Day, the authorities issued an appeal for stability. Tiananmen Square was decorated with red flags, but remained deserted except for a few tourists taking pictures in front of the rostrum. The holiday passed without incident.[36]

Yet tensions were still high. For several weeks both students and intellectuals had been calling for a large-scale demonstration to mark the seventieth anniversary of the May the Fourth Movement.[37] Another landmark event loomed on the horizon, a state visit by Soviet leader Mikhail Gorbachev, scheduled to take place from 15 to 19 May. The leadership viewed the summit as the triumphant conclusion of several years of quiet diplomacy. Three years earlier, in Vladivostok, Gorbachev had announced a series of unilateral concessions to China, paving the way for an improved relationship. Soviet foreign minister Eduard Shevardnadze had visited Beijing and Shanghai in the first week of February 1989 to fix a date for the meeting.

The moment Zhao Ziyang returned from North Korea on 30 April, he began to shift his position. Before consulting his premier or other members of the Standing Committee, he met with his advisers.[38] Even before he had left for North Korea, they had worried that the 'spearhead of the student movement' was turning against him as well as the paramount leader. Now they seemed to suggest that he distance himself strategically from Deng Xiaoping.[39]

At a Standing Committee meeting on 1 May, Zhao Ziyang approved the decisions taken in his absence a week earlier and backed Deng Xiaoping's condemnation of the student demonstrations. He did not question the 26 April editorial. But the following day he had a change of heart and tried to contact Deng through an intermediary, who in turn approached Yang Shangkun, head of state and member of the Standing Committee. Yang refused, pointing out that Deng was unlikely to change his assessment of the student demonstrations overnight.[40]

Before the assembled party leaders at the Great Hall of the People on Wednesday 3 May, Zhao delivered a speech to celebrate May the Fourth, calling on the country to oppose social unrest, and warning that without unity and stability, 'a country of promise will be turned into a country of hopelessness and turbulence.' In a conciliatory gesture, he praised the patriotism of the students and the legitimacy of their demands for 'promoting democracy, fighting corruption and promoting education', all of which corresponded to the aims of the party. He underlined the importance of the Four Cardinal Principles, including the dictatorship of the proletariat as well as Marxism-Leninism-Mao Zedong Thought. But even though other members of the Standing Committee had suggested that he do so after he had circulated an advance draft of his speech, he did not mention the fight against 'bourgeois liberalisation'.[41]

Later that day Du Runsheng, a leading proponent of rural reform in close contact with Zhao Ziyang, convened a meeting at the Science Hall. A dozen senior party members gathered to offer the general secretary their assessment of the situation and advise him on how to handle the situation. They agreed with Zhao Ziyang that the paramount leader was wrong in his assessment of the nature of the student movement and had lost control. 'Deng's reputation has reached rock bottom.' They advised the general secretary to be prudent.[42]

The following day Zhao Ziyang gave another speech, this time in the presence of foreign journalists. At the annual meeting of the board of governors of the Asian Development Bank, the general secretary praised the students, who, he opined, far from opposing the Communist Party or the socialist system, were merely demanding that mistakes in the government's work be corrected. In contrast to his talk a day earlier, he perceived no danger of turmoil, and expressed instead his confidence that the 'demonstrations will gradually calm down'. Reason and restraint, as well as extensive consultations with people from all walks of life, were the way forward.[43]

Students, meanwhile, marched in every major city to commemorate May the Fourth. The demonstrations were peaceful, and the students agreed to return to class and scale back their political activities. They realised that little could be gained by stretching the tolerance of a beleaguered government to breaking point. In Beijing tens of thousands of students marched, far fewer than for the mass parade on 27 April, although they did not leave the square before covering it in small broken bottles. There was a collective sigh of relief. The Hong Kong stock market cheered the news with substantial gains.[44]

Hundreds of journalists, all accredited by the state, had joined the students on May the Fourth, clamouring for the right to 'speak truth'. This turning point was prompted in part by the closure of the *World Economic Herald* in Shanghai. In December 1988 the liberal journal had published Su Shaozhi's speech calling for the rehabilitation of all victims of the campaign against 'bourgeois liberalisation'. Qin Benli, the editor, though warned, seemed undeterred. One week after Hu Yaobang's death, he prepared to publish six pages of tributes to the former general secretary. The propaganda bureau intervened. A passage taking aim at Deng Xiaoping seemed particularly offensive. Jiang Zemin, party secretary of Shanghai, ran out of patience and suspended the editor on 27 April. Qin Benli instantly became a *cause célèbre*. The protesters now had a new demand: press freedom.[45]

Ever larger sections of the official media, including reporters working for CCTV and the *People's Daily*, backed this demand. After Zhao Ziyang's performance at the Asian Development Bank, his advisers recommended that his speech be made public. Radio and television released the general secretary's comments that same day, running the broadcast again for three days. The *People's Daily* printed his conciliatory message on the front page: 'We Need Reason and Restraint, Solve Problems through Democracy and the Law.'[46]

On 5 May the students went back to class, inspired by Zhao Ziyang's promise of a dialogue.[47] The general secretary also encouraged a more conciliatory tone in the media: 'report the student demonstrations a little more openly, there is no danger in doing so,' he instructed Hu Qili, the sympathetic head of the Propaganda Department.[48] People woke up to reports and photographs of the demonstrations splashed over the newspapers. The *China Youth* went so far as to portray the students as patriots, while Zhao Ziyang was quoted as saying that corruption was due partly to 'lack of openness'.[49]

The change in tone encouraged more intellectuals to show their support for the students. On 10 May some 10,000 young protesters rode their bicycles through the capital to demand greater press freedom. Fifty prominent writers, poets and novelists joined them, including Su Xiaokang, who believed that the students 'should not be allowed to stand alone'.[50]

For about a week a strange calm endured, even though behind the scenes a split in the leadership was becoming apparent. Zhao's attempt to extend a hand to the demonstrators was widely welcomed, but his speech contradicted the paramount leader's comments castigating the students for creating turmoil and attempting to overthrow the socialist system. It seemed as if two editorials were pulling in different directions. Either Deng would have to recant his words, or Zhao had made a promise he would be unable to keep.

Leaders who viewed Zhao's speech as a dangerous departure from the party line began to rally behind Li Peng. Among them was Chen Xitong, the mayor of Beijing, who on 7 May demanded that the party abide by the decisions reached by the Standing Committee on 24 April.[51] The committee, on his request, convened the following day. An acrimonious exchange took place. According to several committee members, government officials who had clamped down on student activities felt betrayed by Zhao Ziyang. 'Who betrayed you?' an angry general secretary retorted. 'Only during the Cultural Revolution were people ever betrayed.'[52]

Despite all the promises, there was little dialogue between the government and the protesters. The students insisted that any debate be conducted through their own independent organisations, which the 26 April editorial had outlawed, a demand the general secretary could not meet. Students grew increasingly impatient. They began to worry that after Gorbachev's visit, scores would be settled and the authorities would clamp down again.

On 11 May a poster went up in Peking University calling for a hunger strike on Tiananmen Square.[53] The idea was not new. Like much else, it was part of a tradition of political protest stretching back to the Cultural Revolution. In summer 1966, for example, as students had embraced Chairman Mao's call to sweep away the 'capitalist roaders' allegedly hiding inside the education system, hundreds sat in quiet defiance before the party headquarters in Xi'an, refusing all food and liquids. After several days, chaotic scenes ensued as nurses began to administer intravenous drips to students who had fainted in the summer heat, while ambulances rushed the more serious cases to hospital for emergency treatment. Zhou Enlai was forced to intervene to break the impasse.[54]

An umbrella federation, representing all the autonomous organisations set up by the students, voted against the hunger strike, but the idea was too tempting to discard. Several student leaders decided to proceed on their own. Wang Dan, the history major at Peking University, was one of them. Another was Wuer Kaixi, a charismatic young Uyghur with a full head of thick, curly hair who had been born and raised in Beijing but had spent several years in Xinjiang as a young student. On the night of 19 April he had taken the lead in storming the main gate at Zhongnanhai, pacing up and down the frontline in a faded yellow uniform which had been in vogue during the Cultural Revolution, issuing orders to the students in a booming voice: 'We must hold on to our position here until Li Peng comes out!'[55]

The hunger strikers launched their action on 13 May, two days before the scheduled Sino-Soviet summit. A few hundred students, adorned with red-and-white headbands and wearing sunshades, took an oath, swearing to stay on the square until the government met their demands. 'We can stand hunger,' a banner stuck between two bamboo poles read, 'but we cannot stand dictatorship.' It was a resolute crowd, but not a large one. That evening, at Peking University, a graduate student in psychology called Chai Ling seized the microphone and gave an impassioned plea, bringing a crowd of listeners to tears. 'We, the children, are ready to die,' she cried. 'We want to fight to live with the resolve of death.' Overnight her speech became a manifesto. Twelve prominent intellectuals including Su Xiaokang rallied to support the hunger strikers with an appeal published in the newspapers and broadcast on television. Thousands joined the hunger strike.[56]

The numbers continued to swell. Zhao warned the protesters that they would 'earn the opprobrium of the people' by obstructing the summit, but to no avail. By the time Gorbachev was welcomed at the airport on 15 May, more than 300,000 people crowded the square, including not only the hunger strikers but also 'workers, peasants, government functionaries, working staff of democratic parties, children from kindergartens and elementary schools, and officers and men of justice departments and even of the military academies'.[57] Hundreds of writers, journalists and university professors also joined the fray. The atmosphere was festive, with people from all walks of life expressing themselves freely, many for the first time. They waved their banners, singing songs, greeting each other with the V-for-victory sign. Cui Jian, a 27-year-old guitarist who had introduced the country to rock and roll, made an unannounced appearance. He jammed on his guitar and belted out the lyrics of 'Nothing to My Name', a pop song that had struck a chord with the protesters: 'I am telling you I have waited too long; I am telling you this is my final request, I want to take your hands; So you will come along with me right now.' The music drowned out the sound of ambulance sirens, taking some seventy strikers who had succumbed to heat and lack of food to hospital. Foreign reporters, in town to cover the summit, mingled freely with the crowd, as satellites beamed the show into living rooms all around the world. Standing on the roof of the Great Hall of the People, Zhao Ziyang peered at the students through binoculars.[58]

On 16 May the Soviet leader's black ZIL limousine sneaked into the Great Hall by a back entrance, cordoned off by hundreds of police. Gorbachev shook hands with Deng Xiaoping, who gravely declared that the old disputes between Beijing and Moscow now belonged to the past. In the evening, at the Diaoyutai State Guesthouse, the Soviet leader discussed normalisation between the two communist parties with Zhao Ziyang. The general secretary broke with the traditional fiction of collective leadership, telling his counterpart that the country's paramount leader still made all major decisions. 'We cannot do without him, without his wisdom and experience,' he said, explaining that at the First Plenum of the Thirteenth Party Congress in October 1987 a decision had been made that 'on the most important questions we still need him as the helmsman.' The plenum's decision, Zhao explained, 'has never been published'. Zhao later clarified that he was trying to protect Deng by pointing out that his powers were not arbitrary but stemmed from the party constitution. Nonetheless, he miscalculated, as many observers concluded that Zhao was deflecting responsibility for the handling of the crisis towards his own mentor. One foreign journalist described it as a 'veiled but extraordinary challenge' to Deng.[59]

Zhao Ziyang's mention of the secret resolution was reported in the official press but surprised no one but some of Zhao's own advisers. Yan Jiaqi, a political scientist, seemed to think that the disclosure was a sign to break ranks with Deng Xiaoping, immediately producing a statement denouncing the 'old and decrepit dictator'. 'Down with the Dictator!', 'Dictators Must Go!' he shouted, addressing a crowd on the square.[60]

After his encounter with Gorbachev, Zhao Ziyang rushed to an emergency meeting of the Standing Committee. The only way out of the country's predicament, he told the committee, was to withdraw the 26 April editorial. To protect Deng Xiaoping's reputation, Zhao explained, he was willing to take full responsibility for the editorial by publicly declaring that he had personally drafted it in Pyongyang. But the other members would have none of it, insisting that the editorial reflected the paramount leader's views. The meeting resolved nothing.[61]

The following day, on 17 May, Zhao tried to meet Deng in a private audience. Told to come to Deng's residence in the afternoon, Zhao found the Standing Committee awaiting him. A tense meeting followed, as the committee accused Zhao of having fanned the flames of unrest with his speech at the Asian Development Bank. Deng Xiaoping agreed: 'The turning point was Zhao Ziyang's speech on May the Fourth, it allowed people to see that the leadership was not united, so the demonstrations became even more fierce and many people drew closer to the students.' He issued his verdict, that martial law should be declared and troops brought in. The mood instantly turned sombre, as all but one agreed. Later that evening, as the committee convened again to discuss the logistics of martial law, a gloomy Zhao Ziyang announced that he was unable to carry on with his duties: 'my time is up.'[62]

In a last attempt to defuse the situation, on 18 May a haggard, nervous-looking Li Peng met with student leaders before the cameras, at eleven o'clock in the morning in the Xinjiang Hall of the Great Hall of the People, a large conference room with high ceilings and comfortable sofas. Flowers and teacups stood on end tables between the seats. Wuer Kaixi, who had been taken to hospital after fainting and was still wearing his pyjamas, rebuked the premier for being late, not by a few minutes but by several weeks. Li Peng apologised and embarked on a patronising lecture, only to be interrupted by Wang Dan, who accused him of evading all the issues. Li Peng looked increasingly annoyed. 'Beijing has fallen into a kind of anarchy,' he declared angrily. 'We will not sit idly by, doing nothing,' he warned in a sharp exchange. 'We have to defend our factories. We have to defend our socialist system.' The meeting lasted about an hour.[63]

The government's intransigent attitude resulted in a sudden rise in popular support, with a crowd in the city centre widely estimated at a million. Students from other regions flooded in to join the demonstrations, with eager young people packing the railway platforms and squeezing into every train on its way to the capital. Many managed to board without a ticket, much as two decades earlier the Red Guards had been allowed to travel for free. Work in most factories and offices came to a standstill as throngs of workers joined the students, carrying the official banners of their work units and marching in the streets around the square. They were dressed in their trade uniforms, with cooks wearing chef's hats and clerks shaking their abacuses. Factory workers appeared in their blue uniforms. Cars, trucks and buses, commandeered from work units by their staff, drove along Chang'an Avenue in a show of support. It was a worker protest day, as opposed to a student protest day. The slogans changed in nature, with direct calls for the resignations of Deng Xiaoping, Li Peng and Yang Shangkun.[64]

A festive atmosphere prevailed, with cheering crowds greeting the demonstrators on street corners. Banners supporting the hunger strikers festooned office buildings and apartment blocks. When protesters marched past the ultra-modern CITIC skyscraper, office workers greeted them with ticker-tape confetti thrown out of the windows. Many believed they had reached a turning point in history, with hopes for a democratic China first voiced seventy years earlier at long last about to be fulfilled. It looked like the dawn of a new era.[65]

Support also came from within the party ranks. The previous evening Xiao Ke, a veteran general, had phoned the Central Advisory Commission, dominated by the party elders, to explain that the party was wrong and the masses right. In the provinces, entire party institutions rejected the 26 April editorial. In Zhejiang, a majority of members of the Political Consultative Conference passed a resolution condemning the expression 'oppose and contain the turmoil'. They wired their decision to the leaders in Beijing on 18 May. A similar scenario unfolded in other provinces.[66]

Demonstrations also took place in other cities. Some 100,000 protesters paralysed the centre of Shanghai, disrupting Mikhail Gorbachev's visit, now on the last leg of his four-day trip to China. Across Zhejiang province, the authorities estimated that approximately 400,000 demonstrators marched in Hangzhou, Jinhua, Ningbo, Wenzhou and other cities. In the provincial capital, more than 800 students joined a hunger strike. Similar figures appear in other reports stashed away in the party archives. In Gansu province, far removed from the gaze of foreign reporters, close to a quarter of a million people demonstrated in twelve cities at the height of the movement. In Lanzhou alone some 300 students joined a hunger strike.[67]

The most ominous unrest of all occurred in Urumqi, the capital of Xinjiang province, where some 10,000 students took to the streets to protest against a book entitled *Sexual Customs* that they considered defamatory. It was a pretext to march with banners reading 'Long Live Democracy' and 'Down with Corruption'. The following day the protesters forced their way through a gate leading to a government building and attacked the militia and government workers. On the main square buses were overturned, electricity poles torn down and loudspeaker wires severed. One hundred and fifty people were injured.[68]

On Friday 19 May, at about five o'clock in the early morning, Zhao Ziyang went to the square in the watchful company of Li Peng to express concern for the hunger strikers. 'We have come too late,' Zhao said with tears in his eyes, the microphone trembling in his hand. He explained that he, too, had once been young, and encouraged the students to give up their strike. It would be his last public appearance.

At eleven o'clock that evening, Li Peng addressed a large gathering of party, government and military leaders at the General Logistics Department of the People's Liberation Army, announcing measures to contain the turmoil. Shortly after midnight, the premier appeared on television to read from a prepared script: 'We must adopt firm and resolute measures to end the turmoil swiftly,' he pronounced. 'If we fail to promptly put an end to such a state of affairs and let it go unchecked, it will very likely lead to serious consequences which none of us want to see.' Martial law was proclaimed.[69]

Li Rui, standing on his balcony at three in the morning, saw motorbikes driving up and down Chang'an Avenue to alert the protesters against the army. They called themselves the 'Flying Tigers', wearing headbands resembling those of the hunger strikers and decorating their bikes with flags.[70] They were not the only ones to rally to the defence of the protesters. The moment Li Peng announced martial law, tens of thousands of people rushed out to prevent troops from reaching the square. Beijing was a city with both huge ring roads intersecting with overpasses and crossroads, and small, meandering alleyways. Lorry drivers used their vehicles to block the six main entrances to the capital, while crowds surged forward to surround military convoys, letting out the air in their tyres. The crowds were friendly, offering the troops food and water. They tried to convince them to turn back. By midday they had succeeded in blocking approximately 200 military vehicles belonging to the 65th Army, some 18 kilometres to the west. At the PLA's General Hospital, situated 11 kilometres to the west of Tiananmen Square along the extension of Chang'an Avenue, a crowd also blocked units of the 38th Army. Protesters turned back soldiers from the Beijing garrison as they advanced towards the city from the Ming Tombs, the capital airport and the Summer Palace. In effect, the people of Beijing stopped the army. 'We had not expected that the troops would encounter such huge resistance,' Li Peng noted in his diary.[71]

This scenario repeated itself for several days, as tens of thousands of students camped on the square while others maintained makeshift barricades on all major intersections. On 22 May, the troops began to withdraw. Jubilation took over, as emboldened students called on the soldiers to mutiny. Rumours flew about. Li Peng, who became the most hated party leader after proclaiming martial law, was reportedly in trouble, fighting for his political survival. Deng Xiaoping had resigned. Defections at the highest level inflected the balance of power towards Zhao Ziyang. The tide was turning, as the country was approaching a critical juncture of historical importance. None of these rumours was officially denied. When a letter from six retired generals and an admiral urging the Central Military Commission to refrain from bringing troops to the capital was leaked, the rumour mill went into overdrive.[72]

On 23 May tens of thousands of people took to the streets in Guangzhou, joined by sympathisers from Hong Kong and Macau, even as lightning ripped through the sky and streaming rain blurred the messages on their banners. In Shanghai, a large crowd occupied the waterfront and People's Square. In Lanzhou, deep in the hinterland, tens of thousands of people demanded that 'Deng Xiaoping Step Down' and 'Li Peng Step Down'. A few students shouted, 'Overthrow the Fake Government.' 'Ordinary people support their actions,' the deputy party secretary of the province noted. Students also protested in Nanjing, Changsha, Wuhan and other cities.[73]

In reality, though, the troops had not left, but merely moved into concentration areas on the outskirts. By 25 May their build-up was complete, with over 100,000 soldiers from eleven army groups ready for deployment, together with hundreds of tanks, armoured vehicles, military coaches and trucks. Yao Yilin, behind closed doors, told several ministers that the leadership did not fear foreign pressure. They were determined to close down the entire country and maintain martial law, 'for three or even five years' if necessary. In the evening, after five days when no top leader appeared in public, national television showed Li Peng entertaining three new ambassadors. He looked confident: 'The Chinese government is stable and capable,' he pronounced.[74]

The leadership made the rounds, whipping up support from high officials around the country. The military, addressed by Yang Shangkun in an emergency meeting, closed ranks.[75] Statements supporting martial law arrived from provincial governments, the air force and the navy.[76] On national television elderly party leaders, from Chen Yun, Bo Yibo and Li Xiannian to the widow of Zhou Enlai, were rolled out in a show of unity, some in wheelchairs and barely able to read their message of support themselves.[77] Across the nation, every party member was required to adopt a definite political stance, poring over speeches by the leadership in political study sessions.[78]

Shortly after Li Peng's television appearance, the balance of power shifted towards the hardliners. At every level, doctrinaire party members came to the forefront. In Lanzhou, where protesters had repeatedly assailed the provincial party committee, some cadres urged the leadership to take 'forceful measures towards saboteurs, strike resolutely, and suppress the riot as quickly as possible'.[79] They were far from alone. On 27 May three provincial leaders put Qiao Shi through the wringer, demanding that the Standing Committee take immediate action. At a Central Advisory Commission meeting, Li Peng himself came under fire, interrupted by angry party elders exasperated by the stalemate.[80]

Meanwhile, the local residents manning the road barriers across the capital became less vigilant. The numbers of students dwindled, their organisation obstructed by infighting and dissension. Most foreign journalists had departed, while shortwave radio broadcasts by the BBC and the Voice of America, two of the main sources of information, were jammed. On Monday 29 May a mere 2,000 protesters remained on the square. Their leaders recommended an end to the sit-in. Had they vacated the square, they would have left as victors. They had argued their cause, stared down the regime before international cameras, won support from the local population and, with their backing, forced the army to withdraw.[81]

In Shanghai the mayor adopted a conciliatory approach. Zhu Rongji was warm and sympathetic towards the demonstrators, assuring them that no troops would enter the city. He also excluded martial law. Jiang Zemin, the city's party secretary, shored up support among municipal People's Congress members. Threats of an industrial slowdown or general strike passed. Among ordinary residents, enthusiasm for the movement dimmed. Wall posters were taken down, the city cleaned up. On 27 May red banners and the national flag appeared across city streets to celebrate the fortieth anniversary of the liberation of Shanghai. Students were ready to return to class.[82]

Paradoxically, one of the largest demonstrations took place in Hong Kong. On Saturday 27 May, over 200,000 people gathered at the racecourse in Happy Valley for a benefit concert supporting the Tiananmen students. Celebrities lent their voices to the cause, many in tears as they told television viewers how they felt about the crisis unfolding across the border. Teresa Teng, the popular star from Taiwan, made a cameo appearance, wearing a red and white headband. The following day, an estimated 1.5 million – a quarter of the population – paraded through the streets, trailing through the busy shopping areas of North Point and Causeway Bay to disperse near Victoria Park. There were elderly people, infants wearing yellow headbands hoisted on their parents' shoulders, office workers in business attire and even demonstrators in wheelchairs. The organisers distributed stickers reading 'Today China, Tomorrow Hong Kong'.[83]

On Tuesday 30 May the students in Tiananmen unveiled a plaster statue of the Goddess of Democracy. Ten metres high, proudly lifting a torch with both hands, her stony eyes stared unflinchingly at the Chairman's portrait, replaced after being pelted with ink and eggs the previous week. The goddess seemed to mock forty years of revolution. Most of all, she gave the flagging democracy movement a new lease of life. Numbers began to swell again, as curiosity about the new lady on the square spread to every back alley of the capital. A quarter of a million people defied the government's warning and came to admire the statue. Taxi drivers, unable to cut through the crowd of bicycles and pedicabs, abandoned their cars and joined the crowd on foot instead. They came in silence, without slogans or banners. Few people heeded the government loudspeakers, blaring a message of condemnation across the square: 'This statue is illegal.' In the evening the authorities called the goddess 'an insult to national dignity', demanding she be pulled down.[84]

The previous night, as the sculpture arrived at the square in separate pieces loaded on pedicabs, thousands of university students had reversed their earlier position, vowing to remain for at least three more weeks. By now, large numbers of troops were stationed inside Zhongnanhai, the Great Hall of the People, the Museum of Chinese History and the Forbidden City, supplied through the underground network of tunnels running all the way to the Western Hills outside the city. They had clearly missed by days rather than a few hours their opportunity to quell the unrest without shedding blood.[85]

A new mood of defiance took hold. Donations were collected from the local population, while increased financial and material support flowed in from Hong Kong, where US$1.5 million had been collected during the benefit concert. Contributions from the crown colony included some 200 camping tents, their bright red and blue colours standing out amid the flimsy shanties made of plastic, canvas and cardboard that had so far sheltered the students. But most local students returned to their campuses for the night. The majority of the 5,000 students camping on the square were latecomers from the provinces.[86]

***

On Friday 2 June credible reports began to circulate that elements of the 39th Army were about to move into the capital. Shortly before 11 p.m., a jeep with army plates was seen driving at high speed towards the square from the west. Near Muxidi, where Chang'an Avenue crossed an imperial moat that had protected the old city from intruders, the vehicle lost control and crashed into a group of cyclists, killing three and seriously injuring one. From his balcony, Li Rui saw an angry crowd gathered at the scene.[87]

Later that night, at about 2 a.m. on 3 June, a column of some 8,000 young soldiers in shirtsleeves was seen marching along Chang'an Avenue from the opposite direction. Several motorcyclists who patrolled the city rode ahead of the troops to sound the alarm. 'Come out, come out, the soldiers are coming!' As the soldiers reached the Beijing Hotel, some 300 metres away from the square, local residents sallied out of alleyways to block them, some still in their pyjamas, shouting 'Turn back! You are the people's army!' The troops were unarmed, and apparently without commanding officers. They looked exhausted and disoriented, hiding their faces as they sat on the road, packed together in small groups while local residents taunted and harangued them. When questioned, they answered that they were from the 39th Army, and had been told they would only encounter a few hooligans in the square. They dispersed in the early hours of Saturday morning, some with shirts torn, others hobbling along without shoes. The crowd commandeered buses, dumper trucks filled with coal and sand and even a construction crane to erect barricades outside the Beijing Hotel.[88]

Meanwhile, as a hazy dawn rose over the city, clusters of people gathered all along Chang'an Avenue. Towards the west of the square, near Zhongnanhai, around 500 people surrounded a jeep and four military buses loaded with what appeared to be elite troops. The crowd tried to overturn the jeep, ignoring the automatic weapon one of the officers brandished. They also smashed the windows on both sides of the buses, snatching weapons from the frightened soldiers. Near Liubukou, six or seven young students walked up and down the roof of one of the vehicles, displaying AK-47 rifle magazines, truncheons, knives and bayonets for the cameras. Outside Zhongnanhai, people flourished helmets and shoes on poles, chanting slogans against the government.[89]

A PLA officer later explained that the aim of the operation had been to cordon off the square and avoid harming the students. This stunningly inept plan backfired badly. Throughout the morning, students and their supporters poured back into the square while local residents erected further large-scale barricades along all major intersections within and around the city.[90]

At around noon, troops and armed police began to emerge from Zhongnanhai along the section of Chang'an Avenue running west from Tiananmen to Xidan. They tried to clear some of the barricades and recover the ammunition inside the bus at Liubukou. Residents marching to demand justice for the civilians killed by a jeep the previous evening approached from the west and were met by several hundred armed police and security personnel, who fired tear gas and charged with batons. The crowd fought back, forcing them to scurry back for safety into Zhongnanhai. People were now enraged, throwing stones over the wall into the government compound and setting an abandoned military vehicle on fire. For several hours clashes also took place along other road junctions, resulting in injuries on both sides. Troops and police eventually withdrew later in the afternoon.[91]

The regime now had enough justification for tougher action. At about 4 p.m., at an emergency meeting convened by Qiao Shi, the leadership agreed that a 'shocking counter-revolutionary riot' had broken out in the early morning, referring to the incident at Liubukou when protesters had seized weapons from the military. They took the decision to have the square cleared by dawn through 'peaceful means', although they gave the military permission to defend themselves against acts of violence on the part of the rioters.[92]

At 6.30 p.m. public loudspeakers, radio and television broadcast a warning telling people to stay off the streets.[93]

The military, by now humiliated on two successive occasions, opted for the exact same strategy, a two-pronged attack from east and west along Chang'an Avenue, the main artery running through the city. This time they boosted their fire power, switching from a few thousand unarmed soldiers in canvas shoes to a great wall of steel patiently amassed over two weeks. In Vietnam, a decade earlier, the People's Liberation Army had deployed some 200,000 soldiers and over 200 tanks. Now they were about to unleash comparable forces on the unarmed civilians of their own capital.

The first shots were fired at approximately 11.15 p.m. at Gongzhufen, or Tomb of the Princess, a major roundabout where the third ring road intersects with the extension of Chang'an Avenue to the west of Muxidi. A long procession of tanks, armoured vehicles and soldiers carrying assault rifles approached from the south, where one of the military encampments was located. This was the 38th Army, a fearsome unit which had forged its reputation during the Korean War. Two weeks earlier, its commander, Xu Qinxian, had refused to lead his troops against unarmed civilians; he was arrested and sent to prison, to be court-martialled later. Local residents, who had manned the intersection for weeks, hurled bricks and pieces of concrete at the troops behind their riot shields. After failing to break through the barricades, several hundred soldiers armed with AK-47 rifles advanced, opening fire on the civilians. Red and green tracer bullets streaked across the sky. Tanks fired gas canisters at the crowd. It was a hot and humid night, with most people dressed in T-shirts and shorts, many now splashed in red.[94]

The next intersection was Muxidi, where people also took shelter behind a barricade, trying to hold back the army.[95] Some had improvised weapons, including meat cleavers, bamboo poles, metal chains, even steel rods taken from building sites. Soldiers continued firing their automatic rifles at the crowd, but also shot randomly at residential buildings on both sides of the road. In Li Rui's block of flats, a dumdum bullet killed the son-in-law of a senior prosecutor who was boiling water in the kitchen. A neighbour's maid was found shot dead the following morning. A few days later Li Rui counted roughly one hundred bullet holes on the outside of his building.[96]

The same tragedy repeated itself all the way down to Tiananmen, with thousands of enraged people gathering at intersections to fight the invading army. The armoured vehicles easily crushed through the next roadblock of railings and abandoned bicycles. At the Xidan intersection, where yellow and red public buses had been lined up and set ablaze, they pushed aside the burning vehicles, opening the way to the square. Tanks now moved two or three abreast, followed by armoured vehicles and military trucks loaded with soldiers, felling scores of people at every intersection. Some soldiers chased onlookers down the alleyways, beating them with truncheons, whips and guns. Four people were shot dead deep inside a residential alley near Xidan, including a three-year-old child and an old man.[97]

Around midnight several armoured vehicles entered the square from the south, driving at high speed along the side. A crowd forced three to halt and set them on fire. As the soldiers tried to escape from their burning vehicles, an irate crowd set upon them, beating several to death with their bare fists. One vehicle managed to make it past the square and turned east, smashing through several barricades along Chang'an Avenue, killing and injuring many protesters. Towards the Jianguo Hotel it turned around, careening back at breakneck speed in the direction of the square, but lost control and crashed into several abandoned vehicles surrounded by protesters. A crowd assaulted the soldiers hunkering inside.[98]

One hour later, at around 1.30 a.m., the bulk of the troops approaching from Muxidi reached the north-west corner of the square, regrouping under the hazy yellow glare of street lights. Dozens of tanks rumbled in and parked under the rostrum. A strange lull followed, until one hour later soldiers began to form a line along the Forbidden City to the north of the square.[99]

Some soldiers fired sporadically towards crowds of people to the east of Chang'an Avenue, a section still controlled by the residents. The students assembled on the square could hear the irregular crackle of AK-47s and loud thuds of tear gas canisters, while angry crowds shouted 'fascists'. In the area around the Beijing Hotel, ambulances with flashing blue lights and screaming sirens came out of Wangfujing to help the injured or pick up the dead. Later that night, as ambulances could no longer reach the intersections where the fighting took place, pedicab drivers came to the rescue, evacuating the wounded and driving them to hospital. Doctors were seen marching like pallbearers, carrying the bodies of the slain, closely followed by nurses.[100]

Broadcasts over the loudspeaker system appealed to people to leave the square, where up to 3,000 students were massed around the Monument to the People's Heroes. A strange singing contest followed. Soldiers sang army songs to cheer themselves up, while the protesters boomed the Internationale, singing along with the track played on their own loudspeaker system.[101]

Blinding floodlights illuminated the square, until turned off by the authorities around 4 a.m.[102] Students began to burn some of their tents for lighting. Tens of thousands of soldiers poured into the square from the Great Hall of the People, the Museum of Chinese History and the underground tunnels. Paratroopers from the 15th Army also arrived from the south, having carved a bloody path through the Qianmen district. The soldiers on the square did not open fire, not least because they would have shot each other, while no one wished to desecrate the Monument to the Heroes of the People, let alone the mausoleum where the Chairman was resting. An ultimatum was issued, with several students attempting to negotiate safe passage. Among them was Liu Xiaobo, the young man who three years earlier had savaged the state of literature in his country. Now a professor at Beijing Normal University, he crossed a no-man's-land between the students and the soldiers to bargain with their commanders, reaching a deal whereby the students were instructed to exit through the south-east corner of the square. Some of the protesters still sought to debate whether or not to stay to the bloody end. 'How about a compromise?' Chai Ling proposed. 'Those who want to leave can leave, those who choose to stay can stay.'[103]

At 5 a.m. the students linked hands, walking in two columns towards the designated corner of the square. A huge crowd welcomed them, handing out food and drink. A tank rumbled towards the Goddess of Democracy, toppling the statue and crushing it. Tanks and armoured vehicles also rolled over the tents and continued towards the monument, where loudspeakers still played the Internationale. Soldiers took potshots at the loudspeakers until they began to hiss and crackle, finally falling silent. Students scrambled for safety, as those who had refused to leave were beaten with rifle butts and truncheons.[104]

Only now could a rumble be heard from the east, as a column of tanks emerged from the grey light on Chang'an Avenue. The 39th Army arrived late, but advanced swiftly. The tanks sliced straight through a line of buses strategically deployed across the intersection at Dongdan, the counterpoint to Xidan, some two kilometres to the east of the square. They fired tear gas at the crowds, who pelted the tanks with stones, bottles, broken pavement slabs, bricks brought in on pedicabs and crudely improvised petrol bombs. Patches of flame smouldered all along Chang'an Avenue where Molotov cocktails had failed to hit their targets. As the convoy approached Wangfujing, a group of twenty men pushed a flimsy bus into their way, to no avail. Furious residents, seemingly oblivious to all danger, cycled beside the tanks, screaming for them to turn around and leave. Behind the tanks came armoured personnel carriers, followed in turn by trucks with soldiers in the back, who fired indiscriminately into the crowds. 'One could see the flames of the guns spitting,' one observer recalled. Other vehicles followed in what seemed like an endless convoy, with tankers and trucks laden with drums of fuel, cloth and supplies. This was an army of occupation, bringing their own stores with them.[105]

More vehicles, including 21 tanks, joined this procession using the side roads running north to south. As the tanks passed the Beijing Hotel and entered the north-east corner of the square, just above the museum, they crushed several soldiers as well as civilians.[106]

Even after the tanks of the 39th Army had rumbled through to the square, fighting continued on the stretch of Chang'an Avenue between Tiananmen and Wangfujing. Foreign reporters watched in horror from the Beijing Hotel as soldiers facing east, away from the square, continued firing into the crowd, mainly comprised of relatives of people who had disappeared during the night, who persisted in approaching the soldiers, pleading for information as to where their family members were. 'These were the people who for the rest of the morning we watched being massacred,' one witness noted. There was a pattern to the killings. Soldiers would fire their AK-47s and the crowds would scurry for safety, only to return to their original positions. This took place in broad daylight, until about nine o'clock in the morning. In a separate incident 100 metres further east, at around 10.20 a platoon of soldiers gunned down some forty people who were trying to talk to them on Wangfujing, in full view of journalists watching from the Beijing Hotel.[107]

By now, large parts of the city resembled a war zone. Near the Summer Palace, two dozen tanks stood abandoned, torched by local residents. To the west, near the Babaoshan Revolutionary Cemetery where Hu Yaobang had been cremated, charred military vehicles lined both sides of the road. Another scene of carnage could be found at Gongzhufen, where eighty smouldering hulls of burned-out trucks and armoured personnel carriers blocked the roundabout, while the bodies of people who had been lynched, including several PLA officers, dangled from lamp posts.[108]

Bewildered residents who ventured out on Sunday encountered a chain of destruction all along Chang'an Avenue and its extension. When Li Rui climbed on top of an abandoned tank outside his residence near Muxidi, he could view a whole line of wretched vehicles stretching into the distance. All major intersections were littered with debris, the remains of gutted buses shoved to the side, twisted metal fencing, bicycles and broken street signs crushed together in the middle of the road under tank treads.

Sporadic fire was heard throughout the day, occasionally punctuated by thunder as rain began pouring down. Across from the diplomatic compound near the Jianguo Hotel, more than one hundred armed infantry stood in parade formation in a show of force designed to intimidate the foreign community.[109]

In the evening, a further convoy of 75 tanks and 45 armoured vehicles moved towards the square along Chang'an Avenue from the east. In a vain attempt to stop them, a few hostile residents once again hurled petrol bombs. But overnight almost no one came out.[110]

Hospitals were overwhelmed with casualties. The entrance to the Fuxing Hospital, over a kilometre away from Muxidi, was filled with gunshot victims, some hooked up to intravenous bags. Bloody white sheets covered the dead, as the morgue was overflowing. In the city centre, bodies were piled up in underground passageways. Further north, at Peking University, the students displayed a dozen corpses on blocks of ice outside the health clinic, some with body parts blown away.[111]

Several people kept a running tally of the number of dead. ABC reporter Kate Phillips viewed video tapes brought in by camera crews and phoned local hospitals as well as the Chinese Red Cross. She reached 2,600 before the military moved into all medical facilities and ordered them to stop talking to journalists. The Chinese Red Cross ventured a similar estimate. Alan Donald, the British ambassador, put the death toll between 2,700 and 3,400.[112]

Foreign observers had harsh words for the performance of the People's Liberation Army. Commander M. H. Farr, basing his assessment on the combined intelligence of the British Defence Section and an ad hoc NATO team that had spent weeks tracking the army in the suburbs, opined that the immediate impression was one of 'total military incompetence and complete inability to exploit the chances of almost bloodless victory that were presented to the PLA'.[113]

Large convoys continued to pour into the city on Sunday. Soldiers loaded onto fifty trucks indiscriminately sprayed bullets as they passed in front of the Great Wall Sheraton Hotel. In different parts of the city, near intersections and overpasses, people occasionally emerged from hiding to collect dead bodies, only for the shooting to resume and the crowd to scatter.[114]

The following day, at around noon on Monday 5 June, a man was seen standing on a pedestrian crossing, holding two shopping bags.

He had brought a convoy of tanks leaving Tiananmen Square to a clanking halt. The lead tank tried to manoeuvre around the man, who repeatedly shifted his position to further obstruct its path. An impasse was reached. The man then climbed onto the hull and spoke to the driver. After a brief conversation he climbed down the side of the tank and proceeded to block it again. Two bystanders pulled him to safety and disappeared with him into a nearby crowd. The scene would become one of the most iconic images of the twentieth century.

6

Watershed (1989–1991)

For a few days people huddled nervously at home in the dark, with the power cut off in large sections of the city. Shops were shuttered. No one knew who was in charge. There were no newspapers, and broadcasts merely repeated stern messages warning civilians to observe martial law. The top leaders were silent. Rumours therefore flitted about. Li Peng had been hit by a stray bullet, Yang Shangkun had fled town. Army factions were turning against each other in the outskirts of Beijing, it was whispered.[1]

On Tuesday evening, Yuan Mu, the stern spokesman for the State Council who had alienated the students in a publicly broadcast dialogue, appeared on television to announce that a 'shocking counter-revolutionary rebellion' had occurred in the capital, a plot defeated thanks to the valiant intervention of the People's Liberation Army. He estimated that roughly 300 people had been killed in the military intervention, with most of the losses sustained by the military.[2]

The following days the army began to clean up the city. All along Chang'an Avenue, cranes could be seen lifting the charred remains of buses and armoured vehicles onto flat-bed trucks. Soldiers, with their AK-47s slung across their backs, swept debris into neat piles.[3] It was a desolate city, silent except for a few isolated gunshots. The real frenzy was at the airport, where passport holders were desperate to book flights out of the country. Since all traffic had ground to a halt, groups of people were seen walking to the airport, some 30 kilometres from the city centre, their suitcases piled on pedicabs.[4]

On Thursday 8 June, Li Peng appeared on television in the Great Hall of the People. Wearing a Mao jacket rather than a modern suit, he briskly praised the army for a job well done. 'You have worked hard, comrades,' he told a group of soldiers, who applauded the premier. After the broadcast, a semblance of normality began to return to the city. Buses resumed operation. Residents quietly streamed out, as shops opened for the first time since Saturday. Along the tiny back alleys, old men walked their songbirds. Army platoons patrolled Chang'an Avenue, some of them chanting: 'Protect our Motherland. Long Live the People. Learn from Lei Feng!' Tanks, armoured vehicles and soldiers with rifle in hand guarded the square and all other strategic locations.[5]

As news of the massacre spread, however, people began to demonstrate in other cities. On 5 June protesters rioted in Chengdu, the hometown of Deng Xiaoping and Yang Shangkun, forcing the authorities to declare martial law. A vicious battle between local residents and security forces unfolded over four days, with the main department store burned to the ground. The police were only armed with truncheons, and no shots were fired. Several dozen people died, although rumours put the death toll in the hundreds.[6]

Popular disturbances rocked other cities, too. Prompted by fear of a military crackdown, people blocked the narrow gates of the ancient capital Xi'an. Three thousand demonstrators closed off all the bridges leading into Guangzhou. In Lanzhou tens of thousands of protesters occupied the central square and broadcast the Voice of America over the public loudspeaker system. They also sealed off the railway station and all major roads, only agreeing to disperse five days later.[7]

In Shanghai, unlike most other parts of the country, information about the massacre flowed freely, with photocopies of reports from Hong Kong displayed prominently on public buildings and along bus stops. Protesters commandeered buses and deployed them along makeshift barricades. News from the Voice of America was broadcast in a few neighbourhoods controlled by the students. Many local residents were outraged, but even among the protesters support for more demonstrations began to dwindle. It helped that the authorities avoided direct confrontation and removed the police from the streets.[8]

On 8 June Zhu Rongji launched an appeal for calm on local radio and television. 'Do you want chaos in Shanghai?' he asked rhetorically, appearing in a smart business suit and tie. With a wave of the hand, the mayor ruled out martial law and military intervention, warning instead that those causing disturbances would be 'dealt with by the law'. The people, he continued, would keep a watchful eye on the city. These came in the shape of worker militias, 230,000-strong, fanning out to key intersections in the afternoon, armed with nothing more than bamboo hats. They kept a polite distance from the students.[9]

It was a stellar performance, as Zhu delivered his message almost in the style of a fireside chat. He refused to be drawn on the events in the capital. These, he explained, 'now belonged to the past and would be judged by history'. Next day, the protesters marched on the town hall to deliver their demands, but dispersed quietly afterwards. The consensus appeared to be that they had lost the first round, and must live to fight another day.[10]

***

Even as guns were still firing in Beijing, foreign governments around the world condemned the massacre. On 4 June Margaret Thatcher said she was 'appalled', while the Australian prime minister Bob Hawke cancelled a scheduled visit to Shanghai in a 'message of anger'. In Paris, President François Mitterrand pronounced that a regime that fired on young people who were standing up to fight for freedom had no future. Chancellor Helmut Kohl was outspoken, condemning the 'barbaric use of brutal violence'.[11]

Mikhail Gorbachev was more coy, having only just normalised relations with the People's Republic. The Soviet Congress passed a tepid resolution calling for 'wisdom, sound reason and a balanced approach'. The staunchest supporter of the regime was East Germany, publicly endorsing the repression and stating that the military had intervened 'with the agreement of the masses and the students'. A few days later Egon Krenz, the second highest official in East Berlin, sent a message congratulating the leadership on their firm stance.[12]

A muted response also came from President George H. W. Bush. One day after the massacre, he deplored the use of force and appealed to the leadership to return to their 'policy of restraint'. He expressed his faith in the power of commercial contacts, which would overcome these 'unfortunate events' and inexorably move the country towards democracy. Three days later, on 8 June, he appeared before the cameras in the East Room of the White House. Again he condemned the military violence, but qualified his statement by adding, 'I don't think we ought to judge the whole People's Liberation Army of China by that terrible incident.' Most of all, he tried to exonerate the leadership. Deng Xiaoping, he reminded the reporters, had been purged twice during the Cultural Revolution, and was therefore a 'forward looking' leader. President Bush explained that he had tried to reach Deng by telephone, but 'the line was busy.'[13]

Deng Xiaoping, who had not been seen for weeks, appeared on 9 June to address the troops, looking old and tired, and flanked by Li Peng and Yang Shangkun. His hand was shaky, his speech halting and indistinct. The official statement, widely circulated abroad, blamed a 'very small number of people' for a 'counter-revolutionary rebellion', which had tried to 'overthrow the Communist Party and the socialist system'. In the uncensored version of his speech, Deng singled out 'a few released prisoners who were not properly reformed, a few political hooligans, the residual dregs of the Gang of Four and other social detritus'. He also claimed that 'hostile foreign forces', represented by the Voice of America, had incited the riots and spread rumours.[14]

A barrage of propaganda was unleashed following Deng Xiaoping's address to the troops. 'It would seem,' the British embassy noted on 10 June, 'that the events of 3/4 June are to be expunged from memory.' In order to cover up the massacre, the military were portrayed as the true victims, set upon by hooligans and criminal elements bent on a counter-revolutionary plot. Wounded soldiers recovering in pristine hospital rooms were shown on television, visited by a steady flow of party leaders, some of them holding bouquets of flowers. Pretty nurses in white uniforms simpered at their sides. The programme, shown around the clock, was interspersed with shots of the carbonised bodies of soldiers sitting at the wheels of their charred vehicles. 'Most ghoulish: a soldier boy, naked, guts ripped out, penis bulging upright', the American reporter Harrison Salisbury noted in his diary.[15]

The most rabid language, however, was reserved for foreigners, with the United States bearing the brunt.[16] Even before the massacre, rallies organised by the authorities had singled out Washington. On 2 June, in a sports stadium in Miyun some 60 kilometres outside Beijing, three men had dressed as Uncle Sam, with false noses, blue capes and Stars and Stripes top hats, performing in front of an audience of 10,000 villagers and schoolchildren. They also mocked the democracy movement, most of all Fang Lizhi, accused by the regime of being one of the black hands behind the movement.[17]

Three days later, fearing for their safety, Fang Lizhi and his wife sought refuge in the US embassy, where they were offered sanctuary the following day. On 8 June James Lilley, the ambassador, was summoned to the Foreign Ministry and rebuked for sheltering a criminal element who had helped instigate the counter-revolution, the start of a diplomatic standoff that would last a full year. It seemed to the regime that all along they had been correct in suspecting that Fang Lizhi had been planted by the capitalist camp to plot the overthrow of their socialist system.[18]

Behind the scenes the Americans tried to soften their stance. Since Secretary of State James A. Baker had excluded all high-level exchanges, Henry Kissinger conveyed a private message in mid-June, promising the regime that they could count on him as an old friend of China.[19]

A few weeks later, national security adviser Brent Scowcroft flew to Beijing on a secret mission. He met Deng Xiaoping on 2 July and assured him that 'President Bush is a true friend, a true friend of you and of China.' He added that 'we have both been for many years close associates of Henry Kissinger.' George Bush had personally opposed the use of sanctions against China, and was keen to deepen cooperation.

Deng Xiaoping was blunt, stating that the United States had been involved in the turmoil. Attempts to overthrow the socialist system could 'lead to a war'. He also complained that, while China had many American friends, including Dr Henry Kissinger and Brent Scowcroft himself, the Voice of America was a 'large rumour corporation', while the United States had 'hurt Chinese interests' on a 'considerably large scale'. It was up to Washington to 'untie the knot'.[20]

The mission had one result: after the visiting emissary had come to pay tribute, the regime realised it could ignore much of what was said publicly in Washington.[21]

***

On 8 June orders for the arrest of 'counter-revolutionary elements' and other offenders were broadcast on radio and television. Hotlines were set up around the capital, as the authorities proclaimed that 'each and every citizen' had the 'right and obligation' to report people involved in the turmoil. Two days later more than 400 people were apprehended in Beijing alone. For days on end, national television showed pictures of suspects being taken into custody, their hands tied behind their backs with handcuffs or a piece of rope, their heads forced down by stern security officers. Informers who shopped their neighbours or even relatives also appeared on television, commended for their fortitude. On 13 June arrest warrants for 21 student leaders were issued, their photographs released on television and printed in the newspapers.[22]

Wang Dan went into hiding, but changed his mind a few weeks later, tormented by the idea that his escape put the very people who were trying to help him at risk. He returned to Beijing and turned himself in, to be sentenced later to four years in prison. Ren Wanding, who had already experienced solitary confinement after participating in the 1978 Democracy Wall movement, went back to prison for seven years. Liu Xiaobo, the literary theorist who had persuaded many students to leave the square in the early hours of June the Fourth, was apprehended and sent to the notorious Qincheng prison for nineteen months.

In a daring mission codenamed 'Operation Yellow Bird', smugglers and sympathisers in Hong Kong helped other political activists escape from the mainland. Both Wuer Kaixi and Chai Ling were among seven of the 21 most wanted student leaders who successfully absconded. Yan Jiaqi, a close adviser of Zhao Ziyang, was one of the first intellectuals to make it to Hong Kong, where he promptly published an article condemning the regime and their 'extra-fascist extermination policy'.[23] Su Shaozhi, who had called so boldly for the rehabilitation of all political prisoners, followed soon afterwards. Su Xiaokang, the author of *River Elegy*, spent three months hiding in remote villages before he was smuggled into the crown colony. Hundreds more followed over several years, with extraction teams sent to locate and rescue prominent dissidents. They received temporary shelter in hotels, secluded hideouts and private homes in Hong Kong. Consular officers helped move them past immigration at the airport, from where they travelled on to Europe and the United States to start their new lives.[24]

Towards mid-June the inquisition took a new turn. Summary trials were held, followed by executions in Beijing, Shanghai and Jinan. The procedure was always the same, a bullet in the back of the head before a large crowd. Several party elders on the Central Advisory Commission clamoured for even tougher measures. Huo Shilian, who had served as minister of agriculture from 1979 to 1981, recommended large-scale executions: 'if we don't shoot people this issue can never be resolved.' Yet even while the number of victims put to death remained relatively small, the executions elicited widespread revulsion around the world. Margaret Thatcher said that she was 'utterly appalled'. People in Hong Kong, in particular, found the swift nature of communist justice alarming.[25]

The propaganda was moderated, but the arrests continued. On 30 June, the Central Committee circulated Central Document No. 3 demanding that the 'counter-revolution' be 'resolutely suppressed'. 'We must adopt a resolute attitude and avoid being soft-hearted.' Amnesty International, relying on unofficial sources, estimated that across the country tens of thousands of people were imprisoned, held on various charges, from 'sabotage', looting and disrupting public order to involvement in 'counter-revolutionary activities'.[26]

Those detained included people from all walks of life – students, teachers, journalists, artists, even military officers – but ordinary people bore the brunt of the crackdown. Students were naive and had been 'temporarily confused', whereas the hooligans and criminal elements behind them should be resolutely crushed, Central Document No. 3 explained. Deng Xiaoping had referred to them in his speech as 'social detritus'. These were the bus drivers, factory workers, shop assistants and countless other obscure individuals swept up in the democracy movement, who paid dearly for their idealism, experiencing the full scope of the penal system, including abuse, torture and hard labour followed by social isolation and unemployment after release.

One such was Zhang Maosheng, a mechanic who lit a cloth and set fire to a truck after seeing the mangled body of an eight-year-old girl who had been playing outside when the troops arrived. He received the death penalty in a secret trial, but had his sentence commuted to seventeen years of education through labour. The three workers who had travelled from Changsha to pelt the Chairman's portrait with ink and eggs spent eight to sixteen years in the Hunan Provincial Prison No. 2, beaten repeatedly, sometimes with electric prods. One lost his mind.[27]

Another example was a worker who found an abandoned military supply truck. He and his friends emptied the vehicle, distributing the food to the students. He kept a piece of roast chicken for himself. This constituted the evidence used against him when he was sentenced to thirteen years. 'That was an expensive chicken,' he sighed when telling an interviewer his story. A disabled person was locked up for ten years for 'slamming his crutches on a tank repeatedly before staggering away elated', according to his indictment papers.[28]

Numbers are elusive, but at a secret meeting one year later Gu Linfang, the vice-minister of public security, announced that over a million criminal cases had been cracked in 1989.[29]

Ever since Solidarność (Solidarity) had become the first trade union in the Soviet bloc recognised by the state, the regime had feared that its own workers would set up a labour union. The Beijing Workers' Autonomous Union, established in the heady days leading up to June the Fourth, was suppressed, its leader Han Dongfang sent to prison. 'Solidarność,' Qiao Shi explained in July 1989, 'not only represents the workers, but has also become a political party, it has become a substitute of the Communist Party: that is a lesson for us.' 'If the turmoil had lasted, maybe a Wałęsa would have appeared,' Yao Yilin ventured, referring to the Polish union leader who had won a Nobel Peace Prize in 1983.[30]

Another spectre from Poland was the Catholic Church, which had galvanised opposition to the communist regime. Karol Wojtyła, who became John Paul II in 1978, was an inspiration for the democracy movement in his native Poland and far beyond. Beijing had always viewed Rome as a centre of subversion, and only allowed believers to worship in official churches that had severed all ties to the Vatican. These so-called 'patriotic churches' by 1989 claimed a membership of over 3 million, but as many as 6 million believers remained loyal to the Pope. His ministers were seen as a vanguard for ideological infiltration. 'In the last few years efforts by hostile forces inside and outside our borders to use religion and carry out infiltration and sabotage against us have intensified,' Ren Wuzhi, head of the Bureau for Religion of the State Council, claimed in June 1990. 'Some illegal elements operate private schools as well as underground seminaries and divinity schools to study the scriptures. They vie with us for the younger generation,' he added. The leadership viewed any kind of religion as a threat to the socialist system and demanded that 'underground hostile forces' be 'attacked, split up and dissolved'.[31]

As early as December 1989 more than thirty leaders of underground churches were arrested across the north of the country.[32] More followed the following year. In Guangzhou, the southern city a few hours away from Hong Kong by train, sixty security officials arrived at Reverend Samuel Lam's house, ransacking the place and carting away thousands of Bibles. The church organ was loaded onto a pedicab. In 1991 the number of Catholic leaders arrested soared to over 140.[33]

But repression was fiercest along the fringes of the empire, which were always prone to rebellion. In May 1989, tens of thousands of people in Urumqi, the capital of Xinjiang province, had marched in favour of democracy. An even greater uprising rocked the township of Baren in April 1990, when some 200 demonstrators stormed the local government office, seized weapons from security forces and killed six armed officers. The regime's response was swift, using overwhelming force to crush the uprising. The clergy was purged, mosques closed and thousands arrested.[34]

It was a watershed moment, and not only in Xinjiang. Across the country, the more conciliatory approach that had emerged during the 1980s was seen as a tactical mistake. 'Local party officials must resolutely deal with social unrest the moment it appears,' a new directive from the Central Committee dated 2 April 1990 explained. 'Shoot the bird that takes the lead,' Li Peng repeatedly ordered over the telephone, as he intervened to direct the suppression of turmoil around the country. Whether in a school, mosque or village, he explained, the slightest incident must be nipped in the bud, since with the covert help of foreign hostile forces it could spread at great speed and undermine social stability. On its front page on the first anniversary of the military crackdown, the *People's Daily* proclaimed what for decades to come would be a guiding slogan: 'Social Stability Before All Else'.[35]

***

Purges also took place at the top. One day before imposing martial law, Deng Xiaoping had decided to replace Zhao Ziyang with Jiang Zemin, the party secretary of Shanghai. Zhao Ziyang was brushed aside, cut off from all communications for several weeks. The propaganda chief Hu Qili, another of the five Standing Committee members, was also isolated. One week later, Bao Tong, a close adviser of the general secretary, was arrested for 'revealing state secrets'. He would spend seven years in prison before being consigned to house arrest.[36]

In the days after June the Fourth, leading party officials were ordered to adopt a clear stance and distance themselves from their former general secretary. Deng Xiaoping's speech to the troops was distributed to every party member across the country, to be studied in mandatory sessions.[37]

On 16 June Deng Xiaoping spoke again, this time to members of the Central Committee. 'Only socialism can save China, and only socialism can develop China.' He insisted that the policy of economic reform and opening up to the outside world would not change, and emphasised the importance of rapid development. He returned to his hobby horse, the idea that the economy should quadruple between 1980 and 2000. Deng showed no sign of regret, claiming that military intervention had won the country one or two decades of stability.[38] Party leaders welcomed his speech and distributed it widely. 'Only he can find the right words to win people over,' a former *People's Daily* editor opined.[39]

Now that the party had rallied behind their boss, the ritual denunciation of Zhao Ziyang could begin. From 19 to 21 June, in a series of gruelling meetings, one party elder after another stepped forward to sink in the knife. Three years earlier Hu Yaobang had been degraded for six successive days. Zhao's ordeal was only half as long.[40]

At the Fourth Plenum, held on 24 June, secret voting was abandoned. A unanimous show of hands voted Zhao Ziyang out and welcomed Jiang Zemin instead. The new general secretary's first order of business was to praise the paramount leader and confirm that all the measures taken to fight the counter-revolution had been correct. He congratulated the troops and the armed police. The meeting lasted a mere hour.[41]

Jiang, a 62-year-old with a roundish face and grey hair, had obtained a degree in electrical engineering in Shanghai in 1947 and trained at the Stalin Automobile Works in Moscow in the 1950s, where he had met Li Peng. He was slightly better educated than the premier, with a smattering of foreign languages which he liked to display in small talk with foreign guests. He also occasionally burst into song. He was unpopular in Shanghai, where he had served as mayor before becoming party secretary. The city had a lacklustre economy, and the party secretary had dealt intellectuals a harsh blow during the democracy movement.[42]

Underneath a suave attitude, Jiang Zemin was a staunch Marxist-Leninist. In the following months he vigorously pushed the party line, that hostile foreign forces were using bourgeois propaganda to infiltrate the country and topple the Communist Party. Central Document No. 7, circulated by the Central Committee on 28 July 1989, explained the capitalist plot at length: 'the entire imperialist world tries to make us abandon the socialist road and turn us into a vassal of international monopoly capitalism. They use a variety of methods to politically and ideologically infiltrate our country and spare no effort to propagate the capitalist sham of "democracy", "freedom" and "human rights" to incite and support the ideological trend of bourgeois liberalisation inside our country.' The democracy movement that had culminated in June the Fourth was 'a planned, organised and premeditated political upheaval', the result of a 'nationwide proliferation of bourgeois liberalisation and international anti-communist, anti-socialist forces attempting to infiltrate the country politically and ideologically'.[43]

The name given to this plot was 'peaceful evolution', a concept first formulated in 1957 by US secretary of state John Foster Dulles, who had hoped to use peaceful means to accelerate the evolution towards democracy of countries in the Soviet orbit, thereby shortening the expected life span of communism. Dulles had invoked 'all moral and material support short of war', including loans provided by private investment and credits from the International Bank to support Poland and Hungary, countries 'enslaved behind the iron curtain'. But he did not envisage such support for China. On 4 December 1958 the secretary of state specifically spoke out against diplomatic recognition of Beijing and trade with China, wondering why 'aid and comfort' should be given to a regime 'dedicated to expelling us from the Western Pacific'.[44]

One communist leader who paid attention was Mao Zedong. In November 1959, in the midst of a brutal purge of 3.6 million party members who had expressed doubts about the Great Leap Forward, he convened a meeting to discuss Dulles' ideas. The United States, he noted, 'want to subvert and change us'. 'They want to corrupt us by a peaceful evolution.' Several years later Mao launched the Cultural Revolution, to ensure that no 'capitalist roaders' or 'bourgeois elements' could infiltrate the party and undermine the socialist system.[45]

Central Document No. 7 placed the party on high alert against attempts by 'monopoly capitalism' to 'overthrow' the Communist Party and the socialist system through 'peaceful evolution'. The propaganda machine, now controlled by Li Ruihuan, the party secretary of Tianjin who had risen to the occasion during the December 1986 student demonstrations, cranked into gear. Party members were convened in study sessions and indoctrination meetings, learning the correct interpretation of the events leading to June the Fourth. The students had been manipulated, they were told, as a few 'political conspirators had colluded with foreign hostile forces'. 'Foreign imperialist powers', they were warned, would never abandon 'their desire to annihilate us', quite the contrary: 'the moment an opportunity presents itself they use "peaceful evolution" to win without striking a blow.' The plot against the party had been 'premeditated, organised and meticulously planned': 'from the hunger strike to beating, smashing, looting, burning, killing, every step in this course of events was planned and organised.' Eternal vigilance was required, but also a strong state capable of fighting peaceful evolution. The only way to reach this goal was through a continued policy of economic reform and opening up.[46]

Over the summer the general population was also educated on the true nature of the counter-revolutionary plot and the dangers of 'peaceful evolution', with endless radio and television programmes, as well as a steady flow of articles in the official media. In the Museum of Chinese History, an exhibition was organised to explain how the counter-revolution was quelled. The collection included the remains of two tanks, three armoured personnel vehicles and several trucks, all set on fire by the protesters. There was also an undamaged ambulance donated by the Italian government. Counter-revolutionary posters and leaflets were exhibited in glass-top cabinets, surrounded by crowds of avid readers. A television screen showed videos of the demonstrations, with a stern voice-over explaining how the students had been manipulated. A few weapons used by the rioters were also on display, including one homemade pistol, half a brick and several

Molotov cocktails. Work units across the capital sent their personnel to study the exhibition.[47]

Later in August the second volume of Deng Xiaoping's *Selected Works* was published and distributed to great fanfare. The press hailed the paramount leader as an architect of economic reform and a leading exponent of Mao Zedong Thought.[48]

University students returned to class, but not before undergoing six weeks of political indoctrination, including written confessions of their involvement in the democracy movement. Lei Feng was their role model. Jiang Zemin personally visited several universities, listening with grave concern to the confessions of repentant students. There were no rude interruptions.[49]

First-year students also underwent six weeks of compulsory conscription in the army. An exception was made for new arrivals at Peking University. Since the students there had taken a lead in the democracy movement, they were packed off for a full year to the Military Academy of Shijiazhuang, some 250 kilometres to the south. The rules were strict: up at 6 a.m., a meagre breakfast, followed by physical exercise and political lectures. Books were confiscated, the lights turned off at 9.30 p.m.[50]

A crusade was launched against bourgeois liberalisation. On 25 August, propaganda tsar Li Ruihuan explained in a telephone conference that books and tapes promoting liberal values had proliferated over the past few years and must be eradicated. The campaign came with a twist: hostile foreign forces, he explained, were spreading smut, gambling and drugs to numb the minds of the people. The enemy was waging a battle without gunsmoke. 'Enemy forces abroad have disseminated reactionary, pornographic material on a massive scale: it is a major means for them to carry out "peaceful evolution",' thundered the *People's Daily*.[51]

The anti-pornography crusade had several advantages. After a harsh campaign of repression, the regime was running out of targets. In the absence of additional dissenting intellectuals, manufacturers of pornography became a convenient substitute. The campaign also softened the tone, paving the way for celebrations on 1 October, the fortieth anniversary of the founding of the People's Republic. Most of all, it gave the authorities a pretext to police culture even further, removing from the bookshelves anything smacking even remotely of bourgeois values. The writings of Zhao Ziyang disappeared, while long-forgotten texts of the Great Helmsman appeared again, taking pride of place next to Deng Xiaoping's *Selected Works*. *River Elegy* vanished. Foreign publications critical of China, including *Time*, *Newsweek* and the *International Herald Tribune*, were also missing from the bookstalls.[52]

In many provinces, party secretaries personally supervised the campaign, setting up special censorship committees to determine the nature of every publication. In parts of the country, local cadres were given 'porn quotas', expected to arrest a set number of pornography distributors or confiscate a certain quantity of indecent books. In some places the sweep was perfunctory, in others every book with a title including the word 'love' or 'woman' was removed, regardless of content. By the end of September, zealous commissars had notched up some impressive results, with more than 30 million offensive publications consigned to the paper mills and 400,000 videos destroyed.[53]

On 1 October, celebrated as National Day, Deng Xiaoping, flanked by Jiang Zemin, Li Peng and Yang Shangkun, offered a show of unity on the Tiananmen rostrum. In 1970 Edgar Snow had appeared next to the Chairman. That honour now went to Alexander Haig, the former US secretary of state, who stood side by side with the East German leader Egon Krenz.[54]

For several months the Propaganda Department had prepared for the occasion, intended to 'celebrate the victory of the suppression of the counter-revolutionary turmoil'.[55] Tens of thousands of performers, many of them students selected from high schools and universities against their will, executed a carefully rehearsed dance around a styrofoam statue with the sculpted figures of a peasant, a worker, a soldier and an intellectual, placed at the exact same spot where students had erected their Goddess of Democracy six months earlier. A voice on the loudspeaker praised the 'suppression of the rebellion'. Helmeted soldiers and armed police in riot gear stood on standby at key points along Chang'an Avenue.[56]

***

While martial law was still in effect, not to be lifted until January 1990, the tanks were gone, with single soldiers standing on duty under red and white parasols at major road intersections. The crackdown seemed like a distant memory. Even the beggars along Silk Alley were back, although there were very few foreign tourists. The Friendship Store reluctantly opened its doors to the local population.[57]

While most troops returned to their barracks, soldiers were seen hard at work on building sites around the capital, putting up hotels, restaurants and shopping centres in preparation for the Asian Games.[58]

The regime was fortunate that the Games were scheduled to take place in October 1990, just sixteen months after the massacre. Nothing was quite as effective as the emotional appeal of a sporting extravaganza in shoring up a regime's domestic and foreign legitimacy. The 1936 Berlin Olympics had been a stroke of propaganda genius, setting a very high standard for other regimes to follow. In 1978, a carefully stage-managed World Cup in Argentina had burnished the regime's bloody image as the national football team defeated the Netherlands in the Monumental Stadium, a mere two kilometres away from the Navy Mechanics School, the county's notorious torture camp.

The homes of more than 2,000 families in the capital were demolished to make way for the Games, while bullet holes were filled with plaster, damaged façades given a fresh coat of paint and tank tracks on the tarmac smoothed out. Giant clocks appeared on several billboards in the capital, counting down the days in the hope of uniting a divided population in anticipation of a patriotic showcase event. Daily reports appeared on television screens, including comments from sporting celebrities and other dignitaries. Cui Jian, who had galvanised the protesters with his defiant tunes, experienced a change of heart and went on tour, raising funds for the Games.[59]

The mascot of the Asian Games was Pan-Pan, an adorable, fluffy panda. Pan-Pan set out to woo the world, overcoming the reservations of those who had wanted to boycott the event. By September over 100,000 tourists and 6,500 athletes were expected to attend the Games. Sanitation officials, in a further drive towards unity, ordered local residents to help exterminate the 'four pests', mosquitoes, flies, cockroaches and rats, while children went into the streets to remove cigarette ends and other rubbish. People received orders to police themselves, with individuals assigned to patrol the neighbourhoods and look for potential saboteurs. Chen Xitong, the mayor of the capital, also recruited half a million volunteers to stand along checkpoints across the city and fine or apprehend anyone seen to behave badly. Beggars, migrants and peddlers without proper papers were evicted, and the stalls of vendors closed down. In the run-up to the Games, criminals were executed in the dozens. Along all major streets, not least Chang'an Avenue, red banners fluttered gaily in the wind.[60]

The Games were a triumph, with China taking 183 gold medals out of a possible 310. The spectacle was capped by a magnificent closing ceremony, as some 10,000 performers dressed in national costumes danced in front of 80,000 hand-picked spectators. The final flourish came when a live panda impersonating Pan-Pan was driven into the Beijing Workers' Stadium in a flower-laden cart, with fireworks lighting up the sky. Jiang Zemin, Li Peng and Yang Shangkun, presiding over the closing ceremony, appeared jubilant.[61]

At the Seventh Plenum of the Central Committee a few months later, the superiority of socialism was resoundingly confirmed and Deng Xiaoping's goal of quadrupling the economy between 1980 and 2000 once again endorsed. Words of wisdom from the paramount leader that would become a guiding motto for the party over the next twenty years circulated on the opening day of the meeting: 'do not seek leadership, be modest and prudent, bide your time, he who takes the lead will lose the initiative.'[62]

***

Central Document No. 7 of July 1989 warned party members against 'foreign infiltration' and 'peaceful evolution', but also demanded that 'patriotism' and 'faith in the creative power' of the country be propagated at every level of society. In August the Propaganda Department had taken this theme further: 'we must propagate faith in the superiority of the socialist system,' it noted, 'we must explain that only socialism can save China.' It also highlighted the importance of 'heightening the nation's self-confidence and pride'.[63]

The Asian Games, by all accounts, did much to restore the leadership's confidence. 'The Asian Games mean that the Chinese people have stood up,' Chen Xitong beamed.[64] Other measures were taken, too, above all a campaign of patriotic education which unfolded gradually, over several years, with the aim of building a 'spiritual civilisation' by the turn of the millennium, to coincide with the goal of quadrupling the economy.[65]

The first step was to bring back Lei Feng, whose self-abnegation and unquestioned devotion to the party was always a reliable countervailing force in any fight against decadent bourgeois values. 'Learn from Comrade Lei Feng,' the *People's Daily* enjoined its readers in December 1989, in a front-page tribute to the people's hero. Lei Feng Day, on 5 March 1990, was celebrated with a television series as well as meetings, conferences, symposiums and study groups – over 6,000 in Hunan province alone. The army was invariably keen to support the model soldier. Yang Baibing, half-brother of Yang Shangkun and the general secretary of the Central Military Commission, who had undertaken the job of mobilising the troops in spring 1989, made the rounds, giving speeches and penning articles.[66]

A national meeting in Beijing honoured 45 'living Lei Fengs', plucked from obscurity in farms, factories and barracks. Sergeant Zhang Zixiang, whose many good deeds included rescuing an old man from hooligans and emptying spittoons in a hospital, spoke warmly of his hero. He also sang communist songs in a polished baritone vibrato and named Nikolai Ostrovsky's *How the Steel Was Tempered* as his favourite book.[67]

Two months after Lei Feng Day, Jiang Zemin addressed a gathering of 3,000 youngsters in the Great Hall of the People to mark May the Fourth. 'Patriotism and socialism are one and the same,' he declared, adding that 'only socialism can save China.' He called for extensive patriotic education, most of all among children in primary and secondary schools.[68]

On 3 June, the regime commemorated the 150th anniversary of the Opium War. From elementary school to university, students across the country were required to study the pernicious poppy, which was compared to the modern poison of 'bourgeois liberalisation'. A special conference took place in the Museum of Chinese History, with hundreds of police cordoning off Tiananmen Square.

The leading propaganda figure featured was Lin Zexu, an upright official who had ended the opium trade, taken foreign merchants and their families hostage and destroyed more than 20,000 crates of the poison. Films, lectures and exhibitions sought to provoke national outrage. 'China's modern history is the history of humiliation,' the *China Education News* stated succinctly. Hu Sheng, leading party historian and president of the Chinese Academy of Social Science, opined that 'it is obvious that if we depart from the path of socialism we will again be plunged into the hundred years after the Opium War in which we suffered national humiliation and darkness.'[69]

One year later, 29 August was designated as National Humiliation Day, marking the anniversary of the signing in 1842 of the Treaty of Nanjing, ending the first Opium War, portrayed as the starting point of a century of invasion and exploitation by foreign powers. Countless films, books, newspapers and exhibits resurrected every wrong, from the peddling of opium to wartime atrocities under Japanese occupation. 'Never Forget National Humiliation: Invigorate China' was the message.[70]

***

One key tool in promoting a message of national unity and common destiny was the United Front. At home, the United Front Work Department launched a charm offensive towards public figures outside the Communist Party. 'We must trust them, rely on them and unite them,' the organisation boldly proclaimed at a secret meeting held in the summer of 1989.[71] At a much-publicised tea party later that year, Jiang Zemin personally announced that members of the eight democratic parties would be consulted in all major affairs and allowed to contribute towards 'social stability and unity'. 'The democratic parties accept the leadership of the Chinese Communist Party and work closely with it at socialist projects,' an official document later clarified.[72]

Abroad, a network of groups controlled by the United Front was used to 'win over people's hearts, promote common understanding and ensure that public figures overseas understand and support us'.[73] The effort was heightened one year later with the creation of an Overseas Propaganda Department, which attracted lavish funding despite stringent government cuts elsewhere. 'We must rely on the United Front to defeat the plot of infiltration, subversion and peaceful evolution, carried out by hostile forces at home and abroad,' Jiang Zemin warned darkly in June 1990. The 'antagonism and struggle' between the two camps would take place 'over a long period of time', as 'international hostile forces will never abandon their strategy of overthrowing socialism'. In this long-term struggle the United Front's strategy was to 'unite the majority and isolate the minority'.[74]

The most important contributor to the regime, in terms of goods, services, technology, talent and capital, was Hong Kong. At the height of the democracy movement, euphoria had gripped people from all walks of life, with petitions, rallies and generous donations, but a mood of grim desperation followed the massacre. Tens of thousands in the crown colony decided to migrate, with many more desperately seeking passports. A stampede took place when the Singapore Commission handed out 25,000 application forms for permanent residency. US congressman Stephen Solarz visited the colony from Washington with a proposal to admit more Hong Kongers to the United States. One local businessman even suggested moving the colony to a spot near Darwin, Australia. Another argued that the United Nations should lease Hong Kong and make it the Switzerland of Asia.[75]

All the efforts deployed since 1976 by the mainland to cultivate underground party members and build up a United Front collapsed. Xu Jiatun, the man dispatched by Beijing to plan the resumption of sovereignty and win over community leaders, reported back to his masters that 'all leftist organisations have turned.'[76] Even prominent figures on the left had marched in favour of democracy. Trade unions lost ground. Entire institutions normally loyal to the mainland expressed revulsion over the massacre. The New China News Agency, mouthpiece of the Communist Party and nominally under the thumb of Xu Jiatun, openly sided with the demonstrators, calling on Li Peng to step down. Xu Jiatun himself fled to the United States a few months later.[77]

Beijing concluded that the crown colony was a hotbed of counter-revolutionary activity, a subversive base used by foreign hostile forces to infiltrate the country ideologically and destabilise the Communist Party leadership. The territory, Li Peng argued, posed a threat to national security. Several leaders of the pro-democracy camp, including a legislator named Martin Lee, were condemned for 'supporting subversive activities'.[78]

Every step taken by London was seen as further evidence of deception. When Margaret Thatcher tried to stem the tide of emigration and shore up confidence in the colony by offering the right of abode to 50,000 qualified households, hoping that they would instead remain, Beijing angrily denounced this as a ploy to hijack its own nationals.

It was not all rhetoric. The leadership inserted a new provision into the Basic Law, a document then being drafted to serve as a de facto constitution for Hong Kong after 1997, preventing Chinese citizens on the Legislative Council in Hong Kong from possessing the right of abode in any foreign country. In order to strengthen its ability to control events in future, the regime also introduced a clause prohibiting treason, secession, subversion and theft of state secrets, and prohibited 'political organisations or bodies' from establishing ties with 'foreign political organisations or bodies'.[79] Article 23 was tinder for future unrest, as controversy over the nature of the national security law would divide the territory for decades to come.

The Basic Law, drafted by a committee appointed and dominated by Beijing, was ratified on 16 February 1990. Three years earlier, when meeting members of the committee, Deng Xiaoping had pointedly rejected the separation of powers as a 'Western system' that was unsuitable for Hong Kong.[80] The blueprint therefore merely promised a 'high degree of autonomy' after 1997. It cast aside demands for a democratic framework to protect the colony's rights and freedoms. Instead, it introduced a system so complicated, with indirect balloting and an electoral college appointed by the government, that it all but precluded direct elections. At the very heart of the document was the regime's own understanding of the term 'election': it had in mind the dutiful approval of nominated candidates by limited voting. Still, the idea that elections of any kind in a territory of less than 6 million people might produce a legislative majority hostile to a nation of over a billion haunted the regime. It would intervene repeatedly to rig the system further in its favour.

***

June the Fourth was a milestone in the history of the twentieth century, with parliamentary elections held for the very first time in a country flying the red flag. Although the elections in Poland were rigged, with seats reserved for the Communist Party, Solidarność won a resounding victory, surprising even its own leader, Lech Wałęsa. Widespread strikes and street demonstrations the preceding year had forced the regime to negotiate with Solidarność and agree to open up seats for election in a newly created bicameral legislature. Armed with the agreement, Lech Wałęsa travelled to Rome, where Pope John

Paul II received him in April 1989. Gorbachev did not intervene, as Solidarność led a peaceful transition to democracy in December 1990.

Images of defiant young people with headbands protesting in Tiananmen Square, flickering on television screens across the socialist camp, also galvanised democracy movements elsewhere. On 27 June, the foreign ministers of Austria and Hungary stood before the cameras, cutting through a section of barbed wire that had divided their countries for several decades. Thousands of East Germans headed for Hungary, passing through the gap in the Iron Curtain to join friends and family in West Germany. When the East German authorities closed all borders on 3 October to stem the flow, mass demonstrations erupted in Leipzig, the country's second largest city. Gorbachev, who was in the country on a state visit a few days later, urged the leadership to accept reform. He ruled out intervention by the Soviet troops stationed in more than 200 military barracks across the country. On 9 October some 70,000 protesters thronged the city centre again, despite widespread fears that they would meet the same fate as the student demonstrators on Tiananmen Square. The vastly outnumbered armed police held back, as the order to shoot never came. One month later crowds pushed through crossing points in Berlin, with guards unwilling to use force, some even volunteering to open the gates. The Berlin Wall fell.

A similar scenario unfolded across Eastern Europe, as one dictatorship after another imploded under the weight of its own people. After watching television pictures of PLA soldiers turning their guns on demonstrators, party officials knew the game was up. Their armies would not carry out a 'Chinese solution'. The only exception to the rule was Romania, where a particularly obstinate Nicolae Ceaușescu ordered a military crackdown after people rebelled in the capital, Bucharest. Ordinary soldiers and their commanders switched sides almost immediately, toppling the regime instead.

News of these events was heavily censored in China. 'What we report, what we do not report, when we report it, how we report it: all of this must be determined by us and be beneficial to us,' the Politburo explained in December 1989, concerned over the impact of the events on the population. Behind closed doors, the leaders felt vindicated. Wang Fang, minister of public security, circulated a report blaming Gorbachev for the disaster and concluding that the leadership had been wise to repress the turmoil six months earlier. 'Only China can save socialism,' Bo Yibo opined, turning on its head the old motto that only socialism could save China. The People's Republic was the 'firm rock in the middle of the stream' despite changing winds and clouds.[81]

Gorbachev was now widely reviled, described as a 'traitor' and a 'small clown' in party meetings. Yet when an attempt to remove the general secretary in Moscow failed on 21 August 1991, the leaders fell silent. Deng Xiaoping, who had personally predicted that Gorbachev would be ousted, seemed out of touch. The Chinese military, on Deng's cue, had backed the most conservative elements of the Red Army, who now lingered in prison. Most of all, images of ordinary people pouring into the streets in Moscow to erect barricades against an invading army were an unwelcome reminder of recent events in Beijing. Boris Yeltsin, who climbed on top of one of the tanks to address the crowd, emerged as a popular hero in Russia.[82]

On 23 August a fleet of black Audis and Mercedes-Benzes was seen outside Deng Xiaoping's residence, as the leadership grappled with how to formulate a response. Their answer was to divert even more resources into the fight against 'peaceful evolution'. More shrill propaganda on the perils of 'bourgeois liberalisation' followed.[83]

One of the keenest defenders of the faith was Jiang Zemin. A month earlier, in a speech marking the seventieth anniversary of the founding of the party, he had once again raised the spectre of peaceful evolution, portraying the fight against imperialist infiltration as a life and death issue for the Communist Party. 'Nothing that could poison the minds of the people, pollute society or run counter to socialism should be allowed to spread unchecked,' he vowed in his televised speech, reminding his audience of the importance of the Four Cardinal Principles.

A revised version of his speech, hailed as the new 'Manifesto of the Communist Party', circulated widely in September. Jiang Zemin welcomed economic reform, but pointed out that the private sector would never be more than a mere supplement to the state sector: socialism, not capitalism, was the name of the country's economic system.[84]

Hardliners used this speech to query the extent of economic reform, in particular the private sector. Deng Liqun, the doctrinaire ideologist who never missed an opportunity to rail against capitalism, demanded a more favourable assessment of the Cultural Revolution. One of the Four Cardinal Principles was Mao Zedong Thought, and the Chairman had been right to bombard capitalist roaders within the party ranks. A fifth column of powerful bourgeois cadres, Deng Liqun argued, was trying to lead the country back towards capitalism.[85]

Deng Liqun was not an isolated figure. Others who praised Mao Zedong Thought sallied forth to call for a 'resolute struggle' against 'capitalist reform'. Chen Yun, now aged 86, joined the fray, taking issue with those who believed that the planned economy was outdated. The proper ratio, he pointed out, was 80 per cent of plan versus 20 per cent of market. He scorned the rush towards establishing 'special economic zones' and other 'bonded areas' to hasten the influx of foreign capital.[86]

His protégé Song Ping, one of the five members of the powerful Standing Committee, supervised a campaign of 'socialist education' in the countryside, aimed at transforming 900 million villagers into faithful followers of the collective economy. Tens of thousands of senior cadres went to remote villages to 'educate the peasants about the superiority of socialism and strengthen the organisation of village party cells'. For years, hardliners had deplored that the household contract system had weakened party authority in the countryside. Now came their chance to reverse the trend. In Li Peng's words, 'we must make unremitting efforts to develop the collective economy in the countryside.' Even barefoot doctors, who had criss-crossed the countryside during the Cultural Revolution, offering free medical services, reappeared.[87]

Mao's ghost was conjured up, his call for a crusade against the West revived. As statues of Lenin were falling across the Soviet Union, the *Selected Works of Mao Zedong* became required reading once again in city and countryside alike. *China Youth Daily* applauded young people who steeped themselves in the study of Mao Zedong Thought.[88]

On 25 December the red flag with the hammer and the sickle was lowered from the Kremlin for the last time. For several months, one republic after another had proclaimed their independence from Moscow, transforming the Soviet Union into an empty shell. The People's Republic of China was more isolated than ever before. With hardliners in the ascent, it seemed that the regime was about to retreat back into its Maoist past.

**

When troops had displayed their might in the days following the June the Fourth crackdown, randomly firing automatic weapons from the backs of their military trucks, their bullets had shattered some of the windows of the World Trade Center, still under construction. The largest of several mammoth projects in the capital, with apartment blocks, two hotels, a convention centre and several shopping malls, it stood as a beacon of reform, its 38 floors towering far above the city. The opening date was deferred, as a third of a million dollars had to be spent on special glass imported from Belgium.[89]

More substantial damage came on 15 July, when the world's seven leading industrialised powers met at an economic summit in Paris. They announced the postponement of $2.3 billion in loans earmarked by the World Bank for Beijing. Japan reluctantly followed suit, suspending a package of $5.6 billion scheduled over several years.

The decision came as a blow to the regime. The leaders had assiduously courted foreign governments for preferential loans and interest-free grants, winning generous funding from countries as diverse as Denmark, Italy, Canada, Australia, Japan and Kuwait. The largest share of all came from the World Bank. When Robert McNamara, head of the bank, first travelled to Beijing in April 1980, Deng Xiaoping impressed him by pointing out that an alliance between the United States, Europe, Japan and China was essential in confronting the danger to world peace posed by the Soviet Union.[90] His pitch paid off, as by 1989 China had become the World Bank's largest beneficiary, receiving over $10 billion, roughly half of the credits in the form of interest-free loans that did not have to be repaid for at least 35 years.[91]

Foreign debt reached $42 billion, even as the country was about to enter its peak repayment period. Reserves stood at a mere $10 billion, barely enough to cover nine weeks of imports.[92] Combined with the freeze in foreign loans and the collapse of the tourist industry, it left the regime with only one alternative to earn the required hard currency, namely imposing draconian controls on foreign exchange, curbing imports and increasing exports whatever the cost.

Luxury goods, especially cars, were a predictable target, but over a hundred ordinary products were also subject to stringent new inspection requirements. Central approval was necessary for purchases of key commodities such as grain, sugar, fertiliser, timber, cotton and pesticides, with curbs placed on wool, wood pulp, plywood, chemicals and television tubes. Import of some twenty electronic and machinery products was banned outright, hitting South Korea and Japan particularly hard. Their trade balances became negative, as exports to China slumped.[93]

Export factories, on the other hand, were granted priority access to raw materials, power and transportation, as well as more credit and subsidies. Higher tax rebates were introduced to enhance competition. In a reversal of economic reform, large state enterprises were boosted and small businesses were cut off from state supplies, with village enterprises, in particular, seen as competing unfairly with their larger state counterparts. The number of foreign trade corporations, which had mushroomed after September 1984, was slashed, with roughly one in four, 1,300 in total, forced to close down.[94]

But the greatest change of all was a 21 per cent devaluation against the US dollar at the end of 1989, bringing the dollar to 4.72 yuan. 'Foreigners need our exports,' minister for foreign trade Zheng Tuobin explained after the devaluation was introduced, adding, 'we will resolutely support economic reform and break through the sanctions imposed by foreign countries.'[95]

In August 1990, Zheng Tuobin proudly announced a 60 per cent year-on-year increase in exports, reaching record levels to the United States and the European Union. China, despite an international outcry over the Tiananmen Square massacre and a freeze in loans, had managed to export more than ever before.[96]

There was one exception to external hostility, namely Taiwan. Shortly after President Chiang Ching-kuo died in January 1988, his successor Lee Teng-hui ended a ban on tourism, trade and other contacts with China. Beijing seized the opportunity, making the renegade island a 'strategic priority' with a concerted effort channelled through the United Front to promote economic ties. 'All resources must be deployed under a unified command,' the State Council intoned after June the Fourth, as economic cooperation could 'restrain the trend towards separation and accelerate the peaceful unification of our fatherland'.[97]

Sweeteners were offered, services improved, red tape cut. The charm offensive paid off. Exports to Taiwan soared by more than 250 per cent in 1990. Money from Taiwan poured in, the amounts so voluminous that these compensated for lost revenue from the West. In 1990 alone investment reached $2 billion. Even as Hong Kong recoiled in horror at the massacre, Taiwan took up the financial slack, becoming by 1992 the largest source of foreign investment in China.[98]

Another victory beckoned in July 1990. Fang Lizhi, the dissident sheltering in the American embassy, was quietly ransomed by the regime in exchange for the resumption of international loans. After Brent Scowcroft's secret mission failed to resolve the diplomatic stalemate, President Bush sent Henry Kissinger, China's trusted man in Washington. Deng demanded the lifting of all economic sanctions imposed by Congress. Fang and his wife were forced to pledge that they would not undertake any anti-China activities overseas. On 23 June 1990 all party leaders received a telegram explaining that Fang Lizhi and Li Shuxian had 'confessed to their wrongdoings' and that their release was a 'decision that suits the demands of our international struggle', not least the resumption of international lending and the renewal of the Most Favoured Nation principles. Two days later American officials escorted the couple to the Beijing airport, where they boarded a US Air Force plane.[99]

On 10 July the way was cleared for the World Bank to resume its loans to China. Weeks earlier, the vice-president of the bank, Moeen Qureshi, had already taken up the regime's cause. When visiting Beijing, he repeatedly stressed that the institution's charter did not stipulate any link between financial assistance and human rights. He was toasted by Jiang Zemin.[100] The bank provided $1.6 billion for 1990–91, an amount increased to $2.5 billion the following year, more than any other nation received. The moment the World Bank altered its lending policy, Japan also jumped in with a $5.7 billion package. Its exports to China surged by 40 per cent in what contemporary observers described as a reward to Tokyo for supporting a return to 'normal economic relations'.[101]

The regime learned to appreciate the benefits of hostage diplomacy and the price of even a single dissident. It also acquired a renewed respect for a traditional proverb, 'Money will get the devil to grind the mill.'

***

A further devaluation was introduced on 17 November 1990, bringing the dollar to 5.22 yuan. Devaluation worked miracles for the export market, but carried inflationary risks, making local products cheaper, but raising the prices of foreign goods, including the cost of foreign debt. Denominated in dollars, by the end of 1990 it stood at roughly $55 billion, a modest amount, but one that increased proportionately with every devaluation. In 1984 it represented 5.9 per cent of national output, but by 1990 it amounted to 16 per cent.[102]

More importantly, the benefits derived from a devaluation were rapidly eroded. As in the past, procurement prices began to rise, as did the relative cost of earning a dollar. Zheng Tuobin, fully aware of the conundrum, repeatedly stressed the importance of 'strictly controlling procurement prices for raw materials' and 'preventing random price increases'.[103]

Keen to cap prices, the state began to recentralise portions of the economy, seeking control over raw materials and a monopoly over marketing, whether in plastic sheeting or cotton. Rather predictably, though, the price ceilings had an effect opposite to that desired. Since prices fixed by the state forced many enterprises to sell below the cost of production, they cut output. Enterprise managers, ever inventive, devised other ways of bypassing the price constraints, including forming a partnership with a buyer who would sell on at a higher price; changing the name and classification of a product on the pretext of upgrading; selling products to subsidiary enterprises which then sold them on at market prices; or producing only commodities which were not controlled. The result was reduced economic activity, a fall in product quality and widespread avoidance of price controls.[104]

Although the state was keen to control prices, the dual price system forced it to rely on local governments. When price ceilings were locally enforced, more unintended consequences followed. The price of raw cotton, essential to feed the many looms churning out textiles for foreign markets, was one good example. In Dalian, local controls actually

encouraged a flow of cloth to buyers outside the municipality, willing
to pay the market price. Cloth from Shandong was sold instead in
Dalian at prices 50 per cent higher than the ceiling on local cloth.[105]

The case of cotton illustrated another issue, namely the government's
belief that by holding down procurement prices, a steady supply of
cheap raw materials could find its way to state enterprises. Not only
did cotton management bureaus run by local governments raise prices
by adding all sorts of incidentals, from 'labour service fees' to 'organisation fees', but they also failed to deliver on time. Nor did it help
that they sold sacks of low-grade produce mixed with stones as high-
grade cotton.[106]

The result was disarray in the textile industry. As the overall costs
increased, so did the amount required to earn a dollar. The average cost
of producing enough cotton yarn to earn $1 rose from 4.44 yuan in
1988 to 5.15 yuan in July 1989 and 6.46 yuan in May 1990. The official
exchange rate, after the devaluation of September 1989, was 4.72 yuan
to the dollar. Overall, the net profits of the 1,292 state textile mills had
fallen by over 10 per cent, while the volume of losses increased by 284
per cent – according to official statistics. For every 1,000 metres of
cloth produced, the mills incurred a loss of 200 yuan.[107]

Since price controls increased the losses sustained by state
enterprises, more subsidies were required. Producers attracted subsidies, but so did consumers, since the regime was anxious to avoid
social unrest. In Beijing every increase of 1 per cent in the consumer
price index cost the municipal government 400 million yuan in additional subsidies. 'China is now firmly in a subsidy trap,' one foreign
economist noted. Subsidies were manifold, but increased by roughly
40 per cent per year during the two years of economic retrenchment
that began in September 1988.[108] By one estimate, some 40 per cent of
the budget was earmarked for subsidies. This, in turn, required more
money. In 1990 the money supply grew by roughly 30 per cent.[109]

The regime was driven by fear that it might be unable to pay its
foreign debt. Instead of tackling genuine reform and improving efficiency, the leaders tinkered with the exchange rate to pursue temporary benefits. They built a fragile façade to cope with international
sanctions. They insisted on maintaining a firm hand over prices, capital and labour, but compounded the problem by exercising a weak
hand over fiscal policy, the growing deficit and the money supply. The

overall effect was a rapid fall in economic growth, which dropped to 3.9 per cent in 1989 before sinking to 1.6 per cent in the first half of 1990.[110]

The domestic market slumped and unemployment surged, with one estimate putting the number of people who were not fully employed at 150 million nationwide. In 1989 alone, 3 million of a total 18 million village enterprises vanished.[111]

A familiar scenario revisited an archaic economic system dominated by the dual price system: stockpiles increased, credit froze and debt expanded. The extent of the paralysis, however, was new, and was captured by a phenomenon known as 'triangular debt', the term given to liabilities state companies owed to each other. Superficially, it seemed a relatively benign problem, as state enterprises squeezed for credit decided not to pay their bills or to defer payment for a certain period, spending their capital instead on other priorities. Since their suppliers were not paid, they, too, postponed payment to their own creditors, creating a chain of liabilities. The debt was an informal credit system, a means of raising capital outside the banking system. In some cases state enterprises might even mutually agree to defer payments, or guarantee each other's debts with fake collateral, knowing full well that the state would never allow them to go bankrupt. Debts between state enterprises were therefore evergreen liabilities that could be postponed indefinitely until the state intervened. The moment the state stepped in, ordering the banks to clear up the accumulated debt, the problem of arrears between enterprises surged again.

Most of all, triangular debt was related to inflation. As the price of raw materials and finished products increased, the relative value of working capital decreased. State enterprises were keen to boost short-term profits by entering their inventory at cost value and declaring the gains made from appreciation as direct profit, thereby increasing the nominal surplus profit in excess of the amount turned over to the treasury they could retain. Yet the capital increase was not backed by an equal amount in goods. By one estimate, between 1988 and 1990 the notional profit derived from inventory appreciation amounted to tens of billions of yuan. Soon enough, the state enterprises were no longer able to sustain production, shortages developed, arrears expanded. As consumption was curbed, finished goods that could not find any buyers were stockpiled, sometimes rotting away in warehouses. By the end of 1990, the nationwide inventory had increased by nearly 60 billion year on year.[112] It culminated at 130 billion in 1992. Roughly one-quarter of this stock was worthless, equivalent to a month's salary for every working person.[113]

A related problem was that, in a classic socialist mismatch between supply and demand, many state enterprises excelled at churning out commodities no one wanted. Inflation is generally interpreted as too much money chasing too few goods, but with so few desirable commodities it took surprisingly little cash to reach that threshold. In a recession, enterprises that could not find a market for their products would normally go bankrupt, their assets sold at market value and their liabilities wiped out; but in a socialist economy, when credit dwindled, these companies simply ground to a halt and went into hibernation. Once the economy came back to life, their dormant debts, incurred against worthless assets, were reactivated, attracting more state funds to service deadweight debts and nurture renewed production of goods for which no market existed.[114] As the cycle resumed, these goods once more ended up in storage. All this activity counted towards gross domestic product, a concept formulated by countries with a market economy where all goods produced eventually sold. In the rather elegant phraseology of a branch of the People's Bank of China, 'there is a vicious circle of credit injection, production, overstocking and arrears, and more injection, more production, more overstocking and more arrears.'[115]

In 1990, the state injected 50 billion yuan to clear triangular debt estimated at 160 billion yuan. The problem persisted, and one year later triangular debt reached 300 billion yuan, equivalent to 55 billion dollars (calculated at the parallel market rate of 5.4 yuan per dollar rather than the official rate), roughly equivalent to the total amount of currency in circulation, or one-fifth of all outstanding loans. The crisis came at an inopportune moment, as the socialist world around the leaders was dissolving. 'If this continues any further our economy will collapse,' Li Peng intoned gravely. 'To put it more bluntly, it is a question of life and death for socialism.' Li Rui, in the privacy of his diary, put it slightly less dramatically: 'the debt devours everything.'[116]

Zhu Rongji, elevated to vice-premier in the spring of 1991, was called to the rescue. At this stage, he was one of the few leaders with any idea of how an economy of any kind actually operated. With the exception of Chen Yun, the architect of the planned economy, most of the party elders who made the real decisions were political theorists. Li Peng, in charge of the economy, tended to rely on Yuan Mu, who had worked as a journalist for twenty years before joining the government. Even the people in charge of the country's main financial institutions were political appointees, some with little concrete knowledge of economics. Li Rui, who knew the leaders well, alleged in his diary that Wang Bingqian, the man who had been in charge of the budget for many years, did not understand basic accounting, relying instead on his underlings. Li Guixian, the governor of the People's Bank of China, was a chemical engineer by training, and apparently remained unsure how banking transactions were actually carried out.[117]

Zhu Rongji threw 50 billion yuan at the debt over the following years, demanding that local governments pool funds to clear the debts owed by their enterprises. He also compelled them to sell all the goods stockpiled in warehouses, and proposed that state enterprises that could not sell their output should halt production and develop their facilities instead. He suggested mergers, transfers, even closures. The mergers, he believed, would create powerful state conglomerates in crucial industrial sectors, capable of competing with the most advanced corporations in the world. When asked how he would cope with the loss of fiscal revenue caused by reducing production and selling inventories, his answer was that these revenues existed only on paper. He closed down several state factories in Liaoning province that produced unwanted goods. But when he asked the State Council in September 1991 to extend the experiment to the rest of the country, he was rebuffed. The elders had no desire to risk the social unrest associated with reforms cutting to the heart of the socialist system.[118]

Zhu Rongji's performance had one advantage: he established himself as a committed reformer, even as the regime seemed to be edging back towards the more strictly planned economy of the past. In November 1991 he openly clashed with the ideologue Deng Liqun, who proposed returning to Maoist values. Zhu called instead for 'bigger, bolder reforms', as well as less government interference in business.[119]

Zhu had little authority to push through further reforms. Towards the end of November the more cautious conservatives led by Chen

Yun prevailed at the Eighth Plenum, where Zhu Rongji was not elected as a full Politburo member. Deng Xiaoping, by now 87 and too old to lead from the front, was determined to consolidate his legacy and leave a lasting mark on the economy. To break the deadlock in Beijing, he turned to a political tradition perfected by his erstwhile master Mao Zedong: bypass the party and appeal directly to the people.

7

Capitalist Tools in Socialist Hands
(1992–1996)

Mao was a master of corridor politics, but when he failed to prevail in the capital he would resort to a classic ploy, travelling the country in his personal train to win support from provincial leaders instead.

On 19 January 1992 Deng Xiaoping made a surprise visit to Shenzhen, the special economic zone he had toured in 1984 to extol the benefits of economic reform. On his first public appearance in a year, he cruised an amusement park in a golf cart, admired the city from a revolving restaurant atop the World Trade Center and gave his blessing to the mayor. He was also unusually blunt: 'Reform and opening up is China's only option,' he told journalists, making sure his remarks were widely circulated in Hong Kong. 'Whoever is opposed to reform should leave office.' Crowds clapped and cheered.[1]

This was the highlight of a southern tour during which the para-mount leader vented his frustration at the slow pace of reform to dozens of provincial leaders in Wuhan, Changsha, Guangzhou and Shanghai. The state-run media blacked out the leader's trip, since he was supposed to live in retirement, but his pronouncements, judi-ciously leaked to journalists in Hong Kong, were beamed back across the border.

The patriarch's message was straightforward: there was nothing to fear from increased foreign investment and continued economic reform, since the 'publicly owned sector is the mainstay of the economy.' 'More importantly,' he added, 'political power is in our hands,' meaning that the party exercised political control over all foreign-owned companies, which would be made to serve the nation's interests. This, rather than the balance between central planning and market forces, constituted the true difference between socialism and capitalism. The best defence against peaceful evolution, he maintained, was economic development and enhanced living standards, which would demonstrate the superiority of the socialist system. 'We must experiment, blaze a trail and press ahead boldly,' he opined, an invitation that few were prepared to decline.[2]

Jiang Zemin quickly trimmed his sails to the wind blowing from the south. Two days after the patriarch's private train chugged out of the Beijing railway station to begin his odyssey, the general secretary called for greater reform and opening up to the outside world. On 2 February, marking the Lunar New Year, Jiang made a much-publicised phone call to wish Deng Xiaoping well. In his New Year speech at the Great Hall of the People, he told 4,000 party officials that the country had to make 'bold explorations' and accelerate the pace of reform. On 23 February the *People's Daily* enjoined the country to 'Open to the outside world and make use of capitalism.'[3]

At a Politburo meeting in early March, Jiang Zemin was politically astute enough to offer a self-criticism, taking the blame for having suppressed the paramount leader's southern tour in the official media. His colleagues fell in line, expressing unanimous support for Deng's clarion call for high growth. A glum, defeated Li Peng offered no objection.[4]

A few weeks later the people also spoke, or at least their official representatives at the National People's Congress. After reading the comments the patriarch had made during his southern tour, they, too, demanded an accelerated pace of reform. They also requested more local funds and more local autonomy.[5]

**

The last leg of Deng Xiaoping's tour was Shanghai. In the midst of the regime's campaign of retrenchment, the city was an exception. Even as regional powers were being curtailed and investment cut in the wake of June the Fourth, a huge scheme was launched to turn a marshland located across the Huangpu River into the financial centre of the future. It helped that Jiang Zemin hailed from the city, but the regime was also keen to convince the world that the open-door policy was not only alive, but genuinely flourishing. They also wanted to foster a rival to Hong Kong, viewed as a dangerous base of subversion manipulated by foreign hostile powers. The Pudong Industrial Zone was billed as China's new Hong Kong, a pearl of the Orient that would attract billions in foreign investment.

Li Peng formally inaugurated the project on 18 April 1990, but at first progress was slow. The lion's share of investment was expected to come from foreign investors, who were granted concessions, including the right to lease large tracts of land and set up trading companies in the zone. Profits would be tax free for the first five years. Thousands of foreign delegations arrived in the following months. Mayor Zhu Rongji travelled the world, trying to woo the moneymen. But one year later, a mere forty factories with foreign investment stood amid an uninspiring area with broken roads and ramshackle gas plants. The financial concessions, on closer inspection, turned out to be the gateway into a spider's web of red tape, with endless restrictions on precisely what foreigners were allowed to do. 'I suspect it will just be a bigger cage for different birds,' one foreign banker opined.[6]

Investment picked up after Deng Xiaoping's southern tour. In Shanghai the octogenarian inspected factories, department stores, the securities exchange and even new buildings in Pudong. The moment he left, Huang Ju, the new mayor who had taken over from Zhu Rongji, appeared before the foreign press to pledge more incentives, funding and autonomy. Companies were even allowed to engage in entrepot trade, the backbone of Shenzhen's economy. They could issue stocks and bonds. Over 50 billion yuan had already been committed, he explained, far in excess of what was required for all the infrastructure projects. He invoked the paramount leader's words of wisdom: 'be bold and take faster steps.'[7]

Huang Ju called Pudong a 'socialist metropolis'. In 1992, some 3.3 billion capitalist dollars flowed in, half from Hong Kong and Macau. Over $4.5 billion were contracted in the first half of 1993 alone. By one estimate, a new company was formed every eleven minutes. Fearful of being left behind, big corporations including Ford, Bell, Matsushita, Sharp, Hitachi and Siemens claimed a stake. A tunnel was dug, bridges built and roads laid, with modern skyscrapers appearing in the midst of a forest of cranes, the view occasionally obscured by drift clouds of dust. Pudong was the world's largest building site, transformed by foreign capital and a small army of rural migrants, equipped with nothing but bamboo hats.[8]

The clang of construction also resonated in the heart of Shanghai, with luxury hotels and office buildings rising high above traditional terraced houses in the French Concession. Some celebrated firms that had once been household names returned to Shanghai, including the Wing On department store and Jardine Matheson. On the Bund and beyond, chrome and smoked glass conquered the colonial buildings with their quaint stone façades from the inside out. In modern hotels, dark wood, gilded chandeliers and wall-to-wall mirrors replaced clunky furniture and velvet curtains. Further afield, in the suburbs, luxury residential estates with tennis courts and sprinklers on manicured lawns sprang up right next to the paddy fields.[9]

Pudong was a special project, earmarked by the men at the helm in Beijing. But every town, city and province wanted its share of foreign investment. Less than a month after Li Peng gave the Pudong Industrial Zone his seal of approval, party secretaries in all major coastal cities went on the offensive, offering all sorts of concessions to foreign investors. Delegations from Zhuhai, Guangzhou, Xiamen, Fuzhou, Shantou and Wenzhou went to Hong Kong. They also eyed Taiwan, with investors from the island offered tax exemption for ten years and other preferential policies. Ningbo, to the south-east of Shanghai, boldly announced a sixty-square-kilometre industrial zone with fifty-year land leases for foreign investors. Further north, officials in Tianjin and Dalian pleaded with Beijing for the right to set up their own development zones.[10]

Economic sanctions from abroad, combined with the regime's own policy of retrenchment, kept the trend in check. In the wake of Deng Xiaoping's southern tour, the number of development zones nonetheless exploded. In 1991 there were around 117 nationwide; by the end of 1992 over 8,700, many established without central approval, vied for attention. If government investment were to develop every zone, as Zhu Rongji calculated on the back of an envelope, the total cost would be at least 4.5 trillion yuan.[11]

On offer was land, something even the poorest town could claim. The formula was reasonably straightforward: lease land in exchange for capital to develop infrastructure. A total of 2.2 million square kilometres, equivalent in acreage to roughly 500 cities, was reportedly leased at a cost of over 50 billion yuan, a mere fraction of which went into the state coffers.[12]

Since the country was socialist, and the means of production belonged to the state, the rules determining who could represent the state that owned the land, who could loan it, who would rent it and to whom capital would accrue, were exceptionally vague. Usually, the state was represented by the local government, which assigned the right to use land to state enterprises or state institutions. These institutional users in turn entered the market and sold the land. Since a great many state institutions always existed in a socialist state, the number of institutional users claiming a stake and trying their luck in developing real estate mushroomed. Universities, hospitals, enterprises, but also every conceivable government department at every level of a sprawling state bureaucracy tried to establish real-estate arms.[13]

In the least sophisticated cases, farming land was simply requisitioned and left idle, as development funds were squandered on banquets, cars and prestige buildings. At the other end of the spectrum, on Hainan Island, in 1992 the Japanese company Kumagai Gumi was given the right to develop a zone of thirty square kilometres into a free port. Yangpu, a barren strip of land where only cactus took to the soil, would be the city of the future. The company was granted the right to transfer land rights to local and foreign investors. Instead of developing a port, it sold the land to some 20,000 real estate companies that sprang up on the island, equivalent to one for every eighty local people. Prices went through the roof, reaching a peak of 3,500 yuan per square metre before they collapsed, leaving hundreds of unfinished buildings and 30 billion yuan in debt.[14]

The island was the envy of developers across the country. Similar schemes appeared everywhere. In Zhenyuan, a poverty-stricken county in Gansu province, more was built in two years than in the first three decades of socialism, with extensive marketing on local television, radio and even mobile trucks. As the provincial party committee observed, the wealth that nominally belonged to the state was 'slipping into the hands of a few individuals'.[15] Nationwide, over 110 billion yuan were invested in real estate in 1993, more than double the previous year. Another 160 billion followed in 1994. The State Council deplored that golf courses and luxury hotels proliferated even as housing for ordinary people was torn down.[16]

Since local governments controlled local banks, the latter tended to grant strategic advantages to their own local enterprises. If the state banks refused to provide further credit, cities and provinces could strike out boldly on their own, raising funds on international capital markets. Party secretaries honed their social skills, seeking to lure foreign capitalists with plush investment offices, thick red carpets, eager smiles and attractive brochures. They treated foreign bankers and executives like communist royalty, putting them up in luxury hotels and driving them around in limousines, with police cars opening the procession and shooing traffic out of the way with megaphones. In 1992 some 40,000 foreign-funded projects were approved. Foreign investors pledged over $57 billion, four times the sum reported in 1991 and an amount exceeding the total promised since 1979. In 1993, investment in fixed assets by state enterprises increased in turn by 70 per cent, while investment by local governments soared by 80 per cent.[17]

The numbers were impressive, but could be deceptive. Much domestic capital masqueraded as foreign investment, as billions were smuggled across the border into Hong Kong, where shell companies funnelled the money back into fake joint ventures designed to take advantage of tax concessions. By some estimates as much as two-thirds of foreign investment actually came from China itself. Milton Friedman, for one, was unimpressed, pointing out that the taxpayer had to foot the bill for every special privilege granted to foreign investors in development zones. He described Pudong as a 'Potemkin village built for a reigning emperor'.[18]

Hong Kong played another important financial role: its stock exchange was used to raise money for state enterprises. In 1990, China did not possess functioning bond and stock markets. From 1981 onwards, the state had begun to issue bonds to finance its fiscal deficit, which it could not meet just by collecting taxes. These bonds, however, resembled forced loans rather than securities: state enterprises were obliged to buy them according to quotas set by the central government at interest rates fixed by the central bank. No secondary market existed, meaning there could be no trade in securities. Bonds were sold every year, with additional construction bonds issued from 1987 onwards. The purchase of treasury bonds was also mandatory for households, although individuals received an interest rate slightly higher than state enterprises did. In 1989, for instance, an ordinary worker could see six weeks of income commandeered for the mandatory purchase of a bond.[19]

Since the central government controlled the bonds, it could restructure them whenever it was unable to meet its obligations. This occurred in 1990, when over 24 billion yuan in bonds issued since 1981 reached maturity and the state issued over 9 billion in new bonds instead, rolling over its debt with another batch of 7 billion in 1991.[20]

Since 1982 some state enterprises had also been allowed to issue shares, although these had little in common with their counterparts in a normal economy. Effectively, they resembled bonds, carrying no ownership rights, offering a minimum annual rate of return and also bearing a maturity date.

In 1988, when inflation soared and banks were ordered to curtail lending, state enterprises tried to sell their bond portfolios to market speculators, often at steep discounts, disregarding government injunctions against a secondary market. In 1989 and 1990, an entirely unregulated, over-the-counter market in bonds and shares sprang into existence. It was, in the words of one financial historian, the country's first and only true market for equity and debt capital, and lasted for no more than two years.[21]

In order to rein in the unofficial market, in December 1990 and July 1991 respectively, stock exchanges were opened in Shenzhen and Shanghai. They allowed state regulators to control the trading environment, managing both prices and investors in a way that suited the government's own interests. Trading in a limited range of treasury bonds, corporate bonds and enterprise shares was permitted, with restrictions remaining in place for other types of securities, including financial bonds and conversion bonds. One year later, listed companies were for the first time allowed to issue so-called 'B' shares, limited to foreign investors. Better still, in June 1993 selected state enterprises could issue 'H' shares in Hong Kong, offering investor protections unavailable for 'B' shares. Tsingtao Beer entered history by becoming the first mainland company to list in the crown colony, raising funds that were fully convertible in foreign currency. Within months others followed, although none but the beer company enjoyed any international brand recognition. This marked the beginning of the country's Initial Public Offering fever, with more than HKD8 billion raised before the end of the year.[22]

Whether fuelled by direct foreign investment, sales of real estate or capital raised on stock exchanges, the economy boomed. The entire country seemed like a vast building site, with bamboo scaffolding rising in every major city from strips of land gashed by bulldozers. A whole new world began to take shape amid the old one, with luxury hotels, soaring skyscrapers and modern office buildings standing next to open sewers, rutted roads and shantytowns.

As money poured in along the coast, exports of inexpensive toys, shoes and clothes leaped. Foreign companies were also keen to take advantage of cheap labour, unfettered by cumbersome labour rights or independent unions. Automobile companies – Ford, Volkswagen, Peugeot – produced over a million vehicles, a 50 per cent increase from 1991. Others began to manufacture for the outside world, with Nike exporting 2 million sneakers in 1992 alone.[23]

With so much cash sloshing around, imports surged, from luxury chocolates, electric pianos, shampoo and tampons to whirlpool baths. To foreign sellers it looked like a dream come true, a giant market finally waking from its slumber. In the very heart of Shanghai, Huaihai Middle Road, once called Avenue Joffre, glittered with neon signs, its new shopping malls offering every conceivable designer label. Avon attracted 18,000 local 'Avon ladies' to sell their cosmetics.[24]

Imports of commodities, from aluminium, copper, nickel, cobalt, steel and timber to cement, also soared. Prices, inevitably, rose. In parts of Sichuan, cement prices increased from 200 yuan to as much as 900 yuan a tonne. Outside the gates of one cement factory, a queue of trucks stretched for five kilometres. In Shenzhen, some developers sourced steel and cement from provinces in the north over 2,000 kilometres away. Nationwide, according to one estimate, the cost of cement jumped by 40 per cent, steel by as much as 90 per cent.[25]

Growth in 1992 was 12 per cent, but inflation was also running in double digits. In May 1993, accountants in Beijing dutifully recorded an annualised rate of 19.5 per cent, but shoppers insisted it was closer to 30 or 40 per cent.[26]

Two timely changes the regime introduced reinforced this trend. In spring 1993 most remaining vestiges of food rationing were scrapped and price controls on grain, meat, eggs, cooking oil and other items gradually lifted, meaning that the urban population had to pay higher market prices. The system of fixed prices for coal and other raw materials was also phased out, although the state maintained its grip on production and distribution. Finally, the dual price system, or at least its greatest part, belonged to the past.[27]

Government restrictions on swap centres, which had long served as a means to allow state enterprises to exchange part of the foreign currency they earned among themselves, were also lifted, sparking even greater demand for foreign currency, and therefore leading to further depreciation of the yuan. China had three rates: an official one fixed by the central bank at 5.7 yuan to the dollar; an administered rate for swap centres that was 25 per cent lower, reserved for state enterprises and state banks; and a third rate, the black market, the only one determined by supply and demand. The hope was that an expansion of the swap markets would mean the three would converge.[28]

The exact opposite happened. By the end of May 1993 the dollar was trading at nearly ten yuan on both the swap market and the black market. People realised that with a plunging yuan, purchasing foreign currency was a better hedge against inflation than the miserable rate paid for savings by state banks. In a buying spree reminiscent of the summer of 1988, some consumers turned to jewellery, stocked up on household electrical appliances or bought foreign brand-name goods.[29]

Since wage increases ran ahead of inflation, most urban consumers grumbled but carried on, aware that their living standards were rising. The people left behind were the 900 million villagers in the countryside. In a further example of déjà vu, money earmarked to pay farmers for their produce was diverted away to construction projects. By October 1992, grain-purchasing agents had only 17 per cent of the over 60 billion yuan required to meet contracts for the autumn harvest, forcing local authorities to issue promissory notes once again. To add insult to injury, when villagers tried to cash postal orders sent home by migrant workers, local post offices also issued IOUs. The central bank intervened, injecting more emergency loans into the countryside. One month earlier it had unavailingly banned IOUs, sternly and with equally little effect once more condemning their use one year later.[30]

Villagers were marginalised in other ways, with the terms of trade against them constantly widening by more than 5 per cent every year. The cost of inputs rose as the value of their outputs fell. Higher incomes were eradicated by inflation, but also by hidden taxes, liberally levied by local officials in search of income, supposedly to finance public services, though much of the cash went straight into their pockets. Rural enterprises that had fuelled growth in the countryside in the early 1980s closed down by the million after 1989, as resources were funnelled instead towards larger state enterprises in the cities.[31]

As unemployment in the countryside continued rising, growing numbers joined a mobile army of migrant workers. In front of many railway stations in major cities along the coast, thousands of shabbily dressed people with bales and bundles could be seen sitting on vast concrete plazas, huddling together in small groups, the din of their chatter filling the air. Some held signs advertising their skills. These were new arrivals, lured from inland provinces by novel opportunities offered by economic growth. Many borrowed enough money to buy a ticket and showed up with little more than the clothes on their backs. They were the fuel behind the boom, working on building sites for $2 to $4 a day. It was not only their low wages that made them so attractive. They had no right of free assembly, let alone the right to strike. They did not even have the right of abode in the city. They could be hired and fired at will, shifted around by the tens of thousands, their temporary shacks razed when required. Foreigners were impressed, seeing none of the shantytowns that blotted the cityscapes in so many other developing countries.

***

Yang Shangkun, the country's head of state and keen supporter of greater economic reform, had accompanied Deng Xiaoping on his southern tour. In Zhuhai he waved to hundreds of bystanders, who applauded enthusiastically in return. On the final leg of the tour, he urged leaders in Shanghai to take faster and bolder steps in turning the city into an international trade centre. His half-brother Yang Baibing, general secretary of the powerful Central Military Commission, joined him for the occasion.[32]

As the army's political commissar, Yang Baibing had purged the ranks of officers who had failed to carry out orders three years earlier, replacing them with his own allies. After the southern tour he openly proclaimed his support for the paramount leader's vision, declaring that the military would protect the programme of economic reform.

This caused consternation, since the army was supposed to stay out of politics. A few months later he overplayed his hand, convening a series of secret meetings with military officers to discuss arrangements for Deng Xiaoping's succession. Jiang Zemin rushed to the patriarch's residence, demanding that Yang be stripped of all his positions for engaging in factional politics. Both brothers were demoted in September 1992.[33]

Jiang Zemin emerged from the incident as the undisputed successor of the paramount leader, the holder of supreme power. A few weeks later, as some 2,000 delegates at the Fourteenth Party Congress stuffed their giant red sheets into ballot boxes in the Great Hall of the People, nearly half of the 300-odd members of the Central Committee were replaced. Many outspoken critics of economic reform were voted out. At the end of the largely ceremonial gathering, a frail Deng Xiaoping walked onto the stage, supported by his daughter. The patriarch posed for pictures as the delegates applauded. Then he turned towards Jiang Zemin, standing by his side, and issued his blessing: 'The congress was a great success.'[34]

More changes followed in quick succession. The Central Advisory Commission, packed with elderly leaders grumbling about economic reform, was disbanded. Its chair, the patron of central planners Chen Yun, would not appear in public again.[35]

Jiang Zemin, the rotund engineer with his owlish spectacles, viewed by some colleagues as an insipid technocrat, showed his mettle, using his enhanced status to remove over one thousand military leaders, the most extensive reshuffle of the army since 1949. In a raft of new appointments, he also installed his allies across the propaganda machine and the security apparatus.[36]

Many new appointees came from Shanghai, the general secretary's power base. Among them was Zhu Rongji, promoted to the Standing Committee. After Li Peng suffered a heart attack in April 1993, Zhu took control of economic policy. He immediately found himself buried in an avalanche of telegrams from local banks that were dangerously close to defaulting on deposits.[37]

Jiang Zemin and Zhu Rongji responded to the consequences of the boom unleashed by the patriarch's southern tour with a programme of economic retrenchment eerily similar to the past austerity measures taken by more conservative planners under Chen Yun. A familiar

scenario unfolded in June 1993: infrastructure projects were cut and
the money supply curbed. Lending came to a halt as suddenly as it had
begun in January 1992. The banks were told to recoup tens of billions
of yuan in state loans that had been funnelled towards unauthorised
investment. To ensure compliance, Zhu Rongji sacked Li Guixian, the
director of the People's Bank of China, and took over his position.[38]

Over a thousand development zones were foreclosed and one-third
of the rogue loans collected. Deprived of a steady flow of money, production came to a virtual standstill in factories across the north-eastern
industrial belt and in parts of the manufacturing coast. The scourge
of triangular debt returned with a vengeance. Some state enterprises
found themselves hard pressed to pay their workers. Even in the relatively wealthy province of Jiangsu, 200,000 workers lost their jobs.[39]

Compared to the retrenchment programme launched in September
1988, the austerity measures also encountered much greater resistance
from local governments and state enterprises. Zhu Rongji complained
that the 'rectification teams' he sent to twenty-odd provinces and
cities were welcomed with open 'sabotage'. Guangdong, it transpired,
returned a mere 40 per cent of all the funds it owed to the central
bank.[40]

Unlike his predecessors, Zhu had to compromise, watering down
his austerity measures, extending a deadline for collecting bad debts
and printing yet more money. He sounded resolute before the cameras,
but was weak on the ground. At heart he faced a dilemma that would
bedevil the regime for two decades to come. Deng Xiaoping, on his
southern tour, had proposed that capitalist tools would be safe in
socialist hands. But there was a contradiction in his vision of reform,
one that betrayed his ignorance of basic economic laws. A central
bank in a political system based on the separation of powers had
major financial tools at its disposal, namely interest rates and bank
deposit ratios, whereas in a socialist system the banks belonged to the
state. Following successive waves of decentralisation after 1979, local
banks responded to neither the market nor the plan: they followed
orders from the local party secretary. Despite incessant injunctions
from the central authorities, neither market discipline nor party discipline existed. Since the regime had no intention of abandoning its
hold upon the means of production, including capital, there was only
one solution, namely to wrench power back from local fiefdoms and

impose discipline from above. A strongman willing to purge, slash, burn and punish on a scale vast enough to bring every local leader to heel was required. As one local banker put it, 'What this country needs is an enlightened Mao.'[41] But such a figure was still decades away. Jiang Zemin had neither the will nor the means to fill this role.

One way to whip the regions into line was to get them to deliver more tax revenues to the central treasury. Under the contract system, the precise share of taxes to be remitted was negotiated between local governments and the central authorities, with the ratio perpetually falling. On 1 January 1994, after the failed retrenchment programme, Zhu Rongji revamped the tax system instead, separating national taxes from the local tax service. He also introduced standardised ratios, taking away discretionary powers from local governments and further centralising tax collection.

This was a bitter pill for the provinces to swallow. To mitigate widespread resistance, Zhu Rongji had to accept several concessions, including large central tax refunds for three years, to ensure that local income would not fall below the level reached in 1993, meaning that for several years the central share continued to fall. Overall, however, tax collection increased. Local governments displayed renewed zeal in collecting as much revenue as possible, since this raised the baseline of their retained revenue as well as the size of the refunds the central authorities were committed to paying them.[42]

On the exact same day the new tax system was introduced, the inter-enterprise swap and official exchange rates were merged at 8.70 to the dollar, representing a 33 per cent fall in the official value of the yuan.[43] Like the fiscal overhaul, the move of the currency towards greater convertibility was part of an effort to qualify the country for membership in the General Agreement on Tariffs and Trade (GATT), the precursor of the World Trade Organization. Under GATT rules, members could not discriminate among their trading partners, making entry the equivalent of a permanent Most Favoured Nation status across a whole series of countries with potentially huge markets. Among the pre-conditions for joining GATT was a similar trade regime among all members, including currency convertibility, market access, a transparent legal system, protection of intellectual property and removal of non-trade barriers.

Since the People's Republic was committed to a socialist system of public ownership over the means of production and a monopoly over power – capitalist tools in socialist hands, as Deng Xiaoping had phrased it – such a level playing field was never on the table. But Zhu Rongji's fiscal and currency reforms had the desired effect, creating the impression that the regime was systematically dismantling the plan and moving towards the market. The term 'transition', almost never used before 1993, became popular among foreign experts. As a senior adviser to Bill Clinton explained, China was in a transitional stage, switching from a planned economy to a market economy, meaning its entry into GATT was 'highly desirable'. It was better to have China inside the world trade system than outside, explained Peter Sutherland, the director-general of GATT, who was keen on integrating the country on his watch. Most of all, foreign companies saw a giant untapped market about to open up, with vast future profits beckoning. They wanted more of it, not less.[44]

One effect of bringing the yuan down to a level more in tune with demand was that the 1993 foreign trade deficit of $12.2 billion became a surplus of $5.4 billion in 1994. But as external capital of $30.5 billion flowed in, creating an excess supply of foreign currency, the yuan began to appreciate on the black market, falling from 8.70 to 8.44 to the dollar. For the first time, the People's Bank of China intervened to prevent further appreciation by withdrawing foreign currency from circulation. It marked a key moment in the fiscal history of China, as foreign currency reserves began to increase, rising to $77.9 billion by January 1996. More would follow over the next two decades, reaching several trillion by 2015.[45]

The fiscal and banking reforms looked promising on paper but were immediately sidetracked, as inflation ousted them as the regime's main priority. To prevent the yuan from gaining in value, more money had to be printed to absorb the dollars in the market. In the first quarter of 1995, the currency in circulation stood at 727 billion yuan, an increase of 24.4 per cent over the same period the previous year.[46] As money was churned out, inflation soared, reaching 24 per cent in July 1994, more than double the official target, with cadres from the Statistics Bureau putting the figure at 25 to 30 per cent.[47]

Since a steady supply of yuan was also essential to keep thousands of state enterprises afloat, tightening up credit was a politically fraught task. Zhu Rongji also encountered resistance when trying to impose a lower development rate on booming areas along the coast and inland along the Yangtze. The economic tsar, together with Li Peng, made numerous largely unheeded speeches replete with calls to the regions to observe the 'requirements of the overall situation'. Orders to the industrialised provinces to devote more land to rice and wheat in order to reduce food prices also received a lukewarm response. Price ceilings returned but were widely ignored, except by state shops selling goods that few people wanted to buy.[48]

In June 1995, after two years at the helm of the central bank, Zhu Rongji stepped down, although he remained vice-premier. He had succeeded in reining in inflation from 24 to just under 20 per cent. It was a laudable performance, but one achieved at the expense of fiscal and banking reform, leaving triangular debt rampant and a banking system riddled with bad loans. The money supply had continued to grow by over 20 per cent annually. Plans to create a new commercial banking sector were shunted aside. Rather than moving towards greater independence, the central bank had become the vice-premier personal jurisdiction. Zhu handed the position of next governor of the People's Bank of China to Dai Xianglong, his protégé.[49]

Reform of state enterprises was also put on ice. In 1994 the losses of the state sector amounted to 4.8 billion yuan a month. Some 70 per cent of the nation's factories were unable to pay their employees on a regular basis.[50] Promissory notes were used not only for basic salaries, but also for medical and overtime benefits. Employees in moribund enterprises were sometimes sent home on reduced salaries, or compensated for their labour with unsold factory products. Combined with double-digit inflation, the result was urban poverty on a scale unknown for over a decade. A fully employed clerk working in the general office of one of Beijing's knitting factories, for instance, earned 300 yuan a month, twice the threshold level for absolute poverty. But she could barely make ends meet, struggling to buy essentials, fuel, rice, oil and salt.[51]

Conditions outside the capital were far worse. Industrial unrest was rife, with more than 10,000 incidents registered by the authorities in 1994, from sit-ins to public rallies. In the coal-mining town of Jixi in Heilongjiang province alone, tens of thousands of workers repeatedly went on strike. Beijing feared the mounting unrest. By the early months of 1995, government calls to restructure state enterprises fell silent, with the need for social stability stressed instead.[52]

***

A key tool for imposing the will of the centre was the fight against corruption. Since one-party states did not have an independent judicial system or a free press fed by journalists keen to track down the merest whiff of fraud, corruption was the norm. Chairman Mao had initiated the first campaign against graft inside the ranks of the party a mere two years after liberation, with special squads hunting so-called 'tigers', or party officials who had embezzled large sums of money, as opposed to more trivial suspects, described as mere 'flies'. Similar campaigns unfolded with striking regularity, from the 'Three Anti Campaign' of 1951 and the 'Socialist Education Campaign' of 1963 to the 'One Strike and Three Antis' of 1971, among others. They had two advantages. Since every party member was in one way or another corrupt, they provided a convenient cover for political purges. They were also generally welcomed by the population at large, whether people genuinely believed that the regime was cleaning up its act or whether they merely derived some satisfaction from watching party members tear each other apart.

Under Deng Xiaoping a clampdown on corruption had punctuated the political landscape every three to four years. Yet as the central government devolved greater power to local governments in a bid to stimulate the economy, opportunities for corruption multiplied. Villages, towns, cities, counties and entire provinces became more protective of their own economies, erecting barriers to prevent competition. They became fiefdoms, or 'independent kingdoms' in the parlance of the Communist Party, run by local strongmen or tightly knit groups of trusted associates.

From top to bottom, senior party officials exploited their position to allocate the right to trade, whether in capital, raw resources, energy, land or real estate. Corruption ran the gamut from distributing a more productive plot of land to a farmer in exchange for a gift to sharing in the windfall generated by developing a shopping mall or flipping a piece of land leased for a mere pittance from the state. Additional capital generated more corruption, but most of all high demand for capital in the absence of a capital market created endless opportunities for representatives of the state, who controlled the loans made by the banks.

The higher the position, the greater the opportunity to skim off a share of the cream. During the democracy movement, students had targeted the sons and daughters of the most powerful leaders, seeing them as symbols of the nepotism spawned by a system that placed all power in the hands of a single party. In January 1989, Deng Xiaoping's eldest son had been forced to withdraw from a trading company after it was found to have reaped enormous commissions on imported goods. But after June the Fourth, his other children, like the off-spring of most leaders, continued to forge business deals and lucrative partnerships. Deng's youngest son worked as the chief executive of a Hong Kong subsidiary of the powerful Capital Iron and Steel Works. His youngest daughter was the figurehead of a real estate company based in Shenzhen.[53] The family of the paramount leader was far from an exception. According to one estimate, in 1993 the relatives of 1,700 party leaders controlled 3,100 of the country's top jobs. Another 900 family members ran the country's major trading companies. As Li Rui confided to his diary, public property was their property.[54]

On 25 February 1995, a dozen prominent intellectuals presented a petition to the National People's Congress demanding an independent investigation into corruption within the ranks of the leadership. Corruption, 'in the form of trading power for money', the document explained, was the principal affliction causing public resentment. It was a bold move, as the petitioners viewed the establishment of a constitutional democracy with independent legislative and judicial branches as the only permanent solution. Among the signatories was Wang Ruoshui, the deputy editor of the *People's Daily* who had been sacked in 1983 for publishing an editorial on humanism. Another was Liu Xiaobo, the writer and trenchant critic of the regime's trampling of civil liberties. Rarely since the massacre had a group of such distinction spoken out publicly. Their protest was prompted by the detention of Wei Jingsheng, author of the Fifth Modernisation, who had only just been released from his fifteen-year sentence and had met with John Shattuck, the US State Department's human rights official.[55]

Like so many others, the petition would normally have ended in the dustbin. But its timing was fortunate, coming five days after

Zhou Guanwu, the powerful chairman of the giant Capital Iron and Steel Works, was forced to resign, with his son, who headed the corporation's subsidiary in Hong Kong, dragged from his chauffeured Mercedes-Benz and placed under arrest. The whole affair, notwithstanding years of close connection to the business interests of Deng Xiaoping's family, sent a warning signal to foreign investors and party officials alike. The paramount leader was fading away, the first shot in a battle to inherit his mantle fired. The stock index in Hong Kong dropped by 4.8 per cent.[56]

On 4 April, a bright spring day, vice-mayor of Beijing Wang Baosen left his chauffeur-driven car near a wooded area north-west of the capital, walked up a hillside to smoke a last cigarette and then shot himself in the head, in one of the most sensational scandals to hit the country in decades. Wang was scheduled to meet with investigators from the Central Commission for Disciplinary Inspection, the party's disciplinary watchdog. A few months later they completed their report, charging that he had lived a 'depraved life' that included 'pleasure seeking' in villas and luxury hotel suites. As the main official responsible for the municipal planning committee, he had enjoyed ample opportunities to siphon off millions of yuan. He had reserved one villa in a luxury development for himself, a pale yellow house with a grand staircase leading to a doorway flanked by white marble columns. Half of the money he obtained under the table was lost in business ventures gone awry. The other half he had shared with his younger brother, his mistress and his associates.[57]

One of these turned out to be Chen Xitong, the capital's party secretary. Within weeks he was forced to take responsibility and tender his resignation. A subsequent investigation discovered that he had helped his underling defraud more than 220 million yuan in public funds from the city for an investment scheme in Hong Kong. He, too, had pursued a 'dissolute lifestyle', acquiring several luxury villas in which to throw lavish parties and entertain his mistresses. Wang was posthumously expelled from the party, and Chen sentenced to sixteen years in prison. Work teams arrested dozens of other officials in the capital, encouraging them to denounce each other in order to save themselves. Several were executed, others sacked or disciplined.[58]

Jiang Zemin had struck boldly and decisively, using the corruption drive to consolidate his own status and undermine his rivals. He had bagged a big tiger, and put others on notice. In Guizhou, an impoverished province in the south-east, the top party official was dismissed, his wife executed. Li Peng, sent off to Moscow in May on a state visit, looked even more glum than usual.[59]

A few months later, at a conclave of the party congress, the new helmsman turned upside down the paramount leader's motto on the importance of the economy. Instead of 'more talk about economics, less talk about politics', he sternly invoked the need to 'emphasise politics'. 'Political work is the lifeline of all economic work,' he intoned. Jiang Zemin's opening address was entitled 'On the Correct Handling of the Twelve Major Relations', a direct reference to Chairman Mao's 'On the Ten Major Relations'. Jiang posed as the new philosopher-king, a visionary who had successfully synthesised economic reform with Marxist orthodoxy. The message was unmistakable: the state should control the market, while anything outside the state would merely serve the socialist economy. The boom was over, reform deferred. Central planning was back in fashion.[60]

The plenum ensured the general secretary's supremacy, with several of his protégés promoted to key positions. Since most of them hailed from Shanghai, they were popularly dubbed the Shanghai Faction. One member was a young political theorist from Fudan University who had been among the most vocal opponents of the 1989 democracy movement.[61] A bookish, reticent figure with a poker face and wire-rimmed glasses, he had made a name for himself a few years later with a publication entitled 'America Against America'. Following a well-established Marxist tradition, the book announced the imminent demise of capitalism. Wang Huning, now head of the Political Affairs Division at the mere age of forty, was responsible for penning the slogans behind Jiang Zemin's speech.[62] He would become the party's leading theoretician, the mastermind behind the ideological banner of every successive leader. He was the new Deng Liqun, taking over where the doctrinaire ideologist who had spent a lifetime railing against capitalism had left off.

***

Less than ten kilometres from the Fujian coast, an island fortress of rock and iron rises from the sea. Quemoy, like Matsu to the north, is an offshore island belonging to Taiwan. For decades both islands were the frontline along the Taiwan Strait, reinforced with bunkers, forts, pillarboxes, machine-gun posts and thousands of troops. In 1954 and again in 1958, artillery units on the mainland shelled the islands, trying to dislodge the troops deployed from Taiwan, more than 150 kilometres to the east. On 23 August 1958 alone, during the Second Taiwan Strait Crisis, tens of thousands of shells were fired, prompting the Eisenhower administration to reinforce the US Seventh Fleet in the South China Sea. Heavy shelling alternated with patriotic appeals for reunification. These, too, failed to win over the renegade island.

The tone changed after Taipei lost China's United Nations seat to Beijing in 1971 and the United States moved towards a rapprochement with the People's Republic. In 1974, in comments made to foreign visitors, Deng Xiaoping flatly refused to rule out the right to use force to recover Taiwan, although he was willing to give prior consideration to peaceful reunification. He pointed to Tibet as an example of the gradual integration that would follow once Taiwan had been fully liberated. He also warned Taipei against declaring independence. He repeated his threat in 1982, even as he dangled the idea of 'one country, two systems' as the solution towards bringing the island back into the embrace of the motherland. In 1985, general secretary Hu Yaobang openly envisaged military intervention once the Four Modernisations had resulted in a more powerful army, pointing out that the United States was the main obstacle to uniting the motherland.[63]

The standoff continued, even as Taiwan moved steadily towards democracy. An opposition party, the Democratic Progressive Party, emerged in 1986. Martial law was ended, restrictions on travel lifted and a free press tolerated. Even though the state nominally controlled television for a few more years, the authorities ignored a widespread if illegal cable system that included a 'democracy channel'.[64] Trade across the Taiwan Strait soared. In Quemoy, fish and meat instead of hot shrapnel came from the mainland. Tourists from Taiwan arrived in 1993, as fears of invasion subsided. Instead of blasting propaganda across the waters, the loudspeakers on Quemoy belted out the love ballads of Teresa Teng.[65]

People in Taiwan were not only freer, but also wealthier than ever before. In 1992 their average income was higher than that of Spaniards and Greeks, let alone Poles or Czechs. International investment poured in, making the island the thirteenth largest trader in the world, slightly ahead of China. Highways, railroads, subways, sewage systems, all the infrastructure so badly neglected by the Nationalists began to attract vast amounts of funds. Some also went to modernising the army, including fighter jets, frigates and anti-aircraft missiles acquired from France and the United States.[66]

But Jiang Zemin had nothing new to offer. Like his predecessor, he rigidly insisted on complete sovereignty over the defiant island: 'one nation, one state, one central government'. And, like his predecessor, he did not rule out military force, alternating verbal intimidation and sabre rattling with saccharine messages of goodwill and appeals to patriotism.[67] Subtle it was not. Like many other committed party members, Jiang was in a hurry: socialism meant unification, and they wanted to see it in their own lifetimes.

In May 1994 President Lee Teng-hui requested permission to stay overnight in Hawaii as his plane had to refuel on the way home from a visit to Central America. It was the first visit by a president of the Republic of China since the United States had severed diplomatic relations in 1979, recognising the People's Republic of China instead. Terrified of the consequences of allowing the elected head of an exuberant new democracy to set foot on American soil, the Clinton administration allowed Lee's plane to spend a mere two hours on the tarmac, forcing him to stay on board. Congress protested. Under pressure, President Bill Clinton relented and one year later allowed Lee to speak at his alma mater, Cornell University, provided the occasion be handled as a private visit. Jiang Zemin was livid, threatening that the United States would 'pay the price.'[68]

On 9 June 1995, from his lectern at Cornell University, Lee called on the United States to free his country from diplomatic isolation. 'We are here to stay,' he declared defiantly. His four-day visit was a rousing success. He placed a request for $192 million of fighter air-craft parts, leaving Jiang Zemin apoplectic, accusing the United States of scheming to split China.[69]

Six guided missiles were fired off the coast of Taiwan in July, followed by a second round in August. Another warning came in November, as thousands of soldiers stormed a beach, backed by an array of fighter jets, destroyers, submarines and landing craft. The venue was in Fujian, not far from Quemoy and Matzu, but the message was clear enough. Jiang Zemin watched in rapt admiration on board a command ship. At the end of the military exercise he congratulated the troops: 'Hello, comrades!' he beamed, 'You are certainly working hard!'[70]

More missiles were fired in March 1996. Six years earlier, thousands of students had demonstrated in favour of direct elections, occupying Memorial Square (later renamed Liberty Square) in the centre of Taipei. Speakers wearing protest headbands gave speeches in favour of democracy. A few demonstrators desecrated Chiang Kai-shek's memorial with spray-painted slogans. Some went on hunger strike. Lee Teng-hui, elected as the sole candidate of the Nationalist Party by 641 elderly members of the National Assembly, welcomed a student delegation in the Presidential Building and promised full elections. He stood by his word, as voters went to the ballot box for the first time to elect their president on 23 March 1996. Jiang Zemin, fearful that democracy would lead the island down the road towards independence, made sure the shells landed inside the island's territorial waters, less than 50 kilometres from the coastline. His scaremongering backfired badly. On election day, disgruntled voters increased Lee's majority in Parliament by a comfortable margin.[71]

The Third Taiwan Strait crisis prompted President Clinton to send two aircraft carriers to international waters near Taiwan. After the United States had recognised the People's Republic of China in 1979, it had abrogated the Mutual Defense Treaty with Taiwan but passed instead the Taiwan Relations Act, setting the terms for a non-diplomatic yet substantial relationship. The act was designed both to dissuade Taipei from declaring independence, but also to discourage Beijing from unilaterally annexing the island. Diplomats called it a policy of 'strategic ambiguity'. The goal of the policy was to gain time. Washington hoped that China would gradually moderate its views and make reunification more acceptable to the people of Taiwan. It proved a false hope. As the leaders in Beijing indicated repeatedly, liberation of the renegade province was but a matter of tonnage and timing.

Beijing was equally consistent when it came to the Paracel and Spratly islands, two disputed archipelagos of several hundred small coral islets, sandbanks and reefs in the South China Sea, located in the middle of strategic shipping lanes, off the coasts of China, Vietnam, the Philippines and Malaysia, that had been occupied by the

Japanese during the Second World War. A complicated patchwork of claims followed the end of the war, although both China and Taiwan asserted their title to all of the islands in uncompromising terms. In 1972, following Nixon and Kissinger's visit to China, Beijing tested Washington by protesting the intrusion of American vessels in the Paracels. Henry Kissinger did not contest their claim, instructing ships and aircraft to keep a distance of at least 12 nautical miles from the islands. He also sent ambassador Winston Lord to smooth over the incident, asking him to reassure his counterpart in Beijing that there was 'no policy he believed in more than improving relations with the People's Republic of China'.[72]

One year later, after the Paris Peace Accords effectively removed the United States from the Vietnam War, Saigon reduced its troops on the islands it held in the Paracels. The United States also scaled down the presence of the Seventh Fleet in the South China Sea. Fighting between the north and the south in Vietnam resumed almost immediately. Beijing used the opportunity to capture all of the Paracels, sending four warships, two submarine chasers and aircraft as well as amphibious troops from Hainan. Saigon's request for assistance from the Seventh Fleet was ignored.[73] China had used the appropriate tonnage at the appropriate time.

The Spratlys were further away than the Paracels, although there too both diplomatic and military activity never ceased. In February 1992, Beijing went one step further by passing legislation claiming complete sovereignty over the South China Sea, right up to the shores of Sarawak. The timing was fortunate. Most observers, in Southeast Asia and beyond, found it difficult to take the claim seriously, and were busy courting access to the country's huge market in the wake of Deng Xiaoping's southern tour. But three years later, Filipino fishermen discovered that the Chinese Navy had built fortified bunkers on Mischief Reef, an island less than 200 kilometres west of the Philippines yet more than a thousand kilometres from China. When Manila sent a ship with reporters on board to observe the occupation of the reef, Beijing described the excursion as a 'serious encroachment of China's sovereignty'. Even as missiles were lobbed across the Taiwan Strait, China's suave foreign minister Qian Qichen shuttled around Southeast Asia, professing his country's desire for a peaceful international environment. It was a policy of 'calculated ambiguity', as security analyst Robert A. Manning put it.[74] It consisted in proclaiming one thing but brazenly doing the opposite, not unlike the notion of doublespeak developed by George Orwell.

***

Along the southern banks of the Yangtze, a few hours away from Shanghai, Zhangjiagang greeted travellers with a big banner stretched across the road: 'Welcome to Zhangjiagang, the Most Sanitational City in China'. The thriving port city was a vision of the future, laid out with great geometrical precision. Its immaculate buildings, surrounded by landscaped shrubbery and red azaleas, were set back from a grid of broad avenues lined by fragrant camphor trees. Heavy bronze statues of workers reaching for the sky appeared at major intersections, while coloured spotlights illuminated an immaculately clean shopping street from which all traffic was banned. An army of street sweepers kept the city in pristine condition. Smoking, spitting and littering were strictly prohibited, with fines handed out liberally by city workers lurking on street corners. Hundreds of banners exhorted the residents to 'Be a Model Citizen' and 'Strictly Abide by the Regulations'. In this Orwellian paradise, officials did not hesitate to carry out unannounced inspections of private homes to check that they were clean. In classrooms, sweeping cameras monitored students from the back. It was a stark contrast to the noisy, chaotic, overcrowded cities elsewhere. Unlike boomtowns like Shenzhen, there was no gambling, no prostitution, no swearing and almost no crime. The cars even stopped at red lights.[75]

Zhangjiagang was a socialist utopia, a model to be emulated in a nationwide campaign aimed at combining both a 'spiritual civilisation' and a 'material civilisation'. 'To Be Rich Is Glorious' was the slogan under Deng Xiaoping, but Jiang Zemin aimed to redress the emphasis on material pursuits alone, putting his weight behind a return to the core values of orthodox socialism. People should not only get rich, but also be virtuous.

Most of all, much as Mao had his Dazhai and Deng promoted Shenzhen, Zhangjiagang was Jiang's own showcase. Every day thousands from all corners of the country flocked to the mecca of 'spiritual civilisation'. Dozens of editorials in the official media lauded the virtues of the city, as well as the wisdom and vision of its patron. In

Dalian, a port in the north, mayor Bo Xilai, son of Bo Yibo, took the lead, clearing slums, doubling the amount of green space and issuing fines to people found littering, spitting or swearing. Students were sent to Marxist study groups.[76]

With the drive for 'spiritual civilisation' came a renewed attack on anything smacking of foreign culture, reminiscent of the campaigns against spiritual pollution in 1983 and 1985. 'We must strictly ban the cultural trash poisoning the people,' Jiang intoned on 24 January 1996, lecturing the nation in a khaki Mao jacket before the state cameras. The *Liberation Army Daily*, a few weeks later, quoted directly from Chairman Mao on the dangers of 'blindly learning from and indiscriminately copying' things foreign.[77]

Even as missiles were fired across the Taiwan Strait, the nation was put on high alert against subversion by 'hostile foreign forces'. Foreign ideas and names were portrayed as signs of neo-imperialism, incompatible with the demands of 'spiritual civilisation'. Across the nation, from Xiamen to Chongqing, signs with foreign names were taken off hotels, restaurants and cinemas. In the capital alone, according to the local authorities, colonial or feudal names were removed from 263 streets, 34 commercial centres, 27 tourist attractions and no fewer than 23,873 company names.[78]

Young people were enjoined to avoid McDonald's, KFC and Coca-Cola. Hemlines, once again, came down, as did high heels, also seen to be inspired by decadent capitalist values. Mickey Mouse became the object of a concerted attack, with the general secretary determined to drive him from the minds of children and adults alike. A new cartoon character, Soccer Boy, appeared in his stead, a young footballer whose obedience, hard work and devotion had propelled him all the way to the national team. Lei Feng, a more familiar figure, reappeared, with cities and provinces instructed by Beijing to select a proletarian paragon inspired by the soldier model. In Shanghai, plumber Xu Hu became the hero of the day, extolled for his devotion to unblocking pipes at no expense in his spare time.[79]

The attack on all things foreign went hand in hand with new restrictions imposed on foreign brands. In December 1995, the State Council circulated a report lambasting capitalists for their attempt to conquer the domestic market. They advertised their goods everywhere, on television, radio and newspapers. They sold at a loss in order to establish a monopoly. They behaved like bullies, driving out or incorporating local brands. They refused to hand over their technology. Coca-Cola withheld its recipe. 'Our economy will be colonised,' the report noted, 'our socialist market economy will soon be without a market.' The leaders realised that even with capitalist tools in socialist hands, their economy would collapse the moment it was opened to real market competition.[80]

Foreign capital was still welcomed with open arms, but even more restrictions were imposed to protect local industries. As the vice-minister for foreign trade put it, 'If we set no restrictions on domestic sales, then foreigners can set up all kinds of industrial projects in China and conquer the whole market.'[81]

Financial news provided by foreign agencies was curbed. The Propaganda Department also introduced a moratorium on new magazines, radio programmes and television stations. Restrictions were imposed not only on foreign films, but also on the production of films with foreigners. Several widely admired directors, including Chen Kaige (*Farewell My Concubine*) and Zhang Yimou (*Raise the Red Lantern*), were accused of 'betraying history' and cut off from their links abroad. Popular authors who strayed from the party line to portray the underbelly of the country's rush towards growth, including Wang Shuo and Mo Yan, were taken to task by the official media, their outlets blocked. As Wang Shuo explained, 'their first target of attack is film, then TV, then novels, step by step.'[82]

Dissidents, too, were silenced once more. Liu Xiaobo, who had signed the daring petition against corruption presented to the National People's Congress, was initially arrested and sent back to his parents in Dalian following more than seven months in custody without charge. But once he issued a statement asking the regime to honour a promise it had made in 1945 to protect the freedoms of religion, press and speech, the authorities had a change of heart and sentenced him without trial to three years in a labour camp. Wang Dan, the student leader released on parole in 1993, was condemned to eleven years for 'conspiring to overthrow the party'.[83]

The Strike Hard campaign was revived. In Beijing the paramilitary raided brothels and backyard casinos. People, once again, were asked to snitch on each other. Across the nation, from Dalian to Shenzhen, crowds watched as drug traffickers and other criminals were tied up, shackled and paraded around before being shot in the back of the head.[84]

While novels by controversial writers vanished, books on Jiang Zemin Thought appeared in the bookshops, for the most part controlled by the state. They came with a picture of the general secretary's portly figure on the cover, his hair neatly slicked back. The country's newspapers were filled with reports of his activities, whether he was mingling with peasants, inspecting factories or meeting foreign dignitaries.[85]

On 1 January 1997, for twelve consecutive evenings, national television showed a documentary on the life of Deng Xiaoping. *I Am a Son of the Chinese People* glorified the paramount leader, not seen in public for almost three years. The documentary, viewed by an estimated 224 million people, showed a vigorous leader against a background of golden clouds radiating across the sky. But his southern tour, which had triggered a scramble five years earlier, was barely mentioned. His contribution to building 'spiritual civilisation' was lauded instead. Jiang Zemin, who now controlled the image of his predecessor, personally narrated parts of the documentary. Towards the end of the series, the general secretary appeared on the screen, hailing the paramount leader as an 'outstanding Marxist and a stalwart communist'.[86]

Deng's final gift to Jiang came on the evening of 19 February, when he died at the age of 92 from complications of Parkinson's disease and a lung infection. The timing was auspicious, almost two weeks after the Lunar New Year had been celebrated. On Tiananmen Square, swept by blustery winds, the flag was lowered to half-mast the following day. Police in overcoats patrolled the premises to prevent people from laying wreaths, a precaution that proved unnecessary. One young man approached the square with a floral arrangement, but turned out to be a businessman keen to advertise his flower shop. The death of the paramount leader was met with widespread indifference, although office workers in Shenzhen shed a few tears.[87] It was a measure of his success, not least the peaceful transition of power.

8

Big Is Beautiful (1997–2001)

On 30 June 1997 the union flag at Government House was lowered for the last time to the sound of 'God Save the Queen'. Chris Patten fought back tears in the drizzle. Later that evening, at the official hand-over ceremony inside the newly constructed Hong Kong Convention and Exhibition Centre in Wanchai, a beaming Jiang Zemin strode to the stage to welcome a new dawn. Hong Kong, he announced, had finally returned to the motherland.

The last governor of Hong Kong sailed away later that night on board the Royal Yacht *Britannia*, leaving behind the harbour that had welcomed its first colonial officer in 1842. At dawn, a long convoy of supply trucks and army buses carrying more than 4,000 People's Liberation Army troops crossed the border. They were joined by a dozen armoured personnel carriers, with soldiers in camouflage uniform manning the gun turrets. They had last been seen in action in June 1989. Hundreds of residents waited in the rain to cheer their arrival, a few placing garlands around the necks of leading officers.[1]

Eight years earlier, Jiang Zemin had warned the city against interfering in mainland politics: 'Well water does not mix with river water.' He viewed the crown colony as a subversive base used by foreign hostile forces to undermine the Communist Party. When in October 1989 London had suggested that a new airport be built to instil confidence in the territory's future, Jiang had viewed it as yet another imperialist plot to denude one of its colonies of its assets by handing out lucrative contracts. British prime minister John Major was forced to fly to Beijing and sign a Memorandum of Understanding on the project.[2] The controversy allowed the leadership to achieve its objective, which was to find a way to interfere in every aspect of the territory's affairs. They criticised the budget. They appointed a group of personal advisers who undercut the legislative council and encroached on the role of the government. They suggested that reliable candidates for top government jobs should be hand-picked and groomed. In public they preached stability and prosperity, in private they were rigid. When, in September 1991, a coalition of pro-democracy candidates won a landslide victory in the colony's legislative elections, they expressed their outrage at the outcome to London.[3]

Instead of appeasing his counterparts in Beijing, in October 1992 the newly appointed governor Chris Patten responded to a widespread desire for greater popular representation by proposing that the electoral base for the legislature should be expanded. It enraged Beijing, where the reform package was viewed as a plot to subvert the territory's political system. At first every effort was made to force the governor to retract his proposals, including dire warnings of economic warfare. Then, after the official government gazette published the proposed reforms in March 1993, a carefully orchestrated campaign was unleashed to cover the governor in invective. Li Peng fired the opening shot, telling delegates at the National People's Congress that Patten had 'perfidiously and unilaterally' violated all previous agreements. Lu Ping, the regime's voice in Hong Kong, followed suit a few days later, calling the governor a 'sinner of a thousand years'. The People's Daily described him as a 'small thief in the market place', others a 'serpent', a 'tango dancer' and a 'whore of the East'.[4]

What the regime dreaded, of course, was that the colony could be seen as a model for reform at home. The real fear was political activists who pushed for better representation in Beijing. As Li Peng pointed out at the National People's Congress, dictatorship by the Communist Party remained 'essential'.[5] Weeks earlier, the regime had vetoed a liberal thinker of the China Writers' Association who had been nominated by her home province to become a member of the Political Consultative Conference.[6] She was hardly alone. Yang Zhou, who had organised a 'democracy salon' in Shanghai, sent a letter to the National People's Congress asking that the Four Cardinal Principles be dropped from the constitution. In Beijing, a poll of 1,660 students was publicised, showing that the majority were critical of the Communist Party and demanded the opening of more channels for political participation.[7] In

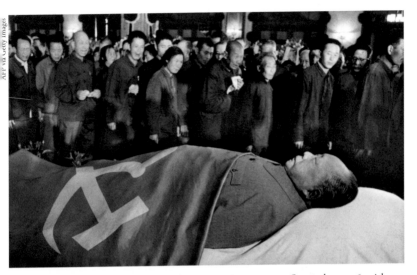

Photo officially released by the New China News Agency on 12 September 1976, with the following caption: 'Peasants from Peking's outskirts, with boundless profound proletarian feelings, paying respects to the remains of the most esteemed and beloved leader Chairman Mao Zedong'.

Hua Guofeng on the rostrum in Tiananmen Square during a rally celebrating his elevation to the post of Chairman of the Chinese Communist Party, followed by Ye Jianying and Li Xiannian, October 1976.

Deng Xiaoping, late 1970s.

A crowd reading handwritten posters at the Democracy Wall in Beijing, February 1979.

Hu Yaobang and Deng Xiaoping in Beijing, 1 September 1981.

Premier Zhao Ziyang during a press conference at the Japan National Press Club in Tokyo, 2 June 1982.

Jiang Qing (Madame Mao) in the dock during sentencing at the trial of the Gang of Four, 25 January 1981.

Peddlers in Guilin, Guangxi, 1982.

A cobbler in Dazu, Sichuan, 1986.

Deng Xiaoping meets Margaret Thatcher in Beijing, 24 September 1982.

Students place flowers and wreaths in front of a portrait of former Chinese Communist Party leader Hu Yaobang at the foot of the Monument to the People's Heroes in Tiananmen Square during an unauthorised demonstration, April 1989.

Soldiers keep demonstrators away from the official memorial for Hu Yaobang at the Great Hall of the People, 22 April 1989.

The Goddess of Democracy, standing tall amidst a huge crowd of demonstrators in front of the Mao Zedong portrait in Tiananmen Square, 1 June 1989.

中华人民共和国万岁

The army confronts the people on Chang'an Avenue, Tiananmen Square, 4 June 1989.

People scrambling for cover along Chang'an Avenue, 4 June 1989.

Walking through Chang'an Avenue, 5 June 1989.

Tanks guarding a key intersection in Beijing, June 1989.

Deng Xiaoping congratulates Jiang Zemin at the end of the Fourteenth Party Congress in Beijing, October 1992.

Migrant construction workers from the countryside in a cramped dormitory, 1995.

New apartment buildings, contrasting with the rudimentary shacks used by the poor, Shanghai, 1994.

Soldiers of the People's Liberation Army cross the border into Hong Kong on the first day of the transfer of sovereignty over the territory from London to Beijing, 1 July 1997.

An abandoned state factory in Shenyang, Liaoning, November 2001.

Job seekers, from electricians and carpenters to painters, in Xuzhou, Jiangsu, June 2002.

Jiang Zemin (second on the right) together with Hu Jintao (on the left), Zhu Rongji (second from the left) and Li Peng, celebrating the 50th anniversary of Communist rule, Beijing, October 1999.

Workers making trainers at a Nike factory, February 2004.

A cotton factory in Shihezi, Xinjiang, October 2005.

An officer admires a statue of Lei Feng during a ceremony to mark the upcoming annual Lei Feng Day in Shenyang, Liaoning, 3 March 2005.

A well-to-do couple poses for the photographer, Shanghai, 2004.

Workers adjust newly installed surveillance cameras on Tiananmen Square ahead of National Day in Beijing, September 2005.

A young boy carefully crosses a heavily polluted stream surrounded by rubbish outside his family's old courtyard house in Beijing, February 2000.

Street vendors sell counterfeit watches and fake luxury brand wallets outside a department store in Shanghai, May 2007.

Thorbjørn Jagland, Chairman of the Nobel Committee, looks at the vacant chair reserved for the Nobel Peace Prize laureate, Liu Xiaobo, in Oslo, Norway, December 2010.

fact, Chris Patten even had his share of supporters across the border from Hong Kong. In Guangdong, as former provincial party secretary Ren Zhongyi pointed out, many party cadres quietly approved the governor's plan for electoral reform, as they followed the saga on satellite television.[8]

The governor's proposals were passed, despite last-ditch efforts by Lu Ping to lobby legislators to abstain or vote against.[9] In September 1994, the pro-democracy camp achieved a landslide victory. In March 1995, the Democratic Party won 23 of the 59 seats for municipal elections. In response to Patten's reforms, Beijing created its own working committee in July 1993, which in turn established a selection committee responsible for identifying the first Chief Executive and members of a Provisional Legislative Council. On 1 July 1997, even as several thousand protesters gathered outside the colonnaded legislative building to protest the takeover, the Provisional Legislative Council replaced the elected Legislative Council, reversed most of the electoral reforms, reintroduced corporate voting and further narrowed the franchise. For good measure the council also introduced new restrictions on demonstrations and other civil liberties. The police were magnanimous, allowing the protesters to disperse.[10]

***

On 2 July, the day after the handover, a beleaguered government in Thailand was forced to float its currency, unable to maintain the peg to the dollar. The baht plunged in value, raising the repayment costs for many local companies with debt denominated in foreign currencies. The collapse of the baht was known locally as the Tom Yam Kung crisis, after the popular hot and sour shrimp soup. But capital flight created a chain reaction, leading to a slump in the currencies of other countries in the region. Within weeks the Malaysian ringgit and the Philippine peso were devalued. Then the Indonesian currency and the South Korean won came under pressure, falling to record lows against the dollar.

It marked the end of what had been known as the 'Asian economic miracle'. For several years the economies of Southeast Asia had experienced high growth rates. They also maintained high interest rates, attracting speculative flows of foreign money that dramatically increased the ratio of foreign debt to gross domestic production.

When the Federal Reserve Bank under Alan Greenspan began raising interest rates on the dollar to head off inflation, the United States became a more attractive investment destination instead. Not only did the flow of money reverse, but a higher dollar also increased the cost of exports for countries in Southeast Asia with currencies pegged to the dollar. As the crisis unfolded in the first half of 1998, currency markets around the world became increasingly risk averse, avoiding emerging markets. In Russia the economy collapsed, forcing a massive devaluation of the ruble. So devastating was the meltdown that the International Monetary Fund had to intervene with several rescue packages worth $40 billion.

China appeared almost impervious to the crisis. It was relatively insulated from capital flight, since the yuan was not convertible on the open market. The yuan had already undergone several steep devaluations between 1989 and 1994, weakening from 3.71 to 8.70 to the dollar. As investment flowed in, creating an excess of foreign currency, the central bank had started to intervene from 1994 onwards to prevent the yuan from appreciating on the black market, strengthening from 8.70 towards 8.44 to the dollar. In 1997, the central bank spent an average of $100 million per day to keep the yuan at the level of 8.30.[11]

The country's incipient stock markets, moreover, were for the most part off-limits to foreigners. Most of all, unlike the flow of hot money into bonds and securities in Southeast Asia, the bulk of foreign investment had gone into factories and real estate, which were much harder to pick up and move elsewhere.

Still, much of the economy depended on exports, and these were badly hit. Even before the crisis, the unrestrained growth of consumer industries, endlessly churning out commodities for which there was no demand, had contributed to an inventory glut. By the end of 1996, an astounding volume of goods languished in government warehouses, including 16 million televisions, 20 million bicycles, 1.3 billion shirts, 10 million watches, a quarter of a million automobiles and 70 per cent of the output of the country's 3,000 cosmetics factories. The goods were worth 64 billion yuan, representing about one-fifth of total production, or roughly 2 per cent of growth. These were the official figures given to foreign journalists, but according to Li Rui, the real amount was around twice as much, with 120 billion in goods occupying some 68 million square metres of storage space. High levels of foreign investment and cheap credit had left the country with over-capacity in almost every major industry. By one estimate, the average factory across the country used less than 60 per cent of its capacity.[12]

Overcapacity pushed down domestic prices, but also fuelled ever cheaper exports overseas. In 1996 China flooded Southeast Asia with cut-price exports, severely crimping their export-driven economies. Even as exports to Thailand, Malaysia, the Philippines and Indonesia surged, these countries experienced sinking export prices and trade deficits. In Thailand, intense competition with China led to a decline of 2 per cent in 1996, compared to growth of more than 20 per cent in each of the previous two years. This was one reason for the attack on the baht.[13]

With the onset of the crisis, more unsold goods were piled up in warehouses, as exports slowed down dramatically in 1997. Prices fell for four consecutive months, with unsold inventory growing faster than the economy, at an annual rate of 11.7 per cent. Among others were a glass glut, due to excessive production, a fertiliser glut, due to excessive imports, a cotton glut, due to excessive procurement prices, a steel glut, due to excessive loans, and an office glut, due to excessive building. Pudong, city of the future, suffered from a glut of real estate. One of the most surreal spectacles was probably a glut of new department stores. In 1992, Beijing only had fifteen major department stores, but by the summer of 1998 it boasted more than seventy, with plans for as many again to open in the next two years. Most were losing money. All slashed prices, offering vouchers, discounts and gift certificates.[14] They presented a scenario that would become familiar across the country for decades to come: gigantic malls of glass and marble with more staff than customers. In order to stimulate domestic production, the central government pumped money into the economy in the first half of 1998, ordering banks to make more loans to state enterprises. The broad monetary supply by the end of July was 15 per cent higher than a year earlier, with massive loans earmarked for state enterprises, resulting in even more output that could not be sold.[15]

For the first time since 1986, negative inflation was officially reported in the last quarter of 1997. In a vortex of falling prices, deflation spread further in the first half of 1998, with prices slipping across the board, from goods and services to the rental and housing market. By the summer, in cities like Shanghai and Qingdao, prices had slumped year on year by 6.5 to 8.4 per cent. According to official figures, in the first half of 1998, growth fell to 7 per cent. Deflation continued for several years, reaching 29 months by March 2000, the longest such spell in the country's modern history.[16]

From oil to fertiliser and metals, commodity prices were particularly vulnerable. Just as heavy industry and hundreds of small steel mills had undergone expensive refitting and renovation programmes, burdening them with heavy loans, the price of pig iron, the base material for all steel products, crashed. Even as domestic demand for everything from cement to cars was slowing in summer 1998, inexpensive goods from East Asia poured into the country. Goods from South Korea led the pack after a sharp plunge in the value of the won against the yuan, although Japan, too, increased its competitive edge. Imports of steel were below the local cost of production, forcing major steel corporations to cut exports by half. The very survival of tens of thousands of factories across the country, from steel mills to cement makers, was at stake.[17]

Deflation raised the appeal of a devaluation, even though Zhu Rongji was adamantly set against tampering with the value of the yuan, appearing in public time and again to reaffirm his country's commitment to maintaining the official exchange rate at roughly 8.30 to the dollar. Even as he spoke, a black market not seen in several years sprang back to life. Touts could be seen loitering outside banks or hanging around luxury hotels, offering 3 per cent above the official rate. They were merely the visible signs of capital flight, fuelled by fear of deflation. Since the yuan had never been convertible, over the years state banks and state enterprises had honed their expertise in circumventing capital controls. Many did not hesitate to falsify letters of credit or import documents to transfer hard currency abroad. According to Dai Xianglong, governor of the People's Bank of China, an audit revealed that in the year following the onset of the Asian financial crisis, more than 2,000 enterprises were 'colluding with outside forces' to export sums amounting to some $6 billion outside approved channels. Wen Jiabao, a mild-tempered and conciliatory geologist brought to Beijing by Hu Yaobang in the early 1980s to serve on the Central Committee, was elevated to vice-premier and put in charge of the Central Financial Work Commission by Zhu Rongji.

The vice-premier's answer to the outflow was to issue a flurry of rules and regulations against foreign currency transactions in July 1998.[18]

More notices, measures, directives, rules and regulations followed, clashing with existing edicts, some of which had been in place for many years. The result was confusion on the ground as well as even greater fear of a future devaluation. State enterprises became even more desperate to get their money across the border. Despite increasingly large trade surpluses with Europe and the United States, foreign reserves stalled at the $145 billion mark, with huge sums shifting abroad. Old scams were fine-tuned and new ones devised, including massive prepayments in hard currency, fictitious deals and dummy contracts. One common ploy was to apply dutifully to the State Administration of Foreign Exchange for a forex allocation. Once permission was granted and the money had left the country, no deal actually took place. The main players were provincial banks in collusion with local industries. The biggest loophole in the system was Hong Kong. While the red flag fluttered in the wind above the legislative council, there was very little that the mainland could do to affect the activities of the territory's banks, finance houses and companies without creating a political outcry.[19]

A campaign against contraband also began in July 1998. For years rampant and deeply entrenched smuggling had been tolerated, not least because, according to Jiang Zemin himself, the worst offenders were party leaders and army officials. It surged during the financial crisis, accounting for roughly 5 per cent of imports, thereby contributing to capital outflow. The contraband involved both foreign and local products, including billions of yuan worth of consumer goods. Many cigarette producers, for instance, exported more than half their output, only to smuggle the cigarettes back into the country to avoid both domestic and import duties.[20]

Despite the economic slump, China appeared like a bastion of stability in the midst of the Asian financial crisis. For most foreign visitors, the only sign of economic distress was the disappearance of Russian traders. Since the collapse of the Soviet Union, they had been ubiquitous in Silk Alley and other informal markets, buying up clothes and household goods in bulk to resell back home in Irkutsk, Khabarovsk, Vladivostok or Moscow. Russian stores and restaurants were scattered around Ritan Park, just north of the old diplomatic district. Once the ruble was devalued, the traders vanished overnight, their individual businesses ruined.[21]

The leadership did all it could to maintain a façade of stability, and was extremely sensitive to any suggestion that the crisis was buffeting the country. When the Royal Bank of Canada decided to close its Shanghai branch, Zhu Rongji personally telephoned the Canadian ambassador to plead against the decision, worried that the outside world might interpret it as a vote of no confidence in the local economy.[22]

Image was everything. But underneath an impression of invulnerability, the crisis exacerbated two problems: bankrupt industry and an insolvent banking system.

Well before the crisis began, state enterprises were in dire straits, with reform repeatedly postponed. In 1996, according to economist Wang Jikuan, they had at most assets of 4 trillion yuan, but debts of 3.2 trillion yuan, meaning a debt ratio of at least 80 per cent. Had these enterprises been able to grow on debt by finding an efficient way to use the money, the ratio might not have been an issue, but year after year the trend was lower profitability. The crisis made it worse. According to Zhu Rongji, in the first quarter of 1997 a combined total of 42,000 state enterprises had squeezed out a miserable profit of 3.37 billion yuan (meaning a return of 0.1 per cent on their loans), which became a collective loss of more than 11 billion one year later. The spread was wide, with more than 56 per cent unable to turn a profit. This was the balance sheet after more than twenty years of reform and untold amounts of credit, not to mention warehouses packed with unsold goods.[23]

China's financial system was fragile. Lending rose, year after year. Loans had two main purposes, to keep the state enterprises afloat and to achieve the magic growth target set by Deng Xiaoping many years earlier. Foreign experts believed that before 1997, some 24 per cent of all outstanding credit consisted of bad loans, a figure that increased to 29 per cent after the crisis, above the estimates for Southeast Asia. But Southeast Asia, besides currencies that were convertible, had something else lacking in China: transparency. In reality non-performing loans were closer to 40 per cent, although no one, not even Dai Xianglong, who headed the People's Bank of China, knew just how much debt was hiding in the system.[24]

This became clear as one local bank after the other turned to the central government for help. In Zhejiang province, just two urban credit cooperatives had accumulated deficits of 12 million yuan. In Ningbo, three trusts had a black hole of 3.4 billion yuan, while the municipality's rural credit cooperatives were unable to meet 836 million yuan in debt payments. In Wenzhou, an investigation of twenty lenders revealed that one-third of all their loans, totalling 200 million yuan, had to be written off. In Dai Xianglong's words, defusing the debt crisis of small and medium fiscal institutions was like 'tenaciously holding on to all positions while fighting a flood'.[25]

These debts were denominated in yuan, a problem easily solved by printing more money, but even the arrears in payments on loans made by foreign governments were so substantial that as early as November 1997 the State Council sounded the alarm, remonstrating that failure to pay interest created a 'bad impression' and affected the country's international reputation. In Zhejiang, a province with a mere 1.2 per cent share of foreign government loans, 40 per cent of these were in arrears, amounting to $50 million.[26]

The true size of the crisis only became apparent in late 1998, when a provincial trust and investment corporation folded. In 1979, with the help of Rong Yiren, an industrialist who had decided to stay behind in 1949 and throw in his lot with the Communist Party, a China International Trust and Investment Corporation, known as CITIC, had been established. Its purpose was to promote the Four Modernisations by attracting foreign capital and advanced technology. Within a few years, hundreds of similar financial vehicles had mushroomed across the country, set up by local governments keen to attract their share of foreign capital. When the State Council decided to intervene in 1982, roughly 620 vied for attention. Fujian had its FITIC, Guangdong its GITIC, Hainan its HITIC, Zhejiang its ZITIC, Shanghai its SITIC and Dalian its DITIC, although the country rapidly exhausted convenient acronyms and had to use the full place name (Shenzhen SITIC or SZ SITIC). Ten years later, after it became clear that most had established subsidiaries across the country to conduct unauthorised transactions and collect deposits with higher interest rates than those offered by the state banks, additional restrictions were introduced. Hundreds managed to survive, thriving in the wave of real-estate speculation unleashed by Deng Xiaoping's southern tour of 1992. Three years later, to mitigate the risk of systemic collapse, all links with commercial banks, their major source of funding, had to be severed, bringing several liquidations and mergers.[27]

Many of the survivors had gleaming office towers with shopping arcades and luxury hotels to advertise their services. In Guangzhou, the provincial Guangdong International Trade and Investment Corporation boasted a GITIC Plaza, not to be confused with the CITIC Plaza, a few kilometres to the east, and the largest concrete building in the world until Donald Trump built his tower in Chicago. As the investment arm of Guangdong province, by 1997 GITIC had expanded into an enterprise group with over 200 subsidiaries.

By contrast with other countries, TICs and ITICs in China basically performed the role of commercial banks for local governments, although they were not closely regulated and were therefore prone to mismanagement. Even before the financial crisis unfolded, it became apparent that the country's third largest investment trust company, CADTIC, the China Agribusiness Development Trust and Investment Corporation, was little more than a pyramid scheme offering high interest rates, sugar smuggling, property speculation and tax evasion. It was closed down in January 1997, and its senior executives arrested for embezzlement, with debts estimated at over 10 billion yuan.[28]

The case spurred renewed scrutiny of China's hundreds of financial institutions. In the following year, as the crisis battered investment trusts, the central bank was forced to intervene in a 'considerable number' of other cases.[29] But the biggest shock came in October 1998, when the liquidators moved into GITIC, the second largest investment trust company, widely believed to be unassailable since it was the investment arm of the wealthiest and most powerful province in China. Its total debts were over $2.5 billion. Rumours began circulating that the country's commercial banks were technically bankrupt.

In the wake of GITIC's implosion, hundreds of other trust companies, plus thousands of urban and rural credit cooperatives across China, were closed. Zhu Rongji used the opportunity to restructure the banking system, bringing control of the four state banks back into the hands of the central government. He recapitalised these banks with 270 billion yuan, a huge amount equivalent to roughly 100 per cent of the total government bonds issued for that year, 25 per cent of foreign reserves and 4 per cent of gross domestic production. He did so by reducing the deposit-reserve ratio from 13 to 8 per cent, in effect taking the required funds from deposits belonging for the most part to ordinary people. The Ministry of Finance paid the banks 7.2 per cent on the 270 billion yuan raised to buy the bonds, while the banks in turn paid the Ministry of Finance 7.2 per cent interest on the 270 billion yuan loan used to increase their capital. As money moved from one pocket to another, the 93 billion yuan used to write off bad loans now nominally rested with the ministry. The next step taken in 1999 was to create four so-called asset management companies, or 'bad banks', tasked with holding the distressed debt, each tethered to a state bank. More bonds were issued to capitalise these asset management companies, with majority ownership resting with the Ministry of Finance. The hope was that by replacing one set of non-performing assets with another, the issue could be deferred well into the future. When the ten-year bonds for the asset management companies came to maturity in 2009, they were postponed for a further ten years.[30]

The crisis also forced the leadership to tackle state enterprises. For several years, plans had been floated to groom potential winners and transform them into huge conglomerates capable of competing on the global stage, while allowing loss-making enterprises to sink. In late 1989, Yao Yilin had suggested fostering a hundred behemoths, starving all others of state resources.[31] The State Commission for Restructuring the Economy relaunched the idea of a hundred national champions in December 1993, but the leadership repeatedly shelved plans for reform, fearful of the social unrest that a wave of unemployment might spark.[32] The Asian financial crisis left them with a stark choice, namely reform or ruin.

In September 1997 Jiang Zemin pledged to break the back of the structural woes plaguing the state sector. Addressing the Fifteenth Party Congress, he summed up the party's new policy: 'Grasp the Big and Let Go of the Small.' The equivalent of 'big is beautiful,' it meant getting rid of thousands of small and inefficient factories and instead grooming industrial giants, in much the same way as South Korea had fostered its chaebols. Instead of allowing entrepreneurial zeal to come to the fore, the party believed that its bureaucrats in the capital could pick future winners and use massive inputs from the state to steer them to great heights. This was, in short, a plan for more, not less, state intervention.[33]

The message to state enterprises was simple: expand or expire. The bureaucrats in Beijing hand-picked enterprises they deemed the best and biggest, showering them with preferential loans, development funds and other forms of state support. In exchange, the winners were expected to take over some ailing state factories and become globally competitive conglomerates. 'Guide Bankruptcies and Encourage Mergers' was the slogan of the Fifteenth Party Congress, as the state saddled its more advanced companies with bloated enterprises in a string of mergers and takeovers.[34]

By January 1998, the central government had selected its first batch of 512 state enterprises designed for expansion into conglomerates. Although they represented a mere handful of candidates from the state sector, they accounted for almost half of its total assets. Industrial giants merged almost overnight, as several thousand pharmaceutical manufacturers, television makers, cotton mills, cement factories, petrochemical plants and even regional airlines were incorporated through mergers and acquisitions. Capital Iron and Steel Works in Beijing was one, the Shanghai Automotive Industry Corporation, maker of the Santana car, another. The ministries that controlled state enterprises, including coal, machine-building, metallurgy, light industry, textiles and petrochemicals were downgraded, placing the conglomerates directly under the control of the Ministry of Finance and the People's Bank of China. A new body, the Central Working Committee of Large-Scale Enterprises, established to enhance control, held the purse strings, deciding which enterprises should merge and which should be liquidated.[35]

At the heart of the wave of mergers was a shift from state ownership to shareholding. New conglomerates and old state enterprises alike were allowed to corporatise and issue shares, raising money from the domestic market. Yet even here the hand of the state was visible, as either the company itself or the government held the controlling stake of such shares. As Jiang Zemin explained at the Fifteenth Party Congress, shareholding was not the same as privatisation.[36]

The flagship conglomerates were listed abroad. In 1993 a limited number of state enterprises had begun to raise capital overseas through initial public offerings. China soon ran out of suitable candidates since few had any international recognition, let alone the scale and profitability required to attract international capital.

The trend changed in October 1997, when China Telecom, one of the behemoths cobbled together by merging and consolidating a string of provincial companies, was listed in both Hong Kong and New York. The initial public offering raised $4.5 billion, making the state asset the world's fifth-largest telecommunications company. It was not just the size of the deal that took investors by surprise. The lead underwriter was Goldman Sachs, with fees rumoured to be over $200 million.[37]

China Telecom showed the way forward: tackle a fragmented industry by amalgamating small enterprises into a large conglomerate, endow it with a bank account supervised by the central bank, funnel the savings of ordinary people towards it, use foreign financial services to ensure compliance with international finance and corporate law, and sell a small number of highly priced shares on foreign stock markets on the basis of future value. It was a perfect illustration of capitalist tools in socialist hands, since China Telecom remained a subsidiary of the Ministry of Posts and Telecommunications. As the small print in the prospectus pointed out, the ministry could 'elect the entire board of directors' and buy assets 'without the concurrence of minority shareholders'.[38]

More listings abroad followed, as international bankers worked hand in hand with the central government to create a series of blockbuster transactions. In all cases, share prices were based not so much on existing assets but on projected estimates of future profitability. When China Telecom was listed, the six independent companies it incorporated had not yet fully merged. The company existed only on the spreadsheets of Goldman Sachs, although its bank account was very real. By 2001, PetroChina, China Unicom, Sinopec, China National Offshore Oil and the Aluminum Corporation of China had all listed in New York, helped by a small army of investment bankers, equity analysts, corporate lawyers, global sales forces, money managers and economists from international banks. More than fifty were listed in Hong Kong.[39]

At the turn of the millennium, after several years of frantic mergers and liquidations, the central bank conducted a survey to discover what had happened to the credit given to state enterprises, including the new national champions. The result showed that for every three yuan lent by the banks, the enterprises increased their output by two yuan. After a quarter of a century of reform, they simply destroyed one-third of the capital they received. State enterprises continued to account for almost half of gross domestic product in 2000, although their share of tax revenue tumbled from 12 to less than 8 per cent.[40]

***

The mergers incorporated thousands of state enterprises into roughly 500 national champions. Since acquisitions were not supposed to bring layoffs, they were favoured by a regime that was always fearful of social unrest. Still, some new conglomerates circumvented the restrictions, for instance by creating shell companies where surplus staff were paid a nominal wage to stay home. But the real problem was that the country had over a quarter of a million state enterprises, few of which were profitable enough to be merged or turned into share-holding companies, even with the help of the best financial advisers. Many of these likewise sent their workers home on reduced pay, keen to avoid having to fork out severance and welfare benefits.

Tens of thousands of others closed, ironworks, pharmaceutical plants, textile makers, coal mines and steel foundries included. Closures were highest across the north-eastern rust belt, birthplace of the country's heavy industry. In Liaoning province alone, home to one in ten large and medium-sized enterprises, by the end of 1997 more than 5,000 firms had gone bankrupt or suspended production. In Shenyang a seemingly endless vista of vacant lots with barred gates and smashed factory windows stretched across the once vibrant industrial zone, with rusty cranes in the Shenyang Steel Complex standing desolate above railway tracks overgrown with grass.[41] One in ten workers in the city were either unemployed or idle, according to Wu Bangguo, the vice-premier in charge of industry. Nationwide, close to 13 million people were dismissed, 17 per cent of the urban state workers accustomed to the cradle-to-grave welfare system the factories had provided. Less than half found jobs elsewhere.[42]

Many more were laid off or put on reduced pay in subsequent years, with the total estimated at 20 to 30 million, although accurate numbers will never be forthcoming, not least because factory managers were not always permitted to declare bankruptcy and instead suspended production. In some cases the nominal owners sold the state assets and pocketed the money, leaving their workers in the lurch without formally dissolving the enterprise. The state, moreover, only counted people who voluntarily registered as unemployed, which a great many never bothered to do. Most of all, many ways existed whereby a manager could make an enterprise appear profitable in order to sell it or attract foreign investment. Time-honoured traditions were to inflate sales figures through fake subsidiaries, disguise major losses as capital expenditure and adjust the number of workers on paper. Wu Bangguo estimated that roughly 90 per cent of those laid off never set foot in one of the employment centres set up by the government.[43]

One in two had no savings. Those unable to find a new job were sometimes allowed to stay in their drab housing blocks, even as some of the windows were bricked up, but without any of the generous pensions, benefits or free health services that had once made heavy industry so attractive. A few bartered unsold goods or rusty scrap metal filched from the factory, in a pale imitation of the plundering common among less scrupulous factory managers. Others tried to make ends meet by peddling all manner of goods, selling socks, hairclips, cherries, toilet seats or skin cream from a cardboard box on the pavement. Some washed cars, repaired shoes or operated pedicabs. In Shenyang the more intrepid could be seen trying to sell cheap steering-wheel covers to passing motorists.[44]

Urban unemployment was merely the more visible aspect of the problems caused by the expansion of state enterprises after 1978. One key engine of growth had been the village enterprises that had mushroomed in the countryside. There were many millions of them, and they had provided up to 40 per cent of the country's national output. In terms of ownership they dwelled in a grey zone, sponsored by town and village governments, but more often than not run like private enterprises. Yet by the time the financial crisis unfolded, they replicated all the problems associated with their urban counterparts: crushing debt, shoddy products, backward technology, huge inventories of unsold goods, poor management and fragmented production. As Yao Yugen, head of the provincial economic committee in Gansu province, observed, a strict isomorphism existed between village enterprises and state enterprises, meaning that their murky ownership structures mirrored each other. Village enterprises complemented state enterprises, exploiting the gap between the plan and the market. 'Seen from a historical perspective, there would not have been any township and village enterprises without state-owned enterprises.' They helped the market, but were also held back by the plan.[45] Most of all, like state enterprises, they had become heavily dependent on credit from local banks. Consequently, there were countless ceramic tile factories, frog farms or mattress plants in the countryside, much as state enterprises duplicated cement plants, steel works and bicycle factories in cities across the nation.[46]

A great many were not only inefficient and riddled with debt, but also dangerous. One reason they had grown so quickly was that they had happily ignored all rules on health and safety, let alone pollution. This was true of small coal mines operated by village teams. In the first nine months of 1992, according to a report compiled by the Ministry of Labour, more than 3,800 workers died in small collieries, representing 65 per cent of all deaths in the mining industry.[47] Casualties were higher than the previous year, and kept on soaring. In 1998, after labour activists estimated the number of fatal accidents at more than 10,000, or one an hour, the central government ordered a clampdown and closed over 25,800 pits. Faced with huge oversupply, coal production fell by an estimated 250 million tonnes. This was the village counterpart to the merger of several hundred large urban state coal mines, kept alive by huge government subsidies.[48]

The state ensured that it funnelled its resources away from the villages and towards the large conglomerates. As Jiang Zemin had decreed, 'Grasp the Big and Let Go of the Small.' Two million other village enterprises across a whole range of industries were cut, reducing the number on the books to 20 million. For the first time in twenty years, village enterprises ceased soaking up not just credit from local banks, but also the massive surplus of rural labour. Unemployment soared to 130 million, reaching almost one-third of the countryside's total work force. To make matters worse, the army of migrant workers who sent back remittances to their home villages began to shrink, falling from a peak estimated at 90 million to around 75 million in 1998. Many were returned to the countryside by municipal governments struggling to provide employment for their own residents. Those still clinging to jobs in the factories and building sites strewn along the coast received lower wages. Some were not paid at all.[49]

Unemployment continued to mount. Since village enterprises contributed to the revenue collected by local governments, who had for that same reason sought to keep them afloat with more bank loans regardless of economic efficiency, state income in the countryside collapsed. As the State Council observed in May 1999, some villages made no distinction between politics and business, taking on endless debt regardless of their ability to pay, and then 'wantonly squandering' the funds.[50] With so much investment in failed rural ventures, a great many sank into debt. By 1999 local governments in large swathes of the countryside, especially in central and western regions of China, could no longer pay their employees. Government officials went without wages for months on end. In Gansu province, tax collections in the countryside fell by roughly 14 per cent, while expenses had risen by 5 per cent. The shortfall for government salaries amounted to more than 250 million yuan.[51]

The problem became even more acute in the following two years. Precise figures, as always in a one-party state keen on image but short on facts, were hard to find. Yet by 2001, according to Zhu Rongji, 59 out of 86 counties in Gansu province had not paid the wages of their government officials in full or on time, equivalent to 68 per cent of all counties. In Sichuan – a relatively wealthy province about the size of France – the proportion was 24 per cent. In Inner Mongolia it was 80 per cent, not including 70 per cent of townships and villages lower down the hierarchy. In Jilin, up in the north-eastern rust belt, it was 46 per cent. Theoretically, of course, these numbers could include an underpayment of one yuan, but in 24 counties in Gansu, to give but one example, the shortfall was 6,000 yuan on average for every government official. In July 2001, some 59 counties in the same province were 300 million yuan in arrears. Governance in parts of the countryside was paralysed, as cadres ceased driving cars, making telephone calls or organising meetings. Some localities took out further loans to cover additional debts, owing the banks tens if not hundreds of millions of yuan.[52]

Credit, in the countryside, was in the hands of rural credit unions, also known as rural credit cooperatives. Established in the 1950s to funnel money from the state to the communes, after 1976 they began to provide credit and savings accounts for villagers. They fell under the purview of the Bank of Agriculture, but by 1996 were so heavily indebted that they were transferred to the People's Bank of China.

In the early 1980s the Ministry of Agriculture introduced a second, more informal network, rural cooperative funds. They tended to cater more to ordinary farmers and individual entrepreneurs who often could not obtain loans elsewhere. Their operating costs were low, and they were seen as competing with and attracting rural deposits away from the unions. Like the unions, they suffered from poor management and lax regulatory oversight. In the countryside outside Wenzhou, one of the country's wealthiest areas, some 175 of these funds vied for customers in 1997. One common feature, according to a team of investigators, was 'anarchy in management' and 'political interference', as local cadres resisted outside scrutiny and handed out loans according to their own predilections. 'It is relatively common to have a local government official appointed as the principal manager of the bank.' Even before the onset of the financial crisis, not a few had lent in excess of 120 per cent of their deposits, a situation replicated across the country, and one so dire that in 1999 the People's Bank of China moved to close them all.[53]

The rural credit unions remained the only financial institution in the countryside. After decades of mismanagement, they had negative net assets by the end of 1999, with total losses amounting to 86.2 billion yuan by 2000. They did not care, knowing that the central government would always bail them out. Had they been allowed to fold, as fiscal expert Lynette Ong points out, tens of millions of rural depositors would have lost their savings. They were offered a 165.6-billion-yuan conditional debt-for-bills swap, as the central bank paid the technically bankrupt credit unions the book value of their toxic assets. It was a rubber stamp, but one that came without reform.[54]

By 2004, a detailed study estimated village debt alone at 370 billion yuan, township debt at 215 billion yuan and county debt at 410 billion yuan. Almost everywhere, the contribution of village enterprises to the local economy was negative. After more than twenty years of economic reform, the countryside was in effect bankrupt.[55]

The rural credit unions were bailed out, as were the local governments which had overseen their lending in pursuit of their own interests. When they could no longer pay their own salaries, they copied the central government, turning debt into bonds and extending the initial maturity to a later date.[56]

Another way of raising money when taxes in the countryside declined was to gouge the local population, both individuals and their enterprises. Across the country, local governments imposed a growing number of fees, levies, dues, tolls, excises and contributions, voluntary or otherwise. In the countryside around Lanzhou, Gansu's provincial capital, in summer 1998 an inspection team counted 57 ways of collecting fees from village enterprises, 42 of them illegal. In the entire Jiuquan region, some 300 kilometres north-west of Lanzhou along the old Silk Road, illegal fees represented 30 per cent of the local government's income.[57]

The problem was by no means confined to Gansu. The State Council became so concerned that in 2001 it sent six investigation teams to various provinces. They discovered a world of iniquity, ranging from fees for slaughtering a cow, keeping a horse or building a house to more extravagant demands. Primary schools, for instance, routinely compelled the villagers to pay for electricity and water, but in Qixian county, Henan, they also demanded a fee of three yuan for pupils to use a bicycle rack, one yuan for missing a lesson and three yuan for undergoing a medical examination. In Yunnan province, insurance fees were common, reaching 44 yuan a year. In Qingxu county, Shanxi, there was a wedding fee of nine yuan, which could be hiked to 50 yuan in some villages. In Mulan county, Heilongjiang, a medical examination was required before a wedding certificate could be granted, costing a crushing 500 yuan. Throughout the country there were forced contributions to dubious investment schemes or public services. Each administrative level tried to squeeze the one below, with counties putting pressure on townships, and townships in turn on villages. In Shangyu city, Zhejiang province, each village was charged 4,000 yuan a year for a compulsory subscription to local newspapers. As a traditional proverb had it, 'there are many monks but not much gruel.'[58]

Since ordinary people were at the bottom of this feudal hierarchy, they ultimately bore the brunt. One rough estimate puts the financial burden of these arbitrary fees at about 25 to 30 per cent of their income across China. A higher figure was ventured by Cao Jinqing, a pioneering sociologist who suggested that in parts of the country, villagers paid as much as 40 per cent of their income in illegal fees, with many, in turn, forced to take out more loans from the rural cooperatives.[59]

***

As the financial crisis unfolded, forcing the regime to reform its collective enterprises, one portion of the overall economy, the private sector, actually succeeded in creating jobs. In a marked change of tone, for the first time since 1978 private entrepreneurs were genuinely welcomed rather than grudgingly tolerated and hemmed in with endless rules and regulations. In cities like Shanghai and Qingdao an estimated two out of every three workers laid off by state enterprises found employment in the private sector. If Lei Feng were alive, the *People's Daily* proclaimed in April 1998, he would be a private entrepreneur. One year later, the constitution was amended to upgrade the status of the individual and private 'non-public sectors' of the economy from a mere 'complement' to an 'important component' of the state economy.[60]

The change was largely symbolic. The same constitution barely mentioned the protection of private property, while declaring 'socialist public property' to be 'sacred and inviolable'. Although private entrepreneurs were welcomed, their numbers remained modest. By 1999, after more than twenty years of reform, registered private enterprises employed a mere 32 million people out of an urban workforce of 239 million – according to official figures.[61]

The numbers were low because private entrepreneurs could not compete with the state sector. The tax collectors sent by the state did not grant them equal treatment. Nor did the banks, also run by the state, or the courts, staffed by party loyalists and retired military officials. From top to bottom, every state institution was run by a party secretary who favoured other state institutions, a situation unlikely to change in the future. As party officials were at pains to explain, under no circumstances would the private sector be allowed to grow and overtake the public sector. 'Now we are allowing the private sector to develop a little bit, because for the time being it is good for the state economy. But that does not mean we are moving towards becoming a capitalist society,' one People's Liberation Army delegate explained. 'China is a communist country because it is led by the Communist Party, and that will never change.'[62]

Time and again, every major leader made similar statements, but many foreigners thought they knew better. In 1993 they had stumbled upon the word 'transition' to convey their vision of a country moving from the plan to the market. In September 1997, after Jiang Zemin announced his determination to change the ownership structure of state enterprises, they began to use the term 'privatisation'. On more than one occasion, Jiang Zemin specifically rejected the idea that anything even vaguely comparable to a move from the state sector to the private sector was taking place on his watch. He did so in September 1997, and gave another clear warning after the constitutional amendment was passed in 1999: 'Some people abroad mistakenly believe that China wants to engage in privatisation, and some of our comrades have developed a similar misunderstanding.' When in 1998 Zhu Rongji explained to George H. W. Bush that the corporatisation of large state assets had nothing to do with 'privatisation', but was just another way of consolidating state ownership, the former American president responded with a nudge and a wink, saying, 'we know what is going on.'[63]

The term used in Chinese was 'change of ownership' or 'equity diversification', not privatisation.[64] In fact party officials could barely bring themselves to utter the word 'private', using instead the more common expression 'non-public sector', by which they meant both individual households and private enterprises. In the vast majority of cases of ownership transfer, whether it was the small enterprises dispersed throughout the countryside or the larger factories in the cities, the move towards shareholding entailed no loss of control by the state or its many representatives. The giant conglomerates listed on the New York Stock Exchange such as China Telecom merely sold a minority stake to outsiders, and retained the right to appoint the entire board of directors. The same was true of most enterprises, as villages, townships, counties, regions, provinces, state ministries or other entities representing the Communist Party took over the majority of shares.

Some shares were also sold to employees, an approach which preserved the ideal of collective ownership. But employee buyouts more often than not turned out to be a means for local governments to force workers to lend more money or leave. In many cases, mergers and acquisitions led to a mere change of name and a shuffling of the figures in the account books. The move towards shareholding redistributed the assets rather than improving the overall efficiency of the state sector. The aim of this redistribution was to strengthen the state and save its enterprises by ousting tens of millions of workers who had devoted their lives to them.[65]

***

The number of labour disputes skyrocketed, reaching 120,000 by 1999 according to official figures. Across the country unpaid workers and retirees besieged their factories, blocked roads and picketed local governments to make their demands heard. In a few cases corruption so angered protesters that they rioted in the tens of thousands, burning cars, smashing windows and fighting pitched battles with the police until the army came to the rescue. This happened, for instance, in the mining town of Yangjiazhangzi, Liaoning province.[66]

Most protesters were state enterprise employees thrown out of work, but the police also had to stop some 10,000 teachers from Jilin province flocking to Beijing to petition the central government. People in the countryside occasionally erupted in protest, with thousands rioting in drought-stricken Shandong province for access to drinking water. Across the country, from one end of the spectrum to the other, unrest was rife.[67]

It was a volatile mix, but in most cases protesters dispersed quietly after their point had been made, resilient yet resigned, fully aware that they stood no chance against the implacable machinery of the state. Their right to strike had been removed from the constitution in 1982, and the unions, as befitted a communist party, were state-controlled. Most salient of all, the protests remained scattered, with no attempt to unite and make common cause across China.

While local authorities often avoided a confrontational approach, making promises that could be broken later on, swift justice was meted out to those who pursued political goals. Jiang Zemin demanded repeatedly that security departments across the country 'nip in the bud' any attempt at political opposition. China's political system 'must not be shaken, weakened or discarded at any time. The Western model of politics must never be copied,' he told party officials in the Great Hall of the People in December 1998. 'We must be vigilant against infiltration, subversive activities and separatist activities of international and domestic hostile forces,' he continued, repeating almost word for word his message to the party in the summer of 1989.[68]

Six months earlier, Bill Clinton had visited the country, lavishing praise on his host. Jiang Zemin, the American president told the international press in June 1998, was a visionary figure nudging his country towards greater freedom. Democracy, he continued, would come to China during his lifetime. Foreign observers, too, proclaimed a new era of political openness. A few weeks before the historic visit, in a goodwill gesture, Jiang had traded some of his dissidents, allowing Wei Jingsheng and Wang Dan to be sent into exile to the United States.[69]

On 25 June 1998, the very day the American president arrived in China, a group of political activists tried to register the China Democracy Party in Hangzhou. Within a few months, preparatory committees were established in 23 provinces and major cities, involving hundreds of volunteers in a tightly coordinated campaign that took the regime by surprise. One of the organisers was Xu Wenli, the veteran dissident of the Democracy Wall movement first detained in 1979. He and the others were promptly arrested. On 5 October 1998, the regime signed the International Covenant on Civil and Political Rights, earning more international praise (although it would never ratify it). Even as the country's ambassador put his name to the document in New York, pledging to grant his citizens basic rights and freedoms, the organisers of the China Democracy Party went on trial, with Xu Wenli once again sent away for thirteen years.[70]

Other arrests followed. Shi Binhai, a columnist for the *China Economic Times* on the liberal fringes of the mainstream, was detained. Fang Jue, an entrepreneur and former government official who wrote about political reform without ever suggesting an end to communist rule, was also sentenced to four years in prison. Labour activists received much harsher sentences. Zhang Shanguang earned a ten-year prison sentence for speaking to Radio Free Asia about rural protests. In June 1999, three men who had tried to set up an independent labour watchdog in Gansu province went on trial for subversion.[71]

***

Ten years after Solidarność had taken control of the political scene in Poland, China's leadership was still haunted by a potential alliance between democracy activists and laid-off workers. Yet despite all their vigilance, they were caught off guard by a far more esoteric protest movement. On 25 April 1999, some 10,000 members of a group calling themselves Falun Gong, or 'Wheel of Law', slipped into the capital and surrounded Zhongnanhai, the vermilion-walled compound where the top leaders lived. Many of the protesters were elderly worshippers. They sat or stood in quiet defiance for hours on end in rows of four or five on Chang'an Avenue. The police were restrained, if only because they were outnumbered. The demonstration was peaceful, but shocked the leadership. Mere weeks before the tenth anniversary of the massacre on June the Fourth, they had been ambushed in their own homes, something not even the students had dared to do.[72]

The movement's founder was Li Hongzhi, who taught his followers a set of physical exercises and breathing techniques to help them achieve peace of mind, if not spiritual enlightenment and a place in the afterlife. Foreign observers were as dumbfounded as the public security forces, unable to decide whether this was a sect, a cult or a religion.

Master Li was in exile in New York, but hailed from Changchun, a city in the middle of the industrial rust belt in the north-east. He had founded the movement in 1992, his blend of Buddhist and Taoist ideas and slow martial art exercises attracting a growing number of followers. By 1999 he could boast tens of millions of supporters, both at home and abroad. His organisation mirrored that of the party, filling the ranks with the disillusioned and the disenfranchised, but also with highly educated people reaching all the way into the top Communist Party echelons. One of them, Li Chang, a retired official from the Ministry of Public Security, was like others in charge of a highly disciplined network organised in cells that supervised thousands of followers. When in April a popular magazine in Tianjin warned its readers against what it described as a cult, supporters felt under threat. During their show of force in Beijing, they demanded legal recognition.[73]

When the demonstrators met Zhu Rongji, they suggested that Falun Gong, not communism, could save the nation. Jiang seethed, lambasting the security agencies for having undermined a clampdown on dissent. 'We called for stability above all, but our stability has fallen through.'[74]

A taskforce was established, headed by Vice-President Hu Jintao, a dull, wooden but tough party operator who had cut his teeth in Tibet, where he had imposed martial law and used troops to suppress mass protests in March 1989. The crackdown against Falun Gong came on 20 July, as the movement was declared illegal, gatherings were broken up, tens of thousands of followers temporarily detained and over a hundred core members arrested. Elderly women were carted off in police vans. Homes were ransacked, material confiscated, books burned, images of the leader smashed. Thousands more were sent to labour camps in the following months.[75]

Towards the end of October the National People's Congress hastily introduced a new law against 'evil cults', defined as 'illegal organisations' that 'deify their founders, spread superstition and heresy to misguide others, or lead members to endanger society'. Tens of thousands of believers came out again, blockading government offices in over thirty cities in silent protest. The police hauled them away, with more lightning raids carried out against the leaders. The numbers in detention soared, reaching some 35,000 by the end of the year. The propaganda machinery conducted a relentless campaign of vilification.[76]

Still more from a seemingly inexhaustible supply of followers appeared, unshakable in their faith. On 25 April 2000, precisely one year after surrounding Zhongnanhai, a hundred adherents briefly demonstrated on Tiananmen Square before plainclothes officers dragged them off. Six months later, as National Day was celebrated on 1 October, hundreds of followers upstaged the meticulously orchestrated festivities on the square, despite tight security. No sooner was one group wrestled away by the police, kicking and punching the protesters, than another emerged from the crowd. A few managed to unfurl a red banner proclaiming 'Falun Gong is Good' below the portrait of Chairman Mao, in full view of tens of thousands of party members and foreign dignitaries attending the celebrations.[77]

But when five members set themselves on fire in Tiananmen Square on the eve of the Lunar New Year in January 2001, many ordinary people concluded that they were indeed a dangerous cult.[78]

The war of attrition intensified in the wake of the immolations, involving a painstaking effort to find and remove followers one work unit at a time, with the police methodically combing entire neighbourhoods to send potential offenders to a network of re-education classes. The use of systematic violence became common, as adherents were beaten, shocked with electric batons or forced to squat on the floor for hours on end. 'I am a broken man,' an electrical engineer confided after having been forced to stand against a wall for nine days. 'Now, whenever I see a policeman and those electric truncheons, I feel sick, ready to throw up.'[79]

Quotas were set for individual cities, counties and provinces, while party secretaries in areas that failed to meet the required numbers faced disciplinary action. Always pragmatic, the leadership allowed local governments that were most successful in converting cult members to sell their services to others. Workers thrown out of a job were hired to help track down believers, with thousands recruited in Beijing alone. Relentless violence worked miracles, as membership dwindled rapidly. A mere handful of forlorn protesters appeared on the square on 20 July 2001, the second anniversary of the crackdown.[80]

The regime also took the opportunity to rein in other religious organisations. Jiang Zemin viewed religion as a threat to socialism, and had presided over a ferocious crusade soon after assuming power in 1989. Like most other political campaigns, for instance the war on crime or the fight against corruption, persecution never went away, its ebb and flow determined by need and opportunity.

An estimated 40 million Christians worshipped in secret house churches, and the leadership viewed their gatherings as a potential challenge to their authority. A few months after the new law aimed at crushing Falun Gong was passed, ten underground churches were denounced as 'evil cults' and more than a hundred of their leaders arrested and sent to labour camps.[81]

The battle of the spirit spread further the following year. In the province of Zhejiang alone, some 1,200 temples, churches and ancestral halls were torn down or blown up. The city of Wenzhou, which by now boasted 7 million inhabitants, was hit hard, with some 200 closures, including a 400-square-metre church blown up with explosive charges. Local people, against all odds, occasionally fought back. When a temple erected in 1986 was earmarked for destruction by the authorities, large crowds took turns to occupy the structure and mount guard. They were no match for the local security forces.[82]

Party members, too, were scrutinised for their religious beliefs. Marxism, Jiang Zemin explained on 1 July 1999, was the 'spiritual ballast' that would prevent party members from drifting towards feudal superstition or money worship. China would be doomed if party members lost faith in communism, he observed. In order to fight the pernicious and widespread influence of Falun Gong within the very ranks of the party, a few weeks later the Central Committee and the Ministry of Propaganda instructed every member to study dialectical materialism and atheism.[83]

The campaign was called the Three Emphases: emphasise the Marxist canon, emphasise politics and emphasise personal righteousness. Hu Jintao, now heir apparent, took charge of the campaign. But heightening the ideology of the party was not quite enough. Its organisation had to be strengthened. In Marxist jargon this was termed 'party building', and according to Jiang Zemin it had been neglected in the rush towards economic growth, leading to slack supervision of party members. The counterpart of the Three Emphases was the Three Represents, launched in May 2000. Its ghost author was Wang Huning, the doctrinaire ideologist who had penned 'On the Correct Handling of the Twelve Major Relations' for Jiang Zemin a few years earlier.[84]

Although few people knew exactly what the formulation meant, the general idea was that the party should not dilute its own political power and must ensure it remained in the vanguard of every area of life. This included the country's 'advanced culture' as well as the 'fundamental interest of the majority of the people'. A third principle posited that the party should 'represent the foremost production forces'. Foreign experts gasped with admiration, as the Three Represents included a decision to end a ban on party membership for private business people. But in typical Orwellian doublespeak, the campaign was designed to extend the hand of the state, not retract it, most of all in the private sector. Since tens of thousands of state enterprises were becoming shareholding companies, shedding millions of jobs along the way, the party insisted on maintaining control. The Three Represents meant that party cells must be established even within private businesses, subjecting them to closer party supervision. These party cells would 'unite, educate and guide the work of private entrepreneurs', making sure that they 'obeyed the law' and also 'supported party policies' and 'contributed to the state and society', Jiang Zemin pronounced.[85]

To mark the launch of the Three Represents, Jiang Zemin visited Wenzhou in May 2000. Some 80 per cent of industrial output in this mecca of capitalism came from the private sector. But a mere 2 per cent of all workers in privately run factories were party members. The secretary general left the city with clear instructions: build a party cell in every private business. 'If we do not properly build up party structures inside those enterprises, then we are abandoning the leadership position of the party.'[86]

More visitors followed, including Hu Jintao and officials from the Organisation Department. A year later, Wenzhou became one of the first cities to formally induct some of its private businessmen into the Communist Party. Among them was Zhou Dahu, owner of the Wenzhou Tiger Lighter Factory, who had been carefully vetted, and was keen to prove his communist credentials. When officials from the Organisation Department asked him what he planned to do with his wealth, he gave the correct answer: 'I told them, in the end, it all belongs to the party.' Zhou would become one of the country's first red capitalists.[87]

The Three Represents further cemented the primacy of the party in regulatory matters. A classic Leninist principle was that the party should be supervised by the party, not by some outside institution, and least of all by an independent judicial system. As Wen Jiabao explained, the requirement that 'the party supervises the party' was stated in the preamble of the constitution. By strengthening the ideology of the party as well as its organisation, the party would be able to supervise and regulate all business more strictly, whether in the state sector or beyond.[88]

Still, a few diehard Maoists, including Deng Liqun, now aged 86, were incensed that the party welcomed entrepreneurs. Yuan Mu, who more than ten years earlier had lectured the students on behalf of the government, viewed it as an attempt to 'restore capitalism'. When two party magazines aired some of these critical views, an enraged Jiang Zemin ordered that they be closed down: the reason was that they failed to conform to one of the Three Principles, namely that the party take a vanguard role in promoting 'advanced culture'. Jiang also made the study of the Three Represents mandatory for every party member.[89] At the Sixteenth Party Congress in November 2002, the Three Represents were enshrined in the party constitution, ranking alongside Mao Zedong Thought and Deng Xiaoping Theory as the party's guiding ideology.

***

On Friday 7 May 1999, less than two weeks after the leadership found itself surrounded by 10,000 Falun Gong practitioners, several stealth bombers delivered five missile-guided bombs over Belgrade, hitting the southern end of the Chinese embassy. The midnight strike demolished the office of the military attaché, but left the northern end of the compound unscathed, including the ambassador's Mercedes-Benz and four flowerpots. During NATO's bombing campaign over Yugoslavia, launched by the Atlantic Alliance after the collapse of peace talks to stop the persecution of ethnic Albanians in Kosovo, hundreds of air defence sites, army headquarters and other military targets were struck. William Cohen, the US secretary of defense, characterised the campaign as 'the most precise application of airpower in history'. But the hit on the embassy turned out to be a tragic mistake, based on wrong information culled from an outdated map. It killed three Chinese journalists and injured twenty more. A statement from NATO the same day declared that it had not intended to target the embassy – as well as a hospital complex and a marketplace in Nis – and regretted any damage and loss of life.[90]

Beijing immediately condemned the 'barbaric' attack and 'criminal conduct' of NATO. Newspapers and the media followed suit, portraying the bombing as a carefully planned act of war designed to divert the country from its economic development by forcing it to increase military spending. China, it was alleged, had been punished for supporting Yugoslavia. The United States was trying to contain China, 'shaking the mountains to scare the tiger'.[91]

Angry crowds erupted almost instantly. In Beijing tens of thousands of incensed students streamed towards the American embassy, pelting the building with rocks, bottles and debris. Onlookers cheered them on as they burned the US flag. In Chengdu a large crowd hurled improvised petrol bombs at the consulate, setting the compound on fire. Similar scenes took place in Shanghai, Hangzhou and Guangzhou. American companies also came under attack. In Changsha, capital of Hunan province, an irate mob tore apart a McDonald's and wrecked two KFC restaurants. In a rare televised speech, Vice-President Hu

Jintao backed the demonstrators, declaring in his wooden manner that the government 'supports and protects, in accordance with the law, all legal protest activities'. Apart from some occasional shoving and pushing, protesters and the police for once seemed to mingle rather happily.[92]

President Bill Clinton apologised in public on 10 May, extending his 'profound condolences' to the victims and their families. The *People's Daily* made no mention of the apology, charging instead that the bombing had been a deliberate attack. 'China Will Not Be Bullied!', its front page editorial proclaimed.[93]

It was a sentiment widely shared across the country, including by the leadership. One day after the bombing, Jiang Zemin had convened the Politburo's Standing Committee, telling them that the attack was 'most certainly not fortuitous'. 'They don't show it but deep in their bones they hate us to death,' he continued, pointing at the threat that the United States presented to the country. Belgrade was a lesson: 'We must further develop our country's economic power, our military strength and our national unity. We must strengthen our preparations for a military conflict.' 'China will not be bullied!' he concluded.[94]

The Standing Committee met again the following day, on 9 May. This time Jiang Zemin invoked Deng Xiaoping's guiding motto: 'keep a low profile and bide your time.' More time was needed, he explained, even though the gap between China and the United States had narrowed. 'We must fight the United States, but not to the point where we break off the relationship,' he opined. 'We must join the WTO but not yield to their demands,' he continued. Maintaining social stability was paramount, as foreign hostile forces were only too keen to exploit turmoil and 'carry out their political plot', which consisted of 'Westernisation' and trying to 'split the country'.[95]

The bombing was an inflection point, as Jiang Zemin's message of an antagonistic capitalist camp bent on destroying a rising socialist power was repeated time and again. At a national conference on public security convened in April 2001, Jiang Zemin and Zhu Rongji warned against 'subversion and infiltration by foreign hostile forces', not least their attempt to 'split the country'. True dictatorship, according to Jiang, could only be found in the West, where the capitalist class had ruled for centuries by maintaining an iron grip on every institution. 'The government, the courts, the police and the army, in the West they use the legislative and the executive as well as advanced technologies to maintain a dictatorship.'[96]

The same vision of entrenched hostility was promoted at every level of government. As Jiang Jufeng, party secretary of Wenzhou, the country's most liberal city, pointed out on the eightieth anniversary of the Communist Party in the summer of 2001, 'hostile forces in the West do not want to see a socialist China develop and grow in strength' and their strategy of 'splitting the country and Westernising it will never change'.[97]

Bill Clinton finally succeeded in reaching Jiang Zemin on 14 May, when he apologised again over the phone. The propaganda machine presented their conversation as a 'serious blow to America's arrogant hegemony'. There was a further silver lining, namely national unity and patriotism. 'We have further united the people in patriotic education,' the Central Committee later pointed out in a secret directive, as the 'great majority of people' could see with even greater clarity the hypocritical nature of 'human rights', 'humanism', 'freedom' and 'democracy', the empty values peddled by the imperialist camp.[98]

The Central Committee had a point. The students who assailed the embassy in Beijing were a world apart from their predecessors. Patriotic education, first launched a decade earlier, had become pervasive in every aspect of the party's propaganda, from school textbooks and radio programmes to television entertainment. There were a hundred patriotic films, a hundred patriotic songs, a hundred patriotic books, all prescribed by the state. When Karoline Kan went to school in the 1990s, there were patriotic quotations on the blackboard and mottos on the wall in every classroom. Like every young child, she was made to endlessly repeat the same mantra: 'Love the country, love the people, and love the Chinese Communist Party.' 'I was constantly told to be loyal, that only the party could make Chinese people's lives better and protect China from the threats of hostile countries like Japan and America.' After the bombing, the national flag in her school was lowered to half-mast, as the headmaster lectured the assembled students on the evils of American imperialism. A few volunteers later plastered anti-American posters outside schools, shopping malls, post offices and hospitals.[99]

A boycott of American products followed the weekend of government-stoked demonstrations. In Beijing two American movies were pulled and replaced by more patriotic films on the Korean War. But the campaign began to run out of steam after a few days. Shouting anti-foreign slogans was one thing, forgoing one's favourite consumer goods, from Nike sneakers to McDonald's hamburgers, another. The leadership, too, began to distance itself from the protests. The ashes of the three journalists killed in Belgrade were returned home, Bill Clinton's apology from the White House broadcast on central television. On 11 May the Foreign Ministry urged the United States to press on with China's accession to the World Trade Organization. An editorial in the influential *China Business News* went further: Washington could make amends for the attack by accelerating talks on Beijing's bid to join the WTO.[100]

9

Going Global (2001–2008)

On 15 November 1999, six months after an angry crowd had besieged the American embassy, the diplomatic compound was once more surrounded, but this time by camera crews eager to capture the moment when a pact was signed between China and the United States. The United States–China Relation Act of 2000 in effect granted the People's Republic permanent normal trade relations, previously known as Most Favoured Nation status, paving the way for China's membership in the World Trade Organization on 11 December 2001.

The timing could not have been more fortunate. Many of the economic problems that Premier Zhu Rongji had tried to solve since he took office turned out to be far more entrenched than he had anticipated. Despite a widespread programme of mergers and acquisitions, carried out with massive subsidies and yet more loans, state enterprises were still operating in the red. In the countryside, millions of village enterprises continued to produce goods that could not be sold at a profit. Overcapacity was so great that deflation returned in 2001, estimated cautiously at 3 per cent, although a few experts suggested the true figure was much higher, obscured by higher prices for services such as banking.[1]

The rural banks that supported local enterprises with loans were technically insolvent, requiring massive intervention on the part of the central bank. Bad loans had also crippled the four state banks, which had to be recapitalised with 270 billion yuan. In large areas of the country, the government could not pay its staff on time. In order to keep the rural economy afloat, the government threw more money at infrastructure projects, building roads, bridges and dams, issuing more treasury bonds in addition to the 150 billion yuan originally planned. Yet by 2000 the coffers were almost exhausted, with the banks awash in red ink, effectively insolvent. A study by Ernst & Young estimated the total amount of unprofitable loans in the financial system at 44 per cent of total lending, equivalent to $480 billion, or 48 per cent of the $1 trillion annual output.[2]

In 1976, according to the World Bank, the country's gross domestic product, when calculated per capita, ranked 123rd in the world. By 2001, after a quarter of a century of relentless emphasis on economic growth, it had dropped to 130th. The International Monetary Fund gave slightly different figures, but likewise highlighted how overall per capita output had barely kept pace with the rest of the world. The figures may have been dubious, given the lack of transparency, and the absence of properly trained accountants operating independently of the government, but they indicated the glacial pace of what some foreigners acclaimed as an economic miracle.

The numbers also hid a structural issue: the household share of gross domestic production was among the lowest of any major economy in modern history. Ordinary people, especially in the countryside, worked very hard, but received a disproportionally small share of growth. They had to save as much as possible in order to make ends meet, besides paying inflated charges for basic services such as schools and hospitals. Despite falling prices, they would not or could not spend. They could deposit their savings in state-controlled banks, buy shares from state-controlled companies or buy bonds issued by the state. They could also buy shares in private companies, but fraud and corruption were so rife that few villagers were willing to take the risk.

Still, China had achieved Deng Xiaoping's goal of quadrupling the economy by the turn of the century, making the country a major player in world trade that could no longer be ignored. Even though the stock, commodity and bond markets that had appeared under Jiang Zemin and Zhu Rongji were underpinned by the hand of the state rather than market forces, they created the impression of an economy firmly in transition from central planning towards the market. When, after 1997, even mergers and acquisitions of state enterprises were encouraged, with initial public offerings in New York, the future of the private sector seemed brighter than ever. But most of all, World Trade Organization members had been suitably impressed by Zhu

Rongji's promise that the much-coveted admission would accelerate economic reform by exposing the state sector to greater competition. As his vice-minister of finance Jin Liqun had observed, 'WTO membership works like a wrecking ball, smashing whatever is left in the old edifice of the planned economy'. There were endless pledges to improve the rule of law, strengthen intellectual property rights and achieve more transparent governance.[3]

The WTO welcomed the country's commitment to cut import tariffs, slash official subsidies and scrap other trade barriers, thus granting greater access to its market, from financial services to the telecommunications industry. So great was the conviction that membership would ensure more reform that China was allowed to join without being required to float its exchange rate, make its capital account convertible or reform its state enterprises.

The deal had its fair share of opponents, not least trade unions concerned over potential job losses as well as human rights groups alarmed by the country's poor track record: 'How can you have free trade without free trade unions?', one labour activist wondered. Others feared rampant counterfeiting and the forced transfer of technology, as well as the risks and costs of doing business in a country where corruption was endemic. Peter Humphrey, an expert in risk management based in Shanghai and later arrested for alleged spying, called the deal a 'honey pot full of sticky promise', highlighting a chaotic regulatory framework. Some wondered how the country's courts could operate independently when judges were party members appointed by the local party secretary. There were also questions about the regime's ability to impose its will upon each of the country's far-flung cities and provinces, not to mention the local fiefdoms that had been so successful in frustrating or deflecting the writ emanating from Beijing.[4]

Yet the lure of a giant market prevailed. All sectors, from agriculture to industry, wanted to sell more to China. For years multinational firms had lobbied for greater access. From telecommunications companies and insurance firms to semiconductor factories, all relished the prospect of taking over the last untapped market on earth. A few private bankers even speculated that since customers in China had no choice but to deposit their savings with local banks, they might withdraw them all at once and leave their money with foreign competitors instead, forcing the state sector into bankruptcy.

Economists joined the fray, pointing out that the deal would reduce the trade deficit between the United States and China. As Nicholas Lardy, a China specialist at the Brookings Institution, explained, Chinese companies already had unlimited access to the American market. It was the People's Republic that was obligated to open its doors and lower its tariffs, making the deal far more profitable for American firms. Fred Bergsten, an economist who had served as assistant for international economic affairs to Henry Kissinger, calculated very precisely that exports from the United States to China would increase by $3.1 billion. As one commentator noted, 'They give. We take. What's not to like?' Observers in the United States considered the arrangement a 'no brainer'.[5]

Not only did economists have at their disposal sophisticated tools that could predict the future of the trade deficit with scientific precision, but they could also talk with great confidence about the unfolding of broader historical forces. Very much as Karl Marx had predicted the collapse of capitalism, some anticipated the inevitable spread of a free society in the wake of free trade. Political reform would succeed economic reform as surely as the cart follows the ox. One scholar calculated that China would become a democracy 'around the year 2015'. Politicians were more prudent, but whether Democrats or Republicans, many in the United States were convinced that they were witnessing the momentous transformation of a state-controlled economy into a free market that would impose a clear set of rules on Beijing.[6]

This was a widely shared view. Although the World Trade Organization prohibited unilateral trade sanctions against countries that violated human rights, even some democracy activists expressed cautious optimism. In New York, Human Rights Watch speculated that membership could 'increase pressure for greater openness, more press freedom, enhanced rights for workers, and an independent judiciary'. In Hong Kong, the pro-democracy legislator Martin Lee joined the chorus, noting that accession would 'pave the way for the early advancement of the rule of law in China'.[7]

***

Within less than a year, the trade surplus with the United States skyrocketed to almost $11 billion a month. By 2008, it stood at more than $266 billion, as China exported goods worth $338 billion but spent only $71.5 billion on imports. The United States was not alone. In Mexico, a manufacturer of clothing, shoes and electronics, the trade deficit increased tenfold between 2000 to 2007, leading the country to file a complaint with the WTO. Overall, the balance of trade between China and other members of the organisation went from $28 billion in 2002 to $348 billion by 2008.[8]

Since 1976, China had doggedly pursued the same strategy: attract foreign investment, improve capacity and export the output abroad to create employment and increase savings at home. Within months of signing the agreement with the United States in November 1999, foreign investment jumped, reversing a steady decline that had hampered the economy since the onset of the 1997 financial crisis. This was the first tangible benefit from the country's decision to join the World Trade Organization. Even as the global economy slowed in the wake of the coordinated terrorist attacks on the United States on 11 September 2001, unprecedented investment funds continued to flood in, rising by 15 per cent to $47 billion. China was a magnet for global capital, with more to come.[9]

Foreign capital inflows came on top of massive overcapacity. In 2001 China could make 36 million television sets a year but managed to sell only 15 million. It churned out 20 million refrigerators even though domestic demand stagnated at 12 million. For decades, both the central government and local officials had encouraged economic growth at all costs, providing enterprises with every incentive needed to continue production even when not profitable. Few factories were ever forced to close, leading to more loans, more debt and more unsold goods, from steel and cement to fans, bicycles and mattresses. Easy credit, cosseted enterprises and warehouses bulging with unwanted goods all went together. Unbalanced output was inherent in a planned economy: the state issued targets, and party officials scrambled to outdo each other in fulfilling and overfulfilling the plan, causing waste in some areas, vast deficits in others. The surge in foreign investment led to even more factories, more equipment and yet more capacity. By 2005 roughly 90 per cent of all manufactured products were in chronic oversupply.[10]

Since supply could not be matched by demand, prices tumbled, playing a part in the record 29 months of deflation that abated somewhat in March 2000. Overcapacity was such that prices then resumed their downward trajectory in 2001. A surplus of cheap labour, coming after several years of mergers and acquisitions with tens of millions of people thrown out of work, contributed to the trend. Prices for locally made motorbikes fell by one-third, those of digital video players by 20 to 30 per cent. Across a whole range of goods, manufacturers competed with each other by ruthlessly slashing prices. In effect, many sold below cost of production. To survive, they had only one option, namely to increase exports overseas.[11]

These cheap exports, compounded with a weak global economy, delivered deflation to the rest of the world. Asia was affected first, but even in the United States the consumer price index fell in a year-on-year decline unparalleled since the Great Depression in the 1930s, except for a brief dip in 1955. In June 2002, an average dress cost as much as it did in 1984. Across a wide array of sectors, from golf clubs to television sets, prices plummeted, personal computers by up to 30 per cent.[12]

Consumers should have rejoiced, but the deflationary forces unleashed by China's export juggernaut savaged corporate profits, causing falling salaries and job cuts. Manufacturing companies across the world faced a choice. Since they could not match the cheap labour on offer in China, where a small army of over 100 million migrants from the countryside could be hired and fired at will, they could either go under or set up shop in China.

Foreign companies flocked to the promised land, outsourcing labour through subcontractors or opening factories. Following the trade deal with China signed by Bill Clinton at the end of 1999, in a mere two years more than 500 foreign-owned factories decamped from Mexico for the People's Republic. One was a golf club manufacturer in Tijuana, where a novice earned $1.50 to $2 an hour, compared with 25 cents in parts of China. Costs were even higher in the United States, where factory closures in parts of Ohio, Illinois, Colorado and Massachusetts were so extensive that by 2004 entire manufacturing centres, some with attractive brick factories and century-old stone buildings, were hollowed out. Although jobs were also outsourced to India, Mexico and Canada, the vast majority went to China. The United States and Mexico were among the first to relocate, but other countries soon followed suit. Almost every week in 2004, a new

Japanese factory opened in China, at the expense of factories and workers not just in Japan, but also in Southeast Asia.[13]

By 2003, roughly 70 per cent of goods sold by Wal-Mart were procured in China. Beleaguered manufacturers from a whole range of sectors cried foul, demanding that a formal complaint be lodged with the WTO, whereas domestic companies and multinational corporations that had invested in China and were turning a good profit had no wish to ruffle any feathers in Beijing. A similar split appeared in other countries, as almost half of China's exports were produced by factories with significant foreign investment, whether American, European or Japanese.[14]

Foreign manufacturers benefited from cheap labour and less stringent environmental and safety standards, but they were forced to pay a price for the privilege. In a familiar pattern insiders termed the 'China price', a foreign company introduced a new product, and within months local manufacturers began cranking out replicas, competing among themselves to cut costs even further. Prices began to slide, until they reached the point where the commodity was selling below its production cost. Fierce entrepreneurial zeal, combined with advanced foreign technology, spawned a widespread copy culture in which virtually every foreign good found its domestic counterpart. The relentless drive to cut costs was such that, barring the knowledge required to counterfeit and reverse-engineer, research and innovation were simply not economically viable. Piracy was not a fringe phenomenon in the rush to produce: it lay at the very heart of the economic boom.[15]

Theft of intellectual property had a long history and was encouraged at the highest levels. China had joined the World Intellectual Property Organization in 1980, but the regime paid mere lip service to its treaty obligations. By 1989 the US Department of Commerce described piracy as 'rampant', as state corporations in China employed teams of engineers devoted to breaking the sophisticated codes protecting foreign software. In 1992 the country joined the Universal Copyright Convention. This, too, was followed by a surge in piracy of music, movies, books and computer software.[16]

A familiar scenario began to play itself out. Time and again, a foreign trade official would declare piracy to be rampant, lodge a complaint and threaten trade sanctions. Several factories were raided, and bootleg videos bulldozed in the presence of foreign journalists. In Beijing's famous Silk Alley, the fake Cartier watches and Louis Vuitton handbags disappeared. A foreign minister solemnly affirmed the importance of intellectual property and the rule of law. A new agreement was signed. On paper, copyright laws were fine-tuned. Even as politicians abroad hailed the breakthrough, piracy and theft of trade secrets resumed. The estimated cost to the United States, measured in billions of dollars, rose annually. While China was by no means the only country where piracy was common, the thefts were by all accounts more blatant and larger in scale than anywhere else. In 2001, as the country was about to join the WTO, China was termed 'the world's number one counterfeiter'.[17]

Paradoxically, one reason why members of the World Trade Organization welcomed China was their hope that the country would abide by the substantial amendments to its trademark, copyright and patent law that membership required. Yet the gap between pledges on paper and piracy on the ground only widened. In November 2002, experts named China 'the worst country in the world for copyright infringement and trademark violations', costing 'artists, writers, computer software developers, designers, drug companies, shampoo makers – just about anyone with a product for sale – billions of dollars a year'.[18]

Over half of some pharmaceutical products sold in China were fake. Prescription drugs not yet released abroad were available in pirated form. Almost every Hollywood blockbuster appeared on DVD in China before its release in the same format in the United States.

Similar problems bedevilled the agrochemical, petrochemical and chemical industries, all of them relying heavily on imitation and reverse engineering of foreign products. Fakes were even copied from other fakes. One example was Harry Potter, with several writers teaming up to write volumes five, six and seven when only four volumes had yet been published in English. One such book, in which the bespectacled young wizard was transformed into a hairy troll, was a copy adapted from a fake. Fake books were big business, with one hundred titles published in early 2005.[19]

Copying was not restricted to relatively simple objects. By 2002, China had highly educated engineers working for powerful state enterprises. When General Motors executives unveiled a new family van at the 2003 Shanghai auto show, at another booth further along the same row, state-owned car manufacturer Chery offered a similar vehicle at two-thirds the price.[20]

By 2004, various estimates assessed the losses to foreign companies at $60 billion, far in excess of direct foreign investment. Yet the costs went beyond those incurred by the original producers. When cheap knock-offs flooded poorer countries, they ravaged local economies. According to the Kenya Revenue Authority, some 80 per cent of fake goods in their country came from China. The local company licensed to produce Bic pens could not compete with the cheaper counterfeits. Since the bulk of fake goods were smuggled across the border, they deprived both local enterprises and cash-strapped governments of millions of dollars per year.[21]

Other indirect costs were generally borne by customers. Electric kettles blew up, golf clubs snapped, brake pads failed. Fake engine oil caused cars to seize up, while imitation shampoo left sores and blisters on the scalp. Since increasing quantities of Chinese counterfeits were smuggled across borders, everywhere customers were at risk from products ranging from cheap batteries and razors to prescription drugs. None were more exposed to the health hazards of copy culture than ordinary people in China. Spices contained paraffin wax, noodles used a red dye that caused cancer and rice wine was made with cheap industrial-grade alcohol. Fake pork, fake rice, even fake eggs appeared on the market. In 2004, cheap infant milk was discovered to lack protein, with some fifty babies dying of malnutrition after parents mistook their symptoms for a sign of overfeeding. Since the central government lacked the clout to impose its writ on local party secretaries, who shielded their enterprises from more thorough scrutiny, even greater disaster struck several years later, when infant formula was adulterated with melanin, a scandal the central government covered up for many months, sickening a reported 300,000 babies, although the real toll was probably higher. Overall, in 2007, the government estimated that one-fifth of the food and consumer goods it had managed to check were substandard or tainted.[22]

In the rush to cut corners, people were hurt even before the goods left the factory. Once wage cuts were banned, safety standards were downgraded or bypassed completely. Here, too, lack of regulatory power compounded the problem, as local party officials colluded with private and state factory owners alike. The biggest obstacle was the absence of basic human rights for tens of millions of migrant workers who filled the factories along the coast. Legally tied to the land, they had no right to urban residence, with their presence tolerated when their hands were required. Like everyone else, they did not enjoy the right of free assembly, let alone the right to strike. They worked long hours, without insurance, sometimes in unlicensed factories where employers could withhold their identity cards and salaries. Work, whether in dimly lit sweatshops or in technologically advanced enterprises, often consisted of endlessly repeating the same sequence of gestures, whether slipping a strip of metal under a mechanical hammer or assembling different parts of a mould. 'If you let your mind wander for just a second, it's over,' commented Wang Chenghua, who had a middle and ring finger reduced to pulp. Digits were generally the first to go, although machines also shredded hands and arms, sometimes even legs, leading to a thriving business in reattachment surgery. In Yongkang, the hardware capital of China to the south of Shanghai, some 7,000 private factories produced hinges, hubcaps, pots, pans, plugs and other goods with metallic innards. Unofficial figures put the number of accidents on their premises at 2,500 each year. Across the country, 140,000 people died of work-related accidents in 2003, while many more were injured. The law prescribed compensation, although in practice few received meaningful payment without costly arbitration that could drag on for years.[23]

Migrant workers with missing fingers were useless, but children had nimble hands that came at an attractive discount. An internal report dated January 2003 noted that the use of children in Wenzhou was 'relatively common' in workshops producing shoes, umbrellas, toys and lamps.[24] Statistics were hard to find, but in 2005 demand increased along the coast, as low wages and poor conditions convinced an increasing number of migrants to stay home and cultivate the land rather than risk life and limb in a factory. There were reports of kidnappings and forced labour involving children as young as ten. Every year a new scandal came to light, whether hundreds of underage workers rescued from slave labour in brick kilns or labour gangs abducting children from impoverished parts of the countryside and sending them to work for 300 hours a month in the factory towns of Guangdong province.[25]

In some villages every family had a child working in a factory. With the rural education system in a state of virtual collapse, some schools contracted out entire classes to work in urban factories to help pay the bills. Cottage industries were common in the countryside, with families working from home for a piece rate. Children joined in, folding paper or bending bamboo.[26]

Exporters were pleased, importers less so, since they could not compete. Two ideologies were clashing on the factory floor. On the one hand, proponents of free trade insisted that unrestricted imports and exports would benefit the greater good, a losing proposition, since free trade with an unfree country was a logical contradiction. On the other, believers in socialism insisted that the state must keep a monopoly over the means of production, also in the name of the greater good. This was a winning proposition. Since the state directly or indirectly controlled all means of production, from raw materials, land, labour and energy to capital, endless subsidies, hidden or otherwise, could be provided. Local governments keen on development could lease the land for free. The cost of some commodities was kept artificially low. The state directed cheap energy towards its enterprises. So massive were subsidies that two of the main state-owned giants, Sinopec in the south and PetroChina in the north, cobbled together from thousands of formerly separate producers and listed in Hong Kong and New York in the rush to create national champions, were left with negligible profit margins. In 2005 retail prices were so low that they did not cover the refiners' costs. In 2008, when spiralling fuel costs left consumers around the world reeling, prices of refined oil in China stood at roughly half of international levels. Capital, too, was in state hands, disbursed generously in pursuit of political goals, whether local or central. With a mere flick of the proverbial hand, private companies and state enterprises could be kept afloat or built up, often without breaking any of the WTO rules.[27]

Tax rebates, first introduced in 1985, were a major tool used to maintain momentum in exports and hence rapid economic growth. They were cranked up in the wake of the Asian financial crisis, varying from 5 to 17 per cent. The rebates imposed a heavy fiscal burden on the central government, consuming from one-fifth to one-third of total expenditure. Other budget items suffered thereby, in particular education and social security.[28]

From the very start there were protests over subsidies, often from China's biggest defenders. 'The honeymoon is over,' the American

Chamber of Commerce in Beijing proclaimed in 2003. Yet complaints lodged with the WTO were costly, time-consuming and in any event made very little difference. The Ministry of Finance, for instance, could easily funnel cash through various assorted organisations instead of transferring funds directly to state enterprises. 'If the WTO says we can't do it this way,' a ministry official explained, 'we just change the methods.' Given the opaque nature of financial transactions and almost every other aspect of governance in a one-party state, this was not a game where outsiders could easily prevail.[29]

An iron law of free trade dictated that the foreign currency earned by the country would be spent abroad, to the benefit of all. Unfortunately, the iron hand of the state subverted the mutual exchanges that justified free trade. Instead of spending, the country was forced to save, accumulating huge surpluses, with savings boosted further by a fixed exchange rate, aimed at keeping imports expensive and exports cheap. This, too, demanded massive state intervention, with constant increases in the money supply needed to maintain the artificial rate of exchange. The economics were quite straightforward: every dollar that came in eventually had to go out. With so much currency entering the country through exports and foreign investment, the cost of the dollar relative to the yuan should have fallen, making the yuan more expensive. To prevent traders from bidding up the yuan, the central bank had to supply an equivalent amount of currency, buying up all the unwanted dollars at a fixed rate of 8.28 yuan and ploughing them into US treasury bonds. Meanwhile, the amount of yuan in circulation steadily increased, surging in August 2003 by 21.6 per cent year on year, with cash piling up in the banks. Since the yuan was undervalued by somewhere between 15 to 25 per cent, not even Bangladesh was able to compete, even though its wages were 20 to 30 per cent lower than those in China.[30]

Not until July 2005 was the yuan allowed to move within a band of 2 per cent. Instead, strict capital controls were used to manage the currency and prevent it rising faster against the dollar. The central bank continued to buy dollars on an enormous scale, amassing foreign reserves of $1.2 trillion by 2007.[31]

Foreign entrepreneurs who imagined they could sell their products to endless multitudes were disappointed. If they found a market, numerous domestic competitors with better connections to the local party secretary piled in and squeezed them out. Even the multinational corporations that had lined up for the gold rush struggled to acquire a mere fraction of the market. In 2002, for instance, more than a hundred international banks were in China, ready to offer their services to the hundreds of millions of customers locked in by technically insolvent state banks. Their first target was the country's new rich. On 21 March 2002, Tang Haisong, a Harvard-educated executive of an internet portal, became Citibank's first local customer, opening an account at its new branch in the iconic Peace Hotel along the Bund in Shanghai. The bank's foray into China was reminiscent of earlier efforts, when in 1902 it had become the first American bank to set up shop in colonial Shanghai, only to flee in 1949 when the communists came to power.[32] But foreign banks encountered tough new restrictions, complex and continually changing regulations. Local officials dragged their feet, favouring local competitors. Most of all, foreign banks never managed to acquire large networks of branches that could win domestic customers. Few people, it turned out, were willing to trek all the way to the Bund to make a deposit. Even by 2011, despite the WTO, foreign banks constituted less than 2 per cent of total domestic financial assets. The country's banking system was an impregnable fortress, protected from outside competition by the regime.[33]

In the telecommunications industry, too, the lowering of tariffs had brought great anticipation, with 1 billion customers waiting to join a 3G network. Foreign carriers were barred outright from the country, meaning that the best they could hope for was to sell equipment. China, however, rapidly developed standards putting it at odds with the rest of the world. In December 2003 a new policy was unveiled, requiring that all imported telecommunication devices conform to the regime's own encryption standard in wireless networking. Industrial giants, from Intel and Nokia to Sony, scrambled to figure out the impact on their business. After the United States threatened to file a complaint with the WTO, the policy was postponed.[34]

Much as the state protected its state-owned banks, it also aggressively shielded its state-owned telecommunication companies from foreign competition. Nokia, Alcatel and others had little choice but to form joint ventures, the traditional means whereby the regime ensured the transfer and sharing of foreign technology with local companies. The state also used a battery of policies to bolster exports by Huawei and ZTE, two of the largest domestic producers. Between 2000 and 2008, the global share of the United States, the European Union and Japan in world exports of telecommunications equipment dropped from a combined 60 per cent to 43 per cent, while that of China saw annual 30 per cent increases, from 6.8 per cent to over 27 per cent.[35]

***

To sustain this manufacturing juggernaut required a constant flow of materials and energy. China acquired a seemingly insatiable appetite for natural resources, from oil, coal, timber and iron ore to cotton. Even as manufacturing countries developed huge trade deficits, commodity exporters thrived. A network of freighters from Australia and Brazil spanned the Pacific Ocean, supplying the country with more than 160 million tonnes of iron ore, a crucial component for the steel used by the automobile and construction industries. Although China was already the world's largest steel producer, it purchased large amounts of scrap steel, resulting in a global drop in metal inventories to their lowest level ever. Even French coins were imported and melted down in the desperate search for more copper, used in air conditioners. Imports of cotton increased sevenfold in the first nine months of 2003. Raw material prices surged, alleviating the deflation caused by the boom in exports. The cost of alumina, a chemical compound extracted from bauxite and used to make aluminium, doubled in less than two years after China joined the WTO. Nickel prices likewise increased by 100 per cent. The entire supply chain for raw materials around the world was strained. To quote one director of research in commodity prices, 'China has sucked the cupboard bare of raw materials.'[36]

The biggest imports were oil and coal, as mammoth tankers the size of three football pitches delivered their loads to the country's ports. No amount could ever quite satiate the country's ravenous appetite for energy, as electric utilities could not keep up with demand. The strain on the grid was such that shortages were endemic, forcing some factories to operate reduced schedules. Many acquired generators, which increased demand for oil. Since legal diesel was also in short supply, some factory operators turned instead to the black market, forgoing the government's generous fuel subsidies.[37]

China had a plan termed 'Go Out', alternatively translated as 'Going Global', to cope with its increased reliance on the world, dating back to

1997, when the Fifteenth Party Congress had declared that 'two kinds of markets, two kinds of resources' existed. It meant, in sum, that the country should take the initiative on the world stage, fully exploiting the comparative advantages of the socialist market at home and the capitalist market abroad, and strive to better utilise their respective resources. More specifically, the policy encouraged state enterprises to export commodities that were plentiful on the domestic market, but also to go abroad to secure natural resources in short supply at home. A few months later Jiang Zemin coined the phrase 'Going Global': it was not sufficient, he opined, to encourage foreigners to invest and set up factories inside China. The state must also 'actively lead and organise powerful domestic enterprises to go abroad to invest and set up factories, using global markets and resources'. 'Going Global' was endorsed at every level, finally becoming part of the country's Five Year Plan in 2001.[38]

One of the first to 'Go Global' was Hu Jintao, who in November 2002 took over from Jiang Zemin as general secretary. He travelled to Latin America, Southeast Asia and Africa, keen to secure the fuel his country needed to keep its economy in overdrive. By June 2005 he had made his third trip to Russia, negotiating for a pipeline to transport Siberian crude directly to Manchurian oil refineries.[39]

Legions of surveyors, prospectors and engineers followed in his footsteps, working for state corporations with preferential financing from state banks. Before 2001 just over 200 enterprises were allowed to invest abroad. The number quadrupled within three years. With plenty of foreign currency available thanks to the gaping trade surplus, the amount invested soared from $500 million in 2000 to $7 billion in 2005.[40] The sums involved recalled Japan in the 1980s, but the strategy was much bolder. In its quest for resource security, the regime sought nothing less than independence from the capitalist camp, roughly defined as the West, a goal it sought to achieve by using its dollars to bind emerging countries together into an alternative supply chain.

From the desert dunes of North Africa to the shores of the Caspian Sea, vast amounts of money were spent on major deals. Within two years, China became a major player in mergers and acquisitions across the globe, picking up distressed companies for their brands, technology or markets, entering joint ventures with local commodity producers, striking exclusive deals for raw materials and purchasing refineries and port facilities. In 2000, China's only energy footprint in Africa was a pipeline built by PetroChina in Sudan. Within a few years, China's oil companies were operating in almost twenty countries across the continent. The procurement of oil was considered a national security issue, meaning that full state resources were used to secure the country's needs. Other commodities also attracted investment, with dozens of state companies extracting copper, manganese, cobalt, zinc, chromium, gold and other base metals. Managers of state companies scoured the continent, buying up raw cotton for export to the weaving machines back home. Even as they shipped raw materials out, they brought in huge volumes of cheap goods, eliminating manufacturing jobs that poor countries desperately needed. However low local salaries were, they could not compete with the yuan. Chinese companies and the banks backing them had one advantage that was difficult to ignore: loans and aid came with few conditions attached, a doctrine of non-interference that abusive regimes in Sudan, Zimbabwe, Eritrea and elsewhere particularly appreciated.[41]

China foraged the globe for metals, minerals and energy, but as its economy expanded so did its appetite for pork, poultry and beef. Soybean was required for animal feed. In a country where water was scarce, it also made sense to import water in the form of grain. When Hu Jintao visited Latin America in 2004, he promised $100 billion of investment over ten years (planned economies generally came with targets and quotas expressed in round numbers). While Ecuador and Venezuela provided oil and Peru and Chile copper, Argentina and Brazil were courted for their protein-packed beans, with exports quadrupling between 2000 and 2005. Brazil, already a major iron ore supplier, shipped 11 million tonnes of soy to China in 2006, overtaking the United States as its largest exporter.[42]

The policy of 'two kinds of markets, two kinds of resources' called not only for the strategic use of overseas raw materials, but also for a more concerted exploitation of domestic assets. When Jiang Zemin proposed to 'Go Out', he counterbalanced it with another initiative, namely 'Go West'. Vast resources beckoned in the country's northwest, nowhere more so than in Xinjiang. Why build a 1,600-kilometre pipeline across mountains and deserts in Sudan when gas from Xinjiang could not even reach Shanghai factories?

The west, seen from Beijing, stretched from the subtropical forests of Yunnan all the way to the deserts and grasslands of Gansu, accounting for more than half of the country's land, but less than one-quarter of its population. Much poorer than the coastal provinces, it attracted little foreign investment. The state dominated large swathes of the economy, especially in Xinjiang, a region three times the size of France. The largest landowner was the Xinjiang Production and Construction Corps, a development corporation the military established after 1949 to tame the wild land and its locals. Boosting their ranks were tens of thousands of demobilised soldiers, political prisoners and rural migrants, sent west to build irrigation canals, plant wheat and grow cotton in giant collective farms. The Corps, in effect, became a state within the state, its tentacles spreading far and wide, with its own schools, hospitals, laboratories, police force and courts, plus a vast network of prisons and labour camps. It oversaw one of the most successful programmes of colonisation in modern history. In 1949 settlers from the east accounted for no more than 3 per cent of the local population, but some four decades later the colonists had expanded to 40 per cent of the province's 17 million people. Many were released prisoners or migrants who arrived with little more than the clothes on their backs, although most were better off than the Uyghurs, who chafed under Beijing's rule.[43]

Tensions increased as the state encouraged greater production of cotton. Zhao Ziyang, visiting the west in 1982, had expressed his admiration for Central Asia, where the cotton yield per square kilometre was higher than in the United States.[44] The Soviet Union, seeking to decrease its dependence on imports, had selected the region for cotton production, sending forced labour to work the fields. The statistics Zhao Ziyang found so impressive were, of course, fake, like most miracles in one-party states. Local officials had falsified the figures, lining their pockets with funds from Moscow. The scheme collapsed in autumn 1983, when satellite pictures revealed that the fields were empty.[45]

Zhao Ziyang and Hu Yaobang toured Xinjiang in 1983, describing the province as a 'new frontier to be tamed', with vast natural resources that had the potential to lead the country's economy into the twenty-first century.[46] In subsequent years, however, the coastal regions were prioritised. Then, after the upheavals of 1989, the drive to develop

Xinjiang resumed. In 1990, Jiang Zemin promised the province more funding, even as tougher measures were used to crack down on local rebels. Xinjiang, the general secretary decreed, should develop a 'production base' for cotton, grain, sugar and animal husbandry, as well as petroleum and natural gas. In the following years, some 500,000 spinners moved to the region, further exacerbating tensions with the local population. In 1995, in an effort to bind the vast territory closer to the rest of the country, the ninth Five Year Plan determined that Xinjiang should become the country's most important cotton producer by the turn of the millennium, a target accompanied by close to 10 billion yuan in aid and subsidies, as dunes were levelled into fields.[47]

With economic development would come social stability and national unity, or so the leaders believed. Yet local resentment simmered, occasionally boiling over into open protests and surging in 1997, when riots erupted in several towns and an explosion rocked Urumqi, the provincial capital. Along the old Silk Road, from neighbouring Afghanistan and Pakistan, came weapons, explosives and religious tracts. A ruthless crackdown followed, with thousands of arrests in the following two years and the execution of an estimated 190 separatists. Even speaking of independence became a crime.[48]

The 1999 conflict in Kosovo was yet another reminder of the danger of ethnic fragmentation. The bombing of the embassy further heightened anxiety over separatist rebellions, as Jiang Zemin warned against hostile foreign forces trying to split up the country. 'It is therefore our sacred task and duty to preserve the great unity of the 56 nationalities of China,' he intoned on the eve of celebrations of the fiftieth anniversary of communist rule. A few months later in 1999, he raised the 'Go West' banner, pledging 100 billion yuan per year for the tenth Five Year Plan. The overall strategy of developing the west was scheduled to take fifty years.[49]

Oil and cotton came top of the list developed by the state planners. In 2002, work began on a 4,000-kilometre pipeline to carry natural gas from Xinjiang to Shanghai, which PetroChina put into operation at the end of 2004. After Hu Jintao visited Kazakhstan in June 2003, an agreement was signed to extend the pipeline all the way to the oilfields on the Caspian Sea. Turkmenistan and Uzbekistan joined in

2007, connecting Shanghai to most of Central Asia. Soon, a network of pipelines carrying massive amounts of liquid wealth criss-crossed the sand.[50]

Highways carved through the desert, with a new railway line inaugurated and some ten airports opened. Migrants arrived in droves. Acreage increased by 50 per cent, with plenty of cheap hands to pick the cotton. Output more than doubled, soaring from under 18 million bales to 37 million in 2007. By 2008, China was not only the world's largest cotton user, absorbing 43 per cent of the world's total, but at 33 per cent also the greatest producer.[51]

***

Even before foreign investment flooded in, a new wave of construction was unleashed, reminiscent of the spree following Deng Xiaoping's 1992 southern tour. Spending had begun after June 1997, when the regime had feared the effects of the Asian financial crisis. Rather than being phased out, after March 2000 even more ambitious infrastructure projects were undertaken in order to cope with the global economic slowdown resulting from the collapse of the dotcom bubble. Everywhere party leaders reached deep into state coffers to finance big projects, keen to maintain growth above the 7 per cent level, a magic number deemed crucial to avoid mass unemployment and urban unrest. The figure represented the rate the regime had singlemindedly pursued since 1982, when Deng Xiaoping had demanded that the economy quadruple by the year 2000. As the country entered a new millennium, the leadership continued to invoke the same rate of growth, decidedly like a mantra, increasing it a few years later to 8 per cent. Despite weakening exports, Shanghai managed to reach annual growth of more than 10 per cent in 2001, as the city widened its highways, built a science exhibition hall, opened an airport services building, upgraded its electric power grid, extended its underground rail system and began work on a magnetic levitation train to link its second airport with the financial district in Pudong. Similar projects were undertaken elsewhere, as Guangzhou, Tianjin and other cities tunnelled through residential areas to install underground railways.[52]

The trend continued: in just eleven months in 2002, the government, state banks, companies and foreign investors collectively sank $200 billion into officially sponsored infrastructure projects. The plan was to add some 14,000 kilometres in railways by 2005, including a high-speed track linking Beijing and Shanghai. In central China, a colossal $60 billion system of channels and pumping stations diverted water from the Yangtze to the Yellow River, while natural gas was sent from the west to the coast.[53]

Party officials followed what they called the 'Shanghai model', referring to the massive financial support Shanghai received after Jiang Zemin and Zhu Rongji became the foremost leaders. Nowhere was this more true than in Chongqing, some 1,500 kilometres inland in Sichuan on the Yangtze, a city hugged by mountains that the leadership had determined would become the capital of the Go West campaign. A complete makeover was required, with billions flowing every quarter towards the city from the treasury. Huang Qifan, who had been vice-mayor of Shanghai in the 1990s, was Beijing's man, tasked with spending as quickly as possible. Since eight was an auspicious number, eight highways and eight new railways were planned, some burrowed through the mountains. Eight bridges were designed to span the city's rivers by the end of the decade. Civic centres, skyscrapers and airports appeared, as well as parks, boulevards and riverside promenades. Huang boasted that he burned more than a billion dollars per month. There was no bottom: 'We will spend like this for ten years,' he told a foreign reporter.[54]

Building was not limited to infrastructure. In anticipation of increased business following the trade agreement, investment in real estate surged, with hundreds of millions of square feet in condominiums, luxury hotels and office blocks, from Dalian to Shenzhen. Beijing had construction cranes hovering above dusty building sites in every direction. One observer counted several thousand dotting the horizon. Entire neighbourhoods were levelled, their residents cast aside. In the first half of 2002, investment in housing surged by some 42 per cent to $2.6 billion, even though the market was struggling with 61.5 million square feet of vacant space. Shopping malls, already plentiful, also multiplied. In Shanghai a ten-storey Super Brand Mall appeared on the Pudong waterfront, claiming to be the largest in Asia. Its corridors gleamed with marble but were for the most part deserted. At least ten more shopping malls were under construction in the city, most financed with bank loans.[55]

This frenzied rush towards the future required vast amounts of steel, cement and other building materials. Long gone were the days of oversupply. 'Everywhere there are steel plants going up,' a former director of the metallurgy ministry grumbled. In 2003, China absorbed roughly half the world's cement production, a third of its steel, a quarter of its copper and a fifth of its aluminium.[56]

The money came from the banks, which the government owned. They were flush with cash. Foreigners invested, much as locals saved. Most of all, given the fixed exchange rate, vast amounts were pumped into the system to maintain the peg to the dollar. The regime pressured the banks to put the money to use. The banks, as a result, lent with relish. Loans went not only to state companies and infrastructure projects, but also to wealthy consumers, often with minimal credit checks and notional penalties for delinquencies. The property sector, in particular, attracted easy money, as more affluent consumers in the cities ploughed their savings into a down payment on an apartment, flipping it every once in a while. 'Everyone believes that property prices will continue to rise, so no one feels any risks,' commented a researcher based at Zhejiang University.[57]

Economists wondered whether the economy was spinning out of control or whether it was smart to invest in the future. Even the government was becoming worried. A report from the Statistics Bureau bemoaned that one province had 800 industrial parks under construction simultaneously, the majority unneeded. A rush to build airports had created overcapacity, with 127 of the country's 143 airports running losses.[58]

The massive investments came without significant change to the economic system. The property bubble that had followed Deng Xiaoping's southern tour in 1992 had fuelled double-digit inflation, eventually leading to a massive increase in bad loans when speculative investments in real estate turned sour. Combined with the losses sustained by state enterprises, the amount of bad debt was so great that Zhu Rongji had been compelled to overhaul the banking system by setting up four companies to take it over. A new tranche of bad loans was now emerging, as between $500 billion and $750 billion of the country's nearly $2 trillion in outstanding loans could not be repaid. The official debt, together with bad loans at state banks and unfinanced pensions of state workers, amounted to 140 per cent of economic output, equivalent to the burden that had crippled Japan.[59]

While the debt was new, the will to change the system had gone. Zhou Xiaochuan, the central banker who took over from Dai Xianglong, created a state-owned corporate entity known as Central Huijin Investment. Huijin, in turn, wholly owned a subsidiary called China Jianyin. Both were independent from the four asset management companies created in 1999 to deal with the toxic assets of the four state banks. Huijin and its subsidiary recapitalised the China Construction Bank and the Bank of China in 2004 with $45 billion drawn from the foreign exchange reserves. Yet when Zhou Xiaochuan proposed that international investors should be allowed to partner with the recapitalised banks, helping them to upgrade their corporate governance and risk management, this brought accusations that foreigners were threatening the nation's financial security. The banks therefore remained beholden to local party officials, and continued to lend at their behest.[60]

After Huijin and its subsidiary bought up bankrupt securities companies, the People's Bank of China had hoped to recover its money by restoring them to health and selling them to new investors, including foreign banks. Here, too, in October 2005 the State Council vetoed the suggestion.[61]

In effect, four years after China joined the WTO, reform ended. The bank restructuring programme forced upon the regime by circumstances in 1998, a time when financial weakness had threatened to unravel the entire system, came to a halt. Now the economy was booming. What could possibly be wrong with huge reserves of foreign currency and a massive trade surplus?

The reform of state enterprises was also put on ice. The economy was dominated by national champions, successfully created after Jiang Zemin had enjoined the party in 1997 to 'Grasp the Big and Let Go of the Small.' By 2004, state-owned businesses accounted for 96 per cent of the assets of the 500 largest companies. In every sector of the economy, from telecommunications, oil, gas, coal, power, tobacco and shipping to aviation, a handful of flagship behemoths prevailed, many of them listed on the stock exchanges of Hong Kong and New York.[62]

They won further protection when barriers against direct foreign investment went up in 2005. In October, for the first time, a foreign equity firm tried to acquire a state-owned company, a tool-making factory called Xugong Construction Machinery Group. A local rival blocked the attempt, but it prompted the regime to publish a raft of rules and regulations limiting foreign investment deemed to constitute a threat to the 'national economic security' of the country. The restrictions extended to petroleum, telecommunications, equipment manufacturing and the automobile industry as well as other 'major industries' and 'famous brands', although most of these remained undefined.[63]

The building of party cells in private enterprises, undertaken after Jiang Zemin launched his Three Represents in 2000, continued apace. Within days of being elected general secretary in November 2002, Hu Jintao went on an inspection tour of Xibaipo, holy ground of revolution where Mao Zedong had set up his headquarters before entering Beijing in 1949. On this highly symbolic visit, the leader made a speech echoing an earlier address by Chairman Mao, warning against complacency in victory and stressing the importance of the party line. On 3 January 2003, the *People's Daily* published Hu's exhortations.[64]

A month later, Hu Jintao launched a drive against corruption, aimed largely at party officials, but also, for the first time, bringing down a number of tycoons in a warning shot to the private sector. Yang Bin, a former wheeler dealer worth $900 million at his peak, was accused of fraud and bribery and sent to prison for eighteen years. Other major players fell, including dealers in real estate and automotive industry executives. In October 2003, Sun Dawu, an outspoken billionaire who championed the rights of poor villagers, was accused of illegally using public deposits and sentenced to three years. The arrests had the desired effect, as the number of individuals owning businesses began to decline. Around the country, in 2004, assorted private projects were wrapped up or forced to slow down, as the government alleged that their owners had infringed land use regulations. In 2006, the private sector had fallen by 15 per cent and amounted to 26 million people in a population of 1.3 billion.[65]

Under Hu Jintao the words 'reform' and 'opening up' were rarely coupled together, while 'opening up' began to disappear altogether, replaced by incessant calls for a 'Harmonious Society', meaning the social stability party officials required to pursue their special interests.

***

The flip side of growth was pollution, although the assault on nature had begun well before the era of reform. Mao had viewed dams as a pillar of development, with huge water conservancy projects carried out by hundreds of millions of villagers at the height of the Great Leap Forward. Many were poorly designed and badly built, resulting in landslides, river silting, soil salinisation and devastating inundations. A prolonged and intense attack on nature, viewed as a force to be tamed, claimed up to half the trees in some provinces. In the rush to transform a predominantly agricultural society into an industrial powerhouse capable of eclipsing the capitalist camp, the amount of sewage and industrial waste released into streams surged. Entire rivers in the industrial north turned into noisome flows of toxic materials, killing fish, poisoning local people and embedding pollutants deep into the soil when diverted through endless conduits and culverts. Belching chimneys covered industrial cities in a brown haze.[66]

Opportunities to pollute diversified after 1976. When nineteen paper factories opened in Zhejiang in 1979, they contributed 100,000 tonnes of the 1.5 million tonnes of untreated industrial waste dumped into the rivers every day throughout the province. More than two-thirds of all drinking water was already unsafe for consumption. The province also discharged millions of tonnes of industrial waste into the air. In Hangzhou, the provincial capital, the concentration of particles in the air exceeded international norms by a factor of ten. Yet that was relatively mild: in Pingyang, where chemical factories produced sulphur, the acid was so corrosive that it ate away clothes, bricks and tiles. 'A sail will rot away in less than two years,' a local resident explained. In parts of the province not even radioactive waste was treated, sickening tens of thousands of people.[67]

Zhejiang was far from an exception. Acid rain was a problem in many cities, from Chongqing inland to Nanjing near the coast. In Lanzhou, where hundreds of factories crowded a narrow corridor along the Yellow River, smog blocked the sun for months on end during winter. In 1981, on what must have been a very conservative estimate, 24 billion tonnes of industrial waste was released into the water nationwide, about three times as much as in Japan, a country with an economy four times as large.[68]

Pledges were made, laws enacted, waste treatment facilities installed. But as Qu Geping, a pioneer in environmental protection and chairman of a committee at the National People's Congress in charge of fighting pollution, pointed out in 1991, there were no incentives to protect the environment. Of all the facilities set up to manage waste, only one-third functioned as intended. Another third was so defective that their equipment only worked intermittently, with the remainder entirely dysfunctional. The State Council estimated the economic losses caused each year by air pollution at 50 billion yuan, and by water pollution at 40 billion yuan.[69]

The trend, over the following decade, was onwards and upwards. By the end of the century, the amount of untreated effluent released into China's waterways reached more than 40 billion tonnes, while 23 million tonnes of sulphur dioxide was pumped into the air. Two out of three cities failed to reach even the lowest standard for particulate matter in the air, and it was estimated that damage due to acid rain alone cost 110 billion yuan annually. Soil erosion, not least deforestation, desertification and alkalinisation, affected 38 per cent of the overall surface, or more than 3.6 million square kilometres.[70]

The country's environmental woes escalated after China joined the WTO. Lax environmental controls were crucial to selling a trillion dollars of goods to the rest of the world, as the companies that dominated the market were also the most polluting, whether they made steel, aluminium, cement, chemicals, plastics, leather or paper. The horizon was blurred, from clouds of brownish smoke spewed into the air by natural gas refineries and coal plants in Xinjiang, all the way to Beijing, buffeted every summer by hazardous sandstorms that turned the sky yellow. According to a government report, 300 million people in the countryside had no alternative but to drink water tainted by chemicals and other contaminants. Entire rivers were dangerous to the touch. Some ran dry before reaching the sea. About 90 per cent of all cities had contaminated underground water. In Shanghai canals bubbled with pollution, even in cold weather. Tap water smelled foul. Roughly one-third of the country was exposed to acid rain.[71]

The pollution, like everything else, went global. Sulphur dioxide spewed from China's coal plants became acid rain in Seoul and Tokyo. Even in Los Angeles, according to the US Environmental Protection Agency, one-quarter of the particulate matter clogging the skies could be traced to China. There were, of course, local benefits, but no global gains. As its polluting factories closed down, with some literally dismantled, shipped to China and reassembled there, Germany emerged as a leader of the green movement. Chancellor Angela Merkel was nicknamed the 'climate chancellor', pushing international agreements to reduce carbon emissions. In the Ruhr Valley, once dominated by coal mines and steel mills, rivers were nursed back to health, contaminated soil cleaned up and turned into parkland. Other countries, too, appeared to benefit from lower carbon emissions as steel production was moved to China. Yet according to the European Parliament, the less efficient mills in China emitted three times as much carbon dioxide for every ton of steel produced as did their counterparts in Germany. Moreover, since China had a socialist economy, once the steel mills were up and running, they rarely shut down, regardless of markets and demand. In 2007 the country had 77 large iron- and steelworks and hundreds of smaller mills, once again producing so much excess capacity that some basic steel products were unprofitable domestically and abroad.[72]

The State Environmental Protection Administration in 2004 had around 1 per cent of the personnel of the Environmental Protection Agency in the United States. Like other state institutions, they produced resounding statements on paper, although their writ ran only as far as their local agent on the ground. When the administration closed a factory, it sometimes reopened within weeks. Local officials often turned a blind eye to environmental edicts to appease polluting factories that paid local taxes.[73]

Protests over environmental degradation took place across the country, and sometimes even pitched battles against riot police. In Xinchang, a factory town some 80 kilometres south of Hangzhou, as many as 15,000 people braved tear gas as they threw stones at the authorities and overturned police cars, demanding the relocation of a pharmaceuticals plant accused of leaking dangerous chemicals into the water supply. Zhou Yongkang, the country's public security minister, reported 74,000 similar incidents in 2004, an increase from 58,000 the previous year. In 2005 the tally rose to 87,000 protests, including a clash with villagers protesting against the construction of a power plant during which the police opened fire, killing at least three people. Most protests escaped wider public attention, and not all concerned the environment, as forced evictions, unpaid wages, land grabs and official corruption likewise angered people. But pollution was a major cause, not least because no public hearings took place when potentially harmful factories were built.[74]

Even in protest, not all people were equal. The economy was lopsided, with a narrow strip along the coast allowed to surge ahead, from Dalian all the way south to Shenzhen. Much of the countryside, meanwhile, remained mired in poverty, as entire villages survived on remittances migrant workers sent home. Local governments could ignore environmental standards, yet they could also decide to apply them to the letter if they came under pressure from their own residents, not least when funding was abundant. Vast amounts of money had come from the central coffers to modernise the infrastructure of showcase cities like Guangzhou and Shanghai. Increasingly these cities used their financial clout to export air, soil and water pollution to less developed parts of the country.

When the gas pipeline from Xinjiang to Shanghai opened on 30 December 2004, it instantly shifted some of the city's air pollution westward by some 4,000 kilometres. As Lake Taihu, on which Shanghai depended for water, became too polluted, construction began in 2007 on four major reservoirs to capture the mainstream of the Yangtze River. The Qingcaosha Reservoir, the first to begin supplying water in 2010, cost the local government 17 billion yuan.[75]

Other cities, too, began to relocate pollution outside their boundaries. In the Pearl River Delta, where around one-third of the country's exports were manufactured, billions were spent on installing sewage treatment plants and moving all major industry towards more remote parts of the province. Shenzhen and Guangzhou introduced new environmental standards in 2006, forcing small enterprises that damaged the environment to migrate further inland. Some factories also moved voluntarily to the countryside, attracted by cheaper land and lower taxes made available by local officials keen to boost growth.[76]

But no city did more than Beijing to clean up its act. The reason was simple: the capital had been selected to host the 2008 Summer Olympics, an event widely seen as the country's 'coming out' party to the world.

***

Jubilation swept the country after the International Olympic Committee announced on 13 July 2001 that Beijing had won its bid to mount the Olympics in 2008. The ballot had taken place in the heavily guarded World Trade Center in Moscow, with a few Tibetan activists protesting outside. In Beijing people danced, cheered and jumped for joy under a dazzling display of fireworks. In a televised speech, a beaming Jiang Zemin congratulated the people of Beijing, also expressing thanks to 'friends all over the world'.[77]

For months the propaganda machine had whipped up popular support for the country's claim, with a barrage of advertising on television and radio. 'New Beijing, Great Olympics', as the campaign was known, portrayed the bid as a matter of national pride in which every Chinese subject had a stake. Critics of the country's human rights record, however, argued that the prestige of hosting the Games would boost the legitimacy of a government that continued to repress its people. Supporters, on the other hand, believed that greater international exposure would speed up the country's transition to democracy, much as its inclusion in the World Trade Organization would encourage the rule of law. Beijing provided reassurances. As Liu Jingmin, vice-mayor of the capital, declared in somewhat clunky language: 'The construction of democracy and the rule of law have been improved and are developing.'[78]

An early test came two years later, as a coronavirus later traced back to a civet began infecting people in Guangdong province in mid-November 2002. Hundreds were infected with what was at first described as 'atypical pneumonia'. The government suppressed news of the outbreak and prevented medical workers from alerting international bodies, including the authorities in neighbouring Hong Kong. After a fishmonger checked into the Sun Yat-sen Memorial Hospital in Guangzhou on 31 January 2003, dozens of hospital staff became infected. By 16 February, rumours of a mysterious bug were so pervasive that millions of people began stockpiling vinegar, supposed to disinfect the air when brought to the boil. Several died from lethal fumes after leaving the brew cooking over coal stoves all night. In Guangzhou shops ran out of face masks, while local residents hoarded rice, edible oil and salt. Officials took to radio and television to quell the panic: 'ignore rumours and trust the government,' pronounced vice-mayor Chen Chuanyu.[79]

On 21 February, Liu Jianlun, an infected doctor from the Sun Yat-sen Memorial Hospital, crossed the border into Hong Kong to attend a wedding. He checked into the Metropole Hotel, passing the disease to more than twenty other hotel guests, who in turn took the corona-virus global, with infected travellers reaching Hanoi, Toronto and Singapore.

On 1 March the World Health Organization issued a global alert. Beijing refused to cooperate: 'No clue indicates that the virus originated in Guangdong province,' a deputy health minister claimed. Even as the world began to take notice, with laboratories around the world racing to probe material from patients, the media in China were instructed not to publish the warning. On 21 March, city health investigators in Hong Kong confirmed that Liu Jianlun had trans-mitted the disease to others. Five days later the Ministry of Public Health finally acknowledged that the virus was far more serious than previously stated, although a World Health Organization team was still denied access to Guangdong province.[80]

The full extent of the cover-up only came to light after Jiang Yanyong, a retired doctor in the People's Liberation Army who called several hospitals to obtain a clearer idea of the number of infected patients, sent a lengthy email on 4 April to Phoenix TV in Hong Kong. His letter was published abroad a few days later, forcing the minister of public health and the mayor of Beijing to resign. Yet when an editorial in the *Wall Street Journal* called for a temporary halt to travel to and from China, the *People's Daily* of 17 April denounced it as 'malicious and unhelpful interference' and repeated the official claim that no evidence pointed to China as the origin of the virus.[81]

In the end, resolute measures taken by the health authorities in Hong Kong kept SARS from ballooning out of control. In total over 8,000 people were infected. More than 700 cases were fatal, the majority in Hong Kong, where the trauma further cemented distrust of the mainland. As one former WHO official put it, 'SARS is the pandemic that did not occur.'[82]

The world, with the exception of Hong Kong, learned very little from the experience. The regime, however, became more adept at suppressing information that might cause instability. Two years later, a virologist whose research on avian flu diverged widely from offi-cial explanations was threatened with detention for revealing 'state secrets'. Jiang Yanyong was arrested in 2004 in one of the regime's customary pre-June the Fourth sweeps. Sixteen years later, in February 2020, he was placed under house arrest again as another coronavirus was setting off on its global journey.[83]

One consequence of the SARS outbreak was that Beijing had to postpone the launch of its marketing campaign for the 2008 Olympics. There were other delays, including a deadline for a contest to compose the official Beijing Olympics song.[84] But construction of all the venues proceeded apace, as gleaming, avant-garde buildings appeared across the capital, many designed by international architects, among them Albert Speer Jr, son of Adolf Hitler's favourite architect who had designed the 1936 Berlin Olympics. Like his father, who had built a magnificent Via Triumphalis cutting through the very heart of Berlin, Speer's son planned an eight-kilometre boulevard stretching from the new railway station past Tiananmen Square to the Olympic Park.

A spending spree of about $40 billion, unmatched by previous host cities, transformed the capital. Roads were expanded, new underground lines installed and dozens of massive structures erected in a steel-and-concrete upheaval that filled the horizon with churning dust. The scale was gargantuan, with more than 1.7 billion square feet of new construction undertaken after 2002. Old neighbourhoods, alleyways and walled courtyard homes were bulldozed and their residents relocated far away from the city centre, sometimes forcibly, with dozens of police and moving vans mobilised to carry out the evictions. The Centre on Housing Rights and Evictions, a non-governmental organisation based in Geneva, estimated that 1.5 million people, roughly one in ten residents, were forced to leave the capital, although the Ministry of Foreign Affairs dismissed the estimate, giving a more reassuring figure of 6,037.[85]

Pollution was a concern, since the organisers had promised a green Olympics. Campaigns were launched to curb vehicle emissions, replace diesel-powered buses with new models fuelled by natural gas and move hundreds of heavily polluting industries beyond the city. Coal-burning stoves and furnaces were replaced by new units fired by electricity. Yet just weeks before the Games opened, a brown haze still covered the city, trapped in a basin surrounded by mountains. Emergency measures were taken, with even factories located hundreds of kilometres away, from Manchuria in the north to the very edge of the Gobi Desert in Inner Mongolia, ordered to shut down. Mine closures caused a shortage of coal, which generated about 80 per cent of the country's power. Prices of thermal coal almost doubled, prompting the central government to introduce new price controls.[86]

On the day of the opening ceremony, the sky was still grey. But no athletes marched into the stadium wearing a mask. By all accounts, the show was dazzling, involving fireworks, drummers, children, dancers, several singers and a pianist, in all 15,000 performers in the National Stadium, a latticed shell popularly known as the Bird's Nest. A security force 100,000-strong ensured that the event went off without a glitch. People around the world were spellbound, with rave reviews of a show many called the 'greatest ever' in the history of the Olympics.[87]

Parts of the show attracted some controversy. An angelic girl in a red dress who had sung a popular tune praising the motherland, capturing the hearts of many viewers, had, it turned out, merely lip-synced along, as the uneven teeth of the seven-year-old who had lent her voice had been considered potentially damaging to the country's international image. A Politburo member had ordered a last-minute switch. The fireworks shown on giant screens and television, with their impressive sequence of explosions moving from Tiananmen Square to the Bird's Nest, were revealed as computer-generated. Most of the 56 children dressed in ethnic costumes, each representing one of the country's minority groups, actually came from the dominant Han, who made up about 92 per cent of the population. Most of the several billion viewers around the world shrugged off these details, with online opinion in the mainland more critical than their counterparts overseas. Even the weather improved after a few days, as a change in the winds at long last brought crystalline blue skies for some of the sporting events.[88]

Yet, despite their obvious success, the Olympics also brought to the fore simmering tensions with the West. There was pride in an event that had shown the world how far the country had come, but also resentment at what were perceived as unfair attempts by foreigners to undermine the country's moment. One growing object of anger had been foreign protests in support of Tibet. On 10 March 2008, the anniversary of a 1959 uprising against Beijing, hundreds of Buddhist monks and nuns held a peaceful protest in Lhasa. After the police used force, the situation spiralled out of control, with demonstrators burning shops and vandalising police vehicles. A fierce crackdown followed, including the use of electric prods, tear gas and shootings. Armed soldiers patrolled the streets, determined to wage what the regime called a 'people's war' against 'hostile forces' and 'reactionary separatist forces', including the Dalai Lama. Casualties numbered in the dozens, although precise numbers remained a matter for conjecture since no foreign journalists were allowed to cover the clashes. Thousands were sent to prison.[89]

The resolute suppression of any form of protest was routine along the country's ethnic belt, but this time protests in support of Tibet erupted in cities around the world. In London, Paris, Delhi and Sydney, demonstrators tried to storm the Chinese embassy, calling for a boycott of the Olympics. On 24 March, the ceremony in Athens to light the Olympic flame was disrupted. The flame became a repeated target on its journey to Beijing, with scuffles between protesters and supporters of the regime. Jin Jing, a wheelchair-bound athlete competing in the Paralympics, became a national icon for fending off protesters in Paris while carrying the flame. In Canberra more than 10,000 Chinese Australians staged a pro-Beijing rally, standing six deep along the 16-kilometre route, with hundreds of cars driving around the city carrying the Chinese flag. In Seoul, more than 8,000 police were not enough to prevent Chinese students from kicking an elderly South Korean protester and hurling rocks at a group that raised banners critical of Beijing. Angry messages appeared on websites in China, demanding that 'China should not be humiliated.' For a great many people steeped in patriotic education, support for Tibet was an intolerable affront to the country's unity, a blatant ploy to prevent the nation's historic rise to greatness. The world, it seemed, was ganging up on China.[90]

The regime tapped into these deep strains of nationalism, using the propaganda machine to present itself as the defender of the motherland. But passion can be dangerous, easily turning inwards. By mid-April, the censors began to rein in the flood of postings, blogs, internet chats and other manifestations of anger towards the West.[91]

The regime also ensured that no form of protest could mar the Olympics. Beijing was transformed into a giant fortress, with tens of thousands of surveillance cameras installed on lamp posts and in internet cafés and bars. Undesirable elements, from migrants, peddlers and beggars to fortune tellers, were sent packing. Civilians wearing red armbands were recruited to patrol the streets. Throughout the country, every unit, factory and school was put on red alert, ordered to watch out for troublemakers who might try to make their way to the capital. Hu Jia, a democracy activist who took the government to task for not improving human rights ahead of the games, was sent to prison for several years.[92]

Following promises made to the International Olympic Committee, 'special zones' were set up in three parks to allow people to express themselves freely. None of the 77 applicants were successful, and two grandmothers aged 77 and 79 were detained. A handful of foreign activists managed to dodge security, unfurling 'Free Tibet' banners before undercover police dragged them away. In a blunt statement just before the Games ended, the American embassy used the opportunity to take Beijing to task for failing to show 'greater tolerance and openness'.[93] But as the leadership watched over the closing ceremony, they had every reason to feel proud of their accomplishments. They had catapulted their economy forward, used a massive trade surplus to transform the capital, defeated calls for a boycott, crushed dissent, tamed pollution, rallied the population around the Games and dazzled foreigners with their clockwork Olympics. Less openness, not more, was clearly the key to success.

10

Hubris (2008–2012)

On 15 September 2008, a global financial services firm called Lehman Brothers, founded in 1847, filed for bankruptcy protection. It had more than $600 billion of debt. Merrill Lynch, another investment company, cut a last-minute deal with Bank of America to avert a financial crisis. The disappearance of two of Wall Street's most powerful firms came barely one week after the US government had taken control of Fannie Mae and Freddie Mac, two mortgage lenders with government backing that had accumulated huge losses in their subprime investments.

Seven years earlier, concerns about the effects of deflation had prompted the Federal Reserve to reduce the interest rate to 1.75 per cent, a level not seen since 1961. A second cut in November 2002 lowered it to 1.25 per cent. At the same time, interest-only mortgages became available, with minimum guarantees, attracting homeowners who could not afford more conventional loans. Since loans were cheap and credit was easy, demand for mortgages increased, in turn driving up housing prices. The percentage of subprime mortgages doubled. But when the interest rate began to rise, up to 5.25 per cent by June 2006, many homeowners could no longer afford their monthly payments. A mortgage crisis began to unfold in 2007, bringing falling house prices and frozen credit markets as well as huge losses in the financial industry, not least among the hedge funds and investment banks that were not subject to the same regulations as depository banks and had repackaged the collateral put up for subprime loans to create new investment products.

The dramatic turn of events underscored the fragile nature of the financial system in the United States, once believed to be unshakable. Markets around the world plummeted, gripped by fear that other banks might collapse. As banks stopped lending to each other, the Federal Reserve intervened, soon followed by central banks in Japan and Europe. In the United States alone, the cost of the bailout package was close to $1.5 trillion, although one-third of this amount was later recouped once assets bought during the crisis were resold at a profit. After years of easy lending, a severe recession brought huge economic damage and widespread human suffering, with unemployment soaring to 10 per cent and millions of people losing their homes.

As the United States, Europe and Japan slipped into recession, their markets dealt a blow to China, which was heavily dependent on exports. Tens of thousands of small- and medium-sized factories were forced to shut down, sending their workers scrambling for jobs or back to the countryside. In Wenzhou, according to an internal investigation by the People's Bank of China, profits were slashed by 50 per cent in the last quarter of 2008. By March 2009 the figure stood at 60 per cent, forcing local enterprises to shed 10 per cent of their workforce. All along the coast, the railway stations, normally teeming with new arrivals, witnessed a great reversal, with surges in the number of passengers returning home. Some enterprise owners simply vanished, while others refused to pay back wages, leading to a rapid rise in protests and labour disputes. Local officials, under pressure to maintain social stability, alternated between shelling out cash and calling in the riot police.[1]

Even before the global financial crisis, many factory owners were reeling from soaring labour and raw material costs, as the yuan had been gaining in value after it was allowed to rise and fall by 2 per cent in July 2005, when it stood at 8.28 to the dollar. It steadily increased to 6.83 in July 2008, when it was fixed again for another two years. In the north, strict environmental standards and intermittent closures before the Games had contributed to the slump.

Inflation disappeared with the financial crisis, but as commodity prices collapsed around the world, the country's steel, cement and construction companies saw their profits evaporate. Building projects ground to a halt, blast furnaces stood idle.[2]

The leadership, who had counted on an economic boom after the Games ended, was taken aback by the financial crisis. Panic set in, as the economy contracted and disgruntled workers took to the streets. Tax rebates for exported goods were introduced that, together with intervention in the currency markets to halt further appreciation of the yuan, made Chinese exports even more competitive abroad. Banks were directed to lend more to small enterprises at lower interest rates. In order to maintain the economic growth on which employment and stability rested, Wen Jiabao proposed a programme of domestic consumption that would wean the country off its reliance on exports. Since ordinary people were too poor to increase their consumption, he proposed a stimulus package worth $586 billion (4 trillion yuan), to be spent mainly on new infrastructure projects, a sum equal to 14 per cent of the country's economic production, compared to the 6 per cent of output represented by the stimulus plan pushed through in Washington. 'They are going to spend like there's no tomorrow,' observed the chief economist at the Hong Kong and Shanghai Banking Corporation.[3]

By the second quarter of 2009, the unprecedented level of credit began to have an impact. The growth rate began to move upward again, despite a decline of 22 per cent in the year-on-year value of exports. One hundred billion dollars was spent on new railways alone. In the spirit of the 'Go West' campaign, a $17.6 billion railway spanned the deserts of Xinjiang province. More than $80 billion was earmarked for intercity rail lines, including a bullet train from Beijing to Guangzhou. Since the spring of 2004, when the economy began to overheat, the regime had barred local and provincial governments from sinking more money into infrastructure. Once the credit spigot was turned on, massive construction projects appeared in every town and city across the country.[4]

Unlike the United States, the country was not short of cash to fund the spending spree. For years, the central bank had prevented the market from bidding up the yuan by buying dollars. As dollar reserves accumulated, the regime was able to maintain the funding imbalance that fuelled its rapid growth. To prevent all the yuan used to buy the dollars from adding to the money supply, it had ordered banks to increase their reserves and buy central bank bonds, which were in effect sterilisation bonds. This huge reservoir of liquidity bottled up in the banking system was now unleashed.[5]

By 2010 the country was absorbing 40 per cent of the world's cement and steel. In the three years following the stimulus, China used more cement than the United States in the entire twentieth century. The country boasted 221 cities with a population of more than a million, each coveting all the accoutrements of modernity, with shopping malls, cinemas and luxury hotels, preferably wrapped in gleaming metal with glass elevators running up the outside. In 2011 alone, 390 new museums were opened, large, small, private or public. Skyscrapers mushroomed everywhere, often in clusters of one or two dozen. Cities rushed to outdo each other in building ever higher towers, with Pudong setting a record with its 127-floor Shanghai Tower. Financial gloom, meanwhile, derailed plans for new towers in Chicago, Moscow, Dubai and other cities around the world.[6]

The money came from the banks, but also from land. In a repeat of the scramble after Deng Xiaoping's southern tour in 1992, local governments sold land to developers at lucrative prices, using the funds to build infrastructure. In 2009, they obtained $219 billion from the sale of land use, an increase of more than 40 per cent over the preceding year. The amount soared to $417 billion in 2010. In their search for growth, they happily seized land from farmers. By the calculations of Wu Jinglian, a noted economist, the farmers whose land was confiscated lost between 20 and 35 trillion yuan, or $3.1 to 5.4 trillion dollars, in land value since 1978. It was the continuation of a familiar pattern of wealth transfer from the countryside to the cities that had started in 1949.[7]

Destruction came knocking on the door before construction. Local governments cheerfully demolished anything and everything blocking their vision of the future. A familiar tale emerged: a community would wake up, find demolition notices affixed to their homes, reject a meagre compensation offer from the state and endure a campaign of harassment only to see bulldozers arrive in the dead of night, leaving them evicted and often dispossessed. Occasionally one could see a family huddled together around a meal in a partially demolished house, the façade torn down but a corner of the living room and a jagged wall around the kitchen still standing. Yet this story came with a twist, as the victims increasingly included the ranks of the privileged, whether doctors, financiers or retired party officials.[8]

Sometimes buildings earmarked for the wrecking ball were no more than five years old. In one neighbourhood in Beijing, several families were evicted from homes only completed that same year. According to the estimate of one research firm, the country demolished 16 per cent of its housing stock between 2005 and 2010. At the height of the stimulus plan, upwards of 2,000 square kilometres, roughly the size of Mauritius, was being expropriated annually. Across the country, shiny new offices and residential towers stood next to fenced-off fields of debris with twisted iron rods protruding from concrete slabs, broken ceramic tiles glistening in the sun.[9]

Listed buildings and other cultural landmarks that had managed to survive war and revolution were torn down. Eminent domain achieved what had eluded Chairman Mao at the height of the Cultural Revolution: the eradication of the last vestiges of the old society. Whether attacking ancient temples, imperial courtyard houses or Art Deco villas, jackhammers tirelessly demolished old architecture. According to Li Xiaojie, the head of the State Administration of Cultural Heritage, an agency with even fewer personnel than the State Environmental Protection Administration, roughly 44,000 of the country's 766,000 registered heritage sites vanished. Developers cheerfully paid the maximum fine of 500,000 yuan.[10]

Developers also cut corners, as hasty construction, shoddy materials and lack of adequate planning shortened the average life-span of a commercial building to about 25 years, roughly one-third of what was expected in Japan, Europe or the United States. Every so often news came of a spectacular failure, whether the collapse of an eight-lane suspension bridge, a building that toppled like a house of cards or an opera house with glass panes falling from the windows. Poorly executed projects were called tofu buildings, as they crumbled when stressed like jiggled blocks of soft bean curd. When in 2008 an earthquake hit Sichuan and killed 87,000 people, a substantial proportion of more than 7,000 school buildings were later found to have collapsed due to substandard construction.[11]

Speculation was rife, with investors driving up prices since people had few alternatives for their cash. This was where the hidden infla-tion was taking place. In Hangzhou, by one expert's reckoning, roughly half of the housing market was in the hands of a small group of speculators selling the same properties to each other to force up their value, each transaction allowing the next seller to obtain an even larger mortgage. Profits were divided once the homes were unloaded to outsiders, with many left unoccupied by their owners. Across the country, empty apartment towers and deserted shopping malls were quite common.[12]

Exports boomed thanks to generous tax rebates. In addition to the $586 billion stimulus package, a flood of new bank loans totalling $1.27 trillion in 2009 kept industry ticking over. The low yuan also helped exporters. Even as the dollar fell steeply against the euro, the yen and most other currencies in the wake of the financial crisis, the central bank continued to intervene heavily, keeping the yuan tightly yoked to the dollar. From March to October 2009 alone, the currency lost 16 per cent of its value against the euro and 31 per cent against the Australian dollar.[13]

Most loans went to large state companies. In an echo of Jiang Zemin's policy of 'Grasping the Big and Letting Go of the Small', Hu Jintao strongly favoured an approach popularly dubbed 'the state advances, the private sector recedes.' A flood of money was channelled into key industries, including airlines, steel, coal, aluminium, even wind turbines. In a continuation of the mergers and acquisitions that had led to the emergence of state behemoths after 1998, state enterprises used political pressure and their economic clout to absorb smaller private rivals. In a whole range of sectors, from steel to real estate, private players were crushed. In a series of virtual hostile takeovers, loss-making state competitors absorbed most of the privately owned airlines set up in the previous couple of years.[14]

For the best part of a decade, state enterprises had been the biggest winners from the country's accession to the WTO. On paper, they were a world apart from their ailing predecessors in the 1990s. Between 2000 and 2010, their profits increased sevenfold, reaching just short of 2 trillion yuan. They created twice as much shareholder value for the government. But when two economists working for the Hong Kong Institute for Monetary Research actually scrutinised the official figures of 250,000 state firms, they discovered that the profits were overstated. Had these enterprises had to pay the same interest rates as their private counterparts, their profits would have been entirely wiped out. In other words, the very structure of the economy had barely budged, as the savings of ordinary people as well as the foreign currency made by export firms along the coast were used to keep the state sector afloat.[15]

Cheap credit, as always, came at the cost of lost efficiency. Fixed investment by state enterprises cost 20 to 30 per cent more than that of private firms and took about 50 per cent longer to complete. Since they had a firm grip on the overall economy, they could also charge extra fees and higher prices that acted as a tax on all consumers.[16] Overcapacity reappeared in key industries, including steel, aluminium and, of course, wind turbines. Manufacturers were keen to unload excess production abroad, further stoking trade tensions. In the United States, President Barack Obama slapped punitive tariffs on imported tyres. Washington also began to investigate evidence of dumping of steel pipes imported from China.[17]

Beijing retaliated by lodging a complaint against protectionism with the WTO. In 2009, after Brussels imposed anti-dumping tariffs on imports of iron and steel fasteners, for the first time it also dragged the European Union into a dispute. The language used by the regime sounded familiar: it mirrored the selfsame objections that officials in the United States and Europe had raised against China.[18]

Hubris set in. The much-vaunted financial system in the United States had failed, while the sixteen members of the eurozone seemed unable to work out a rescue plan for Greece, a country that threatened to default on its sovereign debt. It looked very much like Karl Marx's prediction about the collapse of capitalism was finally coming true, as unemployment soared and growth rates fell in the West. Leading party officials lashed out at the United States, rebuking Washington for failing to properly regulate its markets and control its fiscal deficit. At a world economic forum held in Davos in January 2009, Wen Jiabao blamed capitalism for an unsustainable model of development based on the 'blind pursuit of profit' and lambasted the banks for their 'failure of financial supervision'. Zhou Xiaochuan, governor of the central bank, went further in challenging the global order led by the United States, pronouncing in April 2009 that his country's rapid response to the crisis had demonstrated the superiority of its political system. The leadership felt vindicated. Beijing began to mirror Washington, assuming the role of adviser to the world and offering lessons on how to run an economy. The capitalist model was unsustainable, Beijing explained, and now was the time to promote a new approach which would ultimately prove to be vastly superior, namely 'socialism with Chinese characteristics'. Hu Jintao called it the 'China way'.[19]

***

On 18 December 2008, the leadership convened in the Great Hall of the People to celebrate the thirtieth anniversary of the open-door policy. Hu Jintao gave the keynote address, asking that the country uphold the Four Cardinal Principles, including the 'absolutely correct' leadership of the party and the 'dictatorship of the proletariat'. Beijing, he warned, 'would never copy the political system and the model of the West', but 'continue to hoist high the great flag of socialism'. Stability, he pointed out, was the party's overriding task, 'because nothing can be accomplished without stability'. The message, repeated incessantly by successive leaders, was prompted on this occasion by fear that the global crisis would increase social unrest.[20]

Stability meant repression on the one hand, patriotic education on the other. Even before Hu Jintao delivered his speech, the bludgeon had fallen. Weeks earlier, Liu Xiaobo had been arrested for 'inciting subversion of state power'. This had consisted in contributing to a manifesto entitled Charter 08, inspired by the Charter 77 written by Václav Havel and other dissidents in Czechoslovakia more than thirty years earlier. Charter 08, initially signed by more than 300 people, garnered thousands of signatures once it was published on 10 December 2008, the anniversary of the Universal Declaration of Human Rights. Among other demands, the document called for the separation of powers, an independent judiciary, abolition of the household registration system and freedom of association, expression and religion as well as civic education. One year later, Liu was sentenced to eleven years in prison.

Next came a crackdown on the internet. China already had a sophisticated control mechanism, as all the cables linking the country to the outside world had to pass through one of three large computer centres, where government terminals intercepted all inbound data and checked it against an ever-growing list of banned addresses and forbidden keywords. This was the so-called Great Firewall. But millions of active domestic bloggers still existed. Some of them waged online campaigns against corrupt party officials, posting compromising material or incriminating evidence. Many went quiet, as thousands of websites were closed down in January 2009.[21]

Still, both abroad and at home, social commentators were convinced that the internet would pave the way towards a more open and accountable society. One true believer was Ai Weiwei, a contemporary artist who had helped design the Bird's Nest for the Olympics. Ai, a prominent activist who was openly critical of the government's record on human rights, believed that harsh repression of the internet would only increase the appeal of democracy. His own blog was widely read. But in December 2009 came a second internet crackdown, as new measures were rolled out to limit the ability of an individual to set up a personal website. 'The internet has become an important avenue through which anti-China forces infiltrate, sabotage and magnify their capabilities for destruction,' gravely intoned Meng Jianzhu, the minister for public security. A year later, Google was squeezed out after it refused to censor its search results, while Facebook, YouTube and Twitter were blocked, replaced by clones in state hands. A small army of censors not only monitored the internet, but also flooded chatrooms with online comments supporting the government. They were found wherever there was an internet connection. Jiaozuo, a mining city of some 3 million people in Henan, deployed 35 internet monitors and 120 police officers to censor online messages. Beijing advertised for 10,000 internet censors in 2009.[22]

Activists of every stripe faced increased surveillance or outright arrest. After the Sichuan earthquake in May 2008, the regime had excelled at deploying more than 130,000 soldiers and relief workers, the largest deployment since June the Fourth. Wen Jiabao, who had a background in geomechanics, arrived within hours to oversee the rescue work. The troops, however, were drilled for a potential war with Taiwan, not for disaster relief. Poorly trained and badly equipped, they trawled through the mountains, trying to move the rubble with their bare hands. After a few days, with unusual frankness the regime requested international help. Rescue groups and relief supplies arrived first from Taiwan, then from Japan, Korea, the United States and other countries. Donations also poured in. By far the most generous were the residents of Hong Kong, who raised over HKD1 billion within a week, not counting HKD9 billion allocated by the Legislative Council.[23]

Local governments in the disaster zone promised to investigate the shoddy construction of schools that had collapsed and killed thousands of children. But once the journalists left, very little happened. People who questioned the authorities were detained and harassed, with a few investigated for 'inciting subversion'. The riot police were called in to disperse protests organised by parents whose children died when the schools crumbled. Huang Qi and Tan Zuoren, two human rights activists who tried to give voice to the victims, were put on trial in August 2009 for 'endangering national security'.[24]

One of the most prominent activists to question the government's handling of the rescue effort was Ai Weiwei. On his blog he published his own list of the children killed in the earthquake, determined to give every victim a name. 'No one yet has an explanation for why Mr. Ai is being allowed to speak out so candidly on a government-controlled website,' a foreign journalist wondered in March 2009. Two months later Mr Ai's blog was shut down. When he tried to testify at Tan Zuoren's trial, the police beat him up. For good measure, in January 2011 his studio, deemed to be an illegal structure, was bulldozed.[25]

Repression of legal activists also became more pervasive. In 2006, a blind lawyer who had challenged the coercive implementation of the one-child policy in Linyi, the region of his birth, was locked up for four years. Even after he was released Chen Guangcheng was placed under virtual house arrest, with hundreds of unidentified agents assigned to the sole task of isolating him from the outside world. Their tactics included regular beatings, cutting off the electricity supply and placing metal sheets over the windows of his house. The screws were also tightened on other legal activists. As the drive to build party cells in private enterprises continued apace, Communist Party committees in law firms were tasked with restraining troublesome members. They blocked the renewal of their licences. When law practices refused to bow to the committee's demands, the authorities closed them down.[26]

Repression was helped by new security measures, not least so-called Offices to Maintain Social Security and Rectify Law and Order. The name was clunky, as with so many other institutions in a one-party state, but the underlying task for these new outfits was simple: ferret out 'anti-party elements' and 'nip all destabilising forces in the bud'. They spread like a rash in 2009, with one office in every district in most coastal cities, sometimes one in every major street. Large and medium-sized cities also established Leading Groups on State Security, headed by the municipal party secretary. Minister of State Security Geng Huichang characterised them as a 'people's defence frontline to protect national security'.[27]

The goal of the ever-expanding state security apparatus was to develop a foolproof network that could fight infiltration and subversion. The hand behind these dark forces was the West, or more precisely 'hostile foreign forces' attempting to bring about the country's 'peaceful evolution' towards capitalism in a carefully orchestrated conspiracy. Liu Xiaobo, Ai Weiwei or Chen Guangcheng alike were all seen to have powerful backers in Washington, London and Brussels. When the European Union awarded dissident Hu Jia the Sakharov Prize in December 2008, it became evident that a concerted campaign to undermine the socialist system was underway. Even more damning was the open support offered to the Dalai Lama at a gathering of Nobel Peace laureates by French president Nicolas Sarkozy, who also held the European Union presidency. One year later, in November 2010, Liu Xiaobo was awarded the Nobel Prize. Vice-foreign minister Cui Tiankai denounced the award as a political attack on a rising China, promising that countries which challenged China's judicial system would 'bear the consequences'. The *People's Daily* echoed his sentiments, describing the prize as a 'tool for Western countries to impose peaceful evolution' on 'powers which do not meet their standards'.[28]

Spending on public security skyrocketed, reaching an estimated $77 billion in 2010. According to some media reports, Liaoning province, in the northern rust belt, devoted 15 per cent of its budget to internal security. One city in Guangdong province spent as much in 2010 on so-called 'stability maintenance' as it had in the previous five years, installing surveillance cameras at major intersections and hiring thousands of neighbourhood informants to assist the police in quelling unrest. Urumqi, where deadly clashes between the Uyghurs and Chinese migrants had prompted a ferocious crackdown under security tsar Zhou Yongkang in July 2009, installed 17,000 cameras. Chongqing, the showcase capital of the Go West campaign, added another 200,000, bringing the total to 510,000. Beijing and Shanghai together had more than 3 million. In London, a city which took the lead in camera surveillance in Europe, the police had access to 7,000 closed-circuit television cameras.[29]

A test for the security apparatus came in 2011, when a widespread movement of civil resistance in Tunisia led to the downfall of longtime president Zine al-Abidine Ben Ali. The Jasmine Revolution, as it was also known, ignited a wave of protests across much of the Arab world, culminating in the ousting of dictators in Egypt, Libya and Yemen. After an anonymous online call for a 'Jasmine Revolution' in China, on 20 February 2011 pro-democracy demonstrators appeared in their hundreds on the streets in a dozen cities, including Beijing and Shanghai, to be met by tens of thousands of police, ready to disperse the gatherings. Universities in several provinces were ordered to close their gates to prevent students from leaving campus. One week later, in the midst of a huge police presence, they returned in a silent protest. Since the silent marchers could not be distinguished from ordinary shoppers, the security forces took foreign journalists to task instead, confiscating their cameras, roughing up a BBC crew and arresting some fifteen members of the international press. The regime, clearly terrified of any unrest, apprehended dozens of human rights activists over the following weeks, with many more summoned and placed under close surveillance or house arrest by the police. Jasmine flowers were also banned, causing wholesale prices of the delicate tea leaf to collapse.[30]

The most prominent victim was Ai Weiwei, who was arrested at the airport on 3 April, hooded, thrown into the back of a police van and held in captivity for three months, interrogated no less than fifty times. After an international outcry, Ai was released, made to pay a huge fine for tax evasion and kept under tight surveillance.[31]

Spooked by the uprisings in North Africa and the Middle East, the state once again reined in popular culture. While the hand of the censor had always kept a tight grip on political expression, it had tolerated the increasingly freewheeling realm of entertainment, from raucous talent shows and dance broadcasts on television to microblogs with millions of followers. Concern over 'social integrity' and 'social morality' was expressed by Zhou Yongkang, who ordered a crackdown in October 2011. Television stations were ordered to limit entertainment shows to no more than two programmes of ninety minutes every evening, to be scheduled around two hours of compulsory state news broadcasts. The aim, or so the Orwellian State Administration of Radio, Film and Television claimed, was to root out 'excessive entertainment and vulgar tendencies'. But some of the talent shows curbed were offensive for a different reason. The programmes prompted home viewers to vote for their favourite contestants through mobile phone texting, but voting in any shape or form outside state control was frowned upon. Zhou also called for strict and swift censorship of entertainment on the internet, not least blogs passing on gossip about scandals involving party officials. Supplementing the monitors who already scanned the internet for forbidden posts, some internet companies beefed up their 'rumour rebuttal' departments, staffed by editors whose task it was to investigate and refute information deemed to be 'fake'. A few months earlier, the country had missed a deadline to comply with a World Trade Organization ruling to loosen state controls on access to foreign film, music and books.[32]

On 5 March 2012, Lei Feng made a renewed appearance, as people were once again urged to learn from the model soldier. The campaign strained credulity, with an outpouring of ridicule on the internet. But observers noted that it was the last bout of anonymous criticism, since less than two weeks later new regulations required registration with a verifiable account and posts deemed 'harmful' to national interests to be summarily deleted within five minutes.[33]

By 2012, as a decade of leadership under Hu Jintao and Wen Jiabao was ending, the country was a thoroughly entrenched dictatorship with a sprawling security apparatus and the world's most sophisticated surveillance system, one that their predecessors would have thought the stuff of dreams. Yet throughout, a medley of foreign pundits, ranging from university professors to respected politicians, had announced the imminent arrival of political reform. The mechanism was fairly simple: every once in a while a leader would contrive a smile and use the term 'reform', sending experts into a frenzy of speculation that the true transition towards democracy was about to begin, as carefully hidden forces within the party machine were finally gaining the long-deferred upper hand. A flurry of conjecture came after Wen Jiabao pronounced freedom of speech to be 'indispensable' in an interview with CNN journalist Fareed Zakaria on 3 October 2010. His words were censored at home, and in any event few dissidents believed that he was sincere. Yu Jie, a writer placed under house arrest, had derided the premier in a book entitled *China's Best Actor: Wen Jiabao*, published months earlier. In March 2011 hopes for reform were dashed after Wu Bangguo, chairman of the National People's Congress, once again categorically rejected the 'separation of powers', the 'system of multiple parties holding office in rotation' and the use of a 'bicameral or federal system'. Wu also warned against attempts to 'carry out privatisation'. 'We must maintain the correct political orientation and never waver on key issues of principle such as the fundamental system of the state,' he told the 3,000 delegates in his annual address.[34]

***

With increased repression after the Olympics came another bout of indoctrination. With uncanny timing, the Central Committee launched its campaign on 14 September 2008, precisely one day before the collapse of Lehman Brothers. In a changing world, the leadership opined, a correct understanding of Marxism-Leninism, Mao Zedong Thought, Deng Xiaoping Theory and the Three Represents by Jiang Zemin was more necessary than ever. For eighteen months, party members were required to immerse themselves fully in study of the classics. The works of Marx, Engels and Lenin were also printed for distribution in high schools.[35]

A year later, the regime celebrated sixty years of communist rule with lavish ceremonies and a military parade. 'The development and progress of the new China over the past sixty years fully proves that only socialism can save China, and only reform and opening up can ensure the development of China, socialism and Marxism,' Hu Jintao intoned from the rostrum, dressed in a Mao-style tunic. 'Today a socialist China that faces the future is standing tall and firm in the East,' he proudly declared. Giant portraits of the country's leaders were paraded past the square. Following thousands of goose-stepping troops came a display of military might, including new ballistic missiles. Fighter jets roared overhead in close formation.[36]

A few months after the celebrations, Xi Jinping, head of the Central Party School, the party's top institution that had always taken a lead in ideological indoctrination, sent a congratulatory letter to a study group called the China Marxism Forum, calling on scholars around the country to promote the study of Marxism. Marxism, he explained in his letter, was the ideological foundation of the party and the nation. 'Marxism is the fundamental guiding ideology for the establishment of our party and our nation,' echoed *Qiushi*, or 'Seeking Truth', the flagship magazine of the Central Committee. 'We must truly study, understand, believe in, and apply Marxism. Above all, in promoting the sinicisation, modernisation, and popularisation of Marxism, we must address the issues of correctly understanding and scientifically approaching Marxism.'[37]

A tall and stocky man, his hair always pomaded, Xi Jinping had briefly served as party secretary of Shanghai, where he kept a low profile and confined himself to making a series of bland pronouncements. He hailed from Shaanxi province and had a background in technology, with a degree in chemical engineering from Tsinghua University. Like other technocrats, he had gradually moved up the ladder, from a post in rural Hunan province to party secretary of Zhejiang, where private enterprises dominated the coast.

Xi had several advantages, not least an ability to say or do little of any consequence, thus avoiding closer scrutiny by potential rivals. He rarely took sides, cultivating a neutral persona and a benign smile which revealed nothing. He seemed harmless, and was therefore acceptable to different factions within the party. He also held a trump card. He was a so-called princeling, son of the revolutionary veteran Xi Zhongxun who had helped develop Shenzhen thirty years earlier. An added benefit was his close ties to the People's Liberation Army, who considered him their man. Aged 57, Xi was tipped to become the next general secretary.[38]

Indoctrination at home was standard, but the regime also began to promote its own image aggressively abroad. In January 2008 the leadership had determined that ideological work, too, must 'Go Global'. The goal of its charm offensive was 'to develop a lead in and struggle against international opinion on issues such as Taiwan, Tibet, Xinjiang, human rights and the evil organisation of "Falun Gong"'. 'Culture' was the key word in this exercise in soft power, including a 'Chinese Culture Year', 'Chinese Culture Week' and a 'Cultural China'. One key component was Confucius Institutes, which had first appeared in Uzbekistan in 2004, followed by another on the campus of the University of Maryland near Washington. These institutes were to expand drastically to 'organise and develop' the regime's ideological work.[39]

The propaganda drive overseas came with lavish funding. In 2009, some $10 billion were devoted to the campaign, even as the media in

Europe and the United States were reeling from the economic down-
turn. The lion's share of the funding went to CCTV, the national
television station, which boasted the most expensive single building
in the country, a headquarters soaring some 230 metres into the sky.
With access to six satellites, its stations reached around the world in
several languages (it was renamed CGTN in 2010). The New China
News Agency, for its part, expanded its overseas offices from 100 to
186. The *People's Daily* began to include a new English version of its
subsidiary, called the *Global Times*. As a local propagandist put it,
'we must let the whole world hear the stories that Chinese citizens
have to tell about their democracy, liberty, human rights and the rule
of law.'[40]

By the end of 2010, more than 280 Confucius Institutes were
operating in eighty countries, all controlled by the China Office of
Chinese Language Promotion in Beijing.[41] Consulates and embassies abroad organised 'Chinese Culture Weeks', with help from
the Ministry of Culture. In 2011 a 'Year of Chinese Culture' was
launched in Australia, and in 2012 in Italy, Germany and Turkey.
A few sceptical eyebrows were raised sporadically, with concern
expressed for Ai Weiwei and Liu Xiaobo. But overall the officially
sponsored programmes in dance, theatre and socialist state art were
well received, with the New China News Agency and the *Global
Times* invariably hailing these events as highly successful in 'promoting the understanding and friendship between the peoples of
China' and the rest of the world.

'Culture' was short for 'socialist culture', which in turn stood
for 'socialism with Chinese characteristics'. Hu Jintao called it the
'China way'. At home, this was defined as strict adherence to the
Four Cardinal Principles. Abroad, it was presented in terms of a
more balanced approach between the role of the government and the
market, in contrast to the failed model of the West with its faith in
limited government and open markets. Soon enough it was termed the
'China model', or the 'Beijing consensus', an alternative ideology and
natural counterweight to the 'Washington consensus'. The twentieth
century had been the 'American Century'; the twenty-first would
now belong to China.

Articles, pamphlets and books were churned out on the topic,
conferences and seminars held. One of the most influential volumes

was *The China Model* by Pan Wei, a professor of international politics at Peking University. Another widely read tome was *The China Wave: Rise of a Civilisational State*, published by Zhang Weiwei, professor of international relations at Fudan University in Shanghai. 'China had the capacity to learn from the West, but the West does not have this capacity to learn,' Professor Zhang pontificated. 'We need new thinking and China can humbly offer some wisdom.' Academics toured the world to proffer their advice, lionising the new model and the country's economic miracle. 'The China model has created miracles,' crowed the *People's Daily*; 'it has superseded the belief in a superior "American model", marking its demise.'[42]

In the wake of soft power came more hard power. Since its foreign reserves had ballooned after joining the WTO, the country had embarked on a shopping spree around the globe to develop its military muscle. The military budget more than doubled from $20 billion in 2001 to $42 billion in 2007. Then it rocketed to $90 billion in 2011. These official figures published by a secretive regime represented a mere one-third or one-half of the unofficial estimates produced by a number of international organisations.[43]

One of the regime's priorities was the People's Liberation Navy, as the military underwent a shift from land to sea. The country depended on foreign oil, much of which passed through the narrow Strait of Malacca between Sumatra and peninsular Malaysia. Vast amounts of other raw materials, whether copper, coal or iron ore, were also moved by sea, while a fleet of merchant ships transported the country's exports. Whether civilian container ships or oil tankers, they needed protection. But foremost, the United States had sent carrier battle groups to the region after Jiang Zemin had test-fired missiles near Taiwan in 1996. The leadership was determined to shift the military balance in the South China Sea and the Western Pacific, preventing the United States from lending military support to their long-term regional allies, primarily Taiwan, Japan and South Korea.[44]

The country's blue-water navy expanded to 260 vessels, including frigates, warships and guided-missile destroyers, as well as a fleet of more than sixty submarines, some equipped with Russian-made cruise missiles designed to attack and sink aircraft carriers. Work on intercontinental ballistic missiles proceeded apace in 2012, boosting the country's ability to deliver nuclear warheads to the United States.

By the end of the year sea trials began for the country's first aircraft carrier, a refurbished Soviet-era vessel named *Liaoning* after China's north-eastern province.[45]

The regime's arsenal of missiles arrayed along the coast opposite Taiwan more than doubled after 2002 to reach around 900 by 2007, rising again to as many as 1,200 by 2011. Washington expressed occasional concern, but perpetuated its policy of 'strategic ambiguity', remaining intentionally vague about whether or not it would intervene in a conflict over the island. The goal of the policy, devised in the wake of normalisation, had been to gain time in the hope that the issue would resolve itself peacefully. Beijing made the best of it by steadfastly building up its military clout.

Beijing also projected its power into air and space, adding hundreds of fighter jets to its air force, including a radar-evading stealth plane. Part of its strategy was the development of kinetic and directed-energy weapons capable of destroying the satellites and other space-based assets of potential adversaries. Great strides were also made in cyber warfare, as experts around the world noted a surge in the number of intrusions into computer systems, many apparently originating from China.[46]

As confidence and capability increased, confrontations became more common. The military flexed their muscle, particularly in the South China Sea, which the navy claimed as its own, prompting spats with Japan over the uninhabited Senkaku Islands, clashes with fishing ships in Indonesian waters, veiled threats of invasion against Taiwan and disputes with Vietnam over the Spratly and Paracel island groups. When in July 2010 Secretary of State Hillary Clinton sided with other countries in Southeast Asia in questioning Beijing's claim over the entirety of the South China Sea, Foreign Minister Yang Jiechi could barely contain his anger, calling it an 'attack on China'. He dismissed other countries in the region as mere bit players: 'China is a big country and other countries are small countries, and that's just a fact.' Years earlier, Deng Xiaoping had advised his colleagues to be 'modest and prudent'. His strategy of biding one's time was now replaced by a new assertiveness, based on the unshakable belief that China would be the world's dominant power.[47]

Nor did Beijing hesitate to harass the United States Navy in international waters. In March 2009, five Chinese vessels surrounded the

Impeccable, a submarine surveillance ship, dropping debris in its path some 120 kilometres south of Hainan Island. This was only one in a series of skirmishes, from dangerous near-collisions to aircraft flybys.[48]

Tensions in the South China Sea flared up towards the end of 2012, as China became embroiled in disputes with India, Vietnam, the Philippines and Japan. As leader of a small group of policymakers working in the Maritime Rights Office, Xi Jinping appeared to have a particular interest in the South China Sea, an area that in turn came under the remit of the Foreign Affairs Leading Small Group, which he also headed. In December 2012, Hainan Island announced that it had passed new rules allowing it to intercept, board and search ships in contested areas throughout the South China Sea. Coming less than a month after Xi took office as the country's leader, the escalation was the harbinger of a more rigid hand to come.[49]

Epilogue

In the early 2010s, even as Beijing began to scale back the huge stimulus programme it had launched to fight the global financial crisis, local governments continued to pile up huge debts to maintain economic growth. Dozens of cities undertook massive infrastructure projects, determined to transform themselves into showcases of the country's celebrated economic miracle. Wuhan, for one, pursued a $120 billion master plan that included two new airport terminals and a brand new financial district with extravagant government offices, as well as new highways, tunnels, bridges and an ambitious underground rail system. There were rules, of course, governing how much a local government could borrow. To circumvent them, towns, cities and prefectures created special investment corporations, also called local government financing vehicles. These entities took on new state loans and issued bonds, although their debt never featured on the local government's official balance sheet. More than 10,000 of these local government financing vehicles existed throughout the country. According to one estimate, even before Xi Jinping formally took over from Hu Jintao on 15 November 2012, total local government debt was close to $3 trillion, the equivalent of the country's war chest in foreign reserves.[1]

The collateral was local land. It seemed quite easy: when the local government required credit, it sold land to local developers. Local banks, in turn, valued the land generously, even though prices had soared for the best part of a decade. As liabilities piled up, more land was sold and more money borrowed to roll over the old debts. The process was rather tempting, so much so that by 2010 roughly half the income of local governments came from land transfer fees and land leasing. But there was a catch: if the property market tumbled, local governments would be left exposed to huge liabilities. This, in turn, placed the central government in a conundrum. Should it seek to restrain inflation in the housing market, it ran the risk of being forced to assume more bad debt from local governments. Since local governments in turn took it for granted that an authority higher up the ladder would rescue them if they could not service their debt, there were few restrictions on the borrowing.[2]

Precisely how much was borrowed was difficult to determine, given the endless obfuscation and creative accounting at every level of government, not to mention the extent of shadow banking. The leadership was at a loss, ordering the National Audit Office in 2013 to dispatch inspection teams to tally the outstanding debt. Liu Yuhui, an economist at the Chinese Academy of Social Sciences, estimated in September 2013 that local debt had doubled to roughly 20 trillion yuan ($3.3 trillion) in a mere two years, with 9.7 trillion yuan in direct bank lending, 4 to 5 trillion yuan via shadow lending and another 6 to 7 trillion yuan through various forms of IOUs. Since the central government implicitly backed these liabilities, some economists considered them part of the national debt, pushing the total to 200 per cent of national output, compared to 129 per cent at the end of 2008.[3]

As money flowed towards local governments and big state conglomerates, the state banks were left with too little cash to meet the demands of the real economy, especially smaller companies. Nor did they have the credit to finance new investment. Familiar issues like triangular debt reappeared in 2012, and promissory notes once again became common. The scale of these IOUs was less worrisome than the fact that they indicated the inability or unwillingness of the central government to boost consumption and support the private sector.[4]

Another perennial side effect of the country's top-down approach was chronic overcapacity, since cosseted state enterprises were reluctant to retrench. In 2014 the government estimated that $6.8 trillion had been squandered since 2009 on 'ineffective investment', including steel mills and empty stadiums. Overcapacity, in turn, led to falling prices, causing more stress in the financial system and delaying yet again the shift towards consumer-driven growth.[5]

Yet even as the economy slowed and corporate profits declined, the stock market soared. For years the stock exchanges had remained a minor part of the economy, the vast majority of their shares carefully fenced off from foreign investors. Then in 2014, to attract badly needed investment, Premier Li Keqiang, the country's Number Two in charge of the economy, allowed foreign investors to trade directly in the shares of companies listed on the domestic stock exchange. The leadership also encouraged ordinary people to invest their savings. Tens of millions of investors jumped in, some borrowing money to buy shares. Prices almost tripled in less than a year. At their peak, half the companies listed in Shenzhen and Shanghai were priced at more than 85 times the price-to-earnings ratio. The leadership encouraged investors to ignore warning flags. A crash followed in July 2015. The central bank cut interest rates and reserve requirements to free up more money to save the market, but to no avail. The government then ordered major brokerages to buy $19 billion in shares. When this, too, failed, the regime did what it did best: it outlawed selling and threatened to arrest anyone who interfered with its attempt to shore up prices. Party officials also accused 'foreign forces' of intentionally manipulating the market, promising a crackdown. As one economist put it, the regime 'destroyed its stock market in order to save it'. At long last, some of the foreign experts who had talked so confidently of the country's inevitable march towards the market fell silent.[6]

In August and September, even as the exchange market was still reeling, the central government gradually devalued the yuan by approximately 4.5 per cent to help exporters. Stocks fell again. An exodus of capital followed, with individuals moving close to a trillion dollars from the country, alarmed by the falling value of their savings. Capital flight put pressure on the yuan, forcing the government to step into the markets, selling dollars from its currency reserves to purchase large amounts of yuan. Even greater capital controls were imposed, although over the decades many entrepreneurial individuals had honed their skills and developed techniques to evade the hand of the state, from filing misleading invoices to using friends and family to carry cash.[7]

If 2015 was a key moment in the country's economy, it also marked a shift in terms of politics. Every incoming leader had customarily resorted to a crackdown on corruption to whip his potential opponents into shape. Xi Jinping, in his inaugural speech, vowed to fight corruption, demanding strict discipline from ranking officials and ordinary party members alike. Wang Qishan, who had made a career as an apparatchik in the state banks and worked closely with Zhu Rongji, was asked to lead the Central Commission for Disciplinary Inspection. He sent work teams around the country, bringing down well over a hundred leading figures across a whole range of institutions. One particularly prominent casualty was Bo Xilai, a former mayor of Dalian who was reassigned in 2007 to Chongqing, where he developed a style of governance dubbed the 'Chongqing Model', including a Maoist revival of 'red culture' as well as a sweeping campaign against organised crime and official corruption. When his police chief sought asylum in February 2012 in the American consulate, revealing that Bo Xilai and his wife Gu Kailai had been closely involved in the murder of a British businessman, he fell from power. His close ally Zhou Yongkang, the security tsar, was arrested one year later, together with several other major 'tigers' from the military. By October 2015 more than 100,000 people had fallen foul of the anti-corruption squads.[8]

After a few high-level miscreants were apprehended and party members were put on notice, a corruption drive normally came to an end. But Xi Jinping went much further than his predecessors, making it a permanent feature of the political landscape. In 2015, the campaign turned against the business community, with a string of corporate leaders arrested for fraudulent investments abroad. Several billionaires disappeared, leaving the others scrambling to prove their loyalty to the party.

The Central Commission for Disciplinary Inspection was built up, as were other party institutions. In the 1950s, a series of ad hoc Leading Small Groups had been introduced to advise the party and help coordinate the implementation of party policies that cut across several ministries and government departments. Translated word for word, they were 'small groups of leaders': they sat at the top of the power structure, the party's nerve centre that superseded all other agencies. Leaders used them to bypass opposition and enforce their will. The most notorious one was the Central Leading Small Group on the Cultural Revolution, led by Mao's secretary Chen Boda and the Chairman's wife Jiang Qing.

One of the most important of these informal bodies was the Foreign Affairs Leading Small Group, which Xi Jinping had headed even before 2012. In 2014, two more groups were created to redirect power back to his inner circle. One covered national security, drawing together a patchwork of agencies responsible for domestic and foreign security. The other, the Leading Small Group for the Comprehensive Deepening of Reform, was set up to oversee large policy changes. In 2018, four leading small groups, including that used to overhaul foreign policy, were upgraded to commissions, wielding even more power.[9]

The leading small groups and commissions were part of an effort by Xi to restore power to the centre. Xi personally chaired eleven of them, more than any leader since Mao, giving him a much tighter grip over national security, foreign affairs, financial compliance, the defence sector, military reform and ideological control, among others. As his grasp tightened, the titles multiplied. By 2017 he had garnered no less than seven, from Creative Leader, Core of the Party and Servant Pursuing Happiness for the People to Leader of a Great Country and Architect of Modernisation in the New Era. Xi became the Chairman of Everything, in the words of one observer.[10] In 2018 he became chairman for life, as the National People's Congress enthusiastically voted to abolish limits on their leader's term.

A cult of personality began to blossom, although party officials adamantly insisted that the love ordinary people felt for their leader was entirely natural and heartfelt. 'To follow you is to follow the sun' went a new song launched in Beijing in 2017. Chairman Xi's thoughts became compulsory reading for schoolchildren the same year. His image was everywhere, stamped on trinkets, badges and posters, printed on the front page of every newspaper.[11]

At first people applauded a crackdown on the rampant bribery, kickbacks, theft and waste of public funds, but soon it became clear that the targets extended far beyond just corrupt officials and business moguls. In 2015 lawyers, human rights activists, journalists and religious leaders were confined, exiled and imprisoned in the thousands in what one observer termed the worst crackdown in decades.[12]

The repression was fuelled by a single, overarching conviction on the part of the regime: 'hostile foreign forces' led by the United States were conspiring to undermine the Communist Party. In 2014 alone, the

People's Daily ran 42 articles blaming all manner of ills on 'Western', 'foreign' and 'overseas' forces. Behind every domestic challenge, however seemingly minute, a foreign plot could be detected, demanding a swift and comprehensive response from the security apparatus.[13]

In an echo of the Maoist era, foreign correspondents were considered covert intelligence operatives trying to subvert the regime. In March 2014, a spokeswoman for the National People's Congress told foreign reporters that she knew their purpose in reporting from China was to 'overturn our system of government'. A year later forced departures of foreign journalists began, increasing year after year with a record seventeen expulsions in 2020. One single correspondent of the *New York Times* remained to cover a country of 1.4 billion people.[14]

The pen, Mao had once declared, was a tool as dangerous as the gun. Even as their foreign counterparts were increasingly subject to intimidation and expulsion, 'absolute loyalty' was demanded from local reporters. The country's news outlets, Xi Jinping opined, 'must love the party, protect the party and closely align themselves with the party leadership'. University professors, on the other hand, were ordered to limit foreign textbooks for students and funnel Marxist values directly 'into their heads'.[15]

In this new ideological cold war, censorship increased. *Animal Farm* and *1984*, both written by George Orwell, were banned, while even Winnie the Pooh, rumoured to resemble Xi Jinping, had to go underground. The children's cartoon *Peppa Pig* was deleted from television and books, deemed the subversive symbol of a dangerous foreign ideology. In July 2020, elementary and middle schools across the country conducted a cleansing campaign, removing all books considered politically incorrect. The purged copies were replaced with new books from a list provided by the Ministry of Education, including the Communist Manifesto and poems by Chairman Mao.[16]

The internet was tightened up, to the extent that by 2019 most foreign apps – Google, Facebook, Dropbox, Twitter, YouTube, Reddit, Spotify – and foreign news – BBC, *Financial Times, Wall Street Journal*, Reuters, CNN – were blocked. Two separate internets began to emerge: one for the world and one shielded from the world. People who went abroad took their devices with them, meaning that they were digitally monitored around the clock even when away from home.[17]

But it was along the borders that hostile foreign forces posed the most serious threat, requiring unremitting repression. After Uyghur militants stabbed dozens of people at a railway station in April 2014, Xi called for an all-out 'struggle against terrorism, infiltration and separatism', demanding that the 'organs of dictatorship' be used 'without mercy'. More than a million Uyghurs and other Muslim minorities spent time in re-education camps, officially called 'vocational education and training centres'.[18]

In Hong Kong, protesters demanding that the Chief Executive be elected by universal suffrage took to the streets in September 2014, occupying the heart of the city in a peaceful campaign of civil disobedience. The People's Daily described Occupy Central as an anti-China force manipulated by the United States. One general believed that the demonstrations were part of 'an unprecedented direct and indirect Western encirclement' of the country.[19]

In June 2019 protests in Hong Kong erupted again in response to plans to allow extraditions to mainland China. More than a million people took to the streets, but this time the police and demonstrators became trapped in a spiral of violence, with pitched battles taking place in streets, shopping malls and universities. When later that year 3 million people exercised their right to vote in district council elections, they gave the pro-democracy camp a landslide victory. The election was viewed in Beijing as yet further evidence of the influence hostile foreign forces wielded in the city. Even as the protests died down during the coronavirus pandemic, on 30 June 2020 Beijing introduced a National Security Law with sweeping powers. It all but killed any form of democratic opposition, turning the Legislative Council into the pliable instrument Beijing had tried to introduce on the day of the handover 23 years earlier. World leaders were swift to react, condemning the new legislation as a violation of the Basic Law. A number of countries imposed sanctions and visa restrictions. The United States terminated the city's special regulatory treatment, including export licence exceptions and lower trade tariffs.

Convinced that enemy forces were encircling their country, the regime also adopted a more assertive playbook abroad, pressing border disputes with India, the Philippines, Indonesia, Vietnam, Japan, South Korea, North Korea, Singapore, Brunei, Nepal, Bhutan, Laos, Mongolia and Myanmar, not to mention Taiwan.

Longstanding tensions with the United States culminated in the imposition of tariffs and other trade barriers by Washington in 2018, when the deficit reached $621 billion. The United States accused China of unfair trade practices, intellectual property theft, forced technology transfers and lack of market access. But even without the trade war, more foreign companies were already leaving the country. Rising costs were one reason, endless regulation another. A growing sense of risk was also associated with doing business in China, as foreign companies, too, were targeted in the campaign against corruption. Peter Humphrey, the expert in risk management based in Shanghai, was arrested with his wife in 2013, forced to confess on television and thrown into prison, and only released ahead of schedule due to prostate cancer. Other foreign nationals were held in custody, some for years on end without any charges.

When a coronavirus outbreak in Wuhan quickly spread to the rest of the world in the early months of 2020, distrust of Beijing became entrenched in the United States. In July 2020, US secretary of state Mike Pompeo announced that the era of engagement with China was over. In what appeared very much like a self-fulfilling prophecy, Beijing's belief that the United States was a hostile force bent on containing it actually became true. Against all odds, the regime had succeeded in alienating not just one of its greatest supporters, but also the one power that had created the very conditions on which it had depended for its survival. From the global dollar to global oil, global commodities and global markets for its products, the regime was deeply enmeshed in a world order created by the United States. Deng Xiaoping had warned his colleagues to lie low and bide their time. Instead, they had antagonised a giant.

The coronavirus, combined with a posture so aggressive that it was dubbed 'wolf warrior diplomacy', also alienated other countries, not least India, Japan, Australia, the United Kingdom and the European Union. Beijing conjured enemies out of thin air, from Papua New Guinea to Brazil. It even managed to instil new life in a moribund NATO after its secretary general Jens Stoltenberg repeatedly warned that a stronger alliance was required against a country 'that does not share our values' and 'affects our security'.[20]

By 2021 there was an exodus of foreign firms out of China. Japan even paid its companies to relocate production elsewhere.[21]

The international backlash came even as the country was reaching an impasse in its economy. Growth, for decades, had depended on debt, which had risen slowly from a very low level between 1980 and 2010. Between 2010 and 2020, however, growth doubled while debt trebled, standing at 280 per cent of output. The country's dependence on debt should have been reduced by shifting demand from investment in infrastructure projects towards more domestic consumption. Yet household consumption could not be increased much further, for one very simple reason: most of the wealth flowed to the state, not to the people. As Li Keqiang pointed out in May 2020, more than 600 million people survived on a mere $140 a month, which was insufficient to rent a room in a city. A massive redistribution of income away from party members towards ordinary people would be necessary to spur more consumption, but this was unlikely to happen.[22]

Demographics compounded this issue. With a growing population, for several decades labour had been cheap, but this trend reversed around 2010, as the working population began to decline thanks to the one-child policy. A shrinking workforce required greater growth in productivity, but this, too, was falling steadily.[23] For decades, the countryside had been neglected, used as a reservoir for cheap, unskilled labour. Local governments had invested vast amounts of money in urban infrastructure, but put very little into their own people, least of all those in rural areas. Across the country as a whole, a mere one in three children attended high school, while only a fraction of the nearsighted rural population could afford a pair of glasses. Thanks to decades of wilful neglect, the labour force had one of the lowest levels of education of any comparable country.[24]

The easy options – accept foreign capital, exploit unprotected labour, sell land to raise funds, produce subsidised export goods, list state enterprises abroad, borrow to build and repay tomorrow – were no longer available. The challenge lying ahead for the Communist Party was how to address an entire range of longstanding structural issues of its own making without giving up its monopoly over power and its control over the means of production. It seemed very much like a dead end.

Notes

PREFACE

1 James Palmer, 'Nobody Knows Anything About China: Including the Chinese Government', *Foreign Policy*, 21 March 2018.

2 Zhao Ziyang, 'Yanzhe you Zhongguo tese de shehuizhuyi daolu qianjin' (Advance along the road of socialism with Chinese characteristics), *Renmin ribao*, 4 Nov. 1987; BArch, Berlin, DY 30/2437, Meeting Between Erich Honecker and Zhao Ziyang in Berlin, 8 June 1987, pp. 10–20; Charlotte Gao, 'Xi: China Must Never Adopt Constitutionalism, Separation of Powers, or Judicial Independence', *The Diplomat*, 19 Feb. 2019.

3 Wenzhou, J1-28-51, Conference on Guangdong and Fujian, 24 Dec. 1980, transcript dated 21 Jan. 1981, pp. 43–7.

4 Barry Rubin, *Modern Dictators: Third World Coup Makers, Strongmen, and Populist Tyrants*, McGraw-Hill, New York, 1987.

5 'China Has Over 600 Million Poor with $140 Monthly Income', *PTI News*, 28 May 2020.

6 Xiang Songzuo, 'The Pitiful State of the Chinese Economy', *AsiaNews*, 21 Jan. 2019.

1. FROM ONE DICTATOR TO ANOTHER (1976–1979)

1 On the architectural history of Tiananmen Square, one should read Adrian Hornsby, 'Tiananmen Square: The History of the World's Largest Paved Open Square', *Architectural Review*, 12 Oct. 2009; see also Wu Hung, *Remaking Beijing: Tiananmen Square and the Creation of a Political Space*, Reaktion Books, London, 2005.

2 On the increased freedoms of speech, association, religion, movement and assembly after 1911, see Frank Dikötter, *The Age of Openness: China Before Mao*, University of California Press, Berkeley, CA, 2008.

3 Lu Xun, *Diary of a Madman and Other Stories*, translated by William A. Lyell, University of Hawai'i Press, Honolulu, 1990, p. xxvii.

4 Frank Dikötter, *The Tragedy of Liberation: A History of the Chinese Revolution 1945–1957*, Bloomsbury, London, 2013.

5 Jin Chongji (ed.), *Zhou Enlai zhuan, 1898–1949* (A biography of Zhou Enlai, 1898–1949), Zhongyang wenxian chubanshe, Beijing, 1989, vol. 2, p. 1908.

6 Roderick MacFarquhar and Michael Schoenhals, *Mao's Last Revolution*, Harvard University Press, Cambridge, MA, 2006, pp. 393–7.

7 Li Zhisui, *The Private Life of Chairman Mao: The Memoirs of Mao's Personal Physician*, Random House, New York, 1994.

8 Yan Jiaqi and Gao Gao, *Turbulent Decade: A History of the Cultural Revolution*, University of Hawai'i Press, Honolulu, 1996, pp. 489–92.

9 Roger Garside, *Coming Alive: China after Mao*, Deutsch, London, 1981, pp. 115–28.

10 Hoover Institution, 'Zhongguo Gong Chan Dang Issuances', Box 1, Minutes of Politburo Meeting, 1 April 1976, transcript dated 2 April 1976.

11 Hoover Institution, 'Zhongguo Gong Chan Dang Issuances', Box 1, Minutes of Politburo Meeting, 4 April 1976.

12 Hoover Institution, 'Zhongguo Gong Chan Dang Issuances', Box 1, Mao Yuanxin to Mao Zedong, 5 April 1976.

13 Hoover Institution, 'Zhongguo Gong Chan Dang Issuances', Box 1, Minutes of Politburo Meeting, 6 April 1976; see also Ezra F. Vogel, *Deng Xiaoping and the Transformation of China*, Harvard University Press, Cambridge, MA, 2011, p. 168.

14 Hoover Institution, 'Zhongguo Gong Chan Dang Issuances', Box 1, Minutes of Politburo Meeting, 5 April 1976; Hoover Institution, Li Rui Papers, diary entry dated 18 May 1995.

15 Hoover Institution, 'Zhongguo Gong Chan Dang Issuances', Box 1, Mao Yuanxin to Mao Zedong, 6 April 1976; the role played by Hua Guofeng only came to light a few years later; see Shanghai, B250-5-128, Chen Guoding, Report on the Sixth Plenum, 13 to 15 July 1981, pp. 39–71; Li Zhisui, Mao's doctor, saw Jiang Qing watching the crowd through binoculars: Li, *The Private Life of Chairman Mao*, p. 612; on the contents of the broadcast and lingering questions about Hua's role in the Tiananmen incident, see PRO, FCO 21/1609, 'Your Telno 953: Hua's Watergate', 21 Dec. 1978.

16 Hoover Institution, 'Zhongguo Gong Chan Dang Issuances', Box 1, Mao Yuanxin to Mao Zedong, 7 April 1976; the role played by Hua Guofeng only came to light a few years later; see Shanghai, B250-5-128, Chen Guoding, Report on the Sixth Plenum, 13 to 15 July 1981, pp. 39–71.

17 Pamela Tan, *The Chinese Factor: An Australian Chinese Woman's Life in China from 1950 to 1979*, Roseberg, Dural, New South Wales, 2008, p. 228; PRO, FCO 21/1552, 25 Feb. 1977, 'Internal Situation'; see also MacFarquhar and Schoenhals, *Mao's Last Revolution*, pp. 431–2.

18 The only reference in Mao's official biography to this scrap of paper is to the unpublished diary of Zhang Yufeng, which has been carefully stashed away inside the vaults of the central archives; see Pang Xianzhi and Jin Chongji (eds), *Mao Zedong zhuan, 1949–1976* (A biography of Mao Zedong, 1949–1976), Zhongyang wenxian chubanshe, Beijing, 2003, vol. 2, pp. 1778–9. But Qin Chuan, an editor at the *People's Daily* who had read the diary, claimed otherwise; see Hoover Institution, Li Rui Papers, conversation between Li Rui and Qin Chuan, diary entry dated 27 April 2000.

19 MacFarquhar and Schoenhals, *Mao's Last Revolution*, pp. 443–7.

20 PRO, FCO 21/1493, 'Confidential Wire', 25 Oct. 1976; Hoover Institution, Hongda Harry Wu Collection, Box 2, Document issued by the Central Committee, zhongfa (1976) no. 16, 18 Oct. 1976 as well as Document issued by the Central Committee, zhongfa (1977) no. 10, 6 March 1977; on the removal of all references to the Gang of Four, see Hubei, SZ120-4-380, 23 Oct. 1976.

21 Hoover Institution, 'Zhongguo Gong Chan Dang Issuances', Box 1, Deng Liqun, Talk at the Capital Garrison, 7 and 8 July 1981, pp. 37–42; on posters in Beijing, see PRO, FCO 21/1550, Roger Garside, 'The Force of Public Opinion', 17 Jan. 1977.

22 Hoover Institution, 'Zhongguo Gong Chan Dang Issuances', Box 1, Deng Liqun, Talk at the Capital Garrison, 7 and 8 July 1981, pp. 37–8.

23 Hoover Institution, 'Zhongguo Gong Chan Dang Issuances', Box 1, Deng Liqun, Talk at the Capital Garrison, 7 and 8 July 1981, pp. 37–8; Li Xiannian's attack on Deng is documented in Ruan Ming, *Deng Xiaoping: Chronicle of an Empire*, Routledge, London, 2018, p. 40.

24 PRO, FCO 21/1551, Roger Garside, 'Where Are Hua's Men?', 7 March 1977.

25 Several versions of the speech and three translations, none of them complete, exist; an original version circulated on 16 May 1956 can be found in Shandong, A1-2-387, pp. 2–17; for a more elaborate historical context to the speech and the Hundred Flowers, see Dikötter, *The Tragedy of Liberation*, chapter 14.

26 Dikötter, *The Tragedy of Liberation*, chapter 14.

27 Mao Zedong, *Jianguo yilai Mao Zedong wengao* (Mao Zedong's manuscripts since the founding of the People's Republic), Zhongyang wenxian chubanshe, Beijing, 1998, vol. 13, p. 444.

28 PRO, FCO 21/1550, R. F. Wye, 'Mao Tse-tung's Speech on the 10 Major Relationships', 14 Jan. 1977.

29 MAE, 752INVA/2118, 'La Chine se tourne de nouveau vers les pays occidentaux', 8 Nov. 1976.

30 John P. McKay, 'Foreign Enterprise in Russian and Soviet Industry: A Long Term Perspective', *Business History Review* (Autumn 1974), 48, no. 3, p. 353; a great primary source is the gripping account of Eugene Lyons, *Assignment in Utopia*, George G. Harrap, London, 1938.

31 Frank Dikötter, *Mao's Great Famine: The History of China's Most Devastating Catastrophe, 1958–62*, Bloomsbury, London, 2010, in particular chapter 10 ('Shopping Spree') and chapter 37 ('The Final Tally'). See also chapter 20 ('Housing') on how the capital became a giant building site.

32 Dikötter, *Mao's Great Famine*, p. 79.

33 Frank Dikötter, *The Cultural Revolution: A People's History, 1962–1976*, Bloomsbury, London and New York, 2016, pp. 260–61; on living standards see also the conclusion reached by Lein-Lein Chen and John Devereux, 'The Iron Rice Bowl: Chinese Living Standards 1952–1978', *Comparative Economic Studies*, 2017, no. 59, pp. 261–310.

34 Frederick C. Teiwes and Warren Sun, 'China's New Economic Policy Under Hua Guofeng: Party Consensus and Party Myths', *China Journal*, no. 66 (July 2011), p. 7.

35 PRO, FCO 21/1553, John Gerson, 'The Chinese Leadership Observed', 11 Oct. 1977; Gerson attended a banquet given at a later date in October 1977.

36 PRO, FCO 21/1554, 'PRC Internal Situation', 17 Oct. 1977; on the Four Modernisations see Lawrence C. Reardon, *The Reluctant Dragon: Crisis Cycles in Chinese Foreign Economic Policy*, Hong Kong University Press, Hong Kong, 2002, chapter 3.

37 Hoover, 'Zhongguo Gong Chan Dang Issuances', Box 1, Minutes of Politburo Meeting, 9 Feb. 1978.

38 Teiwes, 'China's New Economic Policy', p. 11. Shanghai, B250-5-128, Chen Guoding, Report on the Sixth Plenum, 13 to 15 July 1981, pp. 39–71.

39 Dikötter, *The Cultural Revolution*, p. 157.

40 Shanghai, B1-8-11, Report from the State Council, 6 Nov. 1978, pp. 14–16; Hebei was one such province: see Hebei, 919-1-148, 11 Dec. 1968.

41 O. Arne Westad, 'The Great Transformation', in Niall Ferguson, Charles S. Maier, Erez Manela and Daniel J. Sargent (eds), *The Shock of the Global: The 1970s in Perspective*, Harvard University Press, Cambridge, MA, 2010, p. 79.

42 Dikötter, *Tragedy of Liberation*, pp. 137–8.

43 Hebei, 979-10-512, Speech by Gu Mu, 13 April 1980, pp. 51–60.

44 'Interest in Technology', *South China Morning Post*, 24 Sept. 1977.

45 Guangdong, 235-2-242, Report on Trade Mission, 20 Oct. 1977, pp. 157–80.

46 Wenzhou, J1-27-60, Nationwide Conference on Foreign Trade, 18 Dec. 1979, p. 189; Hoover Institution, Milton Friedman Papers, Box 188, 'Report of Trip to the People's Republic of China', pp. 6–7 and 20.

47 Ruan, *Deng Xiaoping*, p. 28.

48 Ruan, *Deng Xiaoping*, p. 36.

49 PRO, FCO 21/1609, Roger Garside, 'The April the Fifth Movement', 12 Dec. 1978; Percy Cradock, 'The Politburo and "Democracy Wall"', 18 Dec. 1978.

50 Robert D. Novak, 'China's Saviour', *Washington Post*, 24 Feb. 1997.

51 Hubei, SZ1-4-808, zhongfa 1978 (77), 28 Dec. 1978, including Hua Guofeng's speech at the Central Work Conference on 25 Nov. 1978 and Hua Guofeng and Ye Jianying's talks at the Third Plenum on 13 and 18 Dec. 1978; a detailed disquisition on both the work conference and the subsequent plenum based on officially released records appears in Vogel, *Deng Xiaoping*, pp. 229–47; see also Ruan, *Deng Xiaoping*, pp. 44–8.

52 Westad, 'The Great Transformation', p. 76.

53 See, among others, Katherine G. Burns, 'China and Japan: Economic Partnership to Political Ends', unpublished paper, Stimson Center, accessed on 25 Sept. 2020; Tomozo Morino, 'China-Japan Trade and Investment Relations', *Proceedings of the Academy of Political Science*, 38, no. 2 (1991), pp. 87–94; Wang Hong, *China's Exports since 1979*, St Martin's Press, London, 1993, p. 143.

54 Richard L. Walker, 'What We Should Know About China', *National Review*, 2 May 1980; Walker also quotes Laszlo Ladany, *China News Analysis*, 14 June 1974, pp. 1–2.

55 Hoover Institution, Henry S. Rowen Papers, Box 62, Minutes of Meeting with Committee on the Present Danger, 27 Nov. 1977; see also Box 62, 'Hao Te-ching's Discussion with Governor Edmund G. Brown', 16 July 1977.

56 Fox Butterfield, 'Brzezinski in China', *New York Times*, 24 May 1978.

57 Document 191, 'Telegram from the Liaison Office in China to the Department of State', 11 Jan. 1979, and document 208, 'Memorandum

of Conversation', 30 Jan. 1979, *Foreign Relations of the United States, 1977–1980*, vol. XIII, United States Government Printing Office, Washington: 2013, pp. 709–10 and 778.

58 On normalisation and the MFN status, a profitable read is Jean A. Garrison, 'Explaining Change in the Carter Administration's China Policy: Foreign Policy Adviser Manipulation of the Policy Agenda', *Asian Affairs*, 29, no. 2 (Summer 2002), pp. 83–98.

59 Don Oberdorfer, 'Teng and Khrushchev', *Washington Post*, 5 Feb. 1979.

60 PRO, FCO 21/1686, J. S. Wall, 'Secretary of State's Talks with Mr Vance: China', 23 May 1979.

61 MAE, 752INVA/2090, Claude Arnaud, 'Manifestation paysanne à Pékin', 15 Jan. 1979; PRO, FCO 21/1685, 'Peking's Democracy Wall', January 1979; Roger Garside, 'April 5th Movement: Organisation and Attitudes', 6 Jan. 1979.

62 The essay appears in Gregor Benton (ed.), *Wild Lilies, Poisonous Weeds: Voices from People's China*, Pluto Press, London, 1982; readers should also turn to another invaluable compendium of primary sources, namely Geremie Barmé and John Minford (eds), *Seeds of Fire: Voices of Conscience*, Hill and Wang, New York, 1988.

63 MAE, 752INVA/2093, Claude Arnaud, 'Politique intérieure de la Chine du 9 mars au 5 avril 1979', 4 April 1979; see also 'Strains of Gershwin in Peking', *South China Morning Post*, 17 March 1979.

64 PRO, FCO 21/1685, Percy Cradock, 'My Telno 354: The Internal Situation', 9 April 1979; FCO 21/1686, 'Tightening Political Control', April 1979.

65 Deng Xiaoping, 'Uphold the Four Cardinal Principles', 30 March 1979, *Selected Works of Deng Xiaoping*, vol. 2, various editions.

66 Liu Yan and Wang Tao, '"Jianchi sixiang jiben yuanze" de xingcheng yu lishi diwei' (The emergence and historical position of the 'Four Basic Principles'), *Dangdai Zhongguo shi yanjiu*, 22, no. 2 (March 2015), p. 21.

67 PRO, FCO 21/1686, Christopher O. Hum, 'May Day and After', 7 May 1979.

68 Nigel Wade, 'Brave Editor Who Defied Hua', *Sunday Telegraph*, 21 Oct. 1989; see also the entire folder in PRO, FCO 21/1689, 'Political Prisoners in China', 1979; on the meeting to discuss the Most Favoured Nation status, see 'Trial, Conviction and Imprisonment of Wei Jingsheng', *Hearing before the Subcommittee on International Operations and Human Rights, 18 December 1995*, US Government Printing Office, Washington, 1996, p. 5.

69 Tianjin, X211-1-503, Central Work Conference on Public Security, 25 April 1981.

70 Pitman Potter, *From Leninist Discipline to Socialist Legalism: Peng Zhen on Law and Political Authority in the PRC*, Stanford University Press, Stanford, CA, 2003, p. 113; Tan, *The Chinese Factor*, p. 257.

71 James H. Mann, *About Face: A History of America's Curious Relationship with China, from Nixon to Clinton*, Alfred A. Knopf, New York, 1998, p. 103.

72 Rough pollution measurements can be found in MAE, 752INVA/2117, Claude Martin, 'Pékin: Les embarras d'une capitale', 20 Aug. 1979.

73 Bryan Johnson, 'First Week in Peking is Mental Overload', *Globe and Mail*, 5 Oct. 1979.

74 Wenzhou, J1-27-60, Report by the Ministry of Culture, 4 Jan. 1980, pp. 150-56.

75 PRO, FCO 21/1552, Mark Fenn, 'Culture in China', 13 June 1977; FCO 21/1800, Percy Cradock, 'Youth in China', 27 June 1980; Earl Vinecour, 'The Teresa Teng Craze', *South China Morning Post*, 23 May 1982.

76 Timothy McNulty, 'China Has TV Thirst', *Boston Globe*, 1 Jan. 1980.

77 Bryan Johnson, 'Status in China Now Requires TV and Fan to Cool It', *Globe and Mail*, 1 Jan. 1980.

78 Bryan Johnson, 'Masses Hypnotized by a Doctored Medium', *Globe and Mail*, 2 Dec. 1980.

79 Paul Theroux, *Riding the Iron Rooster: By Train through China*, Houghton Mifflin, New York, 1988, p. 127.

80 On the making of the resolution one should read Robert L. Suettinger, 'Negotiating History: The Chinese Communist Party's 1981', Project 2049 Institute, Washington, 2017.

81 See Hoover Institution, 'Zhongguo Gong Chan Dang Issuances', Box 1, Outline the Sixth Plenum, pp. 19-22, quoting Deng Xiaoping's talk at the Four Thousand Cadre Meeting to discuss the draft resolution on 25 October 1980.

82 'Resolution on Certain Questions in the History of Our Party since the Founding of the People's Republic of China', 27 June 1981, History and Public Policy Program Digital Archive, Wilson Center, translated from the *Beijing Review*, 24, no. 27, 6 July 1981, pp. 10-39.

83 Although an expurgated version of one of these sessions was later made public, all the concrete details have remained secret; however, a summary was presented by Deng Liqun in a lengthy speech given at the Capital Garrison in July 1981; see Hoover Institution, 'Zhongguo Gong Chan Dang Issuances', Box 1, Deng Liqun, Talk at the Capital Garrison, 7 and 8 July 1981, pp. 37-42 in particular; the expurgated version of

Hu Yaobang's talk on 19 November 1980 can be found in Zhonggong zhongyang wenxian yanjiushi (Central Chinese Communist Party Literature Research Office), ed., *Sanzhong quanhui yilai zhongyao wenjian huibian* (Compilation of Major Documents since the Third Plenum), Renmin chubanshe, Beijing, 1982, vol. 2, pp. 735–47; see also Shanghai, B250-5-128, Chen Guoding, Report on the Sixth Plenum, 13 to 15 July 1981, pp. 39–71.

84 'Resolution on Certain Questions'.

2. RETRENCHMENT (1979–1982)

1 Dikötter, *The Tragedy of Liberation*, pp. 215–17.

2 Li, *The Private Life of Chairman Mao*, p. 392.

3 Patrick Tyler, 'Chen Yun, Who Slowed China's Shift to Market, Dies at 89', *New York Times*, 12 April 1995.

4 By far the best analysis of the unintended consequences of the rehabilitations under Hu Yaobang is Ruan, *Deng Xiaoping*, chapter 2.

5 Wenzhou, J1-26-84, Report from the Ministry of Finance, 5 May 1979, pp. 7–25.

6 Nai-Ruenn Chen, *China's Economy and Foreign Trade, 1979–81*, Department of Commerce, Washington, 1982, pp. 1–2.

7 Robert Service, *Comrades: A History of World Communism*, Harvard University Press, Cambridge, MA, 2007, p. 6.

8 Dikötter, *Mao's Great Famine*, chapter 23, 'Wheeling and Dealing'.

9 Dikötter, *Mao's Great Famine*, p. 211.

10 Hebei, 979-10-512, Han Guang, Report on Capital Construction, 23 March 1980, pp. 22–46.

11 Hubei, SZ43-6-183, Speech by Zhao Ziyang at National Conference of Heads of Province, 15 Nov. 1980, pp. 1–5.

12 Wenzhou, J1-26-81, 26 Sept. 1979, pp. 31–46, as well as Report from the Zhejiang Provincial Planning Committee, 31 May 1979, pp. 120–52.

13 Hebei, 979-10-512, Gu Mu, Speech on Capital Construction, 13 April 1980, pp. 51–60.

14 The cut in the state budget is in Wenzhou, J1-26-81, 27 March 1979, pp. 6–30; the figures from local investment were made public and are reported in Chen, *China's Economy and Foreign Trade, 1979–81*, Department of Commerce, Washington, 1982, pp. 1–2.

15 Wenzhou, J51-29-40, 7 Nov. 1979, pp. 90–93.

16 Nanjing, 5093-4-69, 10 Dec. 1979, pp. 1–4; Wenzhou, J1-28-51, 7 March 1981, pp. 49–54; Tianjin, X199-2-1958, 6 July 1979, pp. 37–40.

17 Hubei, SZ48-2-310, Report on Investigation of Prices, 16 Jan. 1979, pp. 20–29; the HSBC estimates are in MAE, 2882TOPO/2936, 'L'économie chinoise en 1981', May 1982, p. 6.

18 Nanjing, 5054-5-216, 4 Aug. 1982, pp. 29–33; Hubei, SZ43-6-183, Speech by Gu Mu at Work Conference on Imports and Exports, 23 Dec. 1980, pp. 134–9; MfAA, Berlin, ZR481/86, 'Sozialökonomische Widersprüche in China', April 1982, p. 4.

19 Hubei, SZ43-6-183, Speech by Gu Mu at Work Conference on Imports and Exports, 23 Dec. 1980, pp. 134–9; the foreign debt is detailed in Yao Yilin, Report to the Politburo, 28 Nov. 1980, pp. 31–7.

20 Hubei, SZ34-11-91, 22 May 1980, Report by State Council on Speculation and Smuggling, pp. 46–51.

21 Wenzhou, J87-31-25, 22 Jan. 1981, pp. 249–51.

22 On the budget see Hubei, SZ43-6-183, Speech by Zhao Ziyang at National Conference of Provincial Leaders, 15 Nov. 1980, pp. 1–15, as well as Speech by Wang Bingqian, 21 Dec. 1980, pp. 76–81.

23 Ruan, *Deng Xiaoping*, p. 98.

24 Hubei, SZ43-6-183, Speech by Zhao Ziyang at National Conference of Heads of Province, 15 Nov. 1980, pp. 1–15.

25 Dikötter, *The Tragedy of Liberation*, p. 81.

26 Dikötter, *Mao's Great Famine*, p. 81.

27 PRO, FCO 21/1687, Christopher O. Hum, 'Back to Basics', 13 Nov. 1979.

28 Hubei, SZ43-6-183, Speech by Zhao Ziyang at National Conference of Heads of Province, 15 Nov. 1980, pp. 1–15; Ruan, *Deng Xiaoping*, p. 98.

29 Michael Parks, 'Dream for a Steel Complex Turns into a Nightmare', *Los Angeles Times*, 29 Nov. 1981; Jonathan Sharp, 'Baoshan: Model of a Planning Disaster', *South China Morning Post*, 24 July 1981; Takashi Oka, 'Peking Shelves Grandiose Plans', *Christian Science Monitor*, 8 Dec. 1980.

30 MAE, 2882TOPO/2935, 'Statistiques monétaires chinoises pour 1981', 19 April 1982, p. 5; Wenzhou, J34-32-57, National Conference on Banking, 30 April 1982, pp. 126–36.

31 Wenzhou, J20-17-23, Report by the State Bureau for Statistics, 31 Oct. 1979, pp. 76–8; the numbers appear in MAE, 2882TOPO/2936, François Lemoine, 'Réformes économiques et finances publiques en Chine', Dec. 1983, p. 5.

32 Wenzhou, J34-32-36, Report by State Council, 9 Dec. 1982, pp. 20–26 as well as Report on Problems with Daily Goods, 24 July 1982, pp. 66–9; Nanjing, 5020-5-208, 6 Sept. 1982, pp. 94–8.

33 Wenzhou, J1-27-60, Nationwide Conference on Foreign Trade, 18 Dec. 1979, p. 197.

34 Wenzhou, J1-27-60, Nationwide Conference on Foreign Trade, 18 Dec. 1979, p. 201.

35 Shanghai, B76-5-112, Comments on Foreign Trade by Zhao Ziyang, Gu Mu and Yao Yilin, 11 Dec. 1980; Shanghai, B1-9-1340, Document by State Council and State Economic Planning Commission, 18 Oct. 1984, pp. 28–30.

36 See Lin Guijun and Ronald M. Schramm, 'China's Foreign Exchange Policies since 1979: A Review of Developments and an Assessment', *China Economic Review*, 14, no. 3 (Dec. 2003), pp. 250–58; see also Nicholas R. Lardy, *Foreign Trade and Economic Reform in China, 1978–1990*, Cambridge University Press, Cambridge, 1992.

37 Lin and Schramm, 'China's Foreign Exchange Policies since 1979', p. 251.

38 Dikötter, *The Cultural Revolution*, chapter 2, 'The Silent Revolution'.

39 Dikötter, *The Cultural Revolution*, pp. 262–3 and 270.

40 Dikötter, *The Cultural Revolution*, pp. 275–6.

41 MAE, 2882TOPO/2951, 'Production et consommation des produits agricoles en Chine', 1 Sept. 1986, p. 4; Guangdong, 235-2-284, Report by State Council, 12 March 1978, pp. 144–8; Hubei, SZ107-6-52, Report by Central Agricultural Committee, 15 Aug. 1979, pp. 3–8.

42 The purchases abroad are detailed in Fox Butterfield, 'China's New Dialectic: Growth', *New York Times*, 5 Feb. 1978; MAE, 2882TOPO/2951, 'Production et consommation des produits agricoles en Chine', 1 Sept. 1986, pp. 3–5; Dong Fureng, *Industrialization and China's Rural Modernization*, World Bank, Washington, 1992, p. 91.

43 Wenzhou, J1-26-81, National Conference on Pricing, 4 Oct. 1979, pp. 188–218; the estimate of 8 billion is from Shanghai, National Conference on Planning, B1-8-113, 17 Jan. 1980, pp. 40–54; the estimate of 30 billion is in MAE, 2882TOPO/2951, 'La fin des communes populaires', 23 Feb. 1983, p. 6.

44 Wenzhou, J1-26-83, Draft by the Centre on Decisions to Speed up Development in the Countryside, 22 Dec. 1978, p. 13.

45 Hebei, 979-10-508, Talk by Deng Xiaoping, Based on Notes by Deng Liqun, 2 April 1980, pp. 10–23.

46 Wenzhou, J1-27-32, Document No. 75 on the Countryside, 14 Nov. 1980, pp. 113–26.

47 Wenzhou, J87-31-25, National Conference on Agriculture, Jan. 1981, pp. 153–8.

48 Wenzhou, J87-31-25, Investigation into the Countryside, Jan. 1981, pp. 159–64; Hebei, 925-2-188, Report on Lulong County, 27 Oct. 1982, pp. 1–7.

49 On living standards, see Dong, *Industrialization*, p. 36; MfAA, ZR 2629/90, Report from Bernd Jordan, 7 Dec. 1983; Kate Zhou, *How the Farmers Changed China: Power of the People*, Westview Press, Boulder, CO, 1996; see also Daniel Kelliher, *Peasant Power in China: The Era of Rural Reform, 1979–1989*, Yale University Press, New Haven, CT, 1992.

50 Dikötter, *The Tragedy of Liberation*, pp. 224–5.

51 MAE, 2882TOPO/2951, 'La fin des communes populaires', 23 Feb. 1983, p. 20; the figure of 100 million is also mentioned in Dong, *Industrialization*, p. 8.

52 Gansu, 216-4-164, 17 Oct. 1983, pp. 136-7; Hebei, 925-2-166, Wan Li, Speech to the State Agriculture Committee, 11 March 1981, pp. 349–54.

53 Hubei, SZ118-5-324, Secretariat of the Communist Party of China, Work Conference on Education, 8 to 12 May 1981, pp. 1–20.

54 Dong, *Industrialization*, p. 53.

55 Dikötter, *The Cultural Revolution*, pp. 230–31.

56 Dikötter, *The Cultural Revolution*, pp. 278–80; the example of Chuansha is from Lynn T. White, *Unstately Power: Local Causes of China's Economic Reforms*, M. E. Sharpe, Armonk, NY, 1998, pp. 94 and 101; one should also read Zhang Qi and Liu Mingxing, *Revolutionary Legacy, Power Structure, and Grassroots Capitalism under the Red Flag in China*, Cambridge University Press, Cambridge, 2019, pp. 189–96.

57 Hubei, SZ43-6-183, Xu Jing'an, Research Paper Circulated by Zhao Ziyang, 8 Nov. 1980, pp. 82–6.

58 Shanghai, B250-5-542, Report on Wuxi, Jiangyin and Shazhou, 9 July 1984, pp. 1–10.

59 Shanghai, B250-5-542, Report on Guangdong, Dec. 1984, pp. 48–65.

60 Shanghai, B250-5-542, Report on Guangdong, Dec. 1984, pp. 48–65.

61 Li Rui, Diary, 19 Sept. 1994.

62 Hubei, SZ43-6-183, Xu Jing'an, Research Paper Circulated by Zhao Ziyang, 8 Nov. 1980, pp. 82–6; imports in statistical table in Chen, *China's Economy and Foreign Trade, 1979–81*, p. 31.

63 Ruan, *Deng Xiaoping*, p. 101.

64 Martin King Whyte, Feng Wang and Yong Cai, 'Challenging Myths About China's One-Child Policy', *China Journal*, no. 74 (July 2015), pp. 144–59. The Shandong figure is in Shandong, A188-1-2, 12 and 30 Dec. 1972, pp. 50 and 155.

65 MAE, 2882TOPO/2917, 'Le contrôle des naissances en Chine', 27 Aug. 1982.

66 Wenzhou, J11-7-20, Comments by Chen Yun at Politburo Meeting, 2 Sept. 1980, pp. 215–16.

67 Chen Yun, 'Pay Attention to Grain Work', translated by Mao Tong and Du Anxia in Chen Yun, *Chen Yun's Strategy for China's Development*, M. E. Sharpe, Armonk, NY, 1983, pp. 67–72.

68 Thomas Sharping, *Birth Control in China 1949-2000: Population Policy and Demographic Development*, Routledge, London, 2003, p. 42.

69 The term 'pseudo-science' is used and justified in Whyte, 'Challenging Myths About China's One-Child Policy'.

70 MAE, 2882TOPO/2917, 'Le contrôle des naissances en Chine', 27 Aug. 1982.

71 MAE, 2882TOPO/2917, 'Renforcement du contrôle des naissances', 14 Jan. 1982.

72 Gansu, 141-1-30, Zhao Ziyang's Comments on Birth Control, 18 Aug. and 8 Sept. 1982, pp. 70–79.

73 Whyte, 'Challenging Myths About China's One-Child Policy'.

3. REFORM (1982–1984)

1 Deng Xiaoping, 'Opening Speech at the Twelfth National Congress of the Communist Party of China', 1 Sept. 1982, *Selected Works of Deng Xiaoping*, vol. 3, various editions.

2 Deng Xiaoping, 'Speech At a Forum of the Military Commission of the Central Committee of the CPC', 4 July 1982, *Selected Works of Deng Xiaoping*, vol. 2, various editions.

3 Dikötter, *The Cultural Revolution*.

4 Yang Zhongmei, *Hu Yao-Bang: A Chinese Biography*, Routledge, London, 1989, pp. 111–12.

5 MAE, 752INVA/2117, 'Quelques aspects du problème des jeunes en Chine', 9 April 1980; Linda Matthews, 'Young Soldier Is New China Hero', *Los Angeles Times*, 1 May 1980.

6 Stanley Oziewicz, 'China Youth Have a New Model Hero', *Washington Post*, 2 Nov. 1982; Christopher Wren, 'Peking's New Line Calls for New Heroes', *New York Times*, 16 Jan. 1983.

7 Christopher Wren, 'Peking's New Line Calls for New Heroes', *New York Times*, 16 Jan. 1983.

8 An excellent analysis appears in Wang Jing, *High Culture Fever: Politics, Aesthetics, and Ideology in Deng's China*, University of California Press, Berkeley, CA, 1996.

9 Song Yuehong, 'Sixiang jiben yuanze cong tichu dao xieru xianfa', *Guangming ribao*, 25 April 2015.

10 Li Rui, Diary, 18 and 21 March 1983.

11 '30,000 Jailed in Clamp on Economic Crime', *South China Morning Post*, 26 July 1983; the quotation is in Amanda Bennett, 'China Starts New Drive Against Crime', *Wall Street Journal*, 24 Aug. 1983.

12 MAE, 2882TOPO/2913, Claude Martin, 'Crime et châtiment', 14 Oct. 1983; Amanda Bennett, 'China Starts New Drive Against Crime', *Wall Street Journal*, 24 Aug. 1983.

13 MAE, 2882TOPO/2913, Claude Martin, 'Crime et châtiment', 14 Oct. 1983; it is unclear whether the figure of 80,000 included the 30,000 sentenced for economic crimes; see also Murray Scot Tanner, 'State Coercion and the Balance of Awe: The 1983–1986 "Stern Blows" Anti-Crime Campaign', *China Journal*, no. 44 (July 2000), pp. 93–125.

14 Deng Xiaoping, 'The Party's Urgent Tasks on the Organisational and Ideological Fronts', 12 Oct. 1983, *Selected Works*, vol. 3, various editions.

15 Michael Weisskopf, 'China Moves to Rescue Itself from Outside "Spiritual Pollution"', *Washington Post*, 2 Dec. 1983.

16 Shanghai, B243-3-149, Report from Shanghai Bureau for Higher Education, 31 Oct. 1983, pp. 51–4; Gansu, 107-5-152, 9 Nov. 1983, pp. 93–6; Shanghai, A76-4-271, 31 Oct. 1983, pp. 1–6.

17 Christopher Wren, 'China's Prey, "Spiritual Pollution", Proves Elusive', *New York Times*, 20 Dec. 1983.

18 MAE, 2882TOPO/2914, 'La réforme agricole et l'évolution du monde rural en Chine', 28 Feb. 1984.

19 Jonathan Mirsky, 'Get Rich Quick Is All the Rage in China', *Observer*, 10 July 1983.

20 Keun Lee, 'The Chinese Model of the Socialist Enterprise: An Assessment of Its Organization and Performance', *Journal of Comparative Economics*, 14, no. 3 (Sept. 1990), p. 385.

21 Lee, 'The Chinese Model of the Socialist Enterprise', p. 386.

22 Wenzhou, J34-32-71, Report by Wenzhou Branch of People's Bank of China, 19 Nov. 1983, pp. 181–4; Tianjin, X110-1-823, 27 Feb. 1985, pp. 109–11; Tianjin, X95-2-2099, Report by Ministry of Commerce, 5 Jan. 1985, pp. 8–13; the example from Taizhou is in MAE, 2882TOPO/2936, United States Mission, 'Tax Reform in China's Provinces', 5 Dec. 1983.

23 MAE, 2882TOPO/2936, United States Mission, 'Attacking China's Deficit Enterprises', 8 Dec. 1983.

24 Hubei, SZ69-7-469, National Conference on the Second Stage of the Tax System (22 June to 7 July 1984), 13 July 1984, pp. 9–22.

25 Vogel, *Deng Xiaoping*, p. 450; see also Li Rui Diary, 21 Jan. 1984.

26 Chen Yulu, Guo Qingwang, Zhang Jie, *Major Issues and Policies in China's Financial Reform*, Enrich Professional Publishing, Honolulu, 2016, vol. 3, p. 24.

27 Lee Zinser, 'The Performance of China's Economy', in Joint Economic Committee (eds), *China's Economic Dilemmas in the 1990s*, US Government Printing Office, Washington, 1991, vol. 1, figures 3 and 4, pp. 112–13.

28 Chen, Guo et al., *Major Issues and Policies in China's Financial Reform*, vol. 3, p. 24; also International Monetary Fund, International Financial Statistics and Wigram Capital Advisors Limited.

29 This was the figure quoted by Wang Renzhong when he met Erich Honecker; he added that for the first five months of 1985, inflation stood at 6 per cent; see BArch, Berlin, DY 30/2436, Minutes of Talk between Erich Honecker and Wang Renzhong, 27 June 1985, pp. 28–34.

30 Hubei, SZ73-6-393, Report on Henan Province Circulated by the People's Bank of China, 3 Sept. 1985, pp. 78–81; Document on Jilin Province Circulated by the People's Bank of China, 29 May 1985, pp. 23–7.

31 Hubei, SZ73-6-599, 1987, pp. 1–15.

32 Hubei, SZ73-6-599, 1987, pp. 1–15.

33 Hubei, SZ73-6-599, 1987, pp. 47–57 and 21 Feb. 1987, p. 82; also Hubei, SZ73-6-623, 24 Dec. 1987, pp. 1–11.

34 See also Donald Hay, Derek Morris, Guy Liu and Shujie Yao, *Economic Reform and State-Owned Enterprises in China 1979–87*, Clarendon Press, Oxford, 1994, p. 178.

35 BArch, Berlin, DY 30/2436, Minutes of Talk between Erich Honecker and Wang Renzhong, 27 June 1985, pp. 28–34.

36 Hubei, SZ73-6-599, 1987, pp. 47–57.

37 Tianjin, X87-2-1673, 26 Dec. 1984, pp. 3–9.

38 MAE, 2883TOPO/3791, 'L'économie chinoise, vers un réformisme de gauche', 14 March 1987.

39 Gansu, 116-4-362, 1985, pp. 58–65.

40 Gansu, 128-7-215, Zhao Ziyang to Heads of Provinces and Municipalities, 11 April 1985, pp. 67–76.

41 Tianjin, X110-1-818, 25 Nov. 1985, pp. 55–6.

42 Tianjin, X110-1-820, Report from the Municipal Economic Committee, 23 Aug. 1985, pp. 107–16; X110-1-804, Tianjin, Report from the No. 1 Light Industry Bureau, July 1985, pp. 259–69.

43 Hubei, SZ1-9-285, 27 Nov. 1984, pp. 114–32.

44 Shanghai, B182-3-199, Feb. 1975, pp. 23–4; quotation from Shanghai, B248-2-1056, 4 Feb. 1977, pp. 3–7.

45 Shanghai, B248-2-810, 11 April 1975, pp. 6–9.

46 Shanghai, B248-2-1056, 4 Feb. 1977, pp. 3–7.

47 Shanghai, B248-4-219, 19 Aug. 1977, pp. 18–27.

48 Shanghai, B248-4-219, 19 Aug. 1977, pp. 18–27.

49 Shanghai, B102-3-57, 13 Dec. 1979, p. 49.

50 Shanghai, B1-9-210, Report on Shenyang, 29 July 1980, pp. 25–34.

51 Nanjing, 5003-4-459, 3 March 1984, pp. 92–103.

52 Shanghai, B123-11-1329, 14 Sept. 1985, pp. 166–70; the estimate for
    unlicensed hawkers is extrapolated from an investigation into the total
    number of fruitsellers; see Shanghai, C47-4-136, 14 March 1986, p. 22.

53 Wenzhou, J51-30-22, 1 Sept. 1980, pp. 252–8.

54 Wenzhou, J34-32-71, 1 June 1983, pp. 127–31.

55 Wenzhou, J80-16-12, Report on Zhao Ziyang's Visit to Wenzhou, 1 Dec.
    1985, pp. 2–10; Report on Hu Qiaomu's Visit to Wenzhou, 12 Nov. 1986,
    pp. 39–45.

56 Kate Xiao Zhou and Lynn T. White III, 'Quiet Politics and Rural
    Enterprise in Reform China', *Journal of Developing Areas*, 29, no. 4
    (July 1995), p. 477.

57 Hubei, SZ80-2-221, 23 Sept. 1985, pp. 124–5.

58 This happened, for instance, in the services sector in Shanghai; see
    Shanghai, B1-10-317, 4 May 1985, pp. 46–9.

59 Jan Prybyla, 'A Systemic Analysis of Prospects for China's Economy'
    in Joint Economic Committee (eds), *China's Economic Dilemmas in
    the 1990s*, US Government Printing Office, Washington: 1991, vol. 1,
    p. 221.

60 Liu Guoguang, 'A Sweet and Sour Decade', *Beijing Review*, 2–6 Jan.
    1989, pp. 22–9, quoted in Prybyla, 'A Systemic Analysis', p. 221.

61 Nanjing, 5020-4-76, 24 Sept. 1985, pp. 46–53.

62 Shanghai, B1-10-317, 27 Sept. 1985, pp. 56–62.

63 Michael Weisskopf, 'Private Squalor and Public Lives', *Guardian*, 23
    Feb. 1985.

64 Susan Young, 'Policy, Practice and the Private Sector in China',
    Australian Journal of Chinese Affairs, no. 21 (Jan. 1989), pp. 61–2; the
    number of people employed by village enterprises is mentioned in MAE,
    2883TOPO/3800, 21 Dec. 1988.

65 Wenzhou, J34-32-180, Talk by Deputy Mayor of Wenzhou, 4 March
    1987, pp. 82 and 85.

66 Terry Cheng, 'A Tale of One City's Rise to Fame', *South China Morning
    Post*, 5 June 1984.

67 Wenzhou, J1-28-51, Conference on Guangdong and Fujian, 24 Dec.
    1980, pp. 43–7; Wenzhou, J87-31-25, Talk by Chen Yun, 18 Jan. 1981,
    pp. 189–92.

68 Terry Cheng, 'A Tale of One City's Rise to Fame', *South China Morning Post*, 5 June 1984.

69 Guangdong, 235-2-242, Sept. 1977, pp. 181–8.

70 Guangdong, 229-6-323, 14 March 1978, pp. 1–31; Shanghai, B1-8-3, 24 Nov. 1977, p. 34.

71 Dikötter, *Mao's Great Famine*, p. 110.

72 Shanghai, A33-7-141, Report on National Conference on United Front Held from 15 August to 3 September 1979, 6 Nov. 1979, p. 1–12; Shanghai, B1-8-130, Conference on Overseas Chinese, 15 Oct. 1981, pp. 114–19.

73 Shanghai, A33-7-141, Report on National Conference on United Front Held from 15 August to 3 September 1979, 6 Nov. 1979, p. 147; MAE, 752INVA/2117, Yves Rodrigues, 'Visite à la municipalité de Shum Chun', 19 June 1979.

74 Frank Ching, 'China Seen Ready to Join Foreign Firms in Ventures in Hong Kong, Macao, China', *Wall Street Journal*, 31 Aug. 1979.

75 Guangdong, 235-2-286, State Council Resolution, 1 Sept. 1978, p. 46.

76 Frank Ching, 'Problems Hobble China Joint Venture', *Wall Street Journal*, 31 Aug. 1979.

77 Barry Kramer, 'Harpers International, China to Establish Vehicle-Assembly Plant near Hong Kong', *Wall Street Journal*, 13 Feb. 1979; MAE, 752INVA/2117, Yves Rodrigues, 'Visite à la municipalité de Shum Chun', 19 June 1979.

78 Guangdong, 253-2-332, Report by the Special Bureau for Zhuhai and Bao'an, 20 Oct. 1978, pp. 102–9.

79 'Where a Different Kind of War Is Being Fought', *South China Morning Post*, 19 Aug. 1979.

80 Reardon, *The Reluctant Dragon*, pp. 207–8.

81 MAE, 2882TOPO/2938, 'Performances économiques et commerciales de la Chine en 1985', 5 May 1986, pp. 30–32; Shanghai, B1-9-1481, 28 April 1984, pp. 1–6.

82 PRO, FCO 21/3738, 'China's Trade and Economic Relations', 1987; the estimate of $1 billion a year is in MAE, 2882TOPO/2938, 'Nuages sur les zones économiques spéciales?', 11 July 1985; MAE, 2882TOPO/2938, 'Performances économiques et commerciales de la Chine en 1985', 5 May 1986, pp. 30–32.

83 Wenzhou, J153-1-27, Speech by Zhao Ziyang at the State Council Conference on the Fourth Industrial Revolution, 9 Oct. 1983, pp. 14–23.

84 Wenzhou, J153-1-27, Ma Hong, 'On a Development Strategy for Our Country', no date, pp. 29–39; MAE, 2882TOPO/2914, Hervé Ladsous, 'La Chine et le choc du futur', 22 March 1984.

85 Shanghai, A33-6-247, Conference on Coastal Cities, 16 April 1984, pp. 17–18; MAE, 2882TOPO/2938, 'Nuages sur les zones économiques spéciales?', 11 July 1985, estimated the input from Beijing at a billion yuan a year.

86 Reardon, *The Reluctant Dragon*, p. 199.

87 Shanghai, A33-6-247, Conference on Coastal Cities, 16 April 1984, pp. 19.

88 Shanghai, B76-5-824, 25 Feb. 1983, pp. 28–31.

89 Shanghai, Notice on Special Material, B76-5-433, 18 March 1982, pp. 4–8.

90 David S. Bennahum, 'Heart of Darkness', *Wired*, 11 Jan. 1997.

91 Shanghai, B103-4-1238, 4 Oct. 1980, pp. 19–22; Shanghai, B1-8-94, 15 Nov. 1980, p. 65.

92 Shanghai, B43-1-70, October 1982, pp. 55–7.

93 Tianjin, X172-2-2292, July 1985, pp. 32–42.

94 Shanghai, B76-5-433, Directive from the State Administration on Guarding State Secrets, 25 May 1982, pp. 12–19; on the precise structure of this institution, see Chen Yongxi, 'Circumventing Transparency: Extra-Legal Exemptions from Freedom of Information and Judicial Review in China', *Journal of International Media & Entertainment Law*, 2018, 7 no. 2, p. 213.

95 Shanghai, B1-10-62, Instructions from the Shanghai Committee on Guarding State Secrets, 20 Oct. 1985, pp. 55–6.

96 MAE, 2882TOPO/2927, École Nationale des Ponts et Chaussées, 'Un voyage en Chine', 1 Dec. 1986.

97 MAE, 2882TOPO/2937, Charles Malo, 'Réforme des structures du commerce extérieur chinois', 20 Sept. 1984; MAE, 2882TOPO/2938, François Gipouloux, 'Les réserves en devises de la Chine', 25 Oct. 1985.

98 Gansu, 128-7-215, Zhao Ziyang to Leaders of Provinces and Municipalities, 11 April 1985, pp. 67–76.

99 MAE, 2882TOPO/2938, François Gipouloux, 'Les réserves en devises de la Chine', 25 Oct. 1985; see also International Monetary Fund, International Financial Statistics and Wigram Capital Advisors Limited.

100 John Burns, 'Scandal Blights Hainan Hope', *New York Times*, 12 Nov. 1985.

101 The figure of 3.20 to the dollar was given by Yao Yilin; see Shanghai, A76-4-351, Documents on the Second Plenum, Reactions to Yao Yilin's Talk at the National Economic Work Conference, 6 Oct. 1983, pp. 56–9.

102 Shanghai, B1-9-1505, 17 March 1984, pp. 59–65.

103 Lin and Schramm, 'China's Foreign Exchange Policies since 1979', pp. 254–6.

104 Tianjin, X78-3-2551, 18 Jan. 1985, pp. 38.

105 Shanghai, B1-10-282, 24 June 1985, pp. 2–5; Shanghai, B1-10-62, Report on Foreign Trade, 9 Aug. 1985, pp. 75–81.

106 Cui, 'China's Export Tax Rebate Policy', p. 340; on 1959, see table XXIV, United Nations Statistical Division, *International Trade Statistics, 1900–1960*, 1962.

107 Wang, *China's Exports since 1979*, p. 145.

108 Louis Kraar, 'A Little Touch of Capitalism', *Fortune*, 107, no. 8, 18 April 1983, p. 125.

109 Margaret Thatcher Foundation, PREM 19/789, 'Mr Heath's Call on Deng Xiaoping', Telno 202, 6 April 1982.

110 Margaret Thatcher Foundation, PREM 19/789, 'Call on the Prime Minister by Lord Maclehose', 23 July 1982.

111 Margaret Thatcher Foundation, PREM 19/790, 'Record of a Meeting Between the Prime Minister and Premier Zhao Ziyang', 23 Sept. 1982.

112 Margaret Thatcher Foundation, PREM 19/790, 'Record of a Meeting Between the Prime Minister and Vice Chairman Deng Xiaoping', 24 Sept. 1982.

113 Margaret Thatcher Foundation, PREM 19/790, 'Record of a Meeting Between the Prime Minister and Officials of the Executive Council of Hong Kong', 26 Sept. 1982.

114 Margaret Thatcher Foundation, PREM 19/788, 'Hong Kong: Sir Y.K. Pao', 28 Sept. 1982.

115 Margaret Thatcher Foundation, PREM 19/1059, 'Chinese Remarks', 7 Nov. 1982.

116 Margaret Thatcher Foundation, PREM 19/1057, 'Future of Hong Kong: Second Phase, Round Four', 22 Sept. 1983.

117 Margaret Thatcher Foundation, PREM 19/1058, 'Future of Hong Kong', 21 Oct. 1983.

118 Deng Xiaoping, 'China Will Always Keep Its Promises', 19 Dec. 1984, *Selected Works of Deng Xiaoping*, vol. 3, various editions.

119 MAE, 2882TOPO/2914, Charles Malo, 'Le triomphe de Deng Xiaoping', 2 Oct. 1984; Deng Xiaoping, 'Speech at the Ceremony Celebrating the 35th Anniversary of the Founding of the People's Republic of China', 1 Oct. 1984, *Selected Works of Deng Xiaoping wenxuan*, vol. 3, various editions.

4. OF PEOPLE AND PRICES (1984–1988)

1 Mao Zedong, 'Combat Liberalism', 7 Sept. 1937, *Selected Works of Mao Tse-tung*, vol. 2, p. 32.

2 Hoover Institution, Hongda Harry Wu Collection, Box 1, Deng Xiaoping, Talk on the Party's Urgent Tasks on the Organisational and Ideological Fronts, 12 Oct. 1983.

3 Ronald Reagan Library, Executive Secretariat: Country File China, Box 6-7, Chas Freeman, 'Situation Message', 31 Aug. 1981.

4 Mao Min, *The Revival of China*, Kindle Direct Publishing, 2017, vol. 3, p. 421.

5 Mao Min, *The Revival of China*, Kindle Direct Publishing, 2017, vol. 3, p. 421; MAE, 2882TOPO/2915, 'Discours de Hu Yaobang sur la propagande', 16 April 1985; see also Vogel, *Deng Xiaoping*, p. 566.

6 Mao Min, *The Revival of China*, Kindle Direct Publishing, 2017, vol. 3, p. 422; Li Rui, Diary, 15 and 20 Dec. 1995.

7 Li Rui, Diary, 20 and 24 Dec. 1995.

8 Zhao Ziyang, *Prisoner of the State*, Simon & Schuster, New York, 2009, pp. 192–3; see also David Bachman, 'Institutions, Factions, Conservatism, and Leadership Change in China: The Case of Hu Yaobang', in Ray Taras (ed.), *Leadership Change in Communist States*, Unwin Hyman, Boston, 1989, p. 95.

9 Li Rui, Diary, 29 Nov. 1998.

10 John F. Burns, '1,000 Peking Students March in Resentment Against Japan', *New York Times*, 19 Sept. 1985.

11 Hubei, SZ118-9-195, Report on Student Unrest, with talks from Li Peng and Hu Qili, Feb 1986, pp. 25–33; John F. Burns, 'Students in Peking Renew Protests against Japan', *New York Times*, 21 Nov. 1985.

12 Hubei, SZ1-9-488, Talk on Student Protests by Hu Qili, 4 Oct. 1985.

13 PRO 21/3305, 'Student Unrest in China', 19 March 1986.

14 Tianjin, X41-1-721, Party Document about the Goals of the Five Year Plan, followed by Talk by Zhao Ziyang, 18 and 23 Sept. 1985, pp. 133 and 196–7.

15 Instructions from Deng Xiaoping to the Standing Committee, Li Rui, Diary, 24 Jan. 1986.

16 Liang Heng and Judith Shapiro, 'China, the Year – and Claws – of the Tiger', *New York Times*, 8 March 1986; '2 Sentenced to Death in China Crackdown', *Boston Globe*, 22 Jan. 1986.

17 Hoover Institution, Hongda Harry Wu Collection, Box 3, Report by Gu Qiliang at the National Working Conference on Laogai and Laojiao, 17 June 1986.

18 'More Flak at Western "Pollution"', *South China Morning Post*, 20 March 1986; Daniel Southerland, 'Popular Singer Is Banned in China', *Washington Post*, 23 Nov. 1985.

19 PRO, FCO 21/1800, Christopher O. Hum, 'Election Fever', 22 Oct. 1980.

20 'China Tries to Muzzle Students Demanding More Democratic Government', *Ottawa Citizen*, 15 December 1986; Julia Kwong, 'The 1986 Student Demonstrations in China: A Democratic Movement?', *Asian Survey*, 28, no. 9 (Sept. 1988), p. 973.

21 Scott Savitt, *Crashing the Party: An American Reporter in China*, Soft Skull Press, Berkeley, CA, 2016, p. 106; also PRO, FCO 21/3308, Confidential Reports by Richard Evans, 23, 24, 29 and 31 December 1986.

22 'Zhenxi he fazhan anding tuanjie de zhengzhi jumian' (Cherish and develop political stability and unity), *Renmin ribao*, 23 Dec. 1986.

23 Wenzhou, J201-5-70, Directive to All Provinces from Central Committee, 24 Dec. 1986, pp. 151–3.

24 'Zhengzhi tizhi gaige zhi neng zai dang de lingdao xia jinxing' (Reform of the political system can only be carried out under the guidance of the party), *Renmin ribao*, 25 Dec. 1986.

25 Kwong, 'The 1986 Student Demonstrations in China', p. 972.

26 Li Rui, Diary, 26 Dec. 1986.

27 Li Rui, Diary, 30 Dec. 1986.

28 'Main Points of Deng Xiaoping's Speech on the Current Problem of Student Disturbance', 30 Dec. 1986, translated in *Chinese Law and Government*, 21, no. 1 (spring 1988), pp. 18–21; see also Li Rui, Diary, 3 Jan. 1987.

29 Zheng Zhongbing, *Hu Yaobang nianpu ziliao changbian* (A chronology of the life of Hu Yaobang), Shidai guoji chubanshe youxian gongsi, Hong Kong, 2005, vol. 2, pp. 1183–5.

30 The accusation was raised in Central Committee Document No. 8, according to Li Rui; see Li Rui, Diary, 19 April 1989; also 'New Offensive from the Left', *Asiaweek*, 19 April 1987, pp. 28–9, and Lu Keng, *Lu Keng huiyi yu chanhuilu* (Memoirs and confessions of Lu Keng), Shibao wenhua chuban qiye youxian gongsi, Taipei, 1997, p. 205.

31 Li Rui, Diary, 19 July 1987.

32 Li Rui, Diary, 29 March 1987.

33 The many ways in which the party constitution was violated in the process leading up to Hu Yaobang's resignation are discussed in Yang, *Hu Yao-Bang*, pp. 155–8; see also Lowell Dittmer, 'China in 1989: The Crisis of Incomplete Reform', *Asian Survey*, 30, no. 1 (Jan. 1990), pp. 25–41.

34 Andrew Nathan, Perry Link and Liang Zhang (eds), *The Tiananmen Papers: The Chinese Leadership's Decision to Use Force against Their Own People*, Little, Brown, London, 2002, p. xxxv; except for the

introduction, I have not otherwise relied on *The Tiananmen Papers*, since the authenticity of some of its documents is questionable.

35 László Ladány, 'China's Communist Old Guard Are Still in Command', *Far Eastern Economic Review*, 17 Dec. 1987.

36 Savitt, *Crashing the Party*, p. 117.

37 Julian Baum, 'Peking Propagandists Bring Back Their '60s Hero', *Christian Science Monitor*, 6 March 1987; Marlowe Hood, 'Tarnished Myth of Socialism's "Rustless Screw"', *South China Morning Post*, 8 March 1987.

38 Hoover Institution, 'Zhongguo Gong Chan Dang Issuances', Box 1, Directive from the Ministry of Propaganda, 9 Jan. 1987; on Liu Xiaobo in 1986, see Geremie Barmé, 'Confession, Redemption, and Death: Liu Xiaobo and the Protest Movement of 1989', in George Hicks (ed.), *The Broken Mirror: China After Tiananmen*, Longman, London, 1990, pp. 52-99.

39 PRO, FCO 21/3738, 'China's External Economic Relations', Oct. 1987.

40 BArch, Berlin, DY 30/2437, Minutes of Meeting between Erich Honecker and Zhao Ziyang, 8 June 1987, pp. 10-20.

41 PRO, FCO 21/3738, 'China's External Economic Relations', Oct. 1987.

42 Chen, Guo et al., *Major Issues and Policies in China's Financial Reform*, vol. 3, p. 26.

43 PRO, FCO 21/3738, Peter Wood, 'Economic Policy After the Congress', 24 Nov. 1987.

44 PRO, FCO 21/3738, Peter Wood, 'Deja Vu: Overheating in the Chinese Economy', 5 Nov. 1987.

45 Thomas M. H. Chan, 'China's Price Reform in the Period of Economic Reform', *Australian Journal of Chinese Affairs*, 18 (July 1987), pp. 85-108.

46 Shanghai, B1-10-409, Report by Ye Gongqi, 14 Sept. 1985, pp. 117-21; Report on National Conference on Price Control, 13 Aug. 1985, pp. 122-5; see also Shanghai, B1-10-40, Directives by State Price Bureau, 23 July 1985, pp. 2-7.

47 Tianjin, X81-1-700, June 1985, pp. 121-30; X81-1-663, 21 May 1984, pp. 25-7.

48 Shanghai, B1-10-409, Report by Ye Gongqi, 14 Sept. 1985, pp. 117-21.

49 PRO, FCO 21/3738, Peter Wood, 'Bread and Circuses', 3 Sept. 1987.

50 PRO, FCO 21/3738, Peter Wood, 'Bread and Circuses', 3 Sept. 1987.

51 Marlowe Hood, 'Deng's Burden', *South China Morning Post*, 15 Oct. 1988.

52 MAE, 2883/TOPO3772, Gérard Chesnel, 'Le protectionnisme provincial en Chine', 29 Nov. 1990.

53 PRO, FCO 21/3736, Charles Parton, 'Investment', 26 March 1987.

54 PRO, FCO 21/3739, Peter Wood, 'China: Economy', 7 Dec. 1987; see also International Monetary Fund, International Financial Statistics and Wigram Capital Advisors Limited.

55 Hubei, SZ273-6-618, Report from the Hubei Branch of the Bank of China, 9 April 1987, pp. 30–38.

56 PRO, FCO 21/4002, Peter Wood, 'The Right Price', 27 Jan. 1988.

57 'Rationing of Pork and Sugar in Beijing', South China Morning Post, 2 Dec. 1987.

58 MAE, 2883TOPO/3791, 'Les difficultés de la réforme économique en Chine', 1 Dec. 1988.

59 MAE, 2883TOPO/3791, 'Les difficultés de la réforme économique en Chine', 1 Dec. 1988.

60 Hubei, SZ69-8-339, Talk by Xiang Huaicheng at National Conference on Controlling Social Spending, 6 April 1988, pp. 28–44.

61 Hubei, SZ69-8-339, Talk by Zhao Ziyang as Reported at National Conference on Controlling Social Spending, 6 April 1988, pp. 28–44.

62 'Protest Action on the Increase by Students', South China Morning Post, 30 Aug. 1988.

63 Ruan, Deng Xiaoping, p. 197.

64 Ruan, Deng Xiaoping, p. 192.

65 Li Rui, Diary, 24 April 1989.

66 'Women de xiwang jiu zai zheili' (This is where our hope lies), Renmin ribao, 19 August 1988.

67 'Panic Buying Prompts Run on Banks in China', Chicago Tribune, 2 Sept. 1988; Wenzhou, J202-8-117, 8 Sept. 1988, pp. 66–7.

68 Wenzhou, J202-8-117, 30 Sept. and 11 Oct. 1988, pp. 114–15 and 118–19.

69 'Panic Buying Prompts Run on Banks in China', Chicago Tribune, 2 Sept. 1988; Wenzhou, J202-8-117, 8 Sept. 1988, pp. 66–7; Robin Pauley, 'Inflation Wounds China's Reformers', South China Morning Post, 21 Sept. 1988.

70 Li Rui, Diary, 23 Aug. 1988.

71 Wenzhou, J202-8-117, 30 Sept. and 11 Oct. 1988, pp. 114–15 and 118–19.

72 Larry Jagan, 'Industrial Unrest Plagues China', Guardian, 26 August 1988.

73 Chen, Guo et al., Major Issues and Policies in China's Financial Reform, vol. 3, p. 26.

74 Hubei, SZ43-7-433, State Council Directive on Economic Discipline, 4 Oct. 1988, pp. 59–63.

75 MAE, 2883TOPI/3800, OECD, Directorate for Food, Agriculture and Fisheries, 'Some Comments on the Grain Crisis in China', 30 Oct.

1989; the quotation from Zhao Ziyang is in Hubei, SZ1-9-332, National Conference on Agriculture, 21 Dec. 1984, pp. 25–9.

76 MfAA, ZR 2629/90, Bernd Jordan, Report on Economic and Social Problems in Agriculture, 27 Feb. 1986.

77 MAE, 2883TOPI/3800, OECD, Directorate for Food, Agriculture and Fisheries, 'Some Comments on the Grain Crisis in China', 30 Oct. 1989.

78 MfAA, ZR 2629/90, Bernd Jordan, Report on Economic and Social Problems in Agriculture, 27 Feb. 1986; Gansu, 216-4-256, Minutes of the Conference on Rural Work, 18 Dec. 1985, pp. 49–68; the compulsory aspect of the new system was made clear by the state in 1986; see PRO, FCO 21/3387, Charles Parton, 'Agriculture: Contracts Are a National Duty', 18 June 1986.

79 PRO, FCO 21/3736, Charles Parton, 'The Rural Sector in 1986', 18 June 1986.

80 MAE, 2883TOPI/3800, OECD, Directorate for Food, Agriculture and Fisheries, 'Some Comments on the Grain Crisis in China', 30 Oct. 1989.

81 Hubei, SZ68-4-362, 26 Oct. 1988, pp. 48–78; also 27 Oct. 1988, pp. 165–209; on Yueqing county see Wenzhou, J34-32-224, 5 Jan. 1989, pp. 95–101; the issue of IOUs is expertly discussed in D. Gale Johnson, 'The People's Republic of China 1978–90', Country Studies, no. 8, International Centre for Economic Growth, San Francisco: ICS Press, 1990, pp. 1–14.

82 Hubei, SZ108-6-271, National Conference on Agriculture, 14 Nov. 1988, pp. 43–51.

83 Gansu, 128-8-236, 28 Dec. 1988, pp. 56–61, followed by 128-8-389, 3 April 1989, pp. 1–10.

84 Zhu Rongji, On the Record: The Shanghai Years, 1987–1991, Brookings Institution Press, Washington, 2018, pp. 240–46; Zinser, 'The Performance of China's Economy', pp. 102–18.

85 One example is Hubei, SZ43-7-462, Document on the Spirit of the Third Plenum of the Thirteenth Congress, 11 Nov. 1988, pp. 56–62.

86 PRO, FCO 21/4251, Peter Wood, 'China: Pre NPC Economic Situation', 9 March 1989.

87 Hubei, SZ108-6-271, National Conference on Agriculture, 14 Nov. 1988, pp. 43–51; an estimate of the number of projects that were scaled back is in Lee Zinser, 'The Performance of China's Economy', p. 109; the figure of 50 million is in MAE, 2883TOPO/3800, 'Evolution de l'emploi en China', 9 March 1989.

88 FCO 21/4192, 'NPC Meeting: Comment', 5 April 1989.

89 Savitt, Crashing the Party, p. 157.

90 Savitt, *Crashing the Party*, p. 157.

91 Savitt, *Crashing the Party*, p. 155.

92 'China Slaps Ban on Video Tapes of Controversial TV Series', *South China Morning Post*, 9 Oct. 1988; the term 'bazooka' is mentioned in Ruan, *Deng Xiaoping*, p. 27.

93 Savitt, *Crashing the Party*, p. 157.

94 Zhao Ziyang, 'Yanzhe you Zhongguo tese de shehuizhuyi daolu qianjin' (Advance along the road of socialism with Chinese characteristics), *Renmin ribao*, 4 Nov. 1987.

95 Ren Wanding, 'Beijing Must Bring Out the Ballot Boxes', *South China Morning Post*, 29 Nov. 1988; see also Savitt, *Crashing the Party*, p. 167.

96 Roderick MacFarquhar (ed.), *The Politics of China*, Cambridge University Press, Cambridge, p. 433; 'Graft "at Worst level in Forty Years"', *South China Morning Post*, 24 Jan. 1989.

97 Marlowe Hood, 'Growing Internal Disquiet Again Focuses on Outsiders', *South China Morning Post*, 11 Dec. 1988.

98 Frank Dikötter and Olivier Richard, Joint Witness Account, 26 May 1986, author's collection.

99 Tim Luard, 'China Wrestles with Student Racial Unrest', *Christian Science Monitor*, 28 Dec. 1988; 'China Racial Unrest Moves to Beijing', *Los Angeles Times*, 3 Jan. 1989.

100 Wenzhou, J201-8-47, National Conference on Legal and Political Work, 19 Jan. 1989, pp. 2–20.

5. THE MASSACRE (1989)

1 FCO 21/3951, Peter Clark, 'Street Level China', Dec. 1988.

2 Kate Phillips, 'Springtime in Tiananmen Square, 1989', *Atlantic*, May 2014.

3 FCO 21/3951, Peter Clark, 'Street Level China', Dec. 1988; Ann Scott Tyson, 'China Sit-In Spotlights Education', *Christian Science Monitor*, 11 April 1988.

4 FCO 21/3951, Peter Clark, 'Street Level China', Dec. 1988.

5 FCO 21/4251, Peter Clark, 'China Economy', 2 Feb. 1989; Uli Schmetzer, 'Chinese Greet New Year with Old Traditions', *Chicago Tribune*, 6 Feb. 1989.

6 'Subdued Welcome for the Year of the Snake', *South China Morning Post*, 8 Feb. 1989.

7 Richard M. Nixon, *1999: Victory Without War*, Simon & Schuster, New York, 1988, p. 251.

8 See the official explanation and chronology of events leading to June the Fourth, compiled on behalf of the party by the mayor of Beijing for the National People's Congress, Chen Xitong, 'Guanyu zhizhi dongluan he pingxi fan geming baoluan de jueyi', 6 July 1989, *Guowuyuan gongbao*, 1989, no. 11 (18 July 1989), pp. 454–5.

9 Fang Lizhi, 'China's Despair and China's Hope', *New York Review of Books*, 2 Feb. 1989; Wenzhou, J201-8-46, Circular from Bureau of the Central Committee, 23 Feb. 1989, pp. 174–6.

10 The entire episode is expertly reconstructed in Mann, *About Face*, pp. 176–9.

11 Seth Faison and Marlowe Hood, 'Keep Out of Our Affairs, Zhao Warns', *South China Morning Post*, 27 Feb. 1989.

12 Ruan, *Deng Xiaoping*, p. 203.

13 Li Rui, Diary, 15 March 1989; also Ruan, *Deng Xiaoping*, p. 209.

14 Nicholas Kristof, 'Power War, Chinese Way', *New York Times*, 23 March 1989.

15 Li Rui, Diary, 18 March and 15 April 1989.

16 MAE, 2883/TOPO3772, Charles Malo, 'Disparition de Hu Yaobang', 17 April 1989.

17 MAE, 2883/TOPO3772, Charles Malo, 'Après la mort de Hu Yaobang', 18 April 1989; 'Agitation étudiante', 19 April 1989; the glass bottles are mentioned in Savitt, *Crashing the Party*, p. 183.

18 Wenzhou, J201-8-47, Directives by Bureau for Public Security, 18 April 1989, pp. 58–61.

19 MAE, 2883/TOPO3772, Charles Malo, 'Agitation étudiante', 19 April 1989; also Wenzhou, J201-8-47, Li Ximing, 'Guanyu Beijing xuechao qingkuang de tongbao' (Report on the circumstances of the student movement in Beijing), 19 May 1989, pp. 66–81; a reliable translation appeared as 'Internal Speech of Li Ximing, Secretary of the Beijing Municipal Party Committee (May 20, 1989)', *Chinese Law and Government*, 23, no. 1 (Spring 1990), p. 58; Eddie Cheng, *Standoff at Tiananmen*, Highlands Ranch, CO: Sensys Corp., 2009, pp. 74–5.

20 MAE, 2883/TOPO3772, Charles Malo, 'Poursuite de l'agitation étudiante', 21 April 1989; Kate Phillips, 'Springtime in Tiananmen Square, 1989', *Atlantic*, 29 May 2014; Cheng, *Standoff at Tiananmen*, pp. 76–7; David Holley, 'Thousands Join Beijing March for Democracy', *Los Angeles Times*, 22 April 1989.

21 MAE, 2883/TOPO3772, Charles Malo, 'Funérailles de Hu Yaobang et agitation sociale', 24 April 1989; also Gansu, 128-8-344, Report by Mu Yongji, Deputy Provincial Governor, 14 July 1989, pp. 37–50.

22   Li Peng, Diary, 21–22 April 1989; Jonathan Mirsky, 'People Power', *Observer*, 23 April 1989.

23   Jonathan Mirsky, 'People Power', *Observer*, 23 April 1989.

24   'Zhao Ziyang zong shuji zai Hu Yaobang tongzhi zhuidaohui shang zhi daoci', *Guowuyuan gongbao*, 13 May 1989, pp. 293–6; 'Can China Find Its Gorbachev?', *Guardian*, 24 April 1989; the decision not to confer the title of 'great Marxist' was taken the previous day; see Li Peng, Diary, 21 April 1989, and also Li Rui, Diary, 21 April 1989; on the different titles and ranks conferred in funerals, see Wen-hsuan Tsai, 'Framing the Funeral: Death Rituals of Chinese Communist Party Leaders', *China Journal*, no. 77 (Jan. 2017), pp. 51–71; the eulogy was also published in the *People's Daily* on 22 April.

25   Li Rui, Diary, 27 April 1989.

26   Li Peng, Diary, 22 April 1989.

27   'Chinese Bid Adieu to Hu Yaobang', *Times of India*, 23 April 1989.

28   MAE, 2883/TOPO3772, Charles Malo, 'Funérailles de Hu Yaobang et agitation sociale', 24 April 1989; Uli Schmetzer, 'Chinese Riots Leave Trail of Looting, Damage', *Chicago Tribune*, 24 April 1989; Seth Faison, 'Students Fear Backlash after Riots in Two Cities', *South China Morning Post*, 24 April 1989; telegram from party secretary mentioned in Li Peng, Diary, 22 April 1989.

29   Li Peng, Diary, 23 April 1989.

30   Chen Xitong, 'Guanyu zhizhi dongluan he pingxi fangeming baoluan de qingkuang baogao' (Report on quelling the counter-revolutionary turmoil), *Zhonghua renmin gongheguo guowuyuan gongbao*, 11, no. 592 (18 July 1989) pp. 453–76; Li Peng, Diary, 24 April 1989; Li Rui, Diary, 24 April 1989; on the student teams, see also MAE, 2883TOPO/3772, Charles Malo, 'Mouvement étudiant', 26 April 1989; volunteers mentioned in Cheng, *Standoff at Tiananmen*, p. 119.

31   Deng Xiaoping's words were widely circulated; a translation appeared in the *South China Morning Post*, reproduced in Michael Oksenberg, Lawrence R. Sullivan and Marc Lambert (eds), *Beijing Spring, 1989: Confrontation and Conflict. The Basic Documents*, Routledge, London, 1990, pp. 203–4; my quotation relies on Chen, 'Guanyu zhizhi dongluan', p. 460.

32   MAE, 2883TOPO/3772, Charles Malo, 'Mouvement étudiant', 26 April 1989; the editorial has been translated in Oksenberg, *Beijing Spring*, doc. 25, although my phrasing is slightly different.

33   MAE, 2883TOPO/3773, 'Mouvement étudiant', 28 April 1989; also Li Rui, Diary, 28 April 1989; Cheng, *Standoff at Tiananmen Square*, pp. 111–13.

34 MAE, 2883TOPO/3773, 'Mouvement étudiant', 28 April 1989; Zhao Ziyang registered Deng's displeasure in his memoir; see Zhao, *Prisoner of the State*, p. 46.

35 Oksenberg, *Beijing Spring*, p. 217; see also Cheng, *Standoff at Tiananmen*, pp. 117–18.

36 Cheng, *Standoff at Tiananmen Square*, pp. 117–18; 'Workers Urged to Support Stability', *South China Morning Post*, 2 May 1989.

37 Daniel Southerland, 'Students Planning New Protest', *Washington Post*, 30 April 1989.

38 Chen, 'Guanyu zhizhi dongluan', p. 461.

39 Li Rui, Diary, 22 April 1989, reporting a meeting of reform-minded intellectuals at the Science Hall that took place in the evening of 22 April; Li Peng, Diary, 30 April 1989.

40 Li Peng, Diary, 1 May 1989; Li Rui, Conversation with Qin Chuan, Diary, 6 May 1989; Zhao, *Prisoner of the State*, pp. 18–19.

41 Li Peng, Diary, 3 May 1989.

42 Li Rui, Diary, notes of meeting at the Science Hall, 3 May 1989.

43 Li Peng, Diary, 4 May 1989; see also Oksenberg, *Beijing Spring*, pp. 251–2.

44 MAE, 2883TOPO/3773, Charles Malo, '70eme Anniversaire du Mouvement du 4 Mai', 5 May 1989; 'Conciliatory Words after the Marches', *South China Morning Post*, 5 May 1989.

45 See the first-rate analysis of Kate Wright, 'The Political Fortunes of Shanghai's *World Economic Herald*', *Australian Journal of Chinese Affairs*, no. 23 (Jan. 1990), pp. 121–32.

46 Chen, 'Guanyu zhizhi dongluan', p. 462; also Li Peng, Diary, 5 May 1989; 'Zhao Ziyang fenxi dangqian guonei xingshi' (Zhao Ziyang analyses the domestic situation), *Renmin ribao*, 4 May 1989.

47 'China Students Show Restraint', *Guardian*, 8 May 1989.

48 Chen, 'Guanyu zhizhi dongluan', p. 465.

49 Cheng, *Standoff at Tiananmen*, p. 126.

50 Seth Faison, '10,000 Cyclists in Beijing Demand More Press Freedom', *South China Morning Post*, 11 May 1989.

51 Li Rui, Diary, 7 May 1989.

52 Chen, 'Guanyu zhizhi dongluan', p. 462.

53 Cheng, *Standoff at Tiananmen*, pp. 130–31.

54 Dikötter, *The Cultural Revolution*, p. 65.

55 Cheng, *Standoff at Tiananmen*, p. 74.

56 Cheng, *Standoff at Tiananmen*, pp. 132–5; '3,500 Students Go on Hunger Strike in China', *Chicago Tribune*, 14 May 1989; 'Huyushu' (Appeal) in *Huo yu xue zhi zhenxiang: Zhongguo dalu minzhu*

yundong jishi (The truth about fire and blood: A true record of the democracy movement in mainland China), Taipei: Zhonggong yanjiu zazhi she, 1989, section 4, p. 22; also Chen, 'Guanyu zhizhi dongluan', p. 465.

57 Li, 'Internal Speech of Li Ximing', p. 64.

58 Peter Gumbel and Adi Ignatius, 'Widening Demonstrations Disrupt Historic Chinese-Soviet Meeting', *Wall Street Journal*, 16 May 1989; Cheng, *Standoff at Tiananmen*, pp. 181–3.

59 See for instance Seth Faison, 'China and USSR Normalize Ties', 17 May 1989; the quotation is from PRO, FCO 21/4193, 'Activities of Chinese Leadership', June 1989; see also Li Peng, Diary, 16 May 1989; Zhao, *Prisoner of the State*, p. 47.

60 Cheng, *Standoff at Tiananmen*, p. 179; the text is in '5.17 xuanyan' (Declaration of 17 May), *Huo yu xue zhi zhenxiang*, part 4, pp. 14–15.

61 Li Peng, Diary, 16 May 1989.

62 Li Peng, Diary, 17 May 1989; also Zhao, *Prisoner of the State*, pp. 27–9.

63 Nicholas Kristof, 'Chinese Premier Issues a Warning to the Protesters', *New York Times*, 19 May 1989; see also Oksenberg, *Beijing Spring*, p. 268.

64 PRO, FCO 21/4193, 'Beijing Troubles', 23 May 1989; 'China's Premier Takes Hard Line', *San Francisco Chronicle*, 18 May 1989; Nicholas Kristof, 'Chinese Premier Issues a Warning to the Protesters', *New York Times*, 19 May 1989.

65 PRO, FCO 21/4197, A. N. R. Millington, 'China: Student Demonstrations', 30 May 1989; Li Rui, Diary, 22 May 1989.

66 Li Rui, Diary, 18 May 1989; Wenzhou, J201-8-47, Li Zemin, Provincial Party Secretary, Talk at Provincial Party Committee, 9 Sept. 1989, pp. 100–3; *Tiananmen Papers*, p. 284.

67 Wenzhou, J201-8-47, Report by Li Zemin, Provincial Party Secretary, 9 Sept. 1989, pp. 88–121, Gansu, 128-8-344, Report by Mu Yongji, Deputy Provincial Governor, 14 July 1989, pp. 37–50.

68 PRO, FCO 21/4199, 'Disturbances in Xinjiang Autonomous Region', 21 May 1989.

69 Oksenberg, *Beijing Spring*, p. 313.

70 Li Rui, Diary, 20 May 1989.

71 Precise figures from PRO, FCO 21/4194, 'PLA Operations in Beijing', 3 July 1989; Li Peng, Diary, 20 May 1989.

72 'People Search for Truth', *South China Morning Post*, 24 May 1989; Cheng, *Standoff at Tiananmen*, p. 201; PRO, FCO 21/4199, 'China: Student Demonstrations', 25 May 1989.

73 'Demonstrations Growing in South China Cities', *Los Angeles Times*, 24 May 1989; MAE, 2883TOPO/3773, 'Situation à Shanghai', 23 and 24 May 1989; 'Clampdown on Protests in Wuhan', *South China Morning Post*, 23 May 1989; for Lanzhou see Gansu, 128-8-344, Report by Mu Yongji, 14 July 1989, pp. 37–50.

74 The build-up is detailed in PRO, FCO 21/4194, 'PLA Operations in Beijing', 3 July 1989; Yao Yilin's comments are noted in Li Rui, Diary, 25 May 1989; Li Peng's appearance on television is described in David Holley, 'Premier Li Peng', *Los Angeles Times*, 27 May 1989.

75 Yang Shangkun's speech to the Central Military Commission was widely circulated; Li Rui came across a copy posted on a telephone pole (Li Rui, Diary, 30 May 1989); this was also noted by the British embassy (PRO, FCO 21/4197, Alan Donald, 'Telno 981'); a partial translation appears in Oksenberg, *Beijing Spring*, pp. 320–27.

76 Li Peng, Diary, 21 and 22 May 1989; also PRO, FCO 21/4194, 'PLA Operations in Beijing', 3 July 1989.

77 MAE, 2883TOPO/3773, Charles Malo, 'Situation intérieure', 29 May 1989.

78 Gansu, 259-2-368, 'Chuanda Li Peng, Yang Shangkun, Yao Yilin de jianghua' (Transmitting talks by Li Peng, Yang Shangkun and Yao Yilin), 26 May 1989, p. 106; also 264-1-61, Wu Jian, 'Chuanda Li Peng, Yang Shangkun de jianghua' (Transmitting talks by Li Peng and Yang Shangkun), 1 June 1989, p. 91.

79 Gansu, 238-1-211, Report by the Provincial Bureau for Environmental Protection, 3 June 1989, pp. 1–4.

80 Li Rui, Diary, 27 May 1989.

81 PRO, FCO 21/4194, 'PLA Operations in Beijing', 3 July 1989.

82 MAE, 2883TOPO/3773, 'Situation à Shanghai', 22, 23 and 24 May 1989; also Jay Matthews, 'In Shanghai and Other Cities, Fervor for Democracy Seems to Wane', *Washington Post*, 28 May 1989.

83 Eamonn Fitzpatrick and Dean Nelson, 'Cash and Tears Flow at Concert', *South China Morning Post*, 28 May 1989; Chris Yeung, 'Another Vast Crowd Joins World-Wide Show of Solidarity', *South China Morning Post*, 29 May 1989.

84 Jay Mathews, 'Goddess of Democracy Rises', *Washington Post*, 31 May 1989; Uli Schmetzer, 'Torch of China's Lady Liberty Rekindles Fervor', *Chicago Tribune*, 31 May 1989.

85 Nicholas Kristof, 'Chinese Students in About-Face', *New York Times*, 30 May 1989; PRO, FCO 21/4194, 'PLA Operations in Beijing', 3 July 1989.

86 David Holley, 'Beijing Students' Bravery Sparked Epic Drama', *Los Angeles Times*, 2 June 1989.

87 Amnesty International, 'People's Republic of China: Preliminary Findings on Killings of Unarmed Civilians, Arbitrary Arrests and Summary Executions since 3 June 1989', London: Amnesty International, document dated 14 August 1989; Li Rui, Diary, 2 June 1989; see also PRO, FCO 21/4194, 'PLA Operations in Beijing', 3 July 1989.

88 Amnesty International, 'People's Republic of China', p. 275; PRO, FCO 21/4194, 'PLA Operations in Beijing', 3 July 1989; Jonathan Mirsky, 'China's Old Men Use Force to Stay in Power', *Guardian*, 4 June 1989; Uli Schmetzer and Ronald Yates, 'Beijing Residents Repel Troops', *Chicago Tribune*, 3 June 1989.

89 PRO, FCO 21/4194, 'PLA Operations in Beijing', 3 July 1989, puts the time at 2.30; PRO, FCO 21/4197, Alan Donald, 'Telno 1002', 3 June 1989; Amnesty International, 'People's Republic of China', put the time at four to five; Jay Mathews, 'Chinese Students Waited Quietly in Tiananmen for Army Action', *Washington Post*, 3 June 1989, witnessed one bus at Liubukou; Amnesty International reported two buses; Alan Donald, 'Telno 1002', 3 June 1989, mentions at least three points where military buses were captured; the most reliable report is from Daniel Southerland, who counted four military buses on the western side of the square: 'Chinese Citizens Block Troops from Reaching Central Square', *Washington Post*, 3 June 1989; the army lorries near the square are mentioned in Colin Nickerson, 'Chinese Civilians Repulse Army Advance on the Square', *Boston Globe*, 3 June 1989.

90 PRO, FCO 21/4194, 'PLA Operations in Beijing', 3 July 1989.

91 PRO, FCO 21/4197, Alan Donald, 3 June 1989, 'Telno 1002'; PRO, FCO 21/4194, 'PLA Operations in Beijing', 3 July 1989; Amnesty International, 'People's Republic of China'.

92 Li Peng, Diary, 3 June 1989; although Li Peng does not use the term 'counter-revolutionary riot' in his notes, it was quoted in a notice issued by the Central Committee and State Council two days later; see PRO, FCO 21/4197, Alan Donald, 'Chinese Internal Situation', 5 June 1989.

93 PRO, FCO 21/4197, Alan Donald, 3 June 1989, 'Telno 1002'; PRO, FCO 21/4194, 'PLA Operations in Beijing', 3 July 1989; Amnesty International, 'People's Republic of China'.

94 PRO, FCO 21/4194, 'PLA Operations in Beijing', 3 July 1989; Savitt, *Crashing the Party*, pp. 192–4.

95 Southerland, 'Remembering Tiananmen'.

96 Li Rui, Diary, 3 and 7 June; also 'Voices from Tiananmen', *South China Morning Post*, p. 1.

97   Liang Jingdong, 'Witness to History', *Salt Lake Tribune*, 3 June 1999; Amnesty International, 'People's Republic of China'.

98   PRO, FCO 21/4194, 'PLA Operations in Beijing', 3 July 1989; also Amnesty International, 'People's Republic of China'.

99   PRO, FCO 21/4194, 'PLA Operations in Beijing', 3 July 1989.

100 Liang, 'Witness to History'; PRO, FCO 21/4194, Letter with Witness Account to Alan Donald, 11 July 1989.

101 Liang, 'Witness to History'.

102 Eyewitness accounts agree on very little, including the time at which the lights were switched off; 4.40 is the time given in PRO, FCO 21/4197, Telnos 1010 and 1012, 'China Internal', 4 June 1989; also Cheng, *Standoff at Tiananmen*, p. 263; Wu Renhua, the foremost historian of these events, says '4.00 precisely'; Wu Renhua, *Liusi shijian quancheng shilu* (A full record of the June Fourth incident), Taipei: Yunchen wenhua shiye gufen youxian gongsi, 2019, n.p.

103 Savitt, *Crashing the Party*, p. 197.

104 Savitt, *Crashing the Party*, p. 197; also Liang, 'Witness to History'.

105 PRO, FCO 21/4194, eyewitness account dated 14 Sept. 1989.

106 PRO, FCO 21/4194, 'PLA Operations in Beijing', 3 July 1989.

107 PRO, FCO 21/4194, 'PLA Operations in Beijing', 3 July 1989; PRO, FCO 21/4194, Letter with Witness Account to Alan Donald, 11 July 1989; also PRO, FCO 21/4197, Telno 1012, 4 June 1989.

108 PRO, FCO 21/4194, 'PLA Operations in Beijing', 3 July 1989.

109 PRO, FCO 21/4194, 'PLA Operations in Beijing', 3 July 1989.

110 PRO, FCO 21/4194, 'PLA Operations in Beijing', 3 July 1989.

111 Savitt, *Crashing the Party*, p. 194.

112 Phillips, 'Springtime in Tiananmen Square, 1989'; PRO, FCO 21/4197, 'Telno 1011', 4 June 1989; PRO, FCO 21/4199, Alan Donald, 'Telno 1196', 22 June 1989; Amnesty, p. 282; Li Rui, in his diary entry dated 25 June 1990, also estimated the death toll at somewhere between 2,700 and 3,400.

113 PRO, FCO 21/4194, M. H. Farr, Commander Royal Navy, 'PLA Operations in Beijing', 3 July 1989.

114 Phillips, 'Springtime in Tiananmen Square, 1989'.

6. WATERSHED (1989–1991)

1   Claudia Rosett, 'Anything Could Happen Next in Tiananmen', *Wall Street Journal*, 7 June 1989.

2   Yuan Mu, 'State Council Spokesman Yuan Mu Holds News Conference',
    Oksenberg, *Beijing Spring*, pp. 348–9.

3   Claudia Rosett, 'Anything Could Happen Next in Tiananmen', *Wall
    Street Journal*, 7 June 1989.

4   James Sterba, 'Chasing for Evidence of China's "Civil War"', *Washington
    Post*, 7 June 1989.

5   Daniel Williams, 'China Hard-Liners Appear in Control', *Los Angeles
    Times*, 9 June 1989.

6   David Chen and Geoffrey Crothall, 'Unrest Growing in the Provinces',
    South China Morning Post, 7 June 1989; this article and others reported
    that at least 300 people died; see also Louisa Lim, *The People's Republic of
    Amnesia: Tiananmen Revisited*, Oxford University Press, Oxford, 2015.

7   David Chen and Geoffrey Crothall, 'Unrest Growing in the Provinces',
    South China Morning Post, 7 June 1989; Gansu, 128-8-344, Report by
    Mu Yongji, 14 July 1989, pp. 37–50.

8   MAE, 2883TOPO/3773, Barroux, 'Situation à Shanghai', 6 June 1989.

9   MAE, 2883TOPO/3773, Barroux, 'Le maire de Shanghai', 9 June 1989;
    also Charles Goddard, 'Shanghai Protest as Calm Returns', *Guardian*,
    10 June 1989.

10 Colin Smith, 'Would-Be Martyrs in Retreat – For Now', *Observer*, 11
    June 1989.

11 Hoover Institution, Jim Mann Papers, Box 2, 'Secretary's Morning
    Summary'; PRO, FCO 21/4197, 'Telno 723' and 'Telno 596', 5 June 1989.

12 Daniel Schorr, 'Washington Notebook', *New Leader*, 12 June 1989.

13 'Excerpts of President Bush's News Conference', *Washington Post*,
    6 June 1989; James Gerstenzang, 'Bush Rejects China Curbs, Urges
    Respect for Rights', *Los Angeles Times*, 9 June 1989.

14 Gansu, 259-2-381, Deng Xiaoping's June 9 Talk to the Troops, 22 June
    1989, pp. 1–8.

15 PRO, FCO 21/4194, 'PLA Operations in Beijing', 3 July 1989; Harrison
    E. Salisbury, *Tiananmen Diary: Thirteen Days in June*, Little, Brown,
    London, 1989, p. 88.

16 PRO, FCO 21/4194, 'PLA Operations in Beijing', 3 July 1989; Salisbury,
    Diary, p. 88.

17 Daniel Southerland, 'Chinese Citizens Block Army Troops in Beijing',
    Washington Post, 3 June 1989.

18 Mann, *About Face*, pp. 201–3.

19 Kissinger sent the message via Huang Hua, the erstwhile foreign min-
    ister and ambassador who had been instrumental in inviting Nixon to
    Beijing; see Li Rui, Diary, 16 June 1989.

20 The National Security Archive, George Washington University, 'Memorandum of Conversation: LTG Brent Scowcroft, Deng Xiaoping et al., July 2, 1989'.

21 Mann, *About Face*, p. 209.

22 PRO, FCO 21/4193, 'Political Situation', 9 June 1989; Amnesty, p. 284; MAE, 2883TOPO/3773, Charles Malo, 'Après la révolte des étudiants', 19 June 1989.

23 'Intellectual Accuses Deng of "Extermination Plan"', *South China Morning Post*, 26 June 1989.

24 Jeffie Lam, '"Operation Yellow Bird": How Tiananmen Activists Fled to Freedom through Hong Kong', *South China Morning Post*, 26 May 2014.

25 Comments by Huo Shilian noted in Li Rui, Diary, 19 June 1989; 'Western Leaders Condemn Executions in Shanghai', *South China Morning Post*, 22 June 1989.

26 Wenzhou, J201-8-47, Directive from the Central Committee, zhongfa (1989) no. 3, 30 June 1989, pp. 122–7; Amnesty International, 'People's Republic of China'.

27 Liao Yiwu, *Bullets and Opium: Real-Life Stories of China After the Tiananmen Massacre*, Atria, New York, 2019, pp. 33–40, 57–8 and 73–88.

28 Liao, *Bullets and Opium*, pp. 33–40, 57–8 and 73–88.

29 Wenzhou, J201-9-70, Report from Vice Minister of Public Security Gu Linfang, 5 May 1990, pp. 209–24.

30 Shanghai, B76-7-872, Jiang Zemin, Yao Yilin, Qiao Shi and others on Labour Unions, 28 July 1989, pp. 2–10.

31 Shanghai, A33-6-466, Jiang Zemin, Yao Yilin, Qiao Shi and others at Conference on United Front, 11 to 15 June 1990, pp. 1–28.

32 James Tyson, 'China Arrests Leaders of Catholic Church', *Christian Science Monitor*, 2 Feb. 1990.

33 Susan Man Ka-po, 'Iron Fist Tightens Around the Church', *South China Morning Post*, 23 Sept. 1990; Beverley Howells, 'How Catholic Cells Will Fight Repression', *South China Morning Post*, 29 Dec. 1991.

34 Justin Hastings, 'Charting the Course of Uyghur Unrest', *China Quarterly*, no. 208 (Dec. 2011), p. 900; also Pablo Adriano Rodriguez, 'Violent Resistance in Xinjiang (China): Tracking Militancy, Ethnic Riots and "Knife-Wielding" Terrorists (1978–2012)', HAO, no. 30 (Winter 2013), p. 137.

35 Wenzhou, J201-9-70, Central Committee, Document on Strengthening Legal Work to Protect Social Stability, 2 April 1990, pp. 1–12; quotation from Li Peng in Wenzhou, J201-9-70, Talk on Law and Politics by Li

Zemin, Party Secretary of Zhejiang Province, 31 March 1990, pp. 31–44; 'Wending yadao yique' (Social stability above all else), *Renmin ribao*, 3 June 1990.

36 Zhao, *Prisoner of the State*.
37 Li Rui, Diary, 15 and 16 June 1989 and following months.
38 Vogel, *Deng Xiaoping*, p. 642.
39 Li Rui, Diary, 27 June 1989.
40 Li Peng, Diary, 19 to 21 June 1989; Zhao, *Prisoner of the State*, pp. 49–50.
41 Li Peng, Diary, 24 June 1989; Li Rui, Diary, 24 June 1989.
42 For reactions in Shanghai to Jiang's rise in June 1989, see Sheryl WuDunn, 'An Urbane Technocrat', *New York Times*, 25 June 1989.
43 Wenzhou, J201-8-46, zhongfa (1989) no. 7, 28 July 1989, pp. 1–17.
44 'Economic Aid for Backward Countries', *South China Morning Post*, 12 May 1957; 'Spending Fails to Curb Reds', *Chicago Daily Tribune*, 7 Jan. 1957; 'Secretary Bars Recognition as Defense Peril', *Washington Post*, 5 Dec. 1989.
45 Pang Xianzhi and Jin Chongji (eds), *Mao Zedong zhuan, 1949–1976* (A biography of Mao Zedong, 1949–1976), Zhongyang wenxian chubanshe, Beijing, 2003, vol. 2, p. 1027.
46 Shanghai, A76-3-645, 28 Aug. 1989, pp. 20–30.
47 PRO, FCO 21/4194, S. C. Riordan, 'How to Quell a Counter-Revolution: The True Story', 1 Aug. 1989; also MAE, 2883TOPO/3772, 'Expositions sur la répression de Pékin', 14 Aug. 1989; a smaller exhibit was organised by the Museum of Fine Arts.
48 MAE, 2883TOPO/3772, 'Culte de la personnalité de Deng Xiaoping', 14 Aug. 1989.
49 MAE, 2883TOPO/3772, 'Les étudiants chinois entre la faucille et le marteau', 11 Sept. 1989.
50 MAE, 2883TOPO/3772, 'Les étudiants de l'université de Pekin à l'ombre des fusils', 7 Nov. 1989; 'Les étudiants chinois entre la faucille et le marteau', 11 Sept. 1989.
51 Wenzhou, J201-8-46, Li Ruihuan, Telephone Conference on Campaign against Pornography, 29 August 1989, pp. 196–200; also State Council and Bureau of the Central Committee, 16 Sept. 1989, pp. 178–87; 'Anti Porn Drive Is Only the Start of Campaign', *South China Morning Post*, 1 Nov. 1989.
52 'Anti Porn Drive Is Only the Start of Campaign', *South China Morning Post*, 1 Nov. 1989; Frederic Moritz, 'China Shackles Its Freer Press', *Christian Science Monitor*, 4 Aug. 1989; see also Richard Curt Kraus, *The Party and the Arty in China: The New Politics of Culture*, Rowman & Littlefield, Lanham, MD, 2004, p. 93.

53 Wenzhou, J201-8-46, Li Zemin, Provincial Party Secretary in Telephone Conference, 5 Sept. 1989, pp. 215–22; Willy Lam, 'Smut Is Only Start of Campaign', *South China Morning Post*, 1 Nov. 1989.

54 MAE, 2883TOPO/3772, Charles Malo, 'Célébrations du 40ème anniversaire', 2 Oct. 1989.

55 Wenzhou, J201-8-46, Telegram by Propaganda Department on Preparations for the Fortieth Anniversary, 29 Aug. 1989, pp. 42–55.

56 MAE, 2883TOPO/3772, Charles Malo, 'Célébrations du 40ème anniversaire', 2 Oct. 1989; also David Holley, 'Under Tight Wraps, China Marks 40th Anniversary of Communist Rule', *Los Angeles Times*, 2 Oct. 1989.

57 PRO, FCO 21/4194, Susan Morton, 'Life Returns to Normal in Peking?', 7 Aug. 1989.

58 'Asian Games', *South China Morning Post*, 8 July 1989.

59 Rajdeep Sardesai, 'Emotional Roller-Coaster', *Times of India*, 14 Oct. 1990; Mark Fineman, 'Beijing Changes Tune', *Los Angeles Times*, 25 Jan. 1990.

60 Ann Scott Tyson, 'Beijing Marshals City Residents to Spruce Up for Asian Games', *Christian Science Monitor*, 21 Sept. 1990.

61 John Kohut, 'Jubilant Beijing Leaders Preside over Asiad Closing', *South China Morning Post*, 8 Oct. 1990.

62 'Buyao dangtou, jia weiba zuoren, taoguang yangmei, zuotou bishi zhudong'; Li Rui, entry dated 28 Dec. 1990, notes on document summarising a 24 December meeting between Deng Xiaoping, Jiang Zemin, Yang Shangkun and Li Peng.

63 Wenzhou, J201-8-46, zhongfa (1989) no. 7, 28 July 1989, pp. 1–17; Telegram by Propaganda Department on Preparations for the Fortieth Anniversary, 29 Aug. 1989, pp. 42–55.

64 Ann Scott Tyson, 'Beijing Marshals City Residents to Spruce Up for Asian Games', *Christian Science Monitor*, 21 Sept. 1990; quotation from Chen Xitong in Simon Long, 'Beijing Washes Whiter for Asian Games Showcase', *Guardian*, 7 Aug. 1990.

65 Willy Lam, 'Role for "United Front" Parties', *South China Morning Post*, 2 Jan. 1990.

66 '"Hero" Lei Resurrected to Win People's Support', *South China Morning Post*, 11 Dec. 1989; Seth Faison, 'A Nation Going Backwards with Tale of Simple Hero', *South China Morning Post*, 4 March 1990.

67 'Model Soldier's Inspiration', *South China Morning Post*, 12 March 1990.

68 'Party Leader Calls on Chinese Youth to Keep Patriotism Alive', *Xinhua News Agency*, 4 May 1990; also 'Party Leader Praises Students', *South China Morning Post*, 4 May 1990.

69 MAE, 2883TOPO/3775, '150ème anniversaire de la Guerre de l'Opium', 8 June 1990; also 'Beijing Revives "Opium War" to Combat Liberalism', *Christian Science Monitor*, 31 May 1990.

70 'When a Five-Year-Old Becomes a Victim of History', *South China Morning Post*, 14 Dec. 1991.

71 Shanghai, A33-6-440, Work on the United Front at the Fourth Plenum, 8–9 Aug. 1989, pp. 50–58.

72 Willy Lam, 'Role for "United Front" Parties', *South China Morning Post*, 2 Jan. 1990.

73 Shanghai, A33-6-440, Work on the United Front at the Fourth Plenum, 8–9 Aug. 1989, pp. 50–58.

74 Shanghai, A33-6-466, Jiang Zemin, Yao Yilin, Qiao Shi and others at Conference on United Front, 11 to 15 June 1990, pp. 1–28 and 127–30.

75 Margaret Scott, 'Hong Kong on Borrowed Time', *New York Times*, 22 Oct. 1989.

76 Li Rui, Diary, 24 June 1989.

77 Christine Loh, *Underground Front: The Chinese Communist Party in Hong Kong*, University Press, Hong Kong, 2019.

78 'Lee, Szeto Subversive, Says China', *South China Morning Post*, 22 July 1989.

79 Loh, *Underground Front*, p. 176.

80 Deng Xiaoping, 'Speech at a Meeting with Members of the Committee for Drafting the Basic Law of the Hong Kong Special Administrative Region', 16 April 1987, *Selected Works of Deng Xiaoping*, vol. 3, various editions.

81 Wenzhou, J201-8-46, Report on How to Report the Political Situation in Eastern Europe, 21 Dec. 1989, pp. 56–61; the report by Wang Fang is mentioned in Li Rui, Diary, 8 Dec. 1989; the quotations are in Li Rui, Diary, 6 Jan. 1990.

82 MAE, 2883TOPO/3773, Claude Martin, 'La montée des inquiétudes', 27 August 1991.

83 MAE, 2883TOPO/3773, Claude Martin, 'La montée des inquiétudes', 27 August 1991; Li Rui, Diary, 8 Oct. 1991; Willy Lam, 'Beijing Set to Fight "Capitalist Trends"', *South China Morning Post*, 26 August 1991.

84 Nicolas Kristof, 'Beijing's Top Priority: Maintain Communism', *New York Times*, 15 Sept. 1991; Li Rui, Diary, 7 Oct. 1991; see also Henry He, *Dictionary of the Political Thought of the People's Republic of China*, Routledge, London, 2000, p. 24.

85 Willy Lam, 'Cultural Revolution Re-Run Waiting in the Left Wing', *South China Morning Post*, 18 July 1991.

86 Willy Lam, 'Cultural Revolution Re-Run Waiting in the Left Wing', *South China Morning Post*, 18 July 1991.

87 'Chen Yun Urges Restraint in Economic Construction', 5 Dec. 1991, in FBIS (FBIS-CHI-91-239), 12 Dec. 1991; Willy Lam, 'Ideology "Boosted" in 390,000 Villages', *South China Morning Post*, 16 Nov. 1991; Daniel Kwan, 'Socialism Ideology Stepped Up', *South China Morning Post*, 28 Aug. 1991; the quotation from Li Peng is in Wenzhou, J201-9-68, Report on Rural Economy by Provincial Party Committee, 22 Jan. 1990, pp. 69–108.

88 Willy Lam, 'Revival for Mao Crusade Against West', *South China Morning Post*, 27 Dec. 1991.

89 PRO, FCO 21/4194, Alan Donald, untitled letter dated 11 July 1989.

90 Library of Congress, 'Meeting With Vice Premier Deng Xiaoping, Beijing, April 15, 1980', Robert S. McNamara Papers, Box 199; my colleague Priscilla Roberts kindly pointed me towards the McNamara Papers in the Library of Congress.

91 Mann, *About Face*, p. 239.

92 PRO, FCO 21/4253, 'Fall in Reserves at End June', 29 Sept. 1989.

93 Seth Faison, 'New Rules on Imports', *South China Morning Post*, 7 Aug. 1989; 'China Tightens Curbs to Narrow Trade Gap', *South China Morning Post*, 18 July 1989; Joint Committee, *China's Economic Dilemmas*, p. 749.

94 Gansu, 151-3-74, Zheng Tuobin, Ministry of Foreign Trade, Conference on Foreign Trade, 1 Aug. 1990, pp. 44–89.

95 Gansu, 151-3-43, Zheng Tuobin, Ministry of Foreign Trade, National Conference on Foreign Trade, 23 Dec. 1989, pp. 85–112; see also Joint Committee, *China's Economic Dilemmas*, p. 749.

96 Gansu, 151-3-74, 1 Aug. 1990, Zheng Tuobin, Ministry of Foreign Trade, Conference on Foreign Trade, 1 Aug. 1990, pp. 44–89.

97 Wenzhou, J34-32-327, Document by State Council, 4 Feb. 1990, guofa (1990) no. 11, pp. 8–15.

98 PRO, FCO 21/4550, PRO, FCO 21/4550, 'Economic Development and Reform Policy in mid-1990', Oct. 1990; 'CIA Report on China's Economy', 20 Aug. 1990; John F. Cooper, 'Tiananmen June 4, 1989: Taiwan's Reaction', *Taiwan Insight*, article posted on 10 June 2019.

99 Wenzhou, J201-9-70, Urgent Telegram Concerning Fang Lizhi, 23 June 1990, pp. 305–8; see also Fang Lizhi, 'The Chinese Amnesia', *New York Review of Books*, 37, no. 14 (27 Sept. 1990), p. 30.

100 MAE, 2883TOPO/3798, Charles Malo, 'Visite à Pékin du vice-président de la Banque Mondiale', 6 April 1990.

101 Mann, *About Face*, pp. 240–41.

102 MAE, 2883TOPO/3793, Cluade Martin, 'Rumeurs de dévaluation du yuan', 20 Dec. 1991.

103 Gansu, 151-3-43, Zheng Tuobin, Ministry of Foreign Trade, National Conference on Foreign Trade, 23 Dec. 1989, pp. 85–112.

104 PRO, FCO 21/4253, Peter Wood, 'Not at Any Price: Markets, Monopolies and Price Controls', 4 Sept. 1989.

105 PRO, FCO 21/4253, Peter Wood, 'Not at Any Price: Markets, Monopolies and Price Controls', 4 Sept. 1989.

106 PRO, FCO 21/4253, Peter Wood, 'Spinning a Yarn: Cotton and the Textile Industry', 28 Sept. 1989.

107 Gansu, 151-3-81, Document by Gansu China Textile Products Import and Export Corporation, 15 May 1990, pp. 4–5; PRO, FCO 21/4253, Peter Wood, 'Spinning a Yarn: Cotton and the Textile Industry', 28 Sept. 1989.

108 PRO, FCO 21/4253, Peter Wood, 'Not at Any Price: Markets, Monopolies and Price Controls', 4 Sept. 1989.

109 The estimate of 40 per cent is in PRO, FCO 21/4550, Andrew Seaton, 'China: Economic Reporting', 7 Dec. 1990; for the money supply see MAE, 2883 TOPO/3793, 'Situation économique et financière de la Chine', 19 April 1991; this document puts the amount of subsidies at 30 to 40 per cent of the budget.

110 PRO, FCO 21/4550, 'Economic Development and Reform Policy in mid-1990', Oct. 1990; the official GDP was 4.2 per cent in 1989 and 3.9 per cent in 1990.

111 PRO, FCO 21/4550, 'Economic Development and Reform Policy in mid-1990', Oct. 1990.

112 Qu Qiang, 'Triangular Debts' in Chen and Guo (eds), *Major Issues and Policies in China's Financial Reform*, vol. 3, pp. 19–36.

113 Wenzhou, J202-12-96, 28 Dec. 1992, pp. 46–57.

114 See PRO, FCO 21/4550, M. Wright, 'China Economy', 12 July 1990.

115 Wenzhou, J202-12-96, 28 Dec. 1992, pp. 46–57.

116 Gansu, 128-9-60, Talks by Li Peng and Zhu Rongji on Triangular Debt, 4 Sept. 1991, pp. 1–11; Li Rui, Diary, 2 Nov. 1991.

117 Li Rui, Diary, 2 Aug. 1991: 'Wang Bingqian does not even have a basic understanding of accounting (credit, debt) and should step down; Li Guixian has even less understanding of banks'.

118 Willy Lam, 'Zhu "Finds Solution to State-Run Firms"', *South China Morning Post*, 1 Oct. 1991.

119 Willy Lam, 'Faction Fighting Out in the Open', *South China Morning Post*, 27 Nov. 1991.

7. CAPITALIST TOOLS IN SOCIALIST HANDS (1992–1996)

1 Paul Marriage, 'Roadshow Points to New Era of Reform', *South China Morning Post*, 2 Feb. 1992.

2 Deng Xiaoping, 'Excerpts from Talks Given in Wuchang, Shenzhen, Zhuhai and Shanghai', 18 January to 21 February 1992, *Selected Works of Deng Xiaoping*, vol. 3, various editions.

3 Bruce Gilley, *Tiger on the Brink: Jiang Zemin and China's New Elite*, 1998, University of California Press, Berkeley, CA, 1998, pp. 185–6; 'China to Speed Economic Reform', *Chicago Tribune*, 6 Feb. 1992; Willy Lam, 'Beijing Breaks Taboo by Calling for Capitalism', *South China Morning Post*, 24 Feb. 1992.

4 Gilley, *Tiger on the Brink*, p. 186.

5 Willy Lam, 'Deng Takes Fight to Headquarters', *South China Morning Post*, 18 March 1992.

6 Shanghai, B109-6-288, Plans for Pudong, 30 June 1991, pp. 28–32; 'Pudong, Symbol of the Future', *South China Morning Post*, 29 April 1991; Geoffrey Crothall, 'Skeptical Greeting for Latest Shanghai Plan', *South China Morning Post*, 10 Aug. 1990; also MAE, 2883TOPO/3793, 'Pudong', April 1991.

7 John Kohut, 'Mayor Expects Shanghai Will Pass Shenzhen', *South China Morning Post*, 11 March 1992; Kenneth Ko, 'Foreign Investment Pours into Pudong', *South China Morning Post*, 3 April 1992.

8 Manoj Joshi, 'Shanghai, City of Contrasts', *Times of India*, 10 Sept. 1993; Martin Wollacott, 'Beware of China's Latest Harbinger', *Guardian*, 19 May 1993.

9 Martin Wollacott, 'Shanghai Aims to Reclaim Its Greatness', *Ottawa Citizen*, 9 Aug. 1993.

10 Geoffrey Crothall, 'Pudong Status Starts Internal Economic War', *South China Morning Post*, 28 May 1990.

11 Kent Chen, 'Development Zones "Wasteful"', *South China Morning Post*, 30 March 1993.

12 Kent Chen, 'Development Zones "Wasteful"', *South China Morning Post*, 30 March 1993.

13 Meg E. Rithmire, *Land Bargains and Chinese Capitalism: The Politics of Property Rights under Reform*, Cambridge University Press, Cambridge, 2015; see also Minxin Pei, *China's Crony Capitalism: The Dynamics of Regime Decay*, Harvard University Press, Cambridge, MA, 2016.

14 'Kumagai Granted Further Rights on Hainan Island', *South China Morning Post*, 18 May 1992; Carl E. Walter and Fraser J. T. Howie, *Red*

Capitalism: The Fragile Financial Foundation of China's Extraordinary Rise, John Wiley, New York, 2012, p. 38; Matthew Miller, 'Real Estate Sector Clean-Up in Hainan', *South China Morning Post*, 21 July 1999.

15   Gansu, 136-1-127, 13 Jan. 1995, pp. 112–30; 136-1-99, 8 Feb. 1993, pp. 111–20.

16   Gansu, 128-9-374, State Council Document on Real Estate, 26 May 1995, pp. 99–104.

17   'China: Will the Bubble Burst?', *South China Morning Post*, 25 May 1993; John Gittings, 'The Patient Has China Syndrome', *Guardian*, 10 July 1993; figures on foreign investment from Sheryl WuDunn, 'Booming China Is Dream Market for West', *New York Times*, 15 Feb. 1993.

18   Sheryl WuDunn, 'Booming China Is Dream Market for West', *New York Times*, 15 Feb. 1993; Hoover Institution, Milton Friedman Papers, Box 188, '1993 Hong Kong–China Trip', unpublished typescript transcribed from a tape, dictated October 1993.

19   MAE, 2883TOPO/3772, Charles Malo, 'Où va la Chine?', 29 Nov. 1989.

20   Wenzhou, J34-32-332, Urgent Telegram from the Ministry of Finance, 14 June 1990, pp. 32–3; also State Council, 13 Oct. 1990, pp. 64–5; the total amounts are calculated in Marc G. Quintyn and Bernard J. Laurens et al. (eds), *Monetary and Exchange System Reforms in China: An Experiment in Gradualism*, International Monetary Fund, Washington, 1996, pp. 24–36.

21   Walter and Howie, *Red Capitalism*, p. 100.

22   Walter and Howie, *Red Capitalism*, pp. 11–14.

23   Sheryl WuDunn, 'Booming China Is Dream Market for West', *New York Times*, 15 Feb. 1993.

24   Sheryl WuDunn, 'Booming China Is Dream Market for West', *New York Times*, 15 Feb. 1993.

25   'Building Boom Sends Cement Price Soaring', *South China Morning Post*, 26 Jan. 1993; Marissa Lague, 'China Aims to Control Cost of Construction', *South China Morning Post*, 10 March 1993.

26   John Gittings, 'The Patient Has China Syndrome', *Guardian*, 10 July 1993.

27   Richard Holman, 'China Lifts Coal Controls', *Wall Street Journal*, 4 Aug. 1992; Sheryl WuDunn, 'China Removes Some Price Controls on Food', *New York Times*, 29 Nov. 1992.

28   Lin and Schramm, 'China's Foreign Exchange Policies since 1979', pp. 257–8; Joon San Wong, 'Yuan's Rate Further Inflates the Bubble', *South China Morning Post*, 7 Jan. 1993.

29   'China: Will the Bubble Burst?', *South China Morning Post*, 25 May 1993.

30 'China Crisis Looms Over IOUs', *South China Morning Post*, 9 Dec. 1992.

31 PRO, FCO 21/4550, 'Teleletter on Record Harvest', 23 Nov. 1990; John Gittings, 'The Patient Has China Syndrome', *Guardian*, 10 July 1993.

32 Geoffrey Crothall, 'Yang Supports Liberal Calls for Faster Reform', *South China Morning Post*, 6 Feb. 1992.

33 Gilley, *Tiger on the Brink*, pp. 195–6; also Li Rui, Diary, 30 Jan., 27 Feb. and 18 April 1993.

34 Sheryl WuDunn, 'Chinese Party Congress Replaces Nearly Half of Central Committee', *New York Times*, 19 Oct. 1992; David Holley, 'China's New Leaders Get a Blessing From Deng', *Los Angeles Times*, 20 Oct. 1992.

35 Geoffrey Crothall and Willy Lam, 'Advisory Body to Be Disbanded', *South China Morning Post*, 12 Oct. 1992.

36 David Holley, 'China Completes Its Biggest Shake-Up of Military Chiefs', *Los Angeles Times*, 16 Dec. 1992; Gilley, *Tiger on the Brink*, pp. 196–9.

37 Gilley, *Tiger on the Brink*, pp. 203–4.

38 'China in Austerity Moves', *New York Times*, 5 July 1993; 'China Names Vice-Premier Bank Governor', *Daily News* (Halifax), 3 July 1993.

39 Patrick Tyler, 'China Austerity Drive is Hurting US Ventures', *New York Times*, 11 Nov. 1993; Willy Lam, 'Zhu Hits Some Bumps on China's Road to Recovery', *South China Morning Post*, 15 Sept. 1993.

40 Willy Lam, 'Zhu Hits Some Bumps on China's Road to Recovery', *South China Morning Post*, 15 Sept. 1993.

41 Steven Mufson, 'As China Booms, Fear of Chaos Fuels New Force', *Washington Post*, 11 Nov. 1995.

42 Wang Shaoguang, 'China's 1994 Fiscal Reform: An Initial Assessment', *Asian Survey*, 37, no. 9 (Sept. 1997), pp. 801–17; see also Pei, *Crony Capitalism*, pp. 53–6.

43 Lin and Schramm, 'China's Foreign Exchange Policies since 1979', p. 258.

44 'Clinton Advisor Says GATT Entry Is Highly Desirable', *South China Morning Post*, 2 June 1994; Sheila Tefft, 'GATT Chief Calls for Chinese Membership', *Christian Science Monitor*, 11 May 1994.

45 Lin and Schramm, 'China's Foreign Exchange Policies since 1979', pp. 258–9.

46 Rowena Tsang, 'Rumours Fail to Dislodge Forex Chief', *South China Morning Post*, 9 May 1995.

47 Willy Lam, 'Zhu Toils to Counter Inflation', *South China Morning Post*, 1 Dec. 1994; 'Inflation and Spiralling Wages Giving Zhu Sleepless

Nights', *South China Morning Post*, 9 May 1995; inflation figures in Li Rui, Diary, 26 Sept. 1994.

48 'Inflation and Spiralling Wages Giving Zhu Sleepless Nights', *South China Morning Post*, 9 May 1995.

49 'Inflation and Spiralling Wages Giving Zhu Sleepless Nights', *South China Morning Post*, 9 May 1995; 'Bank Head Urges Lower Inflation', *South China Morning Post*, 27 July 1995.

50 Wenzhou, J202-13-120, Wang Zhongshu in Telephone Conference on Losses in Industry, 10 March 1994, pp. 94–6.

51 Teresa Poole, *Independent*, 23 Dec. 1994.

52 Willy Lam, 'Unrest on the Cards', *South China Morning Post*, 6 Dec. 1995.

53 Patrick Tyler, 'China's First Family Comes Under Growing Scrutiny', *New York Times*, 2 June 1995; Seth Faison, 'Deng's Son Sidesteps Row', *South China Morning Post*, 19 Jan. 1989.

54 Peter Goodspeed, 'China's "Princelings"', *Toronto Star*, 12 June 1994; Li Rui, Diary, 12 Dec. 1993.

55 Patrick Tyler, '12 Intellectuals Petition China on Corruption', *New York Times*, 26 Feb. 1995.

56 Uli Schmetzer, 'Chinese Executives Find That Deng Connection Is No Longer Protection', *Chicago Tribune*, 23 March 1995.

57 Steven Mufson, 'China's Corruption "Virus"', *Washington Post*, 22 July 1995.

58 Harry Wu papers, Box 1, Central Committee's Report on Chen Xitong, 28 Sept. 1995.

59 Patrick Tyler, 'Jiang Leads Purge of Beijing Party', *Guardian*, 9 May 1995.

60 Jiang Zemin, 'Lingdao ganbu yiding yaojiang zhengzhi' (Leading cadres must emphasise politics), 27 Sept. 1995, *Jiang Zemin wenxuan* (Selected Works of Jiang Zemin), Renmin chubanshe, Beijing, 2006, vol. 1, pp. 455–9; Jiang Zemin, 'Zhengque chuli shehuizhuyi xiandaihua jianshe zhong de ruogan zhongda guanxi' (On the correct handling on a number of major relations in the modernisation of socialism), *Jiang Zemin wenxuan*, vol. 1, pp. 460–75; Willy Lam, 'Jiang's Act Runs into Problems', *South China Morning Post*, 11 Oct. 1995; Kathy Chen, 'China Applies the Brakes to Reforms', *Wall Street Journal*, 7 April 1995.

61 Li Rui, Diary, 3 Aug. 1995.

62 Li Rui, Diary, 28 Jan. 1996.

63 PRO, FCO 21/1371, W. G. Ehrman, 'Mr Teng Hsiao-P'ing on the Situation in China', 5 Feb 1975 and 'Teng Hsiao-P'ing Discusses Economy, Cultural Revolution, Taiwan', 10 Dec. 1974; Selig S. Harrison, 'Taiwan After Chiang Ching-Kuo', *Foreign Affairs*, 66, no. 4 (Spring

1988), pp. 790–808; also 'Hu: Force Last Resort Against Taiwan', *South China Morning Post*, 1 June 1985.

64 Nicholas Kristof, 'A Dictatorship That Grew Up', *New York Times*, 16 Feb. 1992.

65 Patrick Tyler, 'For Taiwan's Frontier Island, the War Is Over', *New York Times*, 4 Oct. 1995.

66 Nicholas Kristof, 'A Dictatorship That Grew Up', *New York Times*, 16 Feb. 1992.

67 Gilley, *Tiger on the Brink*, p. 248.

68 Rone Tempest, 'China Threatens U.S. Over Taiwan Leader's Visit', *Los Angeles Times*, 26 May 1995.

69 'Taiwan Leader to Leave U.S.', *Los Angeles Times*, 11 June 1995.

70 Simon Beck, 'Strengths Across the Strait', *South China Morning Post*, 4 Nov. 1995; Gilley, *Tiger on the Brink*, p. 254.

71 'Taiwan's Democratic Election', *New York Times*, 24 March 1996.

72 Document 219, 'Message from the Government of the United States to the Government of the People's Republic of China', undated, message delivered on the evening of 3 April 1972, 30 Jan. 1979, *Foreign Relations of the United States, 1969–1972*, vol. XVII, US Government Printing Office, Washington, 2006, pp. 873–4.

73 Nayan Chanda, *Brother Enemy: The War After the War*, Harcourt, San Diego, 1987, pp. 19–21.

74 Harvey Stockwin, 'Mischief Reef a Scene of Power Politics', *Times of India News Service*, 9 April 1995; Robert Manning, 'China's Syndrome: Ambiguity', *Washington Post*, 19 March 1995.

75 See, among other witness accounts, reports by Liz Sly, 'Something New in China', *Chicago Tribune*, 28 Oct. 1996; Jasper Becker, 'A Journey Through Jiang's Utopia', *South China Morning Post*, 28 Jan. 1996; Joseph Kahn, 'Envying Singapore, China's Leaders Turn One City Into a Model', *Wall Street Journal*, 19 Dec. 1995; the cameras are mentioned in Maggie Farley, 'The Polite Patriots of China', *Los Angeles Times*, 14 Sept. 1996.

76 Rone Tempest, 'Insults, Spitting, Pigeon Poaching Not Allowed', *Los Angeles Times*, 25 Jan. 1997.

77 'Jiang Calls for Return to Socialist Orthodoxy', *Korea Times*, 26 Jan. 1996; Willy Lam, 'The Party Returns to Mao's Heroes', *South China Morning Post*, 24 April 1996.

78 Willy Lam, 'Liberal Fears Over "Strike Hard" Policy', *South China Morning Post*, 18 July 1996.

79 'Mickey Mouse and Donald Duck Are on the Run in China', *Times of India*, 25 Oct. 1996; Steven Mufson, 'China's "Soccer Boy" Takes on

Foreign Evils', *Washington Post*, 9 Oct. 1996; Joseph Kahn, 'He's the Very Model of a Modem Plumber and a Hero in China', *Wall Street Journal*, 1 July 1996.

80 Wenzhou, J202-15-168, State Council Report on Foreign Brands, 10 Dec. 1995, pp. 1–6.

81 Josephine Ma, 'Beijing to Protect Domestic Brands', *South China Morning Post*, 8 Aug. 1996; Cheung Lai-Kuen, 'Foreign Limits to Go in Stages', *South China Sunday Morning Post*, 28 April 1996.

82 Seth Faison, 'Citing Security, China Will Curb Foreign Financial News Agencies', *New York Times*, 17 Jan. 1996; Sandra Sugawara, 'China Restricts Filmmakers', *Washington Post*, 29 June 1996; Teresa Poole, 'China's Hooligan Author', *South China Morning Post*, 21 Dec. 1996.

83 'Dissident Liu Xiaobo Released and Banished to Dalian', *South China Morning Post*, 20 Jan. 1996; Steven Mufson, 'China Detains Dissident During Party Meeting', *Washington Post*, 9 Oct. 1996.

84 Uli Schmetzer, 'New China Dream', *Chicago Tribune*, 19 June 1996.

85 Willy Lam, 'The Power Players of Beijing', *South China Morning Post*, 12 March 1997.

86 'TV Tribute to Deng's Role Sets the Tone for Next Congress', *South China Morning Post*, 2 Jan. 1997; 'Series on Patriarch Offers No New Glimpse', *South China Morning Post*, 13 Jan. 1997; Willy Lam, 'Shenzhen Plays Up Deng's Reform Views', *South China Morning Post*, 22 Jan. 1997.

87 Seth Faison, 'Beijing after Deng', *New York Times*, 21 Feb. 1997; Kathy Chen, 'After Deng's Death, It's Business as Usual', *Wall Street Journal*, 21 Feb. 1997.

8. BIG IS BEAUTIFUL (1997–2001)

1 Rod Mickleburgh, 'The Handover of Hong Kong', *Globe and Mail*, 1 July 1997.

2 PRO, CAB128/99/13, Meeting of the Cabinet, 11 April 1991; see also Loh, *Underground Front*, pp. 179–80.

3 PRO, PREM 19/3626, 6 March 1992.

4 Fan Cheuk-Wan, 'Hurd Responds to Li Peng Attack with Offer of Talks', *South China Morning Post*, 16 March 1993; Jonathan Mirsky, 'Buddha-Serpent Patten Feels His Colony Tremble', *South China Morning Post*, 28 March 1993.

5 David Holley, 'China's Agenda: Reforms and Dictatorship', *Los Angeles Times*, 6 March 1993.

6   John Kohut, 'One Step Forward, One Step Back', *South China Morning Post*, 13 March 1993; Willy Lam, 'Patriotism Has Now Become the Last Refuge of Li Peng', *South China Morning Post*, 24 March 1993.

7   Willy Lam, 'Activists Bid to Speed Up Democracy', *South China Morning Post*, 13 March 1993.

8   Li Rui, Notes on visit to Guangzhou, Diary, 19 Sept. 1994.

9   Jonathan Dimbleby, *The Last Governor*, Little, Brown, London, 1997, p. 310.

10 Steven Mufson, 'Hong Kong: The Return to China', *Washington Post*, 1 July 1997.

11 'Too Much at Stake to Accept Cheaper Yuan's Temptations', *South China Morning Post*, 2 Jan. 1998.

12 Liz Sly, 'Bloom Is Off China's Boom', *Chicago Tribune*, 4 Feb. 1997; 60 per cent of capacity quoted in Joseph Kahn, 'China's Overcapacity Crimps Neighbors: Glut Swamps Southeast Asia's Exports', *Wall Street Journal*, 14 July 1997; Li Rui, Diary, 9 Jan. 1998.

13 Joseph Kahn, 'China's Overcapacity Crimps Neighbors: Glut Swamps Southeast Asia's Exports', *Wall Street Journal*, 14 July 1997; Somchai Jitsuchon and Chalongphob Sussangkarn, 'Thailand's Growth Rebalancing', Tokyo: Asian Development Bank Institute, 2009.

14 Liz Sly, 'China's Growth May Slip Further', *Chicago Tribune*, 7 March 1998; Kathy Chen, 'China's Retailers Multiply in Spite of Weak Sales', *Wall Street Journal*, 7 Jan. 1998.

15 Wenzhou, J34-33-480, Report by Dai Xianglong, 26 Sept. 1998, pp. 19–31.

16 Wang Xiangwei, 'Fears Grow as China Slides Into Deflation', *South China Morning Post*, 12 Nov. 1997; 'Deflation Worsens as Prices Dip 3.3PC', *South China Morning Post*, 14 Sept. 1998; Karby Leggett, 'The Outlook', *Wall Street Journal*, 13 March 2000.

17 Henny Sender, 'China Faces Flood of Cheap East Asian Imports', *Wall Street Journal*, 24 July 1998; Peter Seidlitz and David Murphy, 'Asian Flu Reaches Mainland', *South China Morning Post*, 19 July 1998.

18 Wenzhou, J34-33-480, Report by Dai Xianglong, 26 Sept. 1998, pp. 19–31.

19 Peter Seidlitz and David Murphy, 'Frustration Rises Over Flood of Forex Edicts', *South China Sunday Morning Post*, 6 Dec. 1998.

20 Mark O'Neill, 'Flat Forex Growth Blamed on Smuggling, Reporting Errors', *South China Morning Post*, 7 Oct. 1998; Seth Faison, 'China Attacks "Hidden" Crime: Smuggling', *New York Times*, 17 July 1998.

21 Howard Balloch, *Semi-Nomadic Anecdotes*, Lulu Publishing Services, Morrisville, NC, 2013, pp. 548–9.

22   Balloch, *Semi-Nomadic Anecdotes*, pp. 547–8.

23   Wang Jikuan quoted in Li Rui, Diary, 4 March 1996; Gansu, 145-12-303, Talk by Zhu Rongji at Conference on Reforming State Owned Enterprises, 16 May 1998, pp. 38–59.

24   John Bartel and Huang Yiping, 'Dealing with the Bad Loans of the Chinese Banks', Columbia University, APEC Study Center: Discussion Paper Series, July 2000; Walter and Howie, *Red Capitalism*, p. vxii; on bad loans see also Carsten A. Holz, 'China's Bad Loan Problem', manuscript, Hong Kong University of Science and Technology, April 1999.

25   Wenzhou, J34-33-480, Report on Banks, 27 Oct. 1998, pp. 225–44; Talk by Dai Xianglong, 26 Sept. 1998, pp. 19–31; on the investigation of Wenzhou, see Wenzhou, J34-33-456, 12 Oct. 1998, pp. 13–23.

26   Wenzhou, J202-16-163, State Council Statement on Outstanding Foreign Loans, 6 Nov. 1997, pp. 1–6; Zhejiang Province Statement on Outstanding Foreign Loans, 4 Sept. 1997, pp. 35–7.

27   Hong Zhaohui and Ellen Y. Yan, 'Trust and Investment Corporations in China', in Chen Beizhu, J. Kimball Dietrich and Yi Fang (eds), *Financial Market Reform in China: Progress, Problems and Prospects*, Westview Press, Boulder, CO, 2000, p. 290, as well as Zhu Jun, 'Closure of Financial Institutions in China', in Bank for International Settlements (eds), *Strengthening the Banking System in China: Issues and Experience*, Bank for International Settlements, Basel, 1999, pp. 311–13.

28   'BoC Digs Deep for CADTIC Debts', *South China Morning Post*, 10 Jan. 1997; Tony Walker, 'China Shuts Debt-Ridden Investment Group', *Financial Times*, 15 Jan. 1997.

29   Wenzhou, J202-17-139, People's Bank of China Report on Investment Trust Companies, 26 Aug. 1998, pp. 76–8.

30   Walter and Howie, *Red Capitalism*, pp. 57–8.

31   MAE, 2883TOPO/3772, 'Réflections de M. Guy Sorman sur la situation en Chine', 28 Nov. 1989.

32   Gansu, 136-1-114, Report by State Commission for Restructuring the Economy, 1 Dec. 1993, pp. 122–38.

33   Foo Ghoy Peng, 'Ambitious Economic Reformists Decree "Big is Beautiful"', *South China Morning Post*, 19 Sept. 1997.

34   Leslie Chang, 'Big Is Beautiful', *Wall Street Journal*, 30 April 1998.

35   Steven Mufson, 'China to Cut Number of State Firms', *Washington Post*, 15 Sept. 1997; 'China: Merger, Acquisition Timely', *China Daily*, 13 Jan. 1998; 'China: Administrative Reform', *Oxford Analytica Daily Brief Service*, 8 May 1998; Russell Smyth, 'Should China Be Promoting Large-Scale Enterprises and Enterprise Groups?', Department of Economics, Monash University, Jan. 1991, p. 24.

36 Daniel Kwan, 'Jiang Backs Shareholding System', *South China Morning Post*, 1 April 1997.

37 Walter and Howie, *Red Capitalism*, pp. 178–9.

38 Erik Guyot and Shanthi Kalanthil, 'China Telecom's IPO Lures Investors', *Wall Street Journal*, 6 Oct. 1997.

39 Walter and Howie, *Red Capitalism*, pp. 182–4.

40 Karby Leggett, 'The Outlook', *Wall Street Journal*, 13 March 2000; Peter Wonacott, 'China's Privatization Efforts Breed New Set of Problems', *Wall Street Journal*, 1 Nov. 2001.

41 'Rust-Belt Unemployment Hits 10pc', *South China Morning Post*, 18 Nov. 1997; Jasper Becker, 'Old Industry Dies Hard', *South China Morning Post*, 9 Aug. 1997.

42 Gansu, 145-12-303, Report by Wu Bangguo on Reform of State Enterprises, 14 May 1998, pp. 60–87.

43 Gansu, 145-12-303, Report by Wu Bangguo on Reform of State Enterprises, 14 May 1998, pp. 60–87.

44 Mark O'Neill, 'No Work, No Future', *South China Morning Post*, 20 June 2000; Mark O'Neill, 'The Growing Pains of Change', *South China Morning Post*, 13 Aug. 1998; Jasper Becker, 'The Dark Side of the Dream', *South China Morning Post*, 12 Oct. 1997.

45 Gansu, 136-1-189, Report by Yao Yugen, Head of Provincial Economic Committee, 25 July 1998, pp. 74–81.

46 Craig Smith, 'Municipal-Run Firms Helped Build China', *Wall Street Journal*, 8 Oct. 1997.

47 Gansu, 128-9-235, Report by Ministry of Labour, 29 Dec. 1992, pp. 1–9.

48 Figures in Gansu, 128-10-175, 5 Dec. 1998, pp. 17–21; see also 'Coal Mines to Face Safety Measures Blitz', *South China Morning Post*, 12 Feb. 1997; mergers of state mines in Mark O'Neill, 'Coal Mines Dosed as Beijing Cleans Up Inefficient Sector', *South China Morning Post*, 14 Sept. 2000.

49 Jasper Becker, 'A Collapse of the Working Class', *South China Morning Post*, 8 Aug. 1998; see also Qin Hui, 'Looking at China from South Africa', on www.readingthechinadream.com, retrieved on 28 Sept. 2019.

50 Gansu, 128-10-289, State Council Document on Debt in the Countryside, 6 May 1999, pp. 70–77.

51 Jasper Becker, 'Slump in Countryside Deepens as Bubble Bursts for Rural Enterprises', *South China Morning Post*, 27 Aug. 1999; Gansu, 128-10-232, Report by Provincial Deputy Governor Wu Bilian, 9 May 1998, pp. 10–32.

52 Gansu, 128-10-551, Talk by Zhu Rongji at the People's Consultative Conference's Economic Committee, 28 Aug. 2001, pp. 120–28; see also

Gerard Greenfield and Tim Pringle, 'The Challenge of Wage Arrears in China', in Manuel Simón Velasco (ed.) *Paying Attention to Wages*, International Labour Organisation, Geneva, 2002, pp. 30–38.

53 Wenzhou, J34-33-318, Document on Rural Cooperative Funds, 10 March 1997, pp. 40–59; Wenzhou, J34-33-417, Feb. 1997, pp. 156–75; on the closure of the funds, see Carsten A. Holz, 'China's Monetary Reform: The Counterrevolution from the Countryside', *Journal of Contemporary China*, 10, no. 27 (2001), pp. 189–217; see also Wen Tiejun, 'Nongcun hezuo jijinhui de xingshuai, 1984–1999' (The rise and fall of rural cooperative funds, 1984–1999), University Services Centre, Chinese University of Hong Kong, Dec. 2000.

54 Zuo Xuejin, 'The Development of Credit Unions in China: Past Experiences and Lessons for the Future', Conference on Financial Sector Reform in China, Harvard University, Cambridge, MA, 11–13 Sept. 2001; Lynette H. Ong, *Prosper or Perish: Credit and Fiscal Systems in Rural China*, Cornell University Press, Ithaca, NY, 2012, p. 156.

55 Ong, *Prosper or Perish*, p. 159.

56 Gansu, 128-10-475, Document on Government Debt and Convertible Loans, 14 May 2001, pp. 90–98; see also Feng Xingyuan, 'Local Government Debt and Municipal Bonds in China: Problems and a Framework of Rules', *Copenhagen Journal of Asian Studies*, 31, no. 2 (2013), pp. 23–53.

57 Gansu, 136-1-189, Report by Zhong Zhaolong, Chairman of the Gansu People's Consultative Conference, 25 July 1998, p. 41.

58 Gansu, 128-10-464, State Council, document 62, 28 Aug. 2001, pp. 72–3, followed by Report by Disciplinary Committee, 27 July 2001, pp. 74–87.

59 Ong, *Prosper or Perish*, p. 138; on deprivation in the countryside, the following two primary sources are essential: Cao Jinqing, *China along the Yellow River: Reflections on Rural Society*, RoutledgeCurzon, London, 2005, p. 4; Chen Guidi and Wu Chuntao, *Will the Boat Sink the Water?: The Life of China's Peasants*, PublicAffairs, New York, 2006.

60 Steven Mufson, 'China's Beefed-Up Private Sector', *Washington Post*, 12 April 1998; Liz Sly, 'China Granting "Important" Private Sector Room to Grow', *Chicago Tribune*, 10 March 1999.

61 Liz Sly, 'China Granting "Important" Private Sector Room to Grow', *Chicago Tribune*, 10 March 1999.

62 Liz Sly, 'China Granting "Important" Private Sector Room to Grow', *Chicago Tribune*, 10 March 1999.

63 Jasper Becker, *The Chinese*, The Free Press, New York, 2000, pp. 148–60;
    Richard McGregor, *The Party: The Secret World of China's Communist
    Rulers*, HarperCollins, New York, 2010, p. 43.

64 The terms were *suoyouzhi gaozao*, or simply *zhuanzhi*, or *gufenhua*.

65 Carsten Holz and Tian Zhu, 'Reforms Simply Shifting Burden', *South
    China Morning Post*, 1 Oct. 1999.

66 Erik Eckholm, 'Unrest Grows at China's Old State Plants', *New York
    Times*, 17 May 2000; John Pomfret, 'Chinese Workers Are Showing
    Disenchantment', *Washington Post*, 23 April 2000.

67 Ted Plafker, 'Incidence of Unrest Rising in China', *Washington Post*, 18
    July 2000.

68 Willy Lam, 'Nip Protest in the Bud, Jiang Tells Top Cadres', *South
    China Morning Post*, 17 Nov. 1998; Jasper Becker, 'Jiang Rejects Political
    Reform', *South China Morning Post*, 19 Dec. 1998.

69 John Harris, 'Jiang Earns Clinton's High Praise', *Washington Post*, 4
    July 1998.

70 Liz Sly, 'On Human Rights, China Takes a 2-Tack Strategy', *Chicago
    Tribune*, 6 Oct. 1998; John Pomfret, 'Politics Stirs Crackdown in China',
    Washington Post, 3 Jan. 1999; one should read the moving story of one of
    the founders of the China Democracy Party in Zha Jianying, 'Enemy of
    the State', *Tide Players: The Movers and Shakers of a Rising China*, The
    Free Press, New York, 2011.

71 Liz Sly, 'On Human Rights, China Takes a 2-Tack Strategy', *Chicago
    Tribune*, 6 Oct. 1998; Henry Chu, 'Chinese Rulers Fear Angry Workers
    May Finally Unite', *Los Angeles Times*, 4 June 1999.

72 John Gittings, 'Cult Descends on Heart of Beijing', *Guardian*, 26
    April 1999.

73 Craig Smith, 'Influential Devotees at Core of Chinese Movement', *Wall
    Street Journal*, 30 April 1999.

74 Charles Hutzler, 'Beijing Seeks to Rein in Falun Gong', *South China
    Morning Post*, 9 May 1999; see also, more generally, James Tong,
    'Anatomy of Regime Repression in China: Timing, Enforcement
    Institutions, and Target Selection in Banning the Falungong, July 1999',
    Asian Survey, 42, no. 6 (Dec. 2002), pp. 795–820.

75 Kevin Platt, 'Another Tiananmen Ahead', *Christian Science Monitor*, 23
    July 1999.

76 John Pomfret, 'Cracks in China's Crackdown', *Washington Post*, 12 Nov.
    1999; Cindy Sui, 'Falun Gong Holds Jail Hunger Strike', *Washington
    Post*, 15 Feb. 2000.

77 Ted Plafker, 'Falun Gong Stays Locked in Struggle with Beijing', *Washington Post*, 26 April 2000; 'Cult Protests Upstage Festivities', *South China Morning Post*, 2 Oct. 2000.

78 Philip Pan, 'Five People Set Themselves Afire in China', *Washington Post*, 24 Jan. 2001.

79 John Pomfret and Philip Pan, 'Torture Is Tearing at Falun Gong', *Washington Post*, 5 Aug. 2001.

80 Mark O'Neill, 'Thousands of Unemployed Recruited to Round Up Falun Gong', *South China Morning Post*, 31 Jan. 2001; Robert Marquand, 'In Two Years, Falun Gong Nearly Gone', *Christian Science Monitor*, 6 Aug. 2001.

81 Michael Sheridan, 'China Crushes the Church', *Sunday Times*, 1 July 1999; Kevin Platt, 'The Wrong Churches in China', *Christian Science Monitor*, 21 Dec. 1999.

82 Vivien Pik-Kwan Chan, 'Officials "Mask Extent of Church Closures"', *South China Morning Post*, 14 Dec. 2000; Wenzhou, J202-20-126, 4 Jan. 2001, pp. 16–17.

83 Daniel Kwan, 'Nation Doomed if Cadres Lose Faith in Communism', *South China Morning Post*, 1 July 1999; Wenzhou, J34-34-93, Urgent Telegram Transmitting Orders on the Study of Important Documents, 15 July 1999, pp. 60–62.

84 Li Rui, Diary, 27 April 2000.

85 'Party Chief Makes "Important Speech" on Party Building in Shanghai', *BBC Monitoring Asia Pacific*, 5 May 2000.

86 Wenzhou, J201-25-9, Document on Party Building, 5 July 2000, pp. 124–63.

87 Clara Li, 'City's Rich Line Up to Be "Red Capitalists"', *South China Morning Post*, 13 Aug. 2001.

88 Wenzhou, J34-34-84, Talk by Wen Jiabao on Party Building Inside the Financial System, 5 April 1999, pp. 5–15, also in the same file his talk dated 14 Sept. 1999, pp. 67–82.

89 Li Rui, Diary, 2 Aug. and 11 Sept. 2001; Mark O'Neill, 'Party Closes Leftist Journal That Opposed Jiang', *South China Morning Post*, 14 Aug. 2001.

90 Steven Lee Myers, 'Deaths Reported', *New York Times*, 8 May 1999.

91 Mark O'Neill, 'Politics, Patriotism and Laying the Blame', *South China Morning Post*, 11 May 1999.

92 Elisabeth Rosenthal, 'China Protesters Rage at America', *New York Times*, 9 May 1999; Erik Eckholm, 'Tightrope for China', *New York Times*, 10 May 1999.

93 John Pomfret and Michael Laris, 'China Suspends Some U.S. Ties', *Washington Post*, 10 May 1999.

94 Wenzhou, J201-24-74, Jiang Zemin, Talk at the Politburo's Standing Committee, 8 May 1999, pp. 33–9.

95 Wenzhou, J201-24-74, Jiang Zemin, Talk at the Politburo's Standing Committee, 9 May 1999, pp. 39–47; Wenzhou, J201-24-74, Series of Telegrams by the Bureau of the Central Commitee, 17 June 1999, pp. 25–8.

96 Wenzhou, J201-26-51, National Conference on Public Security, 5 April 2001, pp. 89–116.

97 Wenzhou, J232-18-17, Talk by Party Secretary Jiang Jufeng, 29 June 2001, pp. 181–97.

98 Wenzhou, J201-24-74, Series of Telegrams by the Bureau of the Central Committee, 17 June 1999, pp. 25–8.

99 Karoline Kan, *Under Red Skies: Three Generations of Life, Loss, and Hope in China*, Hachette Books, New York, 2019, pp. 83–7.

100 John Pomfret, 'Ashes Returned to China', *Washington Post*, 12 May 1999.

9. GOING GLOBAL (2001–2008)

1 Jasper Becker, 'First Money, Then Enlightenment', *South China Morning Post*, 8 Nov. 2001.

2 Clay Chandler, 'Trying to Make Good on Bad-Debt Reform', *Washington Post*, 15 Jan. 2002.

3 Gene Epstein, 'The Tariff Trap', *Barron's*, 82, no. 28 (15 July 2002), pp. 21–2.

4 Alexander Delroy, 'Industries Foresee World Trade Welcome for China', *Chicago Tribune*, 11 Oct. 2001; Peter Humphrey, 'Honey Pot Full of Sticky Promise', *South China Morning Post*, 17 July 2000; Jerome Cohen, 'China's Troubled Path to WTO', *International Financial Law Review*, 20, no. 9 (Sept. 2001), pp. 71–4.

5 Paul Blustein, 'China's Trade Moves Encourage U.S. Firms', *Washington Post*, 6 April 1999; Ian Perkin, 'A New Long March in the Offing', *Hong Kong Business*, Dec. 1999; Steve Chapman, 'The Empty Case Against the China Trade Deal', *Chicago Tribune*, 18 May 2000.

6 Some of these views are summarised in Chalmers Johnson, 'Breaching the Great Wall', *American Prospect*, no. 30 (Feb. 1997), pp. 24–9.

Paul Blustein, 'China's Trade Moves Encourage U.S. Firms', *Washington Post*, 6 April 1999; Ian Perkin, 'A New Long March in the

Offing', *Hong Kong Business*, Dec. 1999; Steve Chapman, 'The Empty Case Against the China Trade Deal', *Chicago Tribune*, 18 May 2000.

7 Kevin Platt, 'A Deal That May Transform China', *Christian Science Monitor*, 16 Nov. 1999; Will Hutton, 'At Last, the Fall of the Great Wall of China', *Observer*, 21 Nov. 1999.

8 United States Census Bureau, Foreign Trade: Trade in Goods with China, at www.census.gov; Marla Dickerson, 'Mexico Files Trade Grievance', *Los Angeles Times*, 27 Feb. 2007.

9 Karby Leggett, 'Economy Stirs as China Gears for WTO', *Wall Street Journal*, 12 April 2000; Karby Leggett, 'Foreign Investment Not a Panacea in China', *Wall Street Journal*, 14 Jan. 2002.

10 Jasper Becker, 'Best-Laid Plans Go Astray', *South China Morning Post*, 16 March 2001; James Kynge, *China Shakes the World: The Rise of a Hungry Nation*, Weidenfeld & Nicolson, London, 2006, p. 61.

11 Jason Booth and Matt Pottinger, 'China's Deflation Puts Pressure on WTO Nations', *Wall Street Journal*, 23 Nov. 2001.

12 Jon Hilsenrath and Lucinda Harper, 'Deflation Fears Make a Comeback', *Wall Street Journal*, 13 Aug. 2002.

13 Mary Jordan, 'Mexican Workers Pay for Success', *Washington Post*, 20 June 2002; Ken Belson, 'Japanese Capital and Jobs Flowing to China', *New York Times*, 17 Feb. 2004.

14 Peter Wonacott and Leslie Chang, 'As Fight Heats Up Over China Trade, Business Is Split', *Wall Street Journal*, 4 Sept. 2003.

15 An excellent account appears in Kynge, *China Shakes the World*.

16 'U.S. Businesses Urge Trade Sanctions to Stop Piracy of Software in China', *Washington Post*, 11 April 1989; Daniel Southerland, 'Piracy of U.S. Software in China Is Big Problem, Commerce Officials Warn', *Washington Post*, 14 Jan. 1989.

17 'U.S. Sidesteps Piracy Trade Issue with China Until After Rights Deadline', *Washington Post*, 1 May 1994; Teresa Poole, 'Peking Backs off US Trade War', *Independent*, 27 Feb. 1995; Miriam Donohoe, 'China Faces Up to Its Counterfeiters', *Irish Times*, 29 June 2001.

18 John Pomfret, 'Chinese Pirates Rob "Harry" of Magic, and Fees', *Washington Post*, 1 Nov. 2002; see also, more generally, William C. Hannas, James Mulvenon and Anna B. Puglisi, *Chinese Industrial Espionage: Technology Acquisition and Military Modernization*, Routledge, London, 2013, and William C. Hannas and Didi Kirsten Tatlow (eds), *China's Quest for Foreign Technology: Beyond Espionage*, Routledge, London, 2021.

19 Li Yahong, 'The Wolf Has Come: Are China's Intellectual Property Industries Prepared for the WTO?', *Pacific Basin Law Journal*, 20, no. 1,

2002, p. 93; John Pomfret, 'Chinese Pirates Rob "Harry" of Magic, and Fees', *Washington Post*, 1 Nov. 2002; Kynge, *China Shakes the World*, p. 57.

20 Karby Leggett, 'U.S. Auto Makers Find Promise and Peril in China', *Wall Street Journal*, 19 June 2003.

21 Janet Moore, 'Intellectual Property', *Star Tribune*, 28 Nov. 2005; Andrew England, 'Counterfeit Goods Flooding Poorer Countries', *Washington Post*, 30 Dec. 2001.

22 Mike Hughlett, 'Counterfeits Pose Real Risks', *Chicago Tribune*, 29 Sept. 2006; Joseph Kahn, 'Can China Reform Itself?', *New York Times*, 8 July 2007; Tania Branigan, 'Chinese Figures Show Fivefold Rise in Babies Sick from Contaminated Milk', *Guardian*, 2 Dec. 2008; David Barboza, 'China Finds Poor Quality in Its Stores', *New York Times*, 5 July 2007.

23 Joseph Kahn, 'China's Workers Risk Limbs in Export Drive', *New York Times*, 7 April 2003.

24 Wenzhou, J202-20-59, Report on Child Labour in Zhejiang Province, 24 Jan. 2003, pp. 7–12.

25 David Barboza, 'China Says Abusive Child Labor Ring Is Exposed', *New York Times*, 1 May 2008.

26 Ching-Ching Ni, 'China's Use of Child Labor Emerges from the Shadows', *Los Angeles Times*, 13 May 2005.

27 Keith Bradsher, 'Fuel Shortages Put Pressure on Price Controls in China', *New York Times*, 18 Aug. 2005; Don Lee, 'China Braces for Leap in Gas Prices', *Los Angeles Times*, 9 June 2008.

28 Cui Zhiyuan, 'China's Export Tax Rebate Policy', *China: An International Journal*, 1, no. 2 (Sept. 2003), pp. 339–49; see also Usha C. V. Haley and George T. Haley, *Subsidies to Chinese Industry: State Capitalism, Business Strategy, and Trade Policy*, Oxford University Press, New York, 2013.

29 Peter Wonacott and Phelim Kyne, 'Shifty, U.S. Investors Intensify Criticism of China Trade Policies', *Wall Street Journal*, 6 Oct. 2003.

30 'China's Money Supply Soars', *Asian Wall Street Journal*, 12 Sept. 2003; David Francis, 'Will China Clothe the World?', *Christian Science Monitor*, 5 Aug. 2004.

31 Keith Bradsher, 'China Finds a Fit with Car Parts', *New York Times*, 7 June 2007.

32 Ching-Ching Ni, 'Citibank Enters China's Consumer Banking Market', *Los Angeles Times*, 22 March 2002.

33 Walter and Howie, *Red Capitalism*, p. 27.

34 Kathy Chen, 'China Sets Own Wireless Encryption Standard', *Wall Street Journal*, 3 Dec. 2003; Evelyn Iritani, 'U.S. Accuses China of Hampering Trade', *Los Angeles Times*, 19 March 2004.

35 World Trade Organization, *International Trade Statistics 2009*, Geneva: WTO, 2009, table II.50, p. 88.

36 Peter Wonacott, 'China Saps Commodity Supplies', *Wall Street Journal*, 24 Oct. 2003.

37 Mark Magnier, 'China Courts the World to Slake a Thirst', *Los Angeles Times*, 17 July 2005.

38 Wenzhou, J156-19-11, Report by the Office for Overseas Affairs, 20 July 2002; see also Li Zhongjie, *Gaige kaifang guanjian ci* (Key words of Reform and Opening Up), Renmin chubanshe, Beijing, 2018, pp. 350–51.

39 Joseph Kahn, 'Behind China's Bid for Unocal: A Costly Quest for Energy Control', *New York Times*, 27 June 2005.

40 Zhongguo guoji maoyi cujin weiyuanhui jingji xinxibu (ed.), 'Woguo "zou chuqu" zhanlüe de xingcheng ji tuidong zhengce tixi fenxi' (An analysis of our country's strategy of 'Going Global'), Jan. 2007, pp. 1–3.

41 Mark Magnier, 'China Courts the World to Slake a Thirst', *Los Angeles Times*, 17 July 2005; James Traub, 'China's African Adventure', *New York Times*, 19 Nov. 2006.

42 'China's Global Reach', *Christian Science Monitor*, 30 Jan. 2007; Alexei Barrionuevo, 'China's Appetites Lead to Changes in Its Trade Diet', *New York Times*, 6 April 2007.

43 Christian Tyler, *Wild West China: The Taming of Xinjiang*, John Murray, London, 2003.

44 Gansu, 128-6-320, Zhao Ziyang's Meeting with Feng Jixin, Head of Gansu Province, 28 July 1982, pp. 113–20.

45 Derek Edward Peterson, 'When a Pound Weighed a Ton: The Cotton Scandal and Uzbek National Consciousness', doctoral dissertation, Ohio State University, 2013; also Riccardo Mario Cucciolla, 'The Crisis of Soviet Power in Central Asia: The "Uzbek Cotton Affair" (1975–1991)', doctoral dissertation, IMT School for Advanced Studies, Lucca, Italy, 2017.

46 MAE, 2882TOPO/2936, 'Controverse sur l'exploitation du Nord-Ouest chinois', 30 Sept. 1983.

47 Willy Lam, 'Jiang Woos Uighurs With Aid Promise', *South China Morning Post*, 4 Sept. 1990; Ivan Tang, 'Boom in Cotton Sows Seeds of Discontent', *South China Morning Post*, 10 June 1997.

48 Liz Sly, 'Ethnic Crisis Brews in China', *Chicago Tribune*, 19 Oct. 1999.

49 Liz Sly, 'Ethnic Crisis Brews in China', *Chicago Tribune*, 19 Oct. 1999; Josephine Ma, 'Go West', *South China Morning Post*, 18 May 2001.

50 Elizabeth Van Wie Davis, 'Uyghur Muslim Ethnic Separatism in Xinjiang', *Asian Affairs*, 35, no. 1 (spring 2008), pp. 15–29.

51 'Half Harvest Remains Unsold in China Major Cotton Producing Region', *Xinhua News Agency*, 6 Nov. 2008; Cotton Economics Research Institute Policy Modeling Group, *Global Cotton Baseline*, Cotton Economics Research Institute, Lubbock, TX, 2009, p. 11.

52 William Kazer, 'Ambitious Building Boom Fuels Growth', *South China Morning Post*, 28 Dec. 2001.

53 Joseph Kahn, 'China Gambles on Big Projects for Its Stability', *New York Times*, 13 Jan. 2003.

54 Ron Glucksman, 'Business: The Chinese Chicago', *Newsweek*, 24 May 2004; Joseph Kahn, 'China Gambles on Big Projects for Its Stability', *New York Times*, 13 Jan. 2003.

55 Phelim Kyne and Peter Wonacott, 'As Investment in China Booms, Some Fear a Real-Estate Bust', *Wall Street Journal*, 10 Oct. 2002; Kathy Chen and Karby Leggett, 'Surge in Lending in China Stokes Economic Worries', *Wall Street Journal*, 3 Oct. 2003.

56 Peter Goodman, 'Booming China Devouring Raw Materials', *Washington Post*, 21 May 2004.

57 Kathy Chen and Karby Leggett, 'Surge in Lending in China Stokes Economic Worries', *Wall Street Journal*, 3 Oct. 2003.

58 Joseph Kahn, 'China Gambles on Big Projects for Its Stability', *New York Times*, 13 Jan. 2003.

59 Kathy Chen and Karby Leggett, 'Surge in Lending in China Stokes Economic Worries', *Wall Street Journal*, 3 Oct. 2003; Joseph Kahn, 'China Gambles on Big Projects for Its Stability', *New York Times*, 13 Jan. 2003.

60 Walter and Howie, *Red Capitalism*, pp. 17–19.

61 Walter and Howie, *Red Capitalism*, pp. 19–20.

62 Peter Goodman, 'Manufacturing Competition', *Washington Post*, 11 Aug. 2004.

63 Jian Dong, 'Foreign Capital M&A to Be Further Regulated', *Jingji daobao*, 2 April 2007; see also Mure Dickie, 'China Moves to Combat Threat of Foreign-Owned Monopolies', *Financial Times*, 11 Nov. 2006; 'China Regulations: Problems with China's New M&A Law', *EIU ViewsWire*, 6 Nov. 2006.

64 Hu Jintao, 'Jianchi fayang jianku fendou de youliang zuofeng' (Persevere and develop the first-rate style of work of arduous struggle), *Renmin ribao*, 3 Jan. 2003.

65 John Gittings, 'China Launches Drive Against Party Corruption',
   Guardian, 21 Feb. 2003; Jia Hepeng, 'The Three Represents
   Campaign: Reform the Party or Indoctrinate the Capitalists?', *Cato
   Journal*, 24, no. 3 (Fall 2004), p. 270; Peter Goodman, 'Manufacturing
   Competition', *Washington Post*, 11 Aug. 2004; Derek Scissors, 'Deng
   Undone', *Foreign Affairs*, 88, no. 3 (June 2009), pp. 24–39.

66 On pollution and the assault on nature during the Great Leap Forward
   see Dikötter, *Mao's Great Famine*; chapter 21; see also Judith Shapiro,
   *Mao's War against Nature: Politics and the Environment in Revolutionary
   China*, Cambridge University Press, New York, 2001.

67 Wenzhou, J1-27-61, Report on Pollution in Zhejiang Province, 2 Feb.
   1980, pp. 167–70.

68 Shanghai, B184-2-732, National Conference on Industrial Pollution, 21
   Jan. 1983, pp. 211–20; Gansu, 238-1-117, Report on Pollution, March
   1985, p. 101.

69 Gansu, 238-1-268, Qu Geping, Report on Pollution, 19 April 1992,
   pp. 87–101; Song Jian, Report on Pollution, 19 April 1992, pp. 72–87.

70 Wenzhou, J173-5-109, 15 Dec. 1998, pp. 140–49; Gansu, 128-10-177,
   Report by State Council, 7 Nov. 1998, pp. 4–28.

71 Jim Yardley, 'Pollution Darkens China's Prospects', *International Herald
   Tribune*, 31 Oct. 2005; 'Millions in China Drink Foul Water, Beijing
   Discloses', *Wall Street Journal*, 30 Dec. 2005; see also Elizabeth Economy,
   The River Runs Black: The Environmental Challenge to China's Future,
   Cornell University Press, Ithaca, NY, 2004; on the more recent years, see
   Huang Yanzhong, *Toxic Politics: China's Environmental Health Crisis
   and Its Challenge to the Chinese State*, Cambridge University Press,
   Cambridge, 2020.

72 Joseph Kahn and Mark Landler, 'China Grabs West's Smoke-Spewing
   Factories', *New York Times*, 21 Dec. 2007.

73 Joshua Kurlantzick, 'China's Blurred Horizon', *Washington Post*, 19
   Sept. 2004.

74 Howard French, 'Riots in a Village in China as Pollution Protest Heats
   Up', *New York Times*, 19 July 2005; Howard French, 'Land of 74,000
   Protests', *New York Times*, 24 Aug. 2005; Ching-Ching Ni, 'China
   Finds Chemical Plants Pose Widespread Risk to Rivers', *Los Angeles
   Times*, 25 Jan. 2006.

75 Zhao Xu, Liu Junguo, Hong Yang, Rosa Duarte, Martin Tillotson and
   Klaus Hubacek, 'Burden Shifting of Water Quantity and Quality Stress
   from Megacity Shanghai', *Water Resources Research*, 52, no. 9 (Sept.
   2016), pp. 6916–27.

76 Simon Montlake, 'China's Pearl River Smells, but Mayor Vows to Swim', *Christian Science Monitor*, 5 May 2006.

77 Mark O'Neill, 'Beijing Wins Olympics in Moscow', *South China Morning Post*, 14 July 2001.

78 Alan Abrahamson, 'Bidding Its Time', *Los Angeles Times*, 1 July 2001.

79 John Gittings, 'Mystery Bug Causes Panic Across China', *Observer*, 16 Feb. 2003.

80 John Pomfret and Peter Goodman, 'Outbreak Originated in China', *Washington Post*, 17 March 2003; Matt Pottinger, 'Hong Kong Hotel Was a Virus Hub', *Wall Street Journal*, 21 March 2003; Michael Lev, 'China Not Sharing Data on Outbreaks, Health Group Says', *Chicago Tribune*, 22 March 2003; Lawrence Altman and Keith Bradsher, 'China Bars W.H.O. Experts from Origin Site of Illness', *New York Times*, 26 March 2003.

81 Matt Pottinger, 'Outraged Surgeon Forces China to Take a Dose of the Truth', *Wall Street Journal*, 22 April 2003; 'China's Other Disease', *Wall Street Journal*, 22 April 2003; 'Eyi chaozuo, yushi wubu' (Malicious interference is unhelpful), *Renmin ribao*, 17 April 2003.

82 'A Shot of Transparency', *The Economist*, 12 Aug. 2006.

83 Cheryl Miller, 'The Red Plague', *New Atlantis* (Winter 2007); Verna Yu, 'Doctor Who Exposed Sars Cover-Up Is Under House Arrest in China, Family Confirm', *South China Morning Post*, 9 February 2020.

84 Peter Wonacott, 'Beijing Postpones Marketing Launch for '08 Olympics', *Wall Street Journal*, 15 May 2003.

85 Jim Yardley, 'Beijing's Olympic Quest', *New York Times*, 29 Dec. 2007; John Boudreau, 'A Marathon of Building for Beijing Olympics', *McClatchy-Tribune News*, 16 Aug. 2007; 'Chinese Spokesman: Has No Forced Evictions for Beijing Olympics', *BBC Monitoring Asia Pacific*, 5 June 2007.

86 Don Lee, 'Chinese Hope Pre-Games Cleanup Will Be Fresh Start', *Los Angeles Times*, 6 Aug. 2008.

87 'Press Hails "Greatest Ever" Olympic Opening Show', *Agence France Presse*, 9 Aug. 2008.

88 Tania Branigan, 'Olympics: Child Singer Revealed as Fake', *Guardian*, 12 Aug. 2008; Jonathan Watts, 'China Faked Footprints of Fire Coverage in Olympics Opening Ceremony', *Guardian*, 11 Aug. 2008; Belinda Goldsmith, 'Ethnic Children Faked at Games Opening', *Reuters*, 15 August 2008.

89 'China Declares "People's War" as Tibet Riots Spread', *Times of India*, 17 March 2008; Robert Barnett, 'The Tibet Protests of Spring 2008: Conflict

Between the Nation and the State', *China Perspectives*, no. 3 (Sept. 2009), pp. 6–23.

90 'Olympic Torch Protests Around the World', *Reuters*, 28 April 2008; Howard French, 'Unrest in Tibet Exposes a Clash of Two Worlds', *New York Times*, 20 March 2008; Jim Yardley, 'Nationalism at Core of China's Angry Reaction to Tibetan Protests', *New York Times*, 30 March 2008.

91 Mark Magnier, 'Dialing Back Chinese Anger', *Los Angeles Times*, 19 April 2008.

92 Edward Wong and Keith Bradsher, 'As China Girds for Olympics, New Violence', *New York Times*, 4 Aug. 2008; Howard French, 'China to Curb Dissidents in Shanghai During Games', *New York Times*, 26 June 2008; 'Olympic Hangover: The Games Are Over, But Hu Jia Is Still in Prison', *Washington Post*, 24 Oct. 2008.

93 'U.S. Seeks Release of Olympic Protesters', *Korea Times*, 25 August 2008.

10. HUBRIS (2008–2012)

1 Wenzhou, J202-22-817, 14 May 2009, pp. 1–14; Don Lee, 'China's Bosses Are Abandoning Ship', *Los Angeles Times*, 3 Nov. 2008; Edward Wong, 'Factories Shut, China Workers Are Suffering', *New York Times*, 14 Nov. 2008.

2 David Barboza, 'Great Engine of China Slows', *New York Times*, 26 Nov. 2008.

3 Edward Wong, 'Factories Shut, China Workers Are Suffering', *New York Times*, 14 Nov. 2008; Keith Bradsher, 'China's Route Forward', *New York Times*, 23 Jan. 2009.

4 Keith Bradsher, 'China's Route Forward', *New York Times*, 23 Jan. 2009.

5 Patrick Chovanec, 'China's Hidden Inflation', *Bloomberg*, 22 Oct. 2010.

6 Michael Wines and David Barboza, 'Fire Trips Alarms About China's Building Boom', *New York Times*, 17 Nov. 2010; Ana Swanson, 'How China Used More Cement in 3 Years Than the U.S. Did in the Entire 20th Century', *Washington Post*, 24 March 2015; Holland Cotter, 'A Building Boom in China', *New York Times*, 21 March 2013.

7 Didi Kirsten Tatlow, 'A Challenge to China's Self-Looting', *International Herald Tribune*, 23 June 2011.

8 Andrew Jacobs, 'Harassment and Evictions Bedevil Even China's Well-Off', *New York Times*, 28 Oct. 2011.

9 Andrew Jacobs, 'Harassment and Evictions Bedevil Even China's Well-Off', *New York Times*, 28 Oct. 2011; Wade Shepard, 'During Its

Long Boom, Chinese Cities Demolished an Area the Size of Mauritius Every Year', *CityMonitor*, 22 Sept. 2015, quoting the research firm GK Dragonomics.

10 Adrian Wan, 'Hong Kong's Architectural Heritage Conservation Is Praised', *South China Morning Post*, 24 July 2013.

11 Christina Larson, 'The Cracks in China's Shiny Buildings', *Bloomberg Businessweek*, 27 Sept. 2012; Choi Chi-yuk, 'The Shame of Sichuan's Tofu Schools', *South China Morning Post*, 6 May 2013.

12 David Pierson, 'A Boom Muffled in China', *Los Angeles Times*, 7 Sept. 2010.

13 Keith Bradsher, 'It's All About the Dollar', *New York Times*, 16 Oct 2009; David Pierson, 'China Bounces Back, But Is It for Real?', *Los Angeles Times*, 21 Oct. 2009.

14 Jamil Anderlini and Geoff Dyer, 'Beijing Accused of Launching Attack on Private Enterprise', *Financial Times*, 26 Nov. 2009; Michael Wines, 'China Fortifies State Businesses to Fuel Growth', *New York Times*, 30 Aug. 2010.

15 Neil Gough, 'What Trade Overhaul?', *South China Morning Post*, 10 Dec. 2011.

16 'Awash in Cash', *China Economic Review*, Aug. 2012.

17 David Pierson, 'China Bounces Back, But Is It for Real?', *Los Angeles Times*, 21 Oct. 2009.

18 Stephen Castle and David Jolly, 'China Escalates Trade Fight Over European Shoe Tariff', *New York Times*, 5 Feb. 2010.

19 Edward Wong, 'Confidence and Disdain Toward U.S. from China', *International Herald Tribune*, 17 June 2008; Carter Dougherty and Katrin Bennhold, 'Russia and China Blame Capitalists for Crisis', *New York Times*, 29 Jan. 2009; Barry Naughton, 'In China's Economy, The State's Hand Grows Heavier', *Current History*, 108, no. 719 (Sept. 2009), pp. 277–83; on the 'China way' (Zhongguo daolu), see for instance 'Zhongguo daolu' (The China way), *Renmin ribao*, 26 June 2012; see also Wang Xiangping, '"Zhongguo moshi" yu Zhongguo tese shehuizhuyi daolu', *Dangdai Zhongguo shi yanjiu*, 2013, no. 5, pp. 89–97.

20 Willy Lam, 'Hu Jintao's Great Leap Backward', *Far Eastern Economic Review*, 172, no. 1 (Jan. 2009), pp. 19–22.

21 Andrew Jacobs, 'Chinese Learn Limits of Online Freedom as the Filter Tightens', *New York Times*, 5 Feb. 2009.

22 Sharon LaFraniere, 'In Second Internet Crackdown, China Squelches Multimedia', *International Herald Tribune*, 18 Dec. 2009; Michael Wines and Sharon LaFraniere, 'Web Censors in Mainland Everywhere But Nowhere', *International Herald Tribune*, 8 April 2010.

23 Jake Hooker, 'Quake Revealed Deficiencies of China's Military', *New York Times*, 2 July 2008; Jennifer Ngo, 'Hong Kong Responds Generously After Latest Sichuan Earthquake', *South China Morning Post*, 21 April 2013.

24 'U.S. House Overwhelmingly Passes Rep. Wu Resolution in Support of Jailed Sichuan Earthquake Activists', *US Fed News Service*, 20 Nov. 2009.

25 David Barboza, 'Prominent Artist Pushes for Candor on Sichuan Earthquake', *International Herald Tribune*, 20 March 2009; 'The Artist's Blog Banned by the Chinese Government', *The Times*, 23 April 2011.

26 Tania Branigan, 'Chen Guangcheng', *Guardian*, 27 April 2012; Peter Ford, 'China's Blind Activist Lawyer, Chen Guangcheng, Released From Prison', *Christian Science Monitor*, 9 Sept. 2010.

27 Willy Lam, 'The Politics of Liu Xiaobo's Trial', in Jean-Philippe Béja, Fu Hualing and Eva Pils (eds), Liu Xiaobo, *Charter 08 and the Challenges of Political Reform in China*, Hong Kong University Press, Hong Kong, 2012, pp. 262–3; Hu Ben, 'Weiwenban rujie jincun' (Offices to Maintain Social Security enter streets and villages), *Nanfang zhoumo*, 18 Aug. 2010.

28 'Beijing Denounces Nobel Prize', *Capital*, 6 Nov. 2010.

29 Andrew Jacobs and Jonathan Ansfield, 'Well-Oiled Security Apparatus in China Stifles Calls for Change', *New York Times*, 1 March 2011; 'China's Urumqi to Install 17,000 Surveillance Cameras', *BBC Monitoring Asia Pacific*, 25 Jan. 2011; 'China: Chongqing Will Add 200,000 Surveillance Cameras', *New York Times*, 10 March 2011; 'The Good and Bad of TV Surveillance', *Kamloops Daily News*, 3 Oct. 2011.

30 'Hundreds Join "Jasmine Revolution"', *South China Morning Post*, 21 Feb. 2011; Andrew Jacobs, 'Catching Scent of Revolution, China Moves to Snip Jasmine', *New York Times*, 10 May 2011.

31 Tania Branigan, 'Ai Weiwei Interrogated by Chinese Police "More Than 50 Times"', *Guardian*, 10 Aug. 2011.

32 Sharon LaFraniere, Michael Wines and Edward Wong, 'China Reins In Entertainment and Blogging', *New York Times*, 27 Oct. 2011; 'China Cracks Down on "Fake Journalists and News"', *Dow Jones Institutional News*, 14 Nov. 2011; David Pierson, 'China Fails to Ease Controls', *Los Angeles Times*, 23 March 2011.

33 Andrew Jacobs, 'Chinese Heroism Effort Is Met with Cynicism', *New York Times*, 6 March 2012.

34 Barbara Demick, 'Chinese Perk Up at Wen's Words: The Premier Has Spoken Out on Political Reform. Some Doubt His Sincerity', *Los Angeles Times*, 16 Oct. 2010; Shi Jiangtao, 'Beijing Slams Door on Political Reform', *South China Morning Post*, 11 March 2011.

35 Wenzhou, J202-22-450, zhongfa (2008) 14, Central Committee Directive on the Study of Marxism, 14 Sept. 2008, pp. 1–16.

36 'China Marks 60 Years of Communist Rule', *Korea Times*, 2–4 Oct. 2009.

37 'Chinese VP Calls for Enhancing Study of Marxism', *Xinhua News Agency*, 10 Dec. 2009; 'Chinese Journal on Sinicization, Modernization, Popularization of Marxism', *BBC Monitoring Asia Pacific*, 19 Dec. 2009.

38 'Xi Jinping: Man for All Factions Is Tip for Top', *South China Morning Post*, 23 Oct. 2007; Jane Perlez, 'China Leader with Close Army Ties Would Be Force for U.S. to Contend With', *New York Times*, 4 Nov. 2012.

39 Wenzhou, J202-22-450, 15 Jan. 2008, zhongban (2008) no. 2, Central Committee Bureau's Directive on Taking Ideological Work Global, pp. 17–32.

40 Rowan Callick, 'China Splashes $10bn in Push for "Soft Power"', *Australian*, 23 Feb. 2009.

41 Zhang Yuwei, 'Confucian Way of Spreading Chinese Culture', *Chicago Tribune*, 21 Jan. 2011.

42 'Beware the Beijing Model', *The Economist*, 26 May 2009; 'Chinese Party Paper Views World's Fascination with "China Model"', *BBC Monitoring Asia Pacific*, 30 June 2009.

43 'China's Real 2010 Defense Spending Estimated at US$240 Bln', *Asia Pulse*, 11 March 2011.

44 Tom Vanden Brook and Calum MacLeod, 'China's Military Flexes Its Muscle', *USA Today*, 28 July 2011.

45 Robert Maginnis, 'China Lies About Its Huge Military Buildup', *Human Events*, vol. 67, no. 14, 11 April 2011, p. 8; Nuclear Threat Initiative, 'China Missile Technology', June 2012.

46 Elisabeth Bumiller, 'U.S. Official Warns About China's Military Buildup', *New York Times*, 25 Aug. 2011.

47 'China's Aggressive New Diplomacy', *Wall Street Journal*, 1 Oct. 2010.

48 Don Lee, 'Run-In at Sea U.S. Fault, Beijing Says', *Los Angeles Times*, 11 March 2009.

49 Jane Perlez, 'Alarm as China Issues Rules for Disputed Area', *New York Times*, 2 Dec. 2012.

EPILOGUE

1 David Barboza, 'China's Cities Piling Up Debt to Fuel Boom', *New York Times*, 7 July 2011.

2   Lynette H. Ong, 'State-Led Urbanization in China: Skyscrapers, Land Revenue and "Concentrated Villages"', *China Quarterly*, no. 217 (March 2014), p. 175; Gabriel Wildau, 'Legacy of Chinese Government's Economic Stimulus Is Mixed', *Financial Times*, 20 Nov. 2015.

3   'Researcher Puts China's Local Government Debt at 20 Trillion Yuan', *Dow Jones Institutional News*, 17 Sept. 2013; Hong Shen, 'China Seeks Clearer View of Government Debt Mountain', *Wall Street Journal*, 21 Oct. 2013; 'China's Hidden Debt Risk', *Korea Times*, 26 March 2013.

4   Dinny McMahon, 'With Cash Scarce in China, IOUs Proliferate', *Wall Street Journal*, 4 April 2014; see also the indispensable Dinny McMahon, *China's Great Wall of Debt*, Little, Brown, London, 2018.

5   Josh Noble and Gabriel Wildau, 'Fear of a Deflationary Spiral', *Financial Times*, 1 Dec. 2014.

6   Patrick Chovanec, 'China Destroyed Its Stock Market in Order to Save It', *Foreign Policy*, 16 July 2015.

7   Keith Bradsher, 'China's Wealthy Move Money Out as Country's Economy Weakens', *New York Times*, 14 Feb. 2016.

8   'Robber Barons, Beware', *The Economist*, 24 Oct. 2015.

9   Gary Huang, 'How Leading Small Groups Help Xi Jinping and Other Party Leaders Exert Power', *South China Morning Post*, 20 Jan. 2014; Nis Grünberg, 'The CCP's Nerve Center', *Merics*, 30 Oct. 2019.

10 'Chairman of Everything', *The Economist*, 2 April 2016, quoting Geremie Barmé.

11 'No Cult of Personality Around Xi, Says Top China Party Academic', *Reuters*, 6 Nov. 2017; Rowan Callick, 'No Turning Back the Tide on Xi Jinping Personality Cult', *The Australian*, 25 Nov. 2017; Viola Zhou, '"Into the Brains" of China's Children: Xi Jinping's "Thought" to Become Compulsory School Topic', *South China Morning Post*, 23 Oct. 2017; Jamil Anderlini, 'Under Xi Jinping, China is Turning Back to Dictatorship', *Financial Times*, 11 Oct. 2017; more generally, see François Bougon, *Inside the Mind of Xi Jinping*, C. Hurst, London, 2018.

12 Tom Phillips, 'Xi Jinping: Does China Truly Love "Big Daddy Xi" – or Fear Him?', *Guardian*, 19 Sept. 2015. Teng Biao, 'What Will This Crackdown on Activists Do to China's Nascent Civil Society?', *Guardian*, 24 Jan. 2015.

13 Peter Ford, 'From Occupy Central to Tibet, China Sees "Hostile Foreign Forces"', *Christian Science Monitor*, 9 Nov. 2014.

14 Edward Wong, 'China Freezes Credentials for Journalists at U.S. Outlets, Hinting at Expulsions', *New York Times*, 6 Sept. 2020.

15 Lucy Hornby and Charles Clover, 'China's Media Pressed Into Service', *Australian Financial Review*, 4 April 2016; 'Foreign Journalists Forced

to Leave China as Diplomatic Tensions Worsen', *Reuters*, 8 Sept. 2020; Leo Lewis, 'Axe Foreign Textbooks, China Tells Universities', *The Times*, 31 Jan. 2015.

16 Robert Fulford, 'Pooh Bear Goes Underground in Xi's China', *National Post*, 17 March 2018; Wu Huizhong, 'In Echo of Mao Era, China's Schools in Book-Cleansing Drive', *Reuters*, 9 July 2020.

17 See Elizabeth C. Economy, *The Third Revolution: Xi Jinping and the New Chinese State*, Oxford University Press, Oxford, 2018.

18 'The Xinjiang Papers', *New York Times*, 16 November 2019.

19 Peter Ford, 'China Targets "Hostile Foreign Forces" in Crescendo of Accusations', *Christian Science Monitor*, 9 Nov. 2014.

20 'China "Does Not Share Our Values", NATO Chief Says', *Reuters*, 30 June 2020; 'Important to "Strengthen" Common Policy on China, Says NATO Chief', *ANI*, 14 June 2021.

21 Adam Dunnett, 'Three Reasons China Is Losing Its Allure for the Foreign Business Community', *South China Morning Post*, 28 May 2021; Shannon Brandao, 'Yes, Manufacturing Really Is Leaving China – And Authorities Are Scrambling to Slow Down the Exodus', *Arabian News*, 11 April 2021.

22 Michael Pettis, 'Xi's Aim to Double China's Economy Is a Fantasy', *Financial Times*, 22 Nov. 2020; 'China Has Over 600 Million Poor with $140 Monthly Income', *PTI News*, 28 May 2020.

23 Michael Pettis, 'Xi's Aim to Double China's Economy Is a Fantasy', *Financial Times*, 22 Nov. 2020.

24 Scott Rozelle and Natalie Hell, *Invisible China: How the Urban-Rural Divide Threatens China's Rise*, University of Chicago Press, Chicago, 2020.

Select Bibliography

ARCHIVES

Principal Non-Chinese Archives

Barch – Bundesarchiv, Berlin
HIA – Hoover Institution Library and Archives, Palo Alto
MfAA – Politisches Archiv des Auswärtigen Amts, Berlin
MAE – Ministère des Affaires Étrangères, Paris
PRO – The National Archives, London

Provincial Archives

GANSU – GANSU SHENG DANG'ANGUAN, LANZHOU

91 Zhonggong Gansu shengwei (Gansu Provincial Party Committee)
107 Gongqingtuan Gansu sheng weiyuanhui (Gansu Committee of the China Youth League)
116 Zhongguo renmin zhengzhi xieshang huiyi Gansu sheng weiyuanhui (Gansu Provincial Committee of the People's Consultative Conference)
128 Gansu sheng renmin zhengfu (Gansu Provincial People's Government)
136 Gansu sheng zhengfu jingji tizhi gaige weiyuanhui (Gansu Provincial Committee for Economic Reform)
141 Gansu sheng jihua shengyu weiyuanhui (Gansu Provincial Committee for Birth Control)
145 Gansu sheng laodongju (Gansu Provincial Bureau for Labour)

151 Gansu sheng duiwai maoyiju (Gansu Provincial Bureau for Foreign Trade)
216 Gansu sheng nongyeting (Gansu Provincial Agricultural Bureau)
238 Gansu sheng huanjing baohuju (Gansu Provincial Bureau for Environmental Protection)
259 Gansu sheng tiyu yundong weiyuanhui (Gansu Provincial Committee on Sports)

GUANGDONG – GUANGDONG SHENG DANG'ANGUAN, GUANGZHOU

235 Guangdong sheng renmin weiyuanhui (Guangdong Provincial People's Congress)

HEBEI – HEBEI SHENG DANG'ANGUAN, SHIJIAZHUANG

879 Zhonggong Hebei shengwei nongcun gongzuobu (Hebei Provincial Party Committee Department for Rural Work)
925 Hebei sheng nongye shengchan weiyuanhui (Hebei Province Agricultural Production Committee)
979 Hebei sheng nongyeting (Hebei Province Agricultural Bureau)
1021 Hebei sheng duiwai jingji maoyiting (Hebei Province Bureau for Foreign Trade)

HUBEI – HUBEI SHENG DANG'ANGUAN, WUHAN

SZ1 Zhonggong Hubei sheng weiyuanhui (Hubei Provincial Party Committee)
SZ29 Hubei sheng zonggonghui (Hubei Province Federation of Trade Unions)
SZ34 Hubei sheng renmin weiyuanhui (Hubei Provincial People's Congress)
SZ75 Hubei sheng liangshiting (Hubei Province Bureau for Grain)
SZ81 Hubei sheng shangyeting (Hubei Province Bureau for Trade)
SZ90 Hubei sheng gongyeting (Hubei Province Bureau for Industry)
SZ107 Hubei sheng nongyeting (Hubei Province Agricultural Bureau)
SZ115 Hubei sheng weishengting (Hubei Province Bureau for Health)

SHANDONG – SHANDONG SHENG DANG'ANGUAN, JINAN

A1 Zhonggong Shandong shengwei (Shandong Provincial Party Committee)

Municipal Archives

HANGZHOU – HANGZHOU SHI DANG'ANGUAN, HANGZHOU, ZHEJIANG

J101 Zhongguo renmin yinhang Hangzhou zhihang (Hangzhou branch of Bank of China)

J132 Hangzhou shi minzhengju (Hangzhou Municipal Bureau for Civil Administration)

NANJING – NANJING SHI DANG'ANGUAN, NANJING, JIANGSU

4003 Nanjing shiwei (Nanjing Municipal Party Committee)

5003 Nanjing shi renmin zhengfu (Nanjing Municipal People's Government)

5019 Nanjing shi jihua weiyuanhui (Nanjing Municipal Planning Committee)

5020 Nanjing shi jingji weiyuanhui (Nanjing City Economic Committee)

5023 Nanjing shi tongjiju (Nanjing Municipal Bureau of Statistics)

5054 Nanjing shi caizhengju (Nanjing Municipal Bureau of Finances)

5071 Nanjing shi nonglinju (Nanjing Municipal Bureau of Agriculture and Forestry)

5093 Nanjing shi duiwai maoyiju (Nanjing Municipal Bureau for Foreign Trade)

SHANGHAI – SHANGHAI SHI DANG'ANGUAN, SHANGHAI

A36 Shanghai shiwei gongye zhengzhibu (Shanghai Municipal Party Committee's Bureau for Industry and Politics)

A38 Shanghai shiwei gongye shengchan weiyuanhui (Committee for Industrial Production of the Shanghai Municipal Party Committee)

B1 Shanghai shi renmin zhengfu (Shanghai Municipal People's Government)

B3 Shanghai shi renmin weiyuanhui wenjiao bangongshi (Shanghai Municipal People's Congress' Bureau for Culture and Education)

B6 Shanghai shi renmin weiyuanhui cailiangmao bangongshi (Shanghai Municipal People's Congress' Bureau for Finances, Grain and Trade)

B45 Shanghai shi nongyeting (Shanghai Municipality's Bureau for Agriculture)

B50 Shanghai shi renwei jiguan shiwu guanliju (Shanghai Municipal People's Congress' Bureau for Office Work)

B74 Shanghai shi minbing zhihuibu (Shanghai City's Militia Command Post)

B92 Shanghai shi renmin guangbo diantai (Shanghai City Radio)

B98 Shanghai shi di'er shangyeju (Shanghai City's Number Two Bureau for Trade)

B104 Shanghai shi caizhengju (Shanghai Municipal Bureau for Finance)

B105 Shanghai shi jiaoyuju (Shanghai Municipal Bureau for Education)

B109 Shanghai shi wuzi (Shanghai Municipal Bureau for Goods and Materials)

B120 Shanghai Shi renmin fangkong bangongshi (Shanghai Municipal Office for Air Defence)

B123 Shanghai shi diyi shangyeju (Shanghai City's Number One Bureau for Trade)

B127 Shanghai shi laodongju (Shanghai Municipal Bureau for Labour)

B134 Shanghai shi fangzhi gongyeju (Shanghai Municipal Bureau for Textile Industry)

B163 Shanghai shi qinggongyeju (Shanghai Municipal Bureau for Light Industry)

B167 Shanghai shi chubanju (Shanghai Municipal Bureau for Publishing)

B168 Shanghai shi minzhengju (Shanghai Municipal Bureau for Civil Administration)

B172 Shanghai shi wenhuaju (Shanghai Municipal Bureau for Culture)

B173 Shanghai shi jidian gongye guanliju (Shanghai Municipal Bureau for Machinery and Electronics)

B182 Shanghai shi gongshanghang guanliju (Shanghai Municipal Bureau of Supervision of Business)

B227 Shanghai shi geming weiyuanhui laodong gongzizu (Shanghai Municipal Revolutionary Committee's Team on Wages)

B228 Shanghai shi renmin zhengfu zhishi qingnian shangshan xiaxiang bangongshi (Shanghai Municipal People's Government's Bureau for Sending Educated Youth to the Countryside)

B244 Shanghai shi jiaoyu weisheng bangongshi (Shanghai Municipal Bureau for Education and Health)

B246 Shanghai shi renmin zhengfu jingji weiyuanhui (Shanghai Municipal People's Government's Committee on the Economy)

B248 Shanghai shi renmin zhengfu caizheng maoyi bangongshi (Shanghai Municipal People's Government's Office for Finance and Trade)

B250 Shanghai shi nongye weiyuanhui (Shanghai Municipal Committee on Agriculture)

TIANJIN – TIANJIN SHI DANG'ANGUAN, TIANJIN

X43 Tianjin shi gongshangye lianhehui (Tianjin Municipal Federation of Industry and Commerce)

X78 Tianjin shi jihua weiyuanhui (Tianjin Municipal Planning Committee)

X81 Tianjin shi wujiaju weiyuanhui (Tianjin Municipal Price Bureau Committee)

X87 Tianjin shi caizhengju (Tianjin Municipal Bureau of Finances))

X95 Tianjin shi liangshiju (Tianjin Municipal Bureau for Grain)

X110 Tianjin shi jingji weiyuanhui (Tianjin Municipal Committee on the Economy)

X172 Tianjin shi yiqingju (Tianjin Municipal No. 1 Light Industry Bureau)

X175 Tianjin shi duiwai maoyiju (Tianjin Municipal Bureau for Foreign Trade)

X199 Tianjin shi wenhuaju (Tianjin Municipal Bureau for Culture)

X211 Tianjin shiwei bangongting (Tianjin Municipal Party Committee Bureau)

X213 Tianjin shi xuanchuanju (Tianjin Municipal Bureau for Propaganda)

WENZHOU – WENZHOU SHI DANG'ANGUAN, WENZHOU

J1 Zhonggong Wenzhou shiwei (Wenzhou Municipal Party Committee)

J20 Wenzhou shi jihua weiyuanhui (Wenzhou Municipal Planning Committee)

J27 Wenzhou shi caimao bangongting (Wenzhou Municipal Bureau for Finance and Trade)

J34 Zhongguo renmin yinhang Wenzhou shi zhihang (People's Bank of China Wenzhou Branch)

J51 Wenzhou shi renmin zhengfu (Wenzhou Municipal People's Government)

J80 Wenzhou shi dang'anju (Wenzhou Municipal Bureau for Archives)

J87 Wenzhou diqu weiyuanhui (Wenzhou Regional Committee)

J153 Wenzhou shi xingzheng ganxiao (Wenzhou Municipal School for Administrative Cadres)

J156 Wenzhou shi qiaowu bangongshi ((Wenzhou Municipal Bureau for Overseas Chinese Affairs)

J173 Wenzhou shi huanbaoju (Wenzhou Municipal Bureau for Environmental Protection)

J201 Wenzhou shiwei bangongshi (Office of the Wenzhou Municipal Party Committee)

J202 Wenzhou shizheng bangongshi (Bureau of the Wenzhou Municipal People's Government)

J232 Wenzhou shi jingji tizhi gaige bangongshi (Wenzhou Municipal Office for Economic Reform)

PUBLISHED WORKS

Amnesty International, 'People's Republic of China: Preliminary Findings on Killings of Unarmed Civilians, Arbitrary Arrests and Summary Executions since 3 June 1989', London: Amnesty International, document dated 14 August 1989

Bachman, David, 'Institutions, Factions, Conservatism, and Leadership Change in China: The Case of Hu Yaobang', in Ray Taras (ed.), *Leadership Change in Communist States*, Unwin Hyman, Boston, 1989

Barmé, Geremie, 'Confession, Redemption, and Death: Liu Xiaobo and the Protest Movement of 1989', in George Hicks (ed.), *The Broken Mirror: China After Tiananmen*, Longman, London, 1990, pp. 52–99

Barmé, Geremie and John Minford (eds), *Seeds of Fire: Dissident Voices of Conscience*, Hill and Wang, New York, 1988

Barnett, Robert, 'The Tibet Protests of Spring 2008: Conflict Between the Nation and the State', *China Perspectives*, no. 3 (Sept. 2009), pp. 6–23

Becker, Jasper, *The Chinese*, The Free Press, New York, 2000

Becker, Jasper, *City of Heavenly Tranquillity: Beijing in the History of China*, Oxford University Press, Oxford, 2008

Béja, Jean-Philippe, Fu Hualing and Eva Pils (eds), Liu Xiaobo, *Charter 08 and the Challenges of Political Reform in China*, Hong Kong University Press, Hong Kong, 2012

Benton, Gregor (ed.), *Wild Lilies, Poisonous Weeds: Dissident Voices from People's China*, Pluto Press, London, 1982

Bougon, François, *Inside the Mind of Xi Jinping*, C. Hurst, London, 2018

Burns, Katherine G., 'China and Japan: Economic Partnership to Political End', unpublished paper, Stimson Center, Accessed 25 September 2020

Cao Jinqing, *China along the Yellow River: Reflections on Rural Society*, RoutledgeCurzon, London, 2005

Callick, Rowan, *The Party Forever: Inside China's Modern Communist Elite*, Palgrave Macmillan, London, 2013

Chang, Leslie T., *Factory Girls: From Village to City in a Changing China*, Random House, New York, 2009

Chen Guidi and Wu Chuntao, *Will the Boat Sink the Water?: The Life of China's Peasants*, PublicAffairs, New York, 2006

Chen Lein-Lein and John Devereux, 'The Iron Rice Bowl: Chinese Living Standards 1952–1978', *Comparative Economic Studies*, 2017, no. 59, pp. 261–310

Chen, Nai-Ruenn, *China's Economy and Foreign Trade, 1979–81*, Department of Commerce, Washington, 1982

Chen Yongxi, 'Circumventing Transparency: Extra-Legal Exemptions from Freedom of Information and Judicial Review in China', in *Journal of International Media & Entertainment Law*, 2018, 7, no. 2, pp. 203–51

Chen Yulu, Guo Qingwang and Zhang Jie, *Major Issues and Policies in China's Financial Reform*, Enrich Professional Publishing, Honolulu, 2016

Cheng, Eddie, *Standoff at Tiananmen*, Sensys Corp., Highlands Ranch, CO, 2009

Creemers, Rogier, 'Cyber China: Upgrading Propaganda, Public Opinion Work and Social Management for the Twenty-First Century', *Journal of Contemporary China*, 26, no. 103 (Sept. 2016), pp. 85–100

Cui Zhiyuan, 'China's Export Tax Rebate Policy', *China: An International Journal*, 1, no. 2 (Sept. 2003), pp. 339–49

Day, Alexander, *The Peasant in Postsocialist China: History, Politics, and Capitalism*, Cambridge University Press, Cambridge, 2013

Dikötter, Frank, *The Age of Openness: China Before Mao*, University of California Press, Berkeley, 2008

——, *Mao's Great Famine: The History of China's Most Devastating Catastrophe, 1958–62*, Bloomsbury, London, 2010

——, *The Tragedy of Liberation: A History of the Chinese Revolution 1945–1957*, Bloomsbury, London, 2013

——, *The Cultural Revolution: A People's History, 1962–1976*, Bloomsbury, London and New York, 2016

Dimbleby, Jonathan, *The Last Governor*, Little, Brown, London, 1997

Dong Fureng, *Industrialization and China's Rural Modernization*, The World Bank, Washington, 1992

Economy, Elizabeth C., *The River Runs Black: The Environmental Challenge to China's Future*, Cornell University Press, Ithaca, NY, 2004

——, *The Third Revolution: Xi Jinping and the New Chinese State*, Oxford University Press, Oxford, 2018

Fang Lizhi, *The Most Wanted Man in China: My Journey from Scientist to Enemy of the State*, Holt and Co., New York, 2016

Feng Xingyuan, 'Local Government Debt and Municipal Bonds in China: Problems and a Framework of Rules', *Copenhagen Journal of Asian Studies*, 31, no. 2 (2013), pp. 23–53

Garrison, Jean A., 'Explaining Change in the Carter Administration's China Policy: Foreign Policy Adviser Manipulation of the Policy Agenda', *Asian Affairs*, 29, no. 2 (Summer 2002), pp. 83–98

Garside, Roger, *Coming Alive: China after Mao*, Deutsch, London, 1981

Gilley, Bruce, *Tiger on the Brink: Jiang Zemin and China's New Elite*, University of California Press, Berkeley, CA, 1998

Greenfield, Gerard and Tim Pringle, 'The Challenge of Wage Arrears in China', in Manuel Simón Velasco (ed.), *Paying Attention to Wages*, International Labour Organisation, Geneva, 2002, pp. 30–38

Haley, Usha C. V. and George T. Haley, *Subsidies to Chinese Industry: State Capitalism, Business Strategy, and Trade Policy*, Oxford University Press, New York, 2013

Hannas, William C., James Mulvenon and Anna B. Puglisi, *Chinese Industrial Espionage: Technology Acquisition and Military Modernization*, Routledge, London, 2013

Hannas, William C. and Didi Kirsten Tatlow (eds), *China's Quest for Foreign Technology: Beyond Espionage*, Routledge, London, 2021

Hastings, Justin, 'Charting the Course of Uyghur Unrest', *China Quarterly*, no. 208 (Dec. 2011), pp. 893–912

Hay, Donald, Derek Morris, Guy Liu and Shujie Yao, *Economic Reform and State-Owned Enterprises in China 1979–87*, Clarendon Press, Oxford, 1994

He, Henry, *Dictionary of the Political Thought of the People's Republic of China*, Routledge, London, 2000

He, Rowena Xiaoqing, *Tiananmen Exiles: Voices of the Struggle for Democracy in China*, Palgrave Macmillan, London, 2014

He Qinglian, *The Fog of Censorship: Media Control in China*, Human Rights in China, New York, 2008

Holz, Carsten A., 'China's Bad Loan Problem', manuscript, Hong Kong University of Science and Technology, April 1999

——, 'China's Monetary Reform: The Counterrevolution from the Countryside', *Journal of Contemporary China*, 10, no. 27 (2001), pp. 189–217

Hong Zhaohui and Ellen Y. Yan, 'Trust and Investment Corporations in China', in Chen Beizhu, J. Kimball Dietrich and Yi Fang (eds), *Financial Market Reform in China: Progress, Problems and Prospects*, Westview Press, Boulder, CO, 2000, pp. 285–98

Hornsby, Adrian, 'Tiananmen Square: The History of the World's Largest Paved Open Square', *Architectural Review*, 12 Oct. 2009

Huo yu xue zhi zhenxiang: Zhongguo dalu minzhu yundong jishi (The truth about fire and blood: A true record of the democracy movement in mainland China), Zhonggong yanjiu zazhi she, Taipei, 1989

Huang Yanzhong, *Toxic Politics: China's Environmental Health Crisis and Its Challenge to the Chinese State*, Cambridge University Press, Cambridge, 2020

Jia Hepeng, 'The Three Represents Campaign: Reform the Party or Indoctrinate the Capitalists?', *Cato Journal*, 24, no. 3 (Fall 2004), pp. 261–75

Jin Chongji (ed.), *Zhou Enlai zhuan, 1898–1949* (A biography of Zhou Enlai, 1898–1949), Zhongyang wenxian chubanshe, Beijing, 1989

Kan, Karoline, *Under Red Skies: Three Generations of Life, Loss, and Hope in China*, Hachette Books, New York, 2019

Kelliher, Daniel, *Peasant Power in China: The Era of Rural Reform, 1979–1989*, Yale University Press, New Haven, CT, 1992

Kraus, Richard Curt, *The Party and the Arty in China: The New Politics of Culture*, Rowman & Littlefield, Lanham, MD, 2004

Kwong, Julia, 'The 1986 Student Demonstrations in China: A Democratic Movement?', *Asian Survey*, 28, no. 9 (Sept. 1988), pp. 970–85

Kynge, James, *China Shakes the World: The Rise of a Hungry Nation*, Weidenfeld & Nicolson, London, 2006

Lam, Willy Wo-Lap, *Chinese Politics in the Era of Xi Jinping: Renaissance, Reform, or Retrogression?*, Routledge, London, 2015

Lardy, Nicholas R., *Foreign Trade and Economic Reform in China, 1978–1990*, Cambridge University Press, Cambridge, 1992

Lee, Keun, 'The Chinese Model of the Socialist Enterprise: An Assessment of Its Organization and Performance', *Journal of Comparative Economics*, 14, no. 3 (Sept. 1990), pp. 384–400

Li Zhisui, *The Private Life of Chairman Mao: The Memoirs of Mao's Personal Physician*, Random House, New York, 1994

Li Zhongjie, *Gaige kaifang guanjian ci* (Key words of Reform and Opening Up), Renmin chubanshe, Beijing, 2018

Liang Zhongtang, *Zhongguo shengyu zhengce yanjiu* (Research on China's Birth Control Policy), Shanxi renmin chubanshe, Taiyuan, 2014

Liao Yiwu, *Bullets and Opium: Real-Life Stories of China After the Tiananmen Massacre*, Atria, New York, 2019

Lim, Louisa, *The People's Republic of Amnesia: Tiananmen Revisited*, Oxford University Press, Oxford, 2015

Lin Guijun and Ronald M. Schramm, 'China's Foreign Exchange Policies Since 1979: A Review of Developments and an Assessment', *China Economic Review*, 14, no. 3 (Dec. 2003), pp. 246–80

Liu Binyan, *A Higher Kind of Loyalty: A Memoir by China's Foremost Journalist*, Pantheon Books, New York, 1990

Loh, Christine, *Underground Front: The Chinese Communist Party in Hong Kong*, Hong Kong University Press, Hong Kong, 2019

Lu Keng, *Lu Keng huiyi yu chanhuilu* (Memoirs and confessions of Lu Keng), Shibao wenhua chuban qiye youxian gongsi, Taipei, 1997

MacFarquhar, Roderick and Michael Schoenhals, *Mao's Last Revolution*, Harvard University Press, Cambridge, MA, 2006

Mann, James H., *About Face: A History of America's Curious Relationship with China, from Nixon to Clinton*, Alfred A. Knopf, New York, 1998

Mao Zedong, *Jianguo yilai Mao Zedong wengao* (Mao Zedong's manuscripts since the founding of the People's Republic), Zhongyang wenxian chubanshe, Beijing, 1998

McKay, John P., 'Foreign Enterprise in Russian and Soviet Industry: A Long Term Perspective', *Business History Review* (Autumn 1974), 48, no. 3, pp. 336–56.

McMahon, Dinny, *China's Great Wall of Debt*, Little, Brown, London, 2018

McGregor, Richard, *The Party: The Secret World of China's Communist Rulers*, HarperCollins, New York, 2010

Morino, Tomozo, 'China-Japan Trade and Investment Relations', *Proceedings of the Academy of Political Science*, 38, no. 2 (1991), pp. 87–94

Naughton, Barry, 'In China's Economy, The State's Hand Grows Heavier', *Current History*, 108, no. 719 (Sept. 2009), pp. 277–83

Ogden, Suzanne, Kathleen Hartford, Nancy Sullivan and David Zweig, *China's Search for Democracy: The Students and Mass Movement of 1989*, Routledge, New York, 1992

Oksenberg, Michael, Lawrence R. Sullivan and Marc Lambert (eds) *Beijing Spring, 1989: Confrontation and Conflict. The Basic Documents*, Routledge, London, 1990

Ong, Lynette H., *Prosper or Perish: Credit and Fiscal Systems in Rural China*, Cornell University Press, Ithaca, NY, 2012

Ong, Lynette H., 'State-Led Urbanization in China: Skyscrapers, Land Revenue and "Concentrated Villages"', *China Quarterly*, no. 217 (March 2014), pp. 162–79

Osnos, Evan, *Age of Ambition: Chasing Fortune, Truth, and Faith in the New China*, Farrar, Straus and Giroux, New York, 2014

Pai Hsiao-Hung, *Scattered Sand: The Story of China's Rural Migrants*, London, Verso, 2012

Pan, Philip, *Out of Mao's Shadow: The Struggle for the Soul of a New China*, Picador, Basingstoke, 2009

Pang Xianzhi and Jin Chongji (eds), *Mao Zedong zhuan, 1949–1976* (A biography of Mao Zedong, 1949–1976), Zhongyang wenxian chubanshe, Beijing, 2003

Pei Minxin, *China's Crony Capitalism: The Dynamics of Regime Decay*, Harvard University Press, Cambridge, MA, 2016

Potter, Pitman, *From Leninist Discipline to Socialist Legalism: Peng Zhen on Law and Political Authority in the PRC*, Stanford University Press, Stanford, CA, 2003

Prybyla, Jan, 'A Systemic Analysis of Prospects for China's Economy', in Joint Economic Committee (eds), *China's Economic Dilemmas in the 1990s*, US Government Printing Office, Washington, 1991, vol. 1, pp. 209–25

Qin Hui, 'Looking at China from South Africa' on www.readingthechinadream. com, retrieved 28 Sept. 2019

Quintyn, Marc G. and Bernard J. Laurens et al. (eds), *Monetary and Exchange System Reforms in China: An Experiment in Gradualism*, International Monetary Fund, Washington, 1996

Reardon, Lawrence C., *The Reluctant Dragon: Crisis Cycles in Chinese Foreign Economic Policy*, Hong Kong University Press, Hong Kong, 2002

Rithmire, Meg E., *Land Bargains and Chinese Capitalism: The Politics of Property Rights under Reform*, Cambridge University Press, Cambridge, 2015

Rodriguez, Pablo Adriano, 'Violent Resistance in Xinjiang (China): Tracking Militancy, Ethnic Riots and "Knife-Wielding" Terrorists (1978–2012)', HAO, no. 30 (Winter 2013), pp. 135–49

Rozelle, Scott and Natalie Hell, *Invisible China: How the Urban-Rural Divide Threatens China's Rise*, University of Chicago Press, Chicago, 2020

Ruan Ming, *Deng Xiaoping: Chronicle of an Empire*, London: Routledge, 2018

Savitt, Scott, *Crashing the Party: An American Reporter in China*, Soft Skull Press, Berkeley, CA, 2016

Rubin, Barry, *Modern Dictators: Third World Coup Makers, Strongmen, and Populist Tyrants*, McGraw-Hill, New York, 1987

Salisbury, Harrison E., *Tiananmen Diary: Thirteen Days in June*, Little, Brown, London, 1989

Shapiro, Judith, *Mao's War against Nature: Politics and the Environment in Revolutionary China*, Cambridge University Press, New York, 2001

Strittmatter, Kai, *We Have Been Harmonised: Life in China's Surveillance State*, Custom House, London, 2020

Suettinger, Robert L., 'Negotiating History: The Chinese Communist Party's 1981', Project 2049 Institute, Washington, 2017

Sullivan, Lawrence R., 'Assault on the Reforms: Conservative Criticism of Political and Economic Liberalization in China, 1985–86', *China Quarterly*, no. 114 (June 1988), pp. 198–222

Tan, Pamela, *The Chinese Factor: An Australian Chinese Woman's Life in China from 1950 to 1979*, Roseberg, Dural, New South Wales, 2008

Tanner, Murray Scot, 'State Coercion and the Balance of Awe: The 1983–1986 "Stern Blows" Anti-Crime Campaign', *China Journal*, no. 44 (July 2000), pp. 93–125

Teiwes, Frederick C. and Warren Sun, 'China's New Economic Policy Under Hua Guofeng: Party Consensus and Party Myths', *China Journal*, no. 66 (July 2011), pp. 1–23

Theroux, Paul, *Riding the Iron Rooster: By Train Through China*, Houghton Mifflin, New York, 1988

Tong, James, 'Anatomy of Regime Repression in China: Timing, Enforcement Institutions, and Target Selection in Banning the Falungong, July 1999', *Asian Survey*, 42, no. 6 (Dec. 2002), pp. 795–820

Tsai, Wen-hsuan, 'Framing the Funeral: Death Rituals of Chinese Communist Party Leaders', *The China Journal*, no. 77 (Jan. 2017), pp. 51–71

Tyler, Christian, *Wild West China: The Taming of Xinjiang*, John Murray, London, 2003

Vogel, Ezra F., *Deng Xiaoping and the Transformation of China*, Harvard University Press, Cambridge, MA, 2011

Walter, Carl E. and Fraser J. T. Howie, *Red Capitalism: The Fragile Financial Foundation of China's Extraordinary Rise*, John Wiley, New York, 2012

Wang Hong, *China's Exports since 1979*, St Martin's Press, London, 1993

Wang Jing, *High Culture Fever: Politics, Aesthetics, and Ideology in Deng's China*, University of California Press, Berkeley, CA, 1996

Wang Shaoguang, 'China's 1994 Fiscal Reform: An Initial Assessment', *Asian Survey*, 37, no. 9 (Sept. 1997), pp. 801–17

Westad, O. Arne, 'The Great Transformation', in Niall Ferguson, Charles S. Maier, Erez Manela and Daniel J. Sargent (eds), *The Shock of the Global: The 1970s in Perspective*, Harvard University Press, Cambridge, MA, 2010, pp. 65–79

White, Lynn T., *Unstately Power: Local Causes of China's Economic Reforms*, M. E. Sharpe, Armonk, NY, 1998

Whyte, Martin King, Feng Wang and Yong Cai, 'Challenging Myths About China's One-Child Policy', *China Journal*, no. 74 (July 2015), pp. 144–59

Wright, Kate, 'The Political Fortunes of Shanghai's *World Economic Herald*', *Australian Journal of Chinese Affairs*, no. 23 (Jan. 1990), pp. 121–32

Wu Hung, *Remaking Beijing: Tiananmen Square and the Creation of a Political Space*, Reaktion Books, London, 2005

Wu Renhua, *Liusi tusha neimu jiemi: Liusi shijian zhong de jieyan budui* (The inside story of the June Fourth massacre: The martial law troops of June Fourth), Yunchen wenhua shiye gufen youxian gongsi, Taipei, 2016

——, *Liusi shijian quancheng shilu* (A full record of the June Fourth incident), Yunchen wenhua shiye gufen youxian gongsi, Taipei, 2019

Yan Jiaqi and Gao Gao, *Turbulent Decade: A History of the Cultural Revolution*, University of Hawai'i Press, Honolulu, 1996

Yan Pengfei and Ding Xia (eds), *Makesizhuyi jingjixue yu Zhongguohua yanjiu* (Research on Marxist economics and sinification), Zhongguo shehui kexue chubanshe, Beijing, 2015

Yang Zhongmei, *Hu Yao-Bang: A Chinese Biography*, Routledge, London, 1989

Zha Jianying, *Tide Players: The Movers and Shakers of a Rising China*, The Free Press, New York, 2011

Zhang Qi and Liu Mingxing, *Revolutionary Legacy, Power Structure, and Grassroots Capitalism under the Red Flag in China*, Cambridge University Press, Cambridge, 2019

Zhao Xu, Liu Junguo, Yang, Hong, Rosa Duarte, Martin Tillotson and Klaus Hubacek, 'Burden Shifting of Water Quantity and Quality Stress from Megacity Shanghai', *Water Resources Research*, 52, no. 9 (Sept. 2016), pp. 6916–27

Zhao Ziyang, *Prisoner of the State: The Secret Journal of Premier Zhao Ziyang*, Simon & Schuster, New York, 2010

Zheng Zhongbing, *Hu Yaobang nianpu ziliao changbian* (A chronology of the life of Hu Yaobang), Shidai guoji chubanshe youxian gongsi, Hong Kong, 2005

Zhonggong zhongyang wenxian yanjiushi (Central Chinese Communist Party Literature Research Office), ed., *Sanzhong quanhui yilai zhongyao wenjian huibian* (Compilation of Major Documents since the Third Plenum), Renmin chubanshe, Beijing, 1982

Zhou, Kate Xiao, *How the Farmers Changed China: Power of the People*, Westview Press, Boulder, CO, 1996

Zhou, Kate Xiao and Lynn T. White III, 'Quiet Politics and Rural Enterprise in Reform China', *Journal of Developing Areas*, 29, no. 4 (July 1995), pp. 461–90

Zinser, Lee, 'The Performance of China's Economy', in Joint Economic Committee (eds), *China's Economic Dilemmas in the 1990s*, US Government Printing Office, Washington, 1991

Zhu Jun, 'Closure of Financial Institutions in China', in Bank for International Settlements (eds), *Strengthening the Banking System in China: Issues and Experience*, Bank for International Settlements, Basel, 1999, pp. 304–19

Acknowledgements

I acknowledge with gratitude a Hsu Long-sing Research Grant from the Faculty of Arts, University of Hong Kong. I should like to thank a number of people who read and commented on draft versions, by name Gail Burrowes, Fraser Howie, Christopher Hutton, Willy Lam and Priscilla Roberts but also other readers who prefer to stay anonymous. Peter Baehr, Jean-Pierre Cabestan, Rowan Callick, Simon Cartledge, Ron Gluck, Paul Gregory, Charles Hill, Carsten Holz, Jean Hung, Li Nanyang and Michael Sheng were very kind with comments, suggestions and answers to queries. Rodney Jones at Wigram Capital Advisors Limited not only read the entire manuscript but also made available invaluable data sets. I also received help from friends and colleagues in mainland China, but prefer not to name them for reasons that are obvious enough.

The staff in the library and archives at the Hoover Institution were unstinting with their help, especially in accessing the Li Rui diaries. At the archives of the Ministère des Affaires Étrangères in Courneuve, Ariane Morais-Abreu was very helpful, not least in making possible the declassification of a whole batch of documents up to 1992. I am also indebted to my publishers, namely Michael Fishwick in London and Ben Hyman in New York, and my copy editor Richard Collins, as well as Francisco Vilhena and all the team at Bloomsbury. I would like to convey my gratitude to my literary agent Andrew Wylie in New York and James Pullen in London. I thank my wife Gail Burrowes, as always, with love.

Index

A Note on the Type

The text of this book is set in Linotype Stempel Garamond, a version of Garamond adapted and first used by the Stempel foundry in 1924. It is one of several versions of Garamond based on the designs of Claude Garamond. It is thought that Garamond based his font on Bembo, cut in 1495 by Francesco Griffo in collaboration with the Italian printer Aldus Manutius. Garamond types were first used in books printed in Paris around 1532. Many of the present-day versions of this type are based on the Typi Academiae of Jean Jannon cut in Sedan in 1615.

Claude Garamond was born in Paris in 1480. He learned how to cut type from his father and by the age of fifteen he was able to fashion steel punches the size of a pica with great precision. At the age of sixty he was commissioned by King Francis I to design a Greek alphabet, and for this he was given the honourable title of royal type founder. He died in 1561.